A CENTURY OF
AMERICAN LIFE INSURANCE

A CENTURY OF

American Life Insurance

A HISTORY OF THE MUTUAL LIFE INSURANCE

COMPANY OF NEW YORK 1843-1943

By SHEPARD B. CLOUGH

GREENWOOD PRESS, PUBLISHERS
WESTPORT, CONNECTICUT

Foreword

BUSINESS ENTERPRISES have a most variable span of life. Their infant death rate is shockingly high; on the other hand, they may live indefinitely. The Bank of England, though not the oldest of British companies, is now in its two-hundred-and-fiftieth year and seems a better "risk" in the twentieth than it seemed in the seventeenth century. No actuary has yet ventured to compute a mortality table for these strange creatures. When one of them becomes a centenarian, there is more occasion for congratulation than when a "natural person" does so. Those who celebrate do not have to repress the thought that dissolution must be close at hand. Also, long life is better evidence of past usefulness in a business enterprise than in a human being. For these man-made beings live on sufferance; if they had not served some lasting purpose, they would not have survived so long.

The biographies of aged people are not always significant. Neither are all the life stories published by old enterprises. Too often the story-teller is one who knows little about the business he extols or about its role in economic evolution. He puts in all available anecdotes and eulogies; he leaves out statistics and complaints. Errors and omissions in management are glossed over unless they are both trivial and amusing. There may be some excuse for saying nothing but good of the dead in a funeral sermon, but that is not becoming conduct in the living when speaking of their own past conduct. Any business enterprise that has rounded out a century can make a genuine contribution to the history of its times if it will let some competent writer use its records candidly.

The Mutual Life Insurance Company of New York provides in this volume a model that other business enterprises may well emulate. When its hundredth anniversary approached, the company sought the services of a professional historian to prepare an account of its career. It put its records at his disposal and gave him a free hand in using them as his judgment dictated. The result is an illuminating history not merely of The Mutual Life but also of the industry in which it has been a leader.

While Dr. Clough has not sought to write a popular book, he has written one that will be read by many men with diverse interests. The development of mortality tables based upon an ever-broadening basis of experience, the diversification of life insurance contracts to fit different needs, methods of selling policies, administrative organization, the relation of trustees to executives, the types of investments made, gross and net yields obtained, governmental investigations that uncovered abuses, the services and the shortcomings of regulatory commissions, the relation of life insurance to the whole economy in which it has expanded so rapidly despite occasional setbacks—all these and many related topics are dealt with faithfully.

American historians have paid scant attention to business enterprises except when they have become involved in political struggles, as did, for example, the second Bank of the United States. Presumably, the basic explanation lies in the secrecy in which business men long shrouded what they thought of as their private affairs. Even the man who had nothing illegal or immoral to conceal did not want competitors to learn overmuch about his costs, his customers, or his profits. A historian who appreciated the role played by business and wished to make it clear was baffled. He could learn far more about technology than about the organizations that apply it. So the nation that entrusted its welfare most unreservedly to business enterprises has known little about the conduct of these agencies, and that little has been a biased sample overweighted with stories of the misdeeds uncovered by muckrakers and prosecutors—two useful but unpopular tribes who often get and give a wrong impression when they are trying to bring out hidden truth.

A combination of developments is now making secretiveness old fashioned—partly pressures from without, partly consciousness within that good business means good service and that the people served are entitled to know how affairs are managed. But there still remains much suspicion of business aims and practices—suspicion that no informed person will say is baseless. Those who hope that the United States will resume the practice of free enterprise after the war and long maintain it recommend a policy of frankness. Business men must win public confidence because of their integrity, efficiency, and fairmindedness if they are to remain the captains of our industry. The first desideratum is to practice these virtues; the second is to make the practice known. If ill has been done along with good, that, too, should be disclosed. But example is better than precept, and the reader holds an example in his hand.

WESLEY C. MITCHELL

New York City
January 15, 1946

Preface

ALL RATIONAL HUMAN ACTION is taken in reference to one's own experience or to the reported experience of others. No machine is built that does not embody many aspects of preceding contraptions; no sales program is undertaken without thought of sales records; no public policy is adopted without some consideration of the effects of analogous policies in the past. Everyone is thus to some extent a historian. The professional historian, however, makes a specialty of studying, recording, representing, and explaining the past of mankind. As a scientist, he endeavors to organize and interpret knowledge, with rigorous restrictions on his personal or environmental biases and a full determination to arrive at those conclusions which are justified by the evidence before him. As a contributor to the formation of public or private policy, the historian indicates long-term trends, shows the position of current problems in these trends, and considers institutions, that is, ways of thought and behavior generally prevalent in a group, in relation to changing environment.

The economic and business historian can, it is believed, throw light upon economic and business problems. By delineating long-term trends and by considering economic and business institutions in the light of changing conditions, he can bring to the attention of executives many of the fundamental issues that become obscured by the everyday handling of detail. Furthermore, he can by the intimate study of the affairs of business increase his own professional competence in organizing and explaining data. In my own case, the experience which I had at The Mutual Life impressed upon me the importance of many issues to which I had previously given inadequate attention. I can recommend heartily the writing of business history to those academicians who would broaden their horizons by a knowledge of practical affairs.

My work at The Mutual Life was, however, done under the most auspicious circumstances. Not only was I permitted access to all the Company's records, but the conclusions which I reached and to which I gave expression were entirely my own. I was shown the greatest courtesy by President Lewis W. Douglas, Executive Vice-President Alexander E. Patterson, and various members of the Board of Trustees. I had access to the expert advice of officers of the Company. To them I wish to extend my grateful thanks for the technical assistance which they gave me and for the time which they devoted to discussing various parts of the book with me.

I would also express my gratitude to a host of other employees of the Company for the help which they rendered me: to Mr. Walter S. Story and Mr. Clarence Emmerson for helping me locate records; to Miss Fannie M. Dana for drawing the charts; to Miss Florence V. Sexton for the laborious task of attending to editorial details; to Mrs. Mildred D. McGrath for typing the manuscript; and to Mrs. Eleanor S. Bagley for overseeing much of the checking of data that is so necessary in a work of this kind. I should also like to extend my thanks to the Insurance Society of New York for use of their library and to the Columbia University Press for the excellent manner in which they handled the intricate details of transforming a complicated manuscript into a book. Especially am I indebted to Miss Ida M. Lynn, whose critical acumen prevented slips that had escaped the practiced eyes of many readers.

SHEPARD B. CLOUGH

New York
January 21, 1946

Contents

Maps and Illustrations

Tables

TABLES xiii

Charts

PART ONE
American Life Insurance
Its Present Position and Beginnings

I. A Sketch of Life Insurance in America

THE LAST CENTURY of American history has witnessed the development of one of the most important social and financial institutions of modern times—life insurance. Since February 1, 1843, when The Mutual Life Insurance Company of New York issued its first policy, life insurance in America has grown, until on January 1, 1943, the assets of three hundred and three life insurance companies domiciled in the United States amounted to $34,931,411,348, a sum which provided insurance of $130,332,848,315.[1] This insurance was written on nearly 134,166,067 policies, was owned by about 67,000,000 persons, and provided on the average a protection of $989 for every man, woman, and child in the land.

The assets of American life insurance companies are approximately equal to the value of the total assets of all Federal Reserve Banks, are almost thrice as much as the assets of mutual savings banks, are double the savings and other time deposits of state and national banks, and are five times as large as the assets of building and loan associations. Even the public debt of the Federal Government and its agencies was about equal to the assets of life insurance companies in 1934.[2] In foreign countries the rise of life insurance has also been tremendous, although it has failed to attain the proportions realized in the United States. On January 1, 1938, the United Kingdom had $16,789,824,000 of life insurance in force, or $354 per capita; the Netherlands, $2,004,470,000, or $233 per head; Germany, $7,919,400,000, or $131 per person; and France, $2,096,253,000, or about $50 per person.[3]

The fundamental reason for this great growth of life insurance, as well

[1] These figures are from *The Spectator Insurance Year Book, 1943 Life Insurance; an Analysis of the Statements for the Year 1942 of All the Life Insurance Companies of the United States*, Philadelphia, pp. 136A–137A. They pertain only to the business of legal reserve life insurance companies, that is, companies which agree to pay a stipulated benefit, collect prescribed rates therefor, and by law maintain a reserve for each policy. These statistics do not include the activity of fraternal orders and assessment societies, which do about 5 percent of the insurance business of the country.

[2] *Statistical Abstract of the United States*, Washington, D.C., Government Printing Office, 1942.

[3] *Hearings before the Temporary National Economic Committee of the Congress of the United States* (Washington, Government Printing Office, 1939), Part 4, p. 1511.

as for all other forms of insurance, is to be found in the very nature of our present-day, capitalistic economy. Time was when society was organized on an essentially agricultural basis, with each small area and even each family largely self-sufficient in an economic sense, and with the exchange of goods conducted mainly on a barter basis. The peasant or farmer had an equity in the land which he tilled, and at his death his sons, or his daughters' husbands, or some other close relatives were glad of the chance to work his fields and in exchange were ready to accept the responsibility of caring for the deceased's dependents. In case of the destruction of a person's buildings by fire, neighbors helped him in the task of reconstruction; and in the event of illness, his friends or even the lord of the manor came to his assistance. In such a self-contained society there was little need for insurance of any kind, for the head of a family left to his survivors a means of livelihood, and misfortunes were alleviated by mutual aid. In fact, the only organizations for sharing risks to which this society gave rise were of a mutual-assistance kind.

With the development of the capitalist system, however, all this gradually changed. To understand why this should have come about, it is necessary to have some idea of capital and the capitalistic economy. Capital may be defined in a historical sense as mobile surplus which can be used for the accumulation of more surplus or profit. And the capitalist system is one in which the means of making a living are primarily based upon the employment of capital.[4] In the long process of economic evolution the growth of our present system has meant that the means of production have in part passed out of the possession or direct control of workers, that the individual himself does not consume what he produces, that he must supply his daily needs by going to the market, and that livelihood is obtained either by money wages, by earnings on capital, or by the expenditure of surplus. In fact, modern society has evolved away from economic self-sufficiency to *economic interdependence*. Division of labor, specialization in all things, exchange of goods by the medium of money, and, what is perhaps the most important consideration for our purpose, the inability of a person to leave to his dependents his own ways of making a living are fundamental characteristics of our present economy.

Early in the evolution of modern capitalism men began to recognize the increasing responsibilities which the changing economic system was forcing upon them. If a person placed all his surplus or capital in a ship-

4 Shepard Bancroft Clough and Charles Woolsey Cole, *An Economic History of Europe* (Boston, 1941), *passim*.

ping venture and the ship were lost, he was ruined. Or if he constructed an expensive building in the search for profits and it was destroyed by fire, he was deprived of a large portion of his earning power. Or if he were an artisan and died, there might not be left a large enough accumulated fund to support his widow or his orphans. As the exigencies of the budding capitalist system became more and more apparent, the wisdom of guarding against such losses became obvious, and the method devised to secure the desired protection was to share risks with others. Thus it was that insurance in its various forms came into being—marine insurance to divide the losses in shipping, fire insurance to disperse losses from the destruction of property by flames, and life insurance to mitigate the loss of a breadwinner.

The exact dates for the beginning of each of these forms of protection is difficult to ascertain, for mutual benefit societies bordered on the edge of insurance, isolated contracts issued by underwriters are steadily turning up which push the origins back a few years, and scholars are not of one mind as to what constitutes bona fide insurance. But if insurance is defined as "the elimination of the uncertain risk of loss for the individual through the combination of a large number of similarly exposed individuals who contribute to a common fund premium payments supposedly sufficient to make good the loss caused any one individual," the activities of mutual aid societies, bets of one individual with another as to whether a ship will come back or a person will die by a certain date, and all contracts by persons not financially interested in the event in question are ruled out. Upon this basis it would seem that marine insurance appeared first in Italy in the fourteenth century; fire insurance in Germany in the sixteenth century; [5] and life insurance in England in the late seventeenth century.[6]

In each case, it will be noted, insurance sprang up where the capitalist system was already becoming important and hence where the consequences of total loss would be most keenly felt. This historical fact tends to substantiate the thesis that insurance came into being to lessen the effects of a situation which a money economy created.

[5] For the early history of insurance see C. F. Trenerry, *The Origin and Early History of Insurance* (London, 1926); Terence O'Donnell, *History of Life Insurance in Its Formative Years* (Chicago, 1936); A. F. Jack, *An Introduction to the History of Life Insurance* (London, 1912); and Richard Ehrenberg, "Studien zur Entwicklungsgeschichte der Versicherung," *Zeitschrift für die gesamte Versicherungswissenschaft* (Berlin, 1901-2).

[6] There were much earlier evidences of life insurance than this. For example, the lives of slaves were insured in Barcelona in the fifteenth century. See R. S. Smith, "Life Insurance in Fifteenth Century Barcelona," *The Journal of Economic History*, New York, May, 1941. In France in the seventeenth century, tontines, if they may be considered life insurance, were sold on a wide scale.

That life insurance has grown hand-in-hand with this kind of an economy is supported by all available evidence—the date of founding of life companies, the development of these companies *pari passu* with the extension of the use of money, and the greater amount of life insurance in force in urban than in agricultural areas. The first important life insurance company in England, The Society for Equitable Assurances on Lives and Survivorships, was founded in 1762; the first successful company in France, in 1819; and the first in Germany, in 1827. In our own country, sporadic attempts to found life insurance companies were made from the end of the eighteenth century onward, but in the period 1843–1851 twelve important companies, which are still in existence today, began to write life policies for the general public. The first of these actually to place insurance on its books was The Mutual Life Insurance Company of New York.

It was not by accident that American life insurance got under way in the "roaring 'forties,' " as we shall see in the next chapter, nor has it been by accident that life insurance has grown as the money economy of America has steadily expanded.

It is a curious fact that, except for the six years following the economic depression inaugurated in 1873 and for the years 1932 and 1933—years also characterized by depression—the amount of life insurance in force in the United States has always shown an upward trend. If the life insurance desired by the public can increase throughout good times and bad (except, perhaps, during the very worst), one may be led to the conclusion that even today life insurance has not assumed the full place destined for it under the capitalist system. But, be that as it may, life insurance has grown concomitantly with the money economy, the advance of science, and the division of labor. In a highly developed capitalist country like the United Kingdom, protection per capita is, as we have seen, $354, while in a more agricultural country, such as Portugal, life insurance per capita is only $3.47. In the United States life insurance protection amounted to $5.47 per capita in 1860; to $40.69 in 1885; to $179.14 in 1910; and to $989 in 1942.

LIFE INSURANCE AFFECTED BY URBANIZATION AND
OCCUPATIONAL SHIFTS

In our own country, fewer persons, irrespective of their wealth, hold life insurance policies in rural areas than in urban areas, as Tables 1 and 2, on page 8, will show.[7]

[7] Data obtained from a special study by the Research Staff of The Mutual Life based on Bureau of Labor Statistics figures.

CHART I

ECONOMIC PROGRESS IN THE UNITED STATES, 1849–1942

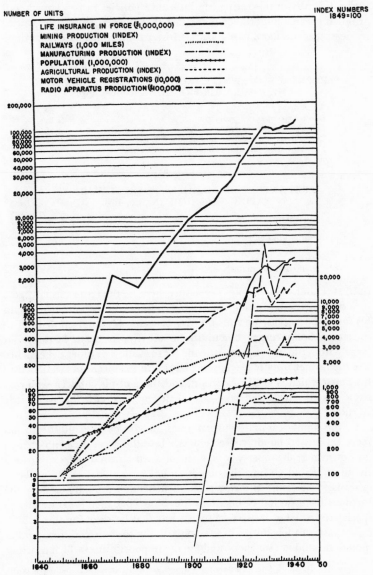

Sources: National Industrial Conference Board, *America's War Effort* (New York, 1942), p. 15; *Statistical Abstract of the United States* (Washington, D.C., 1943).

This situation is not a matter of mere chance. In the first place, there is the difficulty of marketing life insurance policies in rural areas. But of much greater importance is the fact that the responsibilities caused by death can be more easily assumed in a routine manner by agricul-

TABLE 1

PERCENTAGE OF WHITE, NONRELIEF FAMILIES PAYING LIFE INSURANCE PREMIUMS IN 1935–1936

Rural areas	58
Cities, 2,500 to 25,000 population	81
Cities, 25,000 to 100,000 population	86
Cities, 100,000 to 1,500,000 population	88
New York City, Chicago, Philadelphia, and Detroit	90

TABLE 2

PROPORTION OF TOTAL NUMBER OF FAMILIES PAYING PREMIUMS IN 1935–1936

Region	Percentage
New England	82
East North Central	77
South	72
Pacific	69
Plains and mountains	61

turalists than by city people. To be sure, because the farmer usually goes into debt at the beginning of his career either to buy land or to equip his farm and because he runs the risk of seeing his children drift off to the city and of having no one to till the soil after his death, he can profit largely from life insurance to provide for his widow or other dependents. Yet the farmer usually leaves some equity in his means of livelihood to his heirs, which is itself protection, and those of his children who continue his enterprise can take care of dependents with relatively little sacrifice.[8]

In the highly capitalist, urban areas, on the other hand, death has more serious economic consequences. Here the great majority of men do not own real property which can be used by their heirs to make a living or, if sold, to furnish enough capital for sustenance. In our large cities is to be found the very acme of dependence upon wages or the earnings from capital to maintain life. The work men do is usually so specialized or labor is hired in such a way that heads of families cannot easily pass on their means of making a living to their children. And as though this did not sufficiently add to the responsibilities which confront

[8] Hervell F. De Graff, *Life Insurance for Farmers*, Cornell Extension Bulletin 459, April, 1941.

the city dweller, there has been a noticeable diminution in the size of urban families, hence there have been fewer children to care for dependent parents, and there has been a growing inability or unwillingness on the part of children to assume the support of their father's family.[9]

Residents of cities are thus faced with the problem of leaving a surplus to their heirs which will be sufficient for their needs. It may be that this fund can be built up by the accumulation of wealth, but the vast majority (perhaps 90 percent) of the families in metropolitan areas have decided that insurance should be a vital part of their plan to care for dependents after death. That the need for life insurance has been steadily increasing and will probably continue to augment for some time to come is owing in part to the rapid and continuing urbanization of our population and to a shift in the occupations of men from agriculture to commerce and industry—from the more economically self-sufficient to the less economically self-sufficient callings.

LIFE INSURANCE COMPANIES AS FINANCIAL INSTITUTIONS

The role which life insurance has played in the expanding American economy has not been limited to its primary function in the capitalist system, that is, to the distribution of the risks of death. Insurance is a form of savings—and the savings in life companies have been built up more rapidly in recent years than have those in other formal savings institutions.

Life insurance funds in America are amassed from small payments—the average premium per policy in 1942 was $31—made by about 67,000,000 persons on one or more policies. Thus is brought together a tremendous amount of capital or surplus which can be put to use in productive enterprises. Throughout the development of the capitalist system one of the main problems has been to amalgamate the capital of many persons in order to finance great undertakings. Banks were early destined to perform this function, and so, too, were partnerships, sleeping partnerships, and joint stock companies. But life insurance companies, at least in America, have become leading servants in this field. They not only assist the individual in building up a surplus upon which he may fall back at any time, but as of January 1, 1943, they had brought together for investment about $35,000,000,000.

The character of the investments of life insurance companies can

9 Warren S. Thompson, "Urbanization," in *Encyclopedia of the Social Sciences* (New York, 1937); Joanna C. Colcord, "Family Desertion and Non-Support," *op. cit.*; A. M. Carr-Saunders, *World Population; Past Growth and Present Trends* (Oxford, 1936); and Walter F. Willcox, *Studies in American Demography* (Ithaca, 1940).

only be suggested in this place. Suffice it to say that life companies have bought heavily in mortgages, public bonds, railroad bonds, public utilities, and industrial bonds. In 1942 the forty-nine largest life companies, whose assets constituted 91.3 percent of the aggregate for all life com-

CHART II

ASSETS OF SAVINGS INSTITUTIONS IN THE
UNITED STATES, 1910–1942

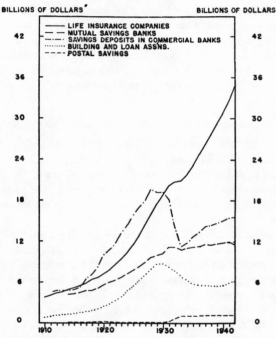

Source: *Statistical Abstract of the United States,* (Washington, D.C., 1930 and 1943).

panies, held 13.7 percent of the total gross long-term private and public debt in the United States.[10]

Furthermore, life insurance companies have provided an element of stability in our unstable world. For the last thirty years not a single life insurance company doing business in the State of New York has gone

[10] Data on assets from the Life Insurance Association of America; on private debt from National Industrial Conference Board; on public debt from the Department of Commerce.

bankrupt with ultimate loss to policyholders [11] and life insurance companies emerged from the depression of the 1930's in much sounder condition than did banks. In the one year 1939 life insurance companies paid out to policyholders or their beneficiaries $2,641,525,955. This vast

TABLE 3

PERCENT OF PRIVATE AND PUBLIC DEBT HELD
BY LIFE INSURANCE COMPANIES IN 1942

Public debt		Private debt	
Federal	9.7	Railway	21.4
State and local	8.6	Industrial	8.6
Total public	9.5	Public utility	**33.3**
		Farm mortgage	11.8
		Urban mortgage	17.8
		Total private	17.9
		Total gross long-term debt	13.7

sum must have done much to provide the security which the modern man so desires.[12]

Yet the effect of life insurance upon our society does not stop here. In the field of sanitation and preventive medicine, life companies have played an important role. During the Civil War they supported the Sanitary Commission—an organization which was a forerunner of the Red Cross. They have impressed upon certain localities the need for better sewage disposal and pure water supplies. Their emphasis upon periodic physical examinations as an element in longevity has popularized the advisability of such checks upon individual health. Life insurance physicians have done pioneer work in amassing health statistics and in investigating the effects of certain diseases or physical conditions on mortality.[13] And, finally, actuaries have made important contributions to the field of mathematics, insurance lawyers to the field of equity, and insurance firms and real estate experts to the field of investment.

Despite the fact, however, that life insurance companies have made their impress upon the legal, mathematical, medical, and financial world, the main function of life companies has been, is, and undoubtedly will continue to be the furnishing of insurance. Their main business is to supply a means whereby the great majority of men can make provision, through a process of sharing risks, for those who will suffer economically from their death or old age.

[11] *Eighty-First Annual Report of the Superintendent of the Insurance Department of the State of New York for the Year Ended Dec. 31, 1939* (Albany, 1940).
[12] *Spectator Yearbook*, 1940, p. 138A.
[13] Edward A. Woods, *The Sociology of Life Insurance* (New York, 1928), chap. ii.

THE HISTORICAL EVOLUTION OF AMERICAN LIFE INSURANCE:
A SYNOPSIS

The history of life insurance in the United States from its meager beginnings, when an underwriter insured not only the cargo of a ship but
also the life of the ship's captain, to the present time, when about
67,000,000 persons own policies having face values aggregating about
$130,000,000,000, is at once a romance and an essential part of our na-
tion's past. It is a romance because of the drama in the growth, management, and operations of life insurance companies. It is an essential part
of our past because of the widespread effects which life insurance has
had upon our social and economic life. There are, however, few aspects
of our economic history which have been so neglected by scholars as
that of life insurance. It is primarily for this reason that the present book
is being written.

Life insurance history is fundamentally the story of life insurance
companies, and yet the enormous task of writing an account from this
comprehensive point of view is, with the present paucity of informative
company histories, practically impossible. The history of The Mutual
Life Insurance Company of New York is, however, probably the best
exemplar of all. This company was the first American life insurance
institution, open to all persons, actually to write policies and to have a
continuous existence down to the present time. It has always been one
of the six largest companies measured in terms of assets. It has shared
in most of the changes that have been made in life insurance, although
it has never written group or industrial insurance.[14] It has been a leader
in the development of nearly all the essential principles upon which
conservative life insurance companies are constituted. And it has experienced the repercussions of the evolving economy of the United
States for the complete span of one century.

14 As defined by the National Convention of Insurance Commissioners in 1918, "Group
life insurance is hereby declared to be that form of life insurance covering not less than
fifty employees with or without medical examination, written under a policy issued to the
employer, the premium on which is to be paid by the employer or by the employer and employees jointly and insuring only all of his employees, or all of any class or classes thereof
determined by conditions pertaining to the employment, for amounts of insurance based
upon some plan which will preclude individual selection, for the benefit of persons other
than the employer; provided, however, that when the premium is to be paid by the employer and employee jointly and the benefits of the policy are offered to all eligible employees, not less than seventy-five per centum of such employees may be so insured." Industrial insurance as defined by the New York Insurance Law, Chapter 201, means that form of
life insurance, either (a) under which premiums are payable weekly, or (b) under which
premiums are payable monthly or oftener, but less often than weekly, if the face amount of
insurance provided in any such policy is less than $1,000.

The history of The Mutual Life, like the history of American life insurance in general, is a continuous story, yet within that history certain stages of development may be discerned. Roughly these stages may be marked by the following years: 1843–1870; 1870–1906; 1906–1943. Significant as this periodization may be, it should be kept in mind that breaks in history are usually not abrupt—that the stream of events flows steadily, sometimes in still waters and sometimes in rapids—and that periods in history are employed by the historian to facilitate exposition, as scenes and acts are used by the dramatist to achieve progression.

The first of the above-mentioned periods in the history of American life insurance and of The Mutual Life, covering the years 1843–1870, were characterized by the beginnings of modern life insurance in this country. Although several attempts had been made to initiate a life insurance business prior to the former date, it was not until the decade of the 1840's that real success was achieved.[15] Between 1843 and 1851 twelve companies, which were to become prominent in the field, began business—most of them on the principle of mutuality—and between 1843 and 1870 the basic principles of modern life insurance were established. An American table of mortality was drawn up, which provided a scientific foundation for determining the size of premiums. Level premiums, that is, premiums which are the same every year throughout the life of the policy, but which vary with the age at which the insured makes his contract with the insurer, were introduced from England. Methods of determining the size of an adequate reserve for each policy were developed. Dividends began to be distributed scientifically on the basis of the proportion of each policyholder's contribution to surplus. Experience showed what physical impairments and what regional and occupational health hazards rendered persons uninsurable or subject to extra premiums. The agency system for marketing life insurance took form. State regulation of life insurance companies came into being.

The rate of growth of the business was very great—the amount of insurance in force quadrupled from the end of the Civil War to 1872.

Whereas in this early period, American life insurance as we know it was born, in the years between 1870 and 1906 it had its growing pains. Although the industry adhered to many of the principles established prior to 1870, it underwent important changes. In the first place, a plethora of new companies was founded toward the end of the 1860's and the beginning of the 1870's, but with the economic depression which

[15] It should be noted, however, that in 1759 the Presbyterian Ministers' Fund had its beginnings.

began in 1873 the number of companies in existence was reduced by half. This situation meant that competition throughout the period was severe, for at first many companies were after the business, and then the depression made business difficult to get. By the time prosperity returned, the surviving newcomers were bent on ousting the old leaders from their positions of primacy. The Equitable Life Assurance Society, founded in 1859 by Henry B. Hyde—the greatest tycoon the business has ever known—the Metropolitan (1867), and the Prudential (1875) are examples of young companies which were to enjoy great growth and to threaten the preeminence of the older concerns. Rivalry and desire for sheer size led to practices which did not always redound to the benefit of policyholders. Rebating, large commissions, raiding competitors' agency forces, "twisting," high expense ratios, concentration on forms of policies that were profitable to the companies and yet expensive for the majority of the policyholders became prevalent.

Managers of the companies worked mightily to get more business. They extended their companies' activities to the West and the South and set up agencies in Europe, Asia, South America, and Africa. If they were successful in vastly expanding their company's business, they thought that the company was heavily indebted to them. They adopted seigniorial attitudes: obtained high salaries, practiced nepotism, built impressive office buildings, and secured favorable legislation. From their activity in placing the large capital accumulations of their companies, they were led to enter investment syndicates, to acquire common stocks and consequently a voice in management, to join the directorates of industrial and financial enterprises, and to link the fortunes of their companies too closely with favored establishments. In spite of the criticisms which can be leveled at these men, however, the fact remains that the insurance managers of this era did greatly expand the institution of life insurance in America, especially from 1884 to 1893 and from 1896 to 1905. Essentially they did aim to serve the public by providing insurance at reasonable rates, and they did pay homage to a code of business ethics which was higher than the one generally employed in their time.

The period of severe competition, of managerial control, and of extremely rapid growth came to a close at the end of 1905 with an investigation of life insurance companies conducted by a committee of the New York State Legislature under the chairmanship of Senator Armstrong. This investigation, in which Charles Evans Hughes played a leading role as counsel for the state, attacked those practices which were not of a conservative nature. So telling were the blows delivered by Mr. Hughes that New York and other states immediately passed legislation which prevented the continuance of the *status quo ante*. Mutualization of companies was extended, and efforts were made to prevent the control of a company by a small group who did not work in the interests of policyholders; investments were limited in New York and in many other states to bonds and mortgages in order to prevent life insurance companies from having their interests inextricably intertwined with those of other enterprises; [16] investment syndicates were forbidden; a limit was placed upon the amounts which could be spent in securing new business, upon total expenses, and upon expansion; and certain types of policies were outlawed. Immediately many new companies were founded—approximately 200 from 1905 to 1915—in some cases by promoters who were attracted to a field in which the investigation showed the harvest to be rich, although many of these companies were soon absorbed by the stronger institutions in a wave of mergers. Companies continued, however, a sharp rivalry for business, and in their eagerness to outdo one another they began to include in their policies insurance against disability and accidental death (the disability benefit and double indemnity policies). Moreover, some of the companies began to write group and substandard insurance. Finally, insurance began to be used on a larger scale for specific purposes—by businesses to insure their key men, and by the individual to meet inheritance taxes, to provide an income for the family after death, and to send his children to college. These new forms of insurance and the new purposes for which insurance was designed added to the general growth of the industry. The total amount of insurance in force more than quadrupled from 1914 to 1930. In this period life insurance achieved the position in our economy which it enjoys today.

The severe economic depression which characterized the decade of the 1930's emphasized the financial aspects of life insurance. In 1931 new business began to fall off, and there was a "run" on the companies which was made possible by policy loans and cash surrenders. The mortality rate increased, owing in part to a large number of suicides; and interest rates declined. Companies found it difficult to invest their funds at favorable yields, and the Federal Government entered the investment field, thus curbing the opportunities for private investment agencies. Corporations refunded their obligations at low rates of interest, and many of the wealthier individuals in society looked to life insurance

16 The New York insurance law of 1928 allowed life insurance companies to invest in preferred and guaranteed stock under certain conditions and limitations.

companies as places to invest their fortunes because of the stability of these institutions.[17] Such changes resulted in reduced dividends and an increased cost of insurance. Gradually, however, life insurance companies began to adjust themselves to the new situation. The amount of insurance in force increased steadily after 1933; the placing of funds in life insurance simply as an investment diminished after 1935; and with an increase in government financing and with the outbreak of World War II, insurance companies began to invest heavily in government bonds.

SCOPE OF OUR STUDY

To understand the history of The Mutual Life Insurance Company of New York it is necessary not only to keep clearly in mind the chronological phases through which American life insurance has passed, but also to trace within each time-period the evolution of the various aspects of the business. Life insurance is many sided, but there are branches of it which are important enough to warrant continuous attention as our story progresses. The first of these functional divisions may be called "organization and management." It is important to know that The Mutual Life has always been owned by its policyholders and that management has been responsible to them; and it is important to discover who the personnel of the Company has been, how it has been organized, and how it has discharged its duties. The second horizontal division of the history of The Mutual Life has to do with the kind of policies written and with such actuarial matters as mortality tables, premium schedules, reserves, and the distribution of dividends. The third embraces the financial side of life insurance—the accumulation of funds, investment policies, and yields. The fourth deals with the marketing of life insurance policies and hence includes the entire activity of the agencies department. The fifth division comprises the work of the department of selection in determining standards required for the assumption of risks and the activity of the law department in defending the Company from unjust claims, in ensuring compliance with legal requirements, and in securing laws or legal decisions which will serve the best interests of the policyholders.

The following history of The Mutual Life Insurance Company of New York will thus be divided into three main chronological periods,

---

[17] The amount received by life companies for annuities increased from $99,170,090 in 1929 to $510,523,390 in 1935. In 1942 this total had fallen off to $428,135,018, in part, because of efforts of the companies to discourage this kind of business. *The Spectator Insurance Year Book*, 1943, pp. 138A–139A.

and in each of these the various branches of the business as outlined above will be treated. More than that, an effort will be made to place the story of The Mutual Life in its setting of American life insurance history and to relate both to the general economic history of the country. To do otherwise would be to write history in a vacuum.

II. Early History of Life Insurance and the Founding of The Mutual Life

IN ITS SIMPLEST TERMS, insurance is a scheme of sharing those risks which are common to a great number of men, and which involve losses that cannot be easily borne by the individual. To make this scheme function successfully it is absolutely necessary to have (1) a fairly definite notion of what losses may be expected to occur among a number of approximately equal risks, (2) a large enough number of persons willing to share these risks so that there will be an average of expected losses, and (3) contributions of some kind from those who are willing to share risks so that those who suffer losses may secure a payment. As applied to life insurance, these essential features of insurance require a knowledge of the rate of mortality of groups of people at all ages living under approximately the same conditions and having approximately the same life expectancy. Once this rate of mortality has been determined, it is necessary to get enough people to agree to share the risks of death so that there will be an average death rate among them; and it is necessary to get them to make contributions to a general fund in proportion to the amount which they expect to receive at death. It is from this fund that each contributor, that is, each insured, may expect his beneficiary to secure at his death the sum insured.[1]

The bringing together of these three factors to produce modern life insurance was accomplished first in England at the end of the seventeenth century. But the development of each factor independently of the others took place much earlier and over a long period. Mortality tables, although known in Rome as early as the fourth decade B. C.,[2] did not come into use in the modern era until the seventeenth century, when they were employed in connection with annuities. At that time various states which wanted to raise money for war purposes hit upon the

[1] For an elucidation of these points see Joseph B. Maclean, *Life Insurance* (New York, 1939) and John H. Magee, *Life Insurance* (Chicago, Business Publications, 1939).

[2] The so-called Ulpian Table. It followed the Falcidian Law of 40 B. C. Under it, if a testator left a beneficiary a certain sum to be paid to the latter annually throughout his lifetime, it became necessary to determine how much should be paid per year and for how many years.

MORRIS ROBINSON, FIRST PRESIDENT OF THE MUTUAL LIFE

scheme of soliciting sums from individuals and of promising to pay to them certain amounts during the remainder of their lives. Such a project necessitated having at least a rough estimate of how long a person of a given age was going to live so that the enterprise would be profitable to the state. Interest in this method of raising money for the war against Louis XIV led John DeWitt, Grand Pensionary of Holland, to get up an illustration of a mortality table in 1671. Similarly, in France the need for money to wage war on the English and the Dutch stimulated the sale of annuities, the making of mortality tables, and the development of a new type of annuity known as the "tontine." This contract, suggested by Lorenzo Tonti to Cardinal Mazarin in 1653, provided that subscribers should be divided into age groups or classes and that the survivors in each class should receive all the money originally earmarked for that class. Finally, in England a desire to use annuities led Edmund Halley, the discoverer of Halley's Comet, to make public (1693) what was really the first modern mortality table, that is, it was the first table which considered from actual experience a large number of persons and showed how many would be alive at each age until all had died.[3]

With this experience in rates of mortality and with the development of the laws of probability by Blaise Pascal and others, life insurance on a scientific basis was possible. Yet it was necessary to have enough people interested in sharing the risks of death before the scientific principles of insurance could operate correctly. That this prerequisite was gradually being met is apparent from the ever-greater number of cases of life insurance which appear in business records. Wager policies, in which parties to the agreement bet that some prominent person—king, emperor, pope, or other dignitary—would not live beyond a certain date, were numerous in the sixteenth century. And at about the same time policies for insurance on lives developed in connection with property insurance. Thus insurance was taken on the lives of slaves, on the lives of debtors by their creditors, on the lives of persons who enjoyed the income from a benefice or an estate and could not leave it to their heirs, and on the lives of merchants and sea captains who placed insurance upon themselves along with the insurance taken on their ships and cargoes. The first mention of persons who insured their own lives for the benefit of their heirs is to be found in Gerard Malynes, *Consuetudo, vel lex mercatoria*, 1622.

These early attempts at life insurance were important, for they pro-

---

[3] For Halley, see Edmund Halley, *Two Papers on the Degrees of Mortality of Mankind*, edited by Lowell J. Reed (Baltimore, 1942).

vided experiences upon which a sounder system could be built. Some of the weaknesses inherent in the initial life insurance projects were clearly discernible. So few persons became insured that the laws of average based on mortality experience were practically inoperative. The insurers were usually marine underwriters who endeavored to distribute the risks which they assumed by taking only part of the insurance on any one man's life and placing the rest with another underwriter—risks thus being shared in part by insurers rather than, as is usual in modern insurance, by the insured. Furthermore, underwriters did not know exactly what the chances of death were and usually charged 5 percent of the face amount of the policy per year, irrespective of age—a rate that was extremely high for young persons. They were willing to make contracts for only short periods in which they knew the conditions under which the insured would be living—a fact that precluded the certainty of providing for one's heirs by means of insurance and gave rise to a desire for insurance to cover the whole of life. Finally, early policies, particularly those of the wager variety, led to so much fraud and to so many murders that gambling insurance on lives was forbidden in Spain (1570), in Genoa (1588), and in France (from 1661 to 1788). Insurance on lives was placed under state control in England as early as 1574 and wager policies were outlawed in the Gambling Act of 1774.[4]

The mere fact that England did not prohibit, but only regulated, life insurance is significant, for she was thus able slowly to develop the institution. Her relatively large marine and marine insurance business presented a fertile field for underwriters who were willing to assume risks on seafarers, while Parliament and the courts built up a body of law which gave life insurance an acceptable legal and social status. By the end of the seventeenth century life insurance in England had reached a point at which modern, scientific insurance was possible.

In England certain changes in the business were clearly becoming ever more desirable. Perhaps the most fundamental of these was for lower costs. Cheaper rates required, however, the association of a large number of policyholders, refinements of the mortality tables, and the issuing of policies which would cover the whole span of life. These changes were only possible by the formation of life companies, which fortunately soon began to put in an appearance. Most of these early companies were, like

---

4 England's decision not to prohibit life insurance as did France and her advance over her continental rival in this field are analogous to the experience of the two countries in the calico industry. France prohibited calico manufacture and hence retarded her development of cotton textiles—so important in the industrial revolution—while England only forbade the importation of calicoes and hence gave a fillip to the cotton industry.

the first of them—The Society of Assurance for Widows and Orphans (1699)—run on an assessment plan, that is, members would contribute their proportionate share whenever a member died. But these assessment societies ran afoul of difficulties which their later prototypes in America were to encounter—they could not attract young members when the original members grew old and assessments began to be high; older members dropped out when their dues began to equal the expected benefits, and sickly persons tended to flock to the insurers in the expectation of early rewards, thus effecting a selection of poor risks—a process known in the trade as adverse selection. Consequently, most of these companies, several of which were sponsored by unscrupulous promoters in the speculative era that was climaxed by the bursting of the South Sea Bubble in 1720, were short-lived.

One of the companies of this period—The Amicable Society for a Perpetual Assurance Office, founded in 1706—had, however, an existence of one hundred and sixty years.[5] It was organized on a mutual benefit basis and operated on a regular contributory plan until 1807. Moreover, two important marine insurance companies were incorporated in 1720 and began to write life insurance for short terms in 1721, being the first stock corporations to appear in the business. The directions in which the life insurance industry was to move were thus becoming clear—the issuing of policies by companies rather than by underwriters, the sharing of risks by many policyholders, and the fixing of regular, annual premiums.

An important milestone in this evolution was reached in 1762 with the founding of The Society for Equitable Assurances on Lives and Survivorships, or as it is called nowadays, "The Old Equitable." It was mutual in its organization,[6] required the payment of stipulated, level premiums based on the probability of death, and issued insurance for specific terms of years. From the first The Equitable was a success, and its managers displayed real perspicacity. They profited not only from improvements which had steadily been made in mortality tables prior to 1762 but they also urged the compilation of new tables, and in 1782 adopted the most famous one of the latter part of the century—the Northampton Table, which had been drawn up by the leading insurance figure of the age, the Reverend Richard Price. They required ap-

---

[5] It was amalgamated with the Norwich Union in 1866.

[6] The Bubble Act of 1720 forbade the establishment of a joint stock company, that is, a stock corporation without a royal charter. The existing companies opposed the granting of a charter to the sponsors of the Equitable and adopted a multiple partnership plan which was essentially mutual. Later the name was changed to the Equitable Life Assurance Society.

plicants for insurance to answer questions regarding their health, charging those who had not had smallpox extra premiums; they demanded extra premiums on the lives of women under fifty years of age and on men in hazardous occupations; they paid dividends, or, as they are called in England, bonuses from their surplus to holders of whole life policies; they employed an actuary; and they maintained a reserve on their policies.

Modern, scientific life insurance may be said definitely to have begun with "The Old Equitable." So successful was this company that by 1816 it voluntarily took measures to limit its growth. Its success encouraged competitors to enter the field. In 1792 the Westminster Society was established as a stock corporation in search of profit, but all the other early companies, like the Globe Insurance Company (1799), and the Scottish Widows' Fund and Life Insurance Society (1815), were organized on a mutual basis. By the first quarter of the nineteenth century the idea of mutuality in life insurance was firmly rooted.

THE BEGINNINGS OF LIFE INSURANCE IN AMERICA

Most American business institutions in the eighteenth and early nineteenth centuries were directly imported from England. This was true of retail trade, wholesaling, private banking, mutual savings banking, bookkeeping, fire insurance and marine underwriting—and it was also true of life insurance. Nor is it strange that this should have been the case, for our intellectual, family, and business ties were closer with England than with any other country in the world.

This borrowing by a youthful from a more mature economy is particularly striking in the case of insurance. It accounts, in large part, for a development of the institution in America that closely paralleled the evolution in England. Thus, the first insurance in the colonies was provided by English underwriters, and when Americans became irked at the time consumed in placing their insurance overseas or in collecting their claims, the business was slowly absorbed by American underwriters who were familiar with English practices. In 1721 a Public Insurance Office was opened in Philadelphia; in 1724 the first Office of Insurance in Boston was established; and shortly thereafter others appeared in New York, Baltimore, Hartford, and similar commercial cities. As in England, the underwriters gravitated toward coffee houses for the conduct of their business, and again, as in England, they employed similar terminology in their contracts, provided the same coverage, and charged about the same premiums. Most of the insurance written by these men was for fire and marine risks. Indeed, it was not until 1780 that the first life contract of which we have record was placed with them in New England.[7] By that time insurance companies were being established, and they were soon to take over the life business of the country.

The transition from the insuring of lives by underwriters to the writing of life insurance by companies was not, however, abrupt or late in appearing. As early as 1759 Presbyterian ministers established a company which has had a continuous existence down to the present and is now known as the Presbyterian Ministers' Fund.[8] At first it provided a means whereby a minister of the Presbyterian faith could buy an annuity for his widow by making annual payments for a specified number of years. Although this system of insurance overcame to some degree a lack of sure mortality data, other steps were taken to offset weaknesses in the process of insurance which had been apparent in other places. Thus, adverse selection was warded off by forbidding ministers to increase their insurance after they had joined the Fund, which they would probably have done if they had fallen into ill health; extra rates were charged for each remarriage on the ground that the new wife would be younger than the former, would live longer, and would thus collect the annuity for a longer period; and the full benefit was not paid out unless fifteen annual premiums had been paid in. So much care was taken in the formulation of these rules and they operated so well that they were adopted by the three Corporations for the Relief of Widows and Children of Clergymen in the Communion of the Church of England in America in 1769.[9]

These denominational insurance organizations had a limited field of action, yet they provided experience and stimulated interest in an institution which was still in its infancy even in England. That this interest was growing in America is evidenced by an abundance of facts. In 1789

[7] Sir Edward R. Hardy, *An Account of Early Insurance Offices in Massachusetts from 1724 to 1801* (Boston, 1901), p. 91, and J. A. Fowler, *History of Insurance in Philadelphia for Two Centuries, 1683–1882* (Philadelphia, 1888), pp. 622–623.

[8] Its original title was The Corporation for the Relief of Poor and Distressed Presbyterian Ministers, and for the Poor and Distressed Widows and Children of Presbyterian Ministers. Its charter was granted by the Proprietary Governors of Pennsylvania. It had been preceded by The Fund for Pious Purposes, established by the Philadelphia Synod in 1717, which had provided for missionary work and for financial assistance to ministers. See *The Presbyterian Ministers' Fund* (Philadelphia, 1938).

[9] Identical charters were granted in this year by Pennsylvania, New Jersey, and New York. In 1784 one was granted by Maryland, but was later dropped. Today they are known as Corporations for the Relief of Widows and Children of Clergymen of the Protestant Episcopal Church. They are very small and are not now classed as insurance companies. The first rules were approved by Richard Price, who studied them at the request of Benjamin Franklin.

Professor Wigglesworth of Harvard presented to the American Academy of Arts and Sciences in Boston the first American mortality table. In 1790 tontines began to be used for raising money for charitable purposes and for the erection of public and private buildings, such as the Tontine Building in Wall Street and the Tontine Hotel in New Haven. And it was a tontine project which led to the establishment in 1794 of the Insurance Company of North America in Philadelphia.[10]

With the outbreak of the French Revolution in 1789, and more especially with the war between the French and English, which began in 1792 and was to continue with scarcely any interruption until 1815, American shipping grew rapidly [11] and America was in many ways thrown upon her own devices. Thus, a fillip was given to American marine insurance and concomitantly to American life insurance. Between 1787 and 1799 charters were granted to at least twenty-four American companies, five of which were authorized along with their fire and marine business to insure lives.[12] The first British company actually to establish a branch office here (1805), The Phoenix Fire, had to close up shop during the War of 1812, and the American agents of English companies mostly severed their connections with their home offices at the same time.[13] The life policies which these new companies wrote were few in number and usually covered risks such as capture by the Barbary pirates, or the loss of life in some such hazardous trip as that to India. Nevertheless, these contracts marked the beginning in America of life insurance for the general public by companies rather than by underwriters.

During the first three decades of the nineteenth century American life insurance entered a new phase, for although life contracts continued to be written by underwriters and by companies doing a mixed fire, life, and marine business, the trend was toward joint stock companies which specialized in the life business. The first of such corporations was the Pennsylvania Company for Insurance on Lives and Granting Annuities which was organized in 1809, was chartered in 1812, and got under way in 1814, and the second was the Massachusetts Hospital Life Insurance

10 Organized in 1792 and chartered in 1794. See T. H. Montgomery, *History of the Insurance Company of North America* (Philadelphia, 1885) and Marquis James, *Biography of a Business* (New York, 1942).

11 J. G. B. Hutchins, *The American Maritime Industries and Public Policy, 1789–1914; an Economic History* (Cambridge, Harvard University Press, 1941).

12 C. K. Knight, *The History of Life Insurance in the United States to 1870* (Philadelphia, 1920), p. 65.

13 Cornelius Walford, *The Insurance Cyclopedia* (New York, 1871). See the article entitled "British Offices in the United States." This encyclopedia was never completed.

Company, chartered in 1818 for the ultimate purpose of providing funds (one-third of its net profits on life insurance) for the Massachusetts General Hospital.[14] The former of these companies followed closely English life insurance practices; in fact one of its directors had been an American agent of an English company,[15] who had lost his job during the War of 1812. The policies which this company adopted indicate great progress in placing life insurance upon a known rather than upon a guesswork basis. The Pennsylvania was the first company in America to employ an actuary—the technician of the life insurance business; it required a signed declaration concerning health, occupation, and residence, based its rates on the Northampton Table, eliminated from its insured risks hazards such as suicide, dueling, long-distance travel, and death because of court sentences, embarked upon a program of mortality rate research, and tried, although not very successfully, modern marketing methods.

The Massachusetts Hospital Life Insurance Company, for its part, adopted approximately the same rules, but it pushed the annuity and trust side of its business rather than life insurance, because it had to make contributions from profits on its life insurance business to the Massachusetts General Hospital. The company which was actively to seek life insurance contracts was the New York Life Insurance and Trust Company,[16] founded as a stock corporation in 1830. By 1839 this company had 694 policies, representing $2,451,958 of insurance in force, and, what was perhaps more important, it popularized the institution of life insurance in the metropolis. A large part of its success was owing to the employment of agents—a practice which has proved to be an integral part of American life insurance experience.

Among the other companies of this period may be mentioned the Aetna Insurance Company of Hartford, which got the privilege in 1820 of writing life insurance, although it did not issue life policies until 1850, the Baltimore Life Insurance Company (1830), and the Girard Life Insurance, Annuity, and Trust Company of Philadelphia (1836)—the

14 The hospital itself had been authorized in 1814 to grant annuities on lives, but since it did not exercise the privilege and since it was believed that some income would accrue to it from a separate company, its privilege was surrendered in 1818. In 1824 stockholders were to receive legal interest before any profits were earmarked for the hospital.

15 J. Owen Stalson, "The Pioneer in American Life Insurance Marketing," *Bulletin of the Business Historical Society*, XII (Nov., 1938), 5–75.

16 Allan Nevins, *History of the Bank of New York and Trust Co.* (New York, 1934). The New York Life Insurance and Trust Co. merged with the Bank of New York in 1922 under the name of The Bank of New York and Trust Co. The name was changed to Bank of New York in 1938.

first company in this country to write life insurance on a commercial basis and to allow its policyholders to participate in the profits. This last-named institution bridged the gap between the proprietary stock companies which were seeking profits and the mutual companies which were profit sharing.

Thus, by 1843 life insurance in America had already made long strides forward. It had passed from simple term contracts, requiring the payment of arbitrary premiums and issued solely by individual underwriters, to term, whole life, or annuity contracts written by stock companies and with premiums determined by the mortality rate of persons in different age groups. English influence had been enormous and had given to America, among other things, an actuarial science, policy forms, company organization, and marketing methods.

In addition to the progress which had been made in life insurance, this business had displayed certain characteristics which were to be more apparent later on. In the first place, insurance activity in these early years reflected the course of the business cycle. Thus several fire and marine insurance companies were chartered in New York State during the upswing of the cycle from 1820 to 1825, only half a dozen new companies came into being during the recession from 1825 to 1830, while twenty-five companies were chartered in the recovery and boom between 1832 and 1837.[17] In the second place, certain forces which determined where life insurance companies were to be established began to be apparent. The first and foremost of these locational influences was the extent to which a money economy had developed in a given area.[18] Consequently, nearly all life companies were founded in commercial centers, where people needed life insurance, could afford to pay premiums, and had enough capital to launch new enterprises. In the third place, life insurance tended to become the sole preoccupation of companies which assumed life risks. All the early companies above mentioned, except the Presbyterian Ministers' Fund, ultimately discontinued their life insurance for their trust business, or went entirely out of existence.[19] In the

[17] Spectator Company, *Charters of American Life Insurance Companies* (New York, 1895).
[18] This applies to Hartford, Conn., where there was a thrifty trade carried on by sloops. See Archibald A. Welch, *A History of Insurance in Connecticut* (New Haven, 1935) and P. H. Woodward, *Insurance in Connecticut* (Boston, 1897).
[19] The Insurance Company of North America abandoned life policies in 1817 and became a leader in the fire and casualty field; the Pennsylvania Company issued no life policies after 1872, concentrating on trust business and reaching an eminent position in that field the Massachusetts Hospital Company retired in 1878; the Baltimore Life's policies were reinsured in the Equitable in 1877; and the Girard Company and the New York Life and Trust Company turned their attention mainly to a trust business.

fourth place, life insurance companies became subject to some state control either by terms of their charters or by laws to prohibit foreign or out-of-state companies from writing insurance within a state (Pennsylvania law of 1810, New York laws of 1814 and 1824, and Massachusetts law of 1827). Finally, life insurance was early regarded by states as a source of revenue, to be tapped by taxation [20] or, as in Massachusetts, for some charitable purpose.

ECONOMIC ENVIRONMENT OF THE FOUNDING OF THE MUTUAL LIFE

Life insurance had by 1840 passed through the stage of pure experimentation and had reached a point at which it could be widely employed to distribute the economic losses occasioned by death. It was on the threshold of a great awakening and the number of successful companies which began business between 1843 and 1851 was large.

TABLE 4

LEGAL RESERVE[a] LIFE INSURANCE COMPANIES COMMENCING BUSINESS PRIOR TO 1852 AND IN ACTIVE OPERATION IN 1942[b]

Name of Company	Home Office	Year and Date of Commencing Business
Presbyterian Ministers' Fund	Philadelphia, Pa.	1759
Mutual Life Ins. Co. of N.Y.	New York, N.Y.	Feb. 1, 1843
New England Mutual Ins. Co.	Boston, Mass.	Dec. 1, 1843
Mutual Benefit Life Ins. Co.	Newark, N.J.	Apr. 1, 1845
New York Life Ins. Co.	New York, N.Y.	Apr. 12, 1845
State Mutual Life Assurance Co.	Worcester, Mass.	June 1, 1845
Conn. Mutual Life Ins. Co.	Hartford, Conn.	Dec. 15, 1846
Penn Mutual Life Ins. Co.	Philadelphia, Pa.	May 25, 1847
Union Mutual Life Ins. Co.	Portland, Me.	Oct. 1, 1849
National Life Ins. Co.	Montpelier, Vt.	Feb. 1, 1850
U.S. Life Ins. Co.	New York, N.Y.	Mar. 4, 1850
Aetna Life Ins. Co.	Hartford, Conn.	July, 1850
Manhattan Life Ins. Co.	New York, N.Y.	Aug. 1, 1850
Phoenix Mutual Life Ins. Co.	Hartford, Conn.	May, 1851
Mass. Mutual Life Ins. Co.	Springfield, Mass.	Aug. 1, 1851
Berkshire Life Ins. Co.	Pittsfield, Mass.	Sept. 4, 1851

[a] The term "legal reserve" means that these companies maintained reserves for their policies according to legal requirements.

[b] In this same period three companies failed and one retired. Frederick L. Hoffman, "Fifty Years of American Life Insurance Progress," *Quarterly Publications of the American Statistical Association*, Sept., 1911, and *Spectator Yearbooks*, 1911 and 1943.

The appearance of so many new companies in the decade after 1843 was owing not only to the fact that the institution of life insurance had attained a stage where its application was practicable but also to the development of the American economy to a level at which there was a

[20] P. L. Gamble, *Taxation of Insurance Companies* (Albany, 1937).

greater demand for life insurance. The reasons for this increased demand are to be found in the growth of the capitalist system in the United States, for, as has already been suggested, life insurance has been a concomitant of a money economy.

By 1843 there was abundant evidence that capitalism had secured a firm foothold in America. Transportation, which makes possible an exchange of goods that in turn results in surplus, had been enormously increased. Roads had been improved; canals had been built; the steamboat had opened up a vast network of rivers; and railroads were being laid down. In 1818 the Cumberland Road was completed by the Federal Government at a cost of $6,821,000. The Erie Canal, which necessitated an expenditure of a little more than $7,000,000, was completed in 1825 and by 1850 was part of a total canal mileage of 3,689. The steamboat was employed so successfully in inland waterways that by 1843 the steam tonnage of the port of New Orleans was twice as much as that of New York. And between 1830 and 1840 the United States put nearly 3,000 miles of railroads in operation and had many more under construction. How much traffic these means of transportation carried, it is impossible to say in the absence of reliable data, but that the rate of increase between 1825 and 1837 was tremendous was apparent to all contemporaries. It was probably greater than the 100 percent increase which was registered in foreign commerce between 1830 and 1840.

Nor was this expansion of transportation an isolated phenomenon. Revenue from the sale of Federal bonds increased from less than $2,000,-000 in 1800 to $25,000,000 in 1836; expenditures of the government doubled between 1830 and 1836; capital invested in manufacturing increased from less than $100,000,000 in 1828 to $300,000,000 in 1838; the population rose from 12,866,020 in 1830 to 17,069,453 in 1840; and the percentage of persons living in cities of 8,000 or more went up from 6.7 to 8.5 in the same ten-year period. In the financial world changes were even more striking. After the War of 1812 the states became large borrowers in order to provide capital for internal improvements. Their loans for these purposes soared from practically nothing when the Erie Canal bonds were marketed in 1817 to $108,000,000 for the years 1836–1839.[21] Loans and discounts of banks were $272,000,000 upon a capital

---

[21] These loans gave rise to the "investment banking" business, the leaders in the field being merchant bankers like Thomas Biddle and Co. of Philadelphia; Astor and Sons; Brown Brothers and Company; Prime, Ward and King; Nevins, Townsend and Company; and the Morris Canal and Banking Company of New York City. The statistical material on this period is taken largely from William J. Shultz and M. R. Caine, *Financial Development of the United States* (New York, 1937).

of $182,000,000 in 1830 and were $525,000,000 on a capital of $291,000,-
000 in 1837. European investments, most of which were British, were
in 1838 between $150,000,000 and $200,000,000. Wholesale prices increased from 1830 to 1837 by more than 25 percent; and the circulating
currency went up from $60,000,000 to $179,000,000.

The great expansion of American economy from 1830 to 1837 did
much to make Americans more dependent on money and moneyed institutions and hence to till the ground for life insurance. But, as in all
periods of great prosperity, the boom engendered certain conditions
which made its continuation impossible. The earnings of many of the
new enterprises fell off as costs increased, a point was reached at which
the prospects for profits were dim, and confidence in the future began
to wane. A business recession, which started in England in 1836, and
President Jackson's policies, which resulted in a restriction of credit,
precipitated the crisis. Bank and railroad stocks, both favorite forms of
investment, collapsed, and there was a general tightening of the money
market.

The influence of the boom and of the recession on life insurance was
great. The prosperity phase of the business cycle had contributed toward
bringing into existence the New York Life and Trust Company (1830),
the Baltimore Life Insurance Company (1830), the American Life Insurance and Trust Company (1836) and toward the chartering of the New
England Mutual Life Insurance Company (1835), although this concern
did not issue its first policy until 1844. Such companies did much, as we
have seen, to popularize the idea of life insurance. On the other hand, the
depression years which followed the crash of 1837 [22] affected life insurance in several ways. The losses which were suffered at first made the
selling of life policies difficult, but when the reaction came, businessmen
desired for their wives some provision which would be immune from
business losses. This feeling was reflected in the famous New York law
of 1840 which stipulated that any married woman might receive benefits
from life insurance free from the claims of her husband's creditors if
the annual premiums on the policy did not exceed $300—a law that was
widely adopted by other states.[23] Secondly, the depression deprived many

[22] In 1839 there was a boom in cotton, but it was only temporary, and its effects were
probably not widespread.

[23] Massachusetts adopted it in 1844.

It is an interesting coincidence that the Mercantile Agency, the first important credit
agency in the country and the forerunner of Dun and Bradstreet, was founded in 1841. This
fact gives further support to the statement that credit was uncertain and liquid capital was
restricted following the panic of 1837. See Roy A. Foulke, *The Sinews of American Commerce* (New York, 1941).

men of their ordinary ways of making a living and encouraged them to turn to other fields, such as life insurance. Thirdly, the period gave a great impulse to the mutual form of organization, for shortage of capital during the depression years made the sale of stock in life insurance companies almost impossible. Furthermore, the great New York fire of December, 1835, resulted in the failure of all but three fire insurance companies in the city—an event which put stock insurance companies under a cloud and led to the establishment of a number of fire insurance mutuals. These forces, the success of mutual life insurance in England, and the practice of the Girard Company of issuing life contracts that allowed the policyholders to share in the profits account in large part for the fact that all the companies in Table 4 which were founded from 1843 through 1849 were mutuals.

THE FOUNDING OF THE MUTUAL LIFE

It was in the general economic environment of the late 1830's and early 1840's that plans for establishing The Mutual Life Insurance Company were formulated. That they should have been made in New York City is not surprising, for by this time New York was more than twice the size of any other American city and since the 1820's had been the nation's financial capital. Nor is it strange that they were drafted mainly by two men who had had some insurance experience and who were known in the financial world. These two men were Alfred S. Pell (1805–1869) and Morris Robinson (1784–1849).

Pell came from a family which had migrated to America in 1635 and had been given letters patent to the manor of Pelham. Alfred S. Pell became, as a fairly young man, a representative of The Mutual Safety Insurance Company, which was engaged in the business of writing marine and fire insurance. Thus, he was familiar with the principles of mutuality, knew something of the problems involved in the insurance business, and had many connections in the insurance field.

Morris Robinson came from an old Virginia family which had moved to New York state prior to the Revolution, but had gone on to Nova Scotia because of its loyalist sympathies during the conflict with England. Young Morris began his business career in a counting house in St. Johns, Newfoundland, came to New York City in 1810, was made cashier of the Orange County Bank at Goshen, N.Y., in 1812, and remained in this position until he was appointed cashier of the New York Branch of the Second Bank of the United States in 1819. He served in this capacity, with offices in what is now the Sub-Treasury Building in Wall Street,

until the Second Bank had lost its fight with President Jackson to get
a new charter and had been incorporated under the laws of Pennsylvania
(1836). After Robinson had resigned from the Second Bank, he seems
to have cast about for a new and lucrative position, for in 1839 he was
in London in the interests of the newly established American Exchange
Bank and was for a time vice-president of the American Life Insurance
and Trust Company of Baltimore—a company that ceased business in
1842.

Pell and Robinson made a good team, for while both were profoundly
interested in the common goal of establishing a life insurance company,
the former knew insurance and the latter knew finance and financial
men. Pell was able, for example, to enlist the active coöperation of
Zebedee Cook, Jr.,[24] who had been president of the Eagle Insurance Company of Boston and was president of The Mutual Safety Insurance Company, and of Joseph B. Collins, secretary of the latter Company and a
future president of The Mutual Life. Robinson, for his part, succeeded
in securing the support of such men as William H. Aspinwall, a shipping
merchant who was said to have control of about $4,000,000,[25] Robert B.
Minturn, who was with a shipping and commission house and had a
fortune of $200,000, James Boorman, an iron merchant with a capital
of $1,500,000, Henry Brevoort, a large real estate owner whose fortune
was valued at $1,000,000, Philip S. Van Rensselaer, Mortimer Livingston,
Joseph Blunt, a lawyer and the Company's first counsel, and John V. L.
Pruyn, an Albany lawyer who later became attorney general for the
New York Central Railroad, chancellor of the University of the State of
New York, and president of the board of trustees of St. Stephen's College
at Anandale-on-the-Hudson, now Bard College.[26]

The first step toward the actual organization of the new company was
to get a charter. This had to be granted by a special act of the state
legislature, for New York's general incorporation law of 1811 did not
apply to a mutual life insurance company. The task of drafting the
charter having been completed in 1841, Mr. Pruyn, aided to some extent by Joseph Blunt, saw the document through its legislative stages

---

24 He was later president of the Astor Insurance Company.

25 These estimates of wealth are from M. Y. Beach, *Wealth and Pedigrees of the Wealthy
Citizens of New York* (New York, 1846). They should not be considered as accurate statements, but as mere guesses.

26 The extent of the services of these gentlemen can be surmised to some degree by the
remuneration which they received when the company got under way. On November 11,
1845, the board voted $400 to Mr. Pruyn and $250 to Mr. Blunt for their services in getting
the charter and for attending to the affairs of the company in the legislature. On February
8, 1848, $1,500 was voted to Mr. Pell for obtaining the charter and for organizing the
company.

at Albany. On April 12, 1842, "The People of the State of New York represented in Senate and Assembly" approved by a two-thirds vote the measure creating the Company.

THE CHARTER [27]

The charter of The Mutual Life Insurance Company of New York is a remarkable document and is often referred to as the magna carta of life insurance in America. The fundamental principles contained in it formed the basis of the life insurance industry in this country, and except for certain details they have never been altered.

The charter granted the right to make "all and every insurance appertaining to or connected with life risks and to grant and purchase annuities." In conformity with the principle of mutuality every policyholder was to become a member of the Company—the Company was to be theirs. The corporate powers of the Company were to be exercised by a board of thirty-six trustees,[28] nine of whom were to be chosen annually from among the policyholders and by members who had insurance amounting to at least $1,000. The president was to be elected annually from among the policyholders by the trustees. This was veritably government of the people and by the people. Whether or not policyholders were to exercise their rights was entirely their concern. On occasion they were to be very active, as we shall see, but in general only a small number were to participate in elections, placing their faith in the trustees to whom power had been delegated.

Government was also for the people. The charter stipulated that premiums, fixed by the trustees, should be paid by all policyholders into a common fund and that from this fund benefits should be paid. Dividends were to be distributed by the Company at first every five years and later annually among members, but liability of policyholders and of officers for the debts of the Company was limited to the actual amount paid into the common fund. No assessments could be made on the policyholders in addition to the contractual premiums for any losses or expenses incurred by the institution.

So far as the investment of moneys received by the Company was concerned, the charter was exceedingly cautious, for experience had taught and was to teach several times in the future that unscrupulous promoters could employ such funds for selfish purposes. Thus the Company was

---

27 For the original text of the charter, see the Appendix.

28 The charter provided that all trustees be citizens of New York State. This provision was soon altered.

permitted to invest only in mortgages on unincumbered real estate within the state of New York (real property to secure such investments being in every case worth twice the amount loaned thereon), or up to one-half the premiums received in the bonds of the United States, New York State, or any incorporated city of New York State.

As further precautions against possible abuse, the charter required the officers to draw up every five years a general financial statement of the affairs of the Company, showing expenses, amount of premiums, amount of losses, the balance remaining with the Company, the nature of the security on which this balance was loaned or invested, and the amount of cash on hand. Every member was to have access to this statement and to the books of the Company. Moreover, the Company was to make a full report of its affairs to the Comptroller of the State on the first of January of each year and to answer those questions which might be asked. Then, as a final safeguard and to make certain that enough members could be obtained to allow the general averages of mortality to operate, no policy was to be issued until applications had been secured for insurance which in the aggregate should amount to at least $500,000.

ORGANIZATION FOR BUSINESS

With the right to conduct a life insurance business on a mutual basis thus obtained, the founders had to set up an organization to carry their plans to realization. In the early months of 1842 Morris Robinson seems to have been busy getting the consent of leaders in the economic life of New York to become trustees or to promise to take out insurance with the proposed company, while Alfred Pell went to London primarily on business for the Mutual Safety, but incidentally to get further details concerning life insurance from the officers of The Old Equitable.

On May 9, 1842,[29] the Board of Trutsees met for the first time in the trustees' room of The Mutual Safety Insurance Company at 44 Wall Street. The Board was composed of the following men, those marked with an asterisk being present.[30]

[29] The minutes of the board begin with this date. The complete minutes from this time to the present have been preserved.

[30] As one can see from the following list of those who signed the petition for the charter, several changes had been made in the personnel of the prospective board: Morris Robinson, William H. Aspinwall, James Brown, Robert B. Minturn, James Boorman, Theodore Sedgwick, Stacy B. Collins, John W. Leavitt, Elihu Townsend, James S. Wadsworth, Philip S. Van Rensselaer, Gouverneur M. Wilkins, John V. L. Pruyn, Thomas W. Olcott, Charles L. Livingston, John C. Cruger, Alfred Pell, David C. Colden, Jacob Harvey, Rufus L. Lord, Arthur Bronson, Henry Brevoort, Robert C. Cornell, Joseph Blunt, Jacob P. Girard, James Campbell, William Moore, Zebedee Cook, Jr., Jonathan Miller, Fitz-Greene Halleck, John A. King, T. Romeyn Beck, Richard V. DeWitt, Gideon Hawley, and James J. Ring.

Alfred Pell called the meeting to order, the trustees divided themselves into four classes of nine each for purposes of future elections, and a quorum of nine was decided upon. Then the Board proceeded to elect Morris Robinson the first president. He received eighteen votes from the twenty persons present, which was tantamount to a unanimous choice—a fact which indicated that the trustees had decided upon Robinson prior to the meeting and that he had expressed his willingness to serve. Finally, the Board asked the president to appoint a committee on organization which was to suggest what other officers and what regulations were needed "to carry into effect the objects of the Company." [31]

At the next meeting of the Board, May 19, 1842, Samuel Hannay, who kept a book and stationery store in Pearl Street, was elected secretary of the new Company, at a salary of $1,000; the president's salary was fixed at the low figure of $1,500 which he was willing to accept until the Company proved to be a success. Joseph Blunt was made counsel, and Dr. Minturn Post was chosen as the Company's examining physician. Meetings of the Board were to be held monthly and there were to be two standing committees—a committee of finance and a committee of insurance. The rates of premiums to be charged were to be the same as those employed by the New York Life Insurance and Trust Company —the most successful company of the day.[32]

With the preliminaries taken care of and with an office established at 44 Wall Street, the Company began to receive subscriptions for insurance. All of the energies of the officers seem to have been directed to this

[31] To this committee were appointed Robert B. Minturn, Mortimer Livingston, Arthur Bronson, Alfred S. Pell, and Joseph Blunt, in addition to the president.

[32] The minutes relate that the rates were to be the same as those of the "New York Life Insurance Company." This obviously means the New York Life Insurance and Trust Company as the present-day New York Life Insurance Co. was not then in existence and was, moreover, at first known as the Nautilus Insurance Company. It did not get its present name until 1848.

tàsk, not even a meeting of the Board of Trustees interrupting their activity. By December 19, 1842, we learn that eleven agents had been appointed to solicit business, the first evidence of an agency system in an American company writing only life business on a mutual basis. The most successful of the agents was Shipman, Ayres, and Company of New York.[33] That the efforts of the officers bore fruit is evidenced by the fact that it was decided to get applications for $1,000,000 of insurance, instead of for the $500,000 required by the charter, before any policies were actually issued.

Finally, at the meeting of the Board on February 1, 1843, the committee on arrangements reported "that having obtained at the office and through the agents of the Company subscriptions to the amount of more than one million of dollars, the sum required by the board before going into operation, they have in consequence thereof taken the necessary steps for commencing business this day, by having the proper books prepared, and applications and policies printed, and also by advertising in several of the morning and evening papers that this Company would be ready to offer policies on the first day of February." In conformity with this report, the Board voted to begin business. Immediately the first two policies were issued—the first a contract on the life of Thomas N. Ayres and the second on the life of George P. Shipman, both partners in Shipman, Ayres, and Company. These were the first policies to have been issued in America by a company which was open to all persons and has had a continuous existence down to the present day. At last The Mutual Life Insurance Company of New York was under way. A new era in American life insurance was inaugurated, an era that was characterized by the placing of life insurance on a scientific and mutual basis.[34]

[33] The other agents were Hale and Welbasky of Boston, Harry A. Brewster, Rochester, N.Y., Osborn Walker, Utica, N.Y., J. V. L. Pruyn, Albany, N.Y., George Merrill, Philadelphia, Pa., William B. Bristol, New Haven, Conn., and John A. Moore, William A. Woodward, J. G. Pierson, and Henry B. Robinson of New York City.

[34] For first policy see p. 52.

PART TWO
1843-1870

III. The Growth of Life Insurance and the Evolution of the Contract

THE TWENTY-SEVEN YEARS which followed the issuance of The Mutual Life Insurance Company's first policy witnessed the establishment of the fundamental procedures and practices which were to make life insurance one of the most successful and one of the largest of American financial enterprises. The amount of insurance in force rose from probably less than $10,000,000 in 1840 to $163,703,455 in 1860 and to $2,023,884,955 in 1870, while the number of companies doing business on the basis of policy reserves and reporting to New York State officials increased from fifteen in 1850 to seventy-one in 1870. In this development of the industry The Mutual Life Insurance Company played a major role. It made several important contributions to the scientific bases of life insurance, and it led all companies in writing insurance, having $242,004,489 of insurance in force in 1870.[1]

During the period from 1843 to 1870 there was not a single aspect of the life insurance business that was not altered or developed to meet the exigencies of the American scene. Rules of selection were established so that people with approximately equal chances of survival should share each other's risks—a problem that required medical examinations to weed out the weak and the infirm and extra premiums from those who lived in unhealthy regions or climates or who engaged in hazardous occupations. A mortality table, based on American experience, was made for no one knew whether or not the mortality rate of a small English town, which was the basis for the table then employed by American life insurance companies, would prove to be the same as the mortality rate in the United States. To allay any doubts on this score The Mutual Life prepared the American Experience Table—a table that was computed from mortality rates among The Mutual's insureds and has proved so satisfactory that it is used by many companies and state insurance commissions at the present time.

---

1 These figures are from William Barnes, *New York Insurance Reports Condensed Edition* (Albany, 1873) and *The Spectator Yearbook* (Philadelphia, 1911).

Premium rates were established in order that members could pay enough into the common fund to cover the costs of insurance. Here, again, The Mutual Life drew up schedules which were widely copied. Reserves on policies were maintained so that adequate funds would always be available to meet death or other claims when they occurred. To this problem Elizur Wright of Massachusetts,[2] the most prominent figure in American life insurance during this period and the first state insurance commissioner, put his active mind and developed tables for the calculation of reserves which were adopted as legal standards by Massachusetts in 1858 and by other states in subsequent years. Moreover, a system was devised by The Mutual Life in 1862 for a more equitable distribution of dividends among policyholders—a system that is today used by most companies. Policies for the investment of insurance funds in safe and remunerative securities were formulated, those pursued by The Mutual Life being particularly conservative and profitable. Finally, The Mutual's investments contributed much to the public improvements of the period, to the development of real estate, particularly in metropolitan New York, and to the financing of the Civil War.

In addition to the formulation of insurance principles and investment policies, the period 1843–1870 witnessed an extension of the agency system of marketing life insurance. Although most of the insurance was at first sold by and at home offices, the proportion placed by agents working on a commission basis, having exclusive territories, and actually engaged in personal solicitation, steadily increased. In the early years of its existence, The Mutual Life, like other companies, obtained most of its business in the large cities of the East, but gradually it opened a market along the routes to the West, in the cities of the Middle West, and in the South. With the outbreak of the Civil War, the Southern market was lost, but compensating areas were secured by opening agencies in the West and on the Pacific Coast. By 1870 life insurance had become nation-wide in its scope, and consideration was being given to extending it overseas. Also, by the same date competition within the industry had become severe and practices which were to become exaggerated between the years 1870–1906 had been inaugurated. In order to obtain more business, some companies took personal notes instead of cash for premiums and some issued scrip for dividends. Moreover, commissions to agents mounted steadily; "twisting," that is, the changing of insurance from one company to another, had put in an appearance, and the raiding of agency forces had become a not uncommon practice.

[2] Elizur Wright, *Reports and Biography* (Chicago, 1932).

Finally, the quarter of a century of life insurance history prior to 1870 was marked by an increasing amount of state regulation. This governmental intervention followed two major lines—to further the business of companies domiciled in a particular state and to safeguard the interests of policyholders. To achieve the former goal, some states levied discriminatory taxes on out-of-state companies and hindered their activity by enforcing nuisance requirements—a kind of state protectionism which has not been entirely wiped out to this day. To protect policyholders, states began to publicize information concerning the operations of life companies, but when this did not prove sufficient, they established legal standards for various aspects of the business and appointed commissioners to see that the laws were obeyed. By the late 1860's states had such a variety of these laws that the companies contemplated the wisdom of seeking Federal control. This move was, however, stopped by a famous decision of the United States Supreme Court in the case of *Paul vs. Virginia* (1868), which declared that insurance was not interstate commerce and not subject to Federal jurisdiction. State regulation had come to stay. The problem was to make it intelligently effective.

THE GROWTH OF LIFE INSURANCE AND AMERICAN ECONOMIC DEVELOPMENT, 1843–1870

As was stated in the first chapter of this book, insurance came into being when our economy reached a point at which risks could not easily be sustained by the individual. And life insurance developed on a large scale when relatively more and more people were engaged in commercial or industrial enterprises; when they had to rely on daily wages or the earnings from capital for subsistence; and when dependents absorbed large portions of these persons' wages or earnings. Many of these conditions were met in the period 1843–1870 on account of the great expansion of the American economy—an expansion which is too frequently minimized because of a still greater extension of business activity after 1880. Moreover, a rapid growth of life insurance was possible because the new industry, with its relatively late start, had to make up for lost time—it had to satisfy a long pent-up demand.

The history of new countries has usually been characterized by problems of territorial acquisition and of settlement and by the necessity of securing sufficient capital for getting the economy under way. Such questions were paramount in the American scene in the middle decades of the nineteenth century, but they were complicated and conditioned by certain other factors. Most prominent of these was the mechanization of

CHART III

GROWTH OF ORDINARY LIFE INSURANCE, 1843–1870

*Peaks in business are indicated by broken vertical
lines; troughs by solid vertical lines*

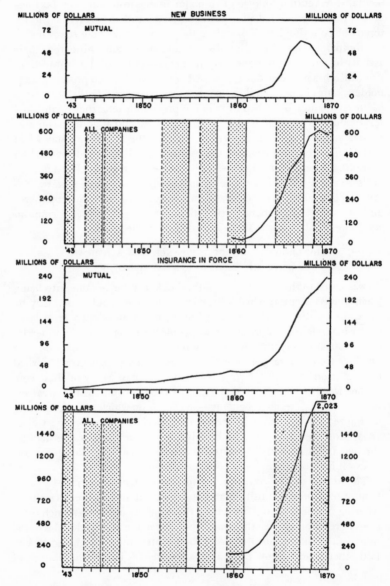

Sources: New York Insurance Department, *Reports* (Albany, N.Y.), 1861–1871; turning points
of the business cycle were made public by the National Bureau of Economic Research (1941).

industrial production, which profoundly altered man's ways of living and of earning a livelihood. Secondly, a new commercial revolution, effected by the building of railways, the use of steamboats, and the widening of the market, decidedly influenced the course of events. And thirdly, the Civil War gave a fillip to the metallurgical industries and to transportation, but resulted in a great drain upon the capital resources of the nation.

Shortly after the founding of The Mutual Life, the United States completed its acquisition of contiguous territory on the American mainland. In 1846 the long-standing dispute between Great Britain and this country over the Oregon territory was definitely settled by the recognition of the forty-ninth parallel as the northern boundary of the United States. In 1845 Texas was annexed and, although this action led to war, the conflict with Mexico resulted (1848) not only in confirming the claim to the Lone Star state but also in the addition of most of the area of California, Nevada, Utah, Arizona, New Mexico, and part of Colorado to the territory of the country. Finally, in 1853 the Gadsden Purchase rounded out the lands of this nation by securing the southern part of Arizona and southwestern New Mexico. The resulting total area of three million square miles made the United States nearly fifteen times as large as France and Germany. It contained rich and varied natural resources which were unsurpassed in any other national state.

The settlement of this vast expanse of land was one of the great undertakings of modern times. By 1843 the fertile plains of the Mississippi valley had drawn white farmers from the East and had given rise to wheat farming, cotton growing, and cattle raising. The California gold rush in 1848 and 1849 led great numbers of people to the Pacific Coast, while the discovery of gold on Pike's Peak in 1858 and of silver in the Comstock Lode of Nevada in 1859 started new migrations to Colorado and Nevada. The hardy souls who ventured forth in the quest of a modern Eldorado blazed trails which were soon followed by those who were content to make a living from agriculture and commerce. These people obtained land from the Government at low prices, especially by the terms of the Homestead Act of 1862, while land grants to canal companies, railroads, and states helped to provide them with transportation facilities, low tax rates, and educational institutions. But despite all these initial steps, only about 14 percent of the population lived west of the Mississippi River in 1870 (the percentage was 31 in 1940) and the frontier was not far beyond the Missouri River, approximately at the ninety-seventh meridian. Completion of western settlement remained to be accomplished after 1870.

While trails were being blazed westward, manufacturing was steadily growing in the northern states of the East. Here, where the merchant-employer, or putting-out, method of production had never been firmly established, the factory system was introduced with comparative ease. Machines and techniques imported from England and further developed on this side of the Atlantic gave rise to the great cotton and woolen industries of New England, New York, and Pennsylvania. The use of coke for smelting iron ore and of coal for steam led to an increase in coal production from 4,535,000 short tons as a yearly average between 1841 and 1850 to an annual average of 31,706,000 short tons for the years 1866–1870. The invention of shoemaking machinery and of the sewing machine made possible the manufacture of boots and clothes in small shops or factories. The demand for machines, railroad equipment, and steam engines revolutionized the metallurgical trades. From 1849 to 1869 the value added to products by manufacturing increased from $463,-983,000 to $1,395,119,000—an increase of about 300 percent.

In agriculture methods were generally wasteful and exhaustive of the soil, but in spite of cheap land, technological improvements were made. Knowledge of soil chemistry led to the use of artificial fertilizers, particularly phosphate, and to a more scientific rotation of crops. Reapers, hay mowers, horse rakes, the chilled plow, and many other implements came into use. The quality of livestock was improved by the importation of good strains and by the exercise of more care in breeding. The amount of land under cultivation grew by leaps and bounds, and the total as well as the per acre production of farm products was greatly increased. In 1839 the wheat crop was 84,823,000 bushels, but by 1870 it had reached the sizable figure of 254,429,000 bushels. The cotton crop, which had been 160,000,000 pounds in 1820, attained 2,200,000,000 pounds in 1860, and this product, although "king" in the economy of the South, was only equal in value to wheat. Corn, the great staple, was by far the leader of all farm produce, its annual value being twice that of wheat or cotton. Finally, the prices for agricultural products were particularly good from 1845 to 1865 and the farming community enjoyed relative prosperity during these years.

Much of the success of the farmer, as well as of the manufacturer, was owing to revolutionary improvements in transportation. The building of canals, the introduction of the steamboat in the great Mississippian system, the construction of railroads, and the use of clippers and ocean-going steam vessels ushered in a new era in commerce. In 1847 the steamboat tonnage on Western rivers was said to have exceeded that of the entire British Empire, and in 1861 the tonnage of American sea vessels amounted to 2,500,000—a figure not again equaled for fifty years. The mileage of railroads increased from 4,026 in 1842 to 52,922 in 1870,[3] lines were built from the Eastern seaboard to beyond Chicago, and transcontinental routes were planned. Some measure of this increase in trade is provided by statistics of foreign commerce, which indicate that exports, including reëxports, rose from a yearly average of $122,620,000 for the years 1841–1850 to $320,842,000 for the years 1866–1870, while imports increased from $121,123,000 to $408,295,000 in the same period.

With the increase in the physical production of goods and in their transportation to market, new challenges were presented to the financial institutions of the country. The number of banks and the amount of business which they transacted expanded greatly, and the national banking system established during the Civil War added much to their stability.

TABLE 5

ALL ACTIVE BANKS IN 1840 AND 1870

(In millions of dollars)

Year	Number of Banks	Loans and Discounts	Investments	Cash and Balances with Other Banks	Total Assets	Capital Surplus and Undivided Profits	Circulation	Deposits
1840	901	462.9	42.4	98.7	657.7	358.4	107.0	119.9
1870	1937	863.8	469.7	405.6	1,780.8	648.3	336.1	775.1

Considerable sums of capital were borrowed abroad, especially from Great Britain, but there was such a large accumulation of national capital that during the Civil War no appreciable amount of specie was drained off to foreign lands. Nevertheless, the public debt increased to nearly $2,700,000,000 in 1865, and this proved to be a serious burden to the American economy. Finally, individual wealth increased and became somewhat more concentrated—a fact that had a direct bearing upon the life insurance industry.

The economic expansion from 1843 to 1870 made possible a large increase in the population. Not only was the native birth rate high, particularly in rural areas where children were economically necessary, but immigration was large. The Irish potato famine of 1846 and the revolutionary events of 1848 sent large numbers of Irish and Germans to our shores. In 1854, 427,000 citizens of other lands arrived in the United States, and although the number subsequently dropped, workers from abroad were in demand to build the railroads, to man the factories, and to take the places of those farmers who moved on to the West. From

[3] All figures are from the *U.S. Statistical Abstract, 1940*.

1840 to 1870 the population of the United States increased from 17,069,-453 to 38,558,371, and at the latter date was comparable in size to those of the great states of western Europe. Moreover, this American population was slowly becoming urbanized [4] and was hence placed in a position where life insurance protection was of exceptional importance.

TABLE 6

LEGAL RESERVE LIFE COMPANIES COMMENCING BUSINESS BETWEEN 1851 AND 1875 AND IN ACTIVE OPERATION IN 1942

Name of Company	Home Office	Year and Date of Commencing Business
German Mutual Life Ins. Co.[a]	St. Louis, Mo.	Apr. 12, 1858
Northwestern Mutual Life Insurance Co.	Milwaukee, Wis.	Nov. 25, 1858
Equitable Life Assurance Society of U.S.	New York, N.Y.	July 28, 1859
Home Life Insurance Co.	New York, N.Y.	May 1, 1860
Germania Life Ins. Co.[b]	New York, N.Y.	July 16, 1860
John Hancock Mutual Life Ins. Co.	Boston, Mass.	Dec. 27, 1862
Maryland Life Ins. Co.	Baltimore, Md.	July 12, 1865
Provident Life & Trust Co. of Philadelphia [c]	Philadelphia, Pa.	July 31, 1865
Conn. General Life Ins. Co.	Hartford, Conn.	Oct., 1865
Travelers Insurance Co.	Hartford, Conn.	July, 1866
Metropolitan Life Ins. Co.	New York, N.Y.	Jan., 1867
Equitable Life Ins. Co. of Iowa	Des Moines, Ia.	March, 1867
Union Central Life Ins. Co.	Cincinnati, Ohio	1867
Pacific Mutual Life Ins. Co.	Los Angeles, Cal.	April, 1868
Masonic Mutual Relief Ass'n.[d]	Washington, D.C.	Mar. 3, 1869
Mutual Life Ins. Co. of Baltimore [e]	Baltimore, Md.	1870
Pennsylvania Mutual Ins. Co.	Philadelphia, Pa.	1870
Life Insurance Co. of Virginia	Richmond, Va.	April, 1871
Prudential Insurance Co. of America	Newark, N.J.	Oct. 13, 1875

    [a] Name changed to St. Louis Mutual Life Insurance Co., 1919.

    [b] Name changed to Guardian Life Insurance Co. of America, 1918.

    [c] Name changed to Provident Mutual Life Insurance Co. of Philadelphia, 1922.

    [d] Name changed to Masonic Mutual Life Ass'n. of the District of Columbia, 1908; in 1922 to the Acacia Mutual Life Ass'n.; in 1932 to the Acacia Mutual Life Ins. Co.

    [e] Name changed to Monumental Life Ins. Co., 1935.

In view of the great growth of business activity, of population, of individual wealth, and of economic relationships based on money, the rapid progress made by life insurance is more readily understood. Yet it should not be imagined that either the general economy or life insurance advanced at an even pace without any setbacks. There was, indeed, a close correlation between life insurance activity and the business cycle. New life companies were founded in the revivals from the troughs after 1843, 1848, 1858, and 1867. Failures or retirements from business were most pronounced in the California gold inflation period of 1852–1853, in the recession of the cycle in 1856–1857, and in the revival years 1868–1869—a record which indicates that booms gave rise to new and unstable companies, which were soon to founder.

    [4] *Ibid.*, "Area and Population," pp. 1–72.

As can be seen from the Appendix tables, the fluctuation of "new business" follows closely the business cycle—more closely than "total insurance in force," for the simple reason that the latter was of an incremental nature. The Mutual Life's "new business," on the other hand, was not so faithful a follower of the cyclical curve as was the new business of all companies, because managerial policies tend to be reflected more sharply in a single case than in many. Nevertheless, the falling off of new business after 1849, the increase after 1852, the slight fall after 1858, then the steady increase to 1867, and the subsequent decline make the connection fairly clear. Another matter in the above tables, which is worthy of note, is the tremendous increase in the amount of insurance outstanding during the Civil War. This shows that the endangering of life by war brings home to people the wisdom of carrying life insurance.

KINDS OF INSURANCE, 1843–1870

A policy of insurance was defined by Blackstone as a "contract between A and B, that upon A's paying a premium equivalent to the hazard run, B will indemnify or insure him against a particular event." [5] Simple as these fundamentals are, the life insurance contract can be a most complicated document. It can be made to cover a specified number of years (term insurance); it can demand payments for the whole of life (ordinary life policy); it can require payments for only a specified number of years (limited payment life); it can provide for the payment of the sum insured at the end of a given period or at prior death (endowment policy); or it can combine life insurance with an annuity, with disability, and with other risks, such as death by accident.

The terms of life insurance contracts are legion, but they fall into two general classifications: (1) those which aim to meet specific needs or desires of the insured and (2) those which are designed to permit the insurer successfully to distribute nearly equal risks over a large number of cases. In the early history of life insurance in the United States the kinds of policies which were offered the public were very limited, but they became ever more numerous as the financial demands upon the

[5] For a *bona fide* insurance contract five elements must be present: (1) the insured possesses an interest of some kind susceptible of pecuniary estimation, known as insurable interest; (2) the insured is subject to risk of loss through the destruction or impairment of that interest by the happening of designated perils; (3) the insurer assumes that risk of loss; (4) such assumption is part of a general scheme to distribute actual losses among a large group of persons bearing similar risks; (5) as consideration for the insurer's promise, the insured makes a ratable contribution to a general insurance fund, called a premium. *Blackstone Commentaries* (Lewis ed.), xxx, p. 458. On the question of insurable interest see *The Mutual Life vs. Armstrong*, 117 U.S. 591 (1886).

individual became increasingly complex. On the other hand, the insurer tried to protect his business from almost the very first not only by charging premiums which were ample, but also by establishing restrictions on such exceptional hazards as long-distance travel, residence in unhealthy localities, dangerous occupations, and war service. By about 1870 the peak of this trend had been reached, and from then to recent times there was a general movement toward the liberalization of the life insurance contract.

When The Mutual Life opened its books for business on February 1, 1843, it advertised that "persons may effect insurance on their own lives, or upon the lives of others, and for the whole duration of life, or for a limited period." The Company thus made available ordinary whole life insurance and term insurance and allowed persons to insure their own lives or the lives of others. In the last case it was necessary that those who took insurance have a financial stake (insurable interest) in the person insured—for example, a wife in the life of a husband or a creditor in the life of a debtor.

Very shortly the Company greatly expanded the kind of wares that it was offering, and its annual reports, which combined a report of the Company's affairs with advertising, rates, and insurance information, were replete with new types of contracts. The third report, published in 1846, contained rates for ordinary term and endowment policies, for annuities, that is, for annual payments during the life of an annuitant in return for a sum paid to the Company, and for policies on two lives, the death benefit being paid in one of the following contingencies—(1) upon the death of the first of two lives, (2) upon the death of the last of two lives, and (3) upon the death of both of two lives.[6] The experience with term insurance was not very satisfactory, for persons who were insured for short periods were frequently debtors who were "worried to death," [7] or they were in poor physical condition, or they were about to run some exceptional risk. Hence, in 1853 it was decided that new term policies should be nonparticipating, that is, should not be paid dividends, and that all old term policies should receive less dividends than whole life policies. When this system did not prove satisfactory, the Company stopped (1859) issuing term contracts pending a revision of the table of premiums. In 1864 these policies were reinstituted provided that they

---

[6] The first joint life policy was number 1,544, issued in 1845; endowments were at first payable at a given age, not as at present at the end of 10, 20, or more years. The Union Mutual Life Ins. Company of Maine issued such a policy in 1850; The Mutual Life issued its first one in 1855.

[7] *Fifteenth Annual Report*, p. 32.

were taken with an endowment policy, but they were not again sold alone until 1886.

The dropping of term insurance did not, however, substantially reduce the Company's list of policies, for new arrangements were steadily being concocted. In 1853 the accumulative policy [8] was put on the market —a contract which allowed the insured to buy small amounts of insurance whenever he had the funds available and freed him from the usual procedure of having to meet stipulated payments at regular intervals for a given amount of insurance. In the same year deferred annuities were also offered to the public. Unlike the customary type of annuity, which requires a person to pay down a given sum and then provides him at once with a steady income, the deferred annuity might be paid for either in a lump sum or by annual premiums, but the annuitant would not begin to receive any money until he had attained a certain age— 60 or 70 years.

The year 1859, moreover, witnessed a plethora of new contracts. Children's endowments were created so that a fund could be amassed which would allow parents to set their sons up in business, to give them an advanced education, or to provide daughters with a dowry.[9] Plans were announced and were soon put into effect for *post obit,* or survivorship, annuities and for installment policies. These contracts provided that the Company would pay beneficiaries, not the usual lump insurance sum, but either annuities during their lifetime or the amount of insurance in regular annual installments. They were designed to relieve women and children, unversed in financial matters, from the responsibility of investing money.[10] Finally, the Company began to write contracts which would provide for paid up policies at the more advanced ages when the

[8] Also called deposit insurance. This policy did not prove popular and, although pushed by the Company for a time, was abandoned by 1859.

[9] These endowments would be payable when the child arrived at a given age—18, 21, 25, or more years. Two kinds of contracts were made available, the one which provided that all premiums paid to the Company would revert to the Company in case the child died before attaining the endowment age and the other which provided that such premiums would be returned to the one who had paid the premiums. The premiums on the former were, of course, lower than on the latter.

[10] See the *Sixteenth and Eighteenth Annual Reports.* The first policy form designed for survivorship annuities was printed in 1865, and the first installment policy was issued in 1866. The latter was the forerunner of the Continuous Installment policy which provided payments certain to the beneficiary and was first issued in 1893. Some of these early survivorship annuities provided that the premiums paid be surrendered to the Company in case of the death of the beneficiary before the death of the insured, while others stipulated that they should be returned. The premiums on the latter policy were higher than on the former. Prior to the development of these new contracts the Company would by special arrangement pay the death claim in installments. The first survivorship annuity was issued in 1855, policy no. 14,229, as a special favor.

earning power of the insured would presumably be less than in his earlier years. This arrangement was a forerunner of the limited payment life policy—a policy that would be paid up in a given number of years and which was issued on a special form for the first time in 1864.

TABLE 7

KIND AND AMOUNT OF INSURANCE IN FORCE: THE MUTUAL LIFE

Kind	FEB. 1, 1848 [a] Number	Amount	FEB. 1, 1858 [b] Number	Amount	JAN. 1, 1870 [c] Number	Amount
Life	2,685		9,478	$27,528,065	39,339	$122,218,703
10 payments					9,163	36,142,925
5 payments					306	1,621,500
15 payments					163	454,750
20 payments					87	268,300
Paid up					914	1,216,267
Endowments			154	609,800	13,547	39,386,866
10 payments					3,539	13,812,884
5 payments					105	346,800
Paid up					561	644,629
Irregular					137	467,500
Premiums cease at certain ages					}	
Joint lives			7	13,100	} 24	63,000
Deferred annuities					}	
Survivorship annuities					37	16,500
Children's endowments					141	246,100
End. paid up					4	6,100
Annuities					58	18,458
Accumulative			1	287		
Seven-year term	781		572	1,738,300		
Other short term	154		178	591,750		
Average size of policy (annuities excluded)		$2,762		$2,934		$3,187

    a Board of Trustees, *Minutes*, February 8, 1848. Separate amounts for each kind of insurance not available.

    b Insurance Committee, *Minutes*, February 12, 1858.

    c Insurance Committee, *Minutes*, April 21, 1870.

The Mutual Life was frequently the first to make these various contracts available to the public, although the New York Life prepared a ten-year limited-payment life policy in 1860,[11] and nearly all companies were quick to adopt the new forms. Competition induced insurance institutions to provide ways of distributing more and more of the risks of life, for increased coverage meant more business. Rivalry among companies was, however, to lead in the latter part of the period under consideration, more especially in the period between 1870 and 1906, to the sale of tontine and semi-tontine, or deferred dividend, policies— policies which, as we shall see, were not advantageous, as administered,

    11 James M. Hudnut, *Semi-Centennial History of the New York Life Insurance Company, 1845–1895* (New York, 1895), p. 61n.

44 WALL STREET IN 1842

to the mass of policyholders. All the earlier contracts, on the other hand, were basically sound and form today the backbone of insurance offerings. All except annuities were insurance policies in the strict sense of the word, for they distributed the risks of death, were free of sheer gambling, and paid a benefit to survivors; even ordinary annuities met all but the last requirement. As is the case today, ordinary whole life policies soon became the most popular of all contracts, early supplanting term policies, while ten-year endowments and ten payment life followed, in that order.

EVOLUTION OF THE INSURANCE CONTRACT, 1843–1870

The early life insurance contracts were brief, simple in form, and loosely worded, as can be seen from the first policy issued by The Mutual Life.

This first policy form was similar to that used by the Girard Life Insurance Company as far back as 1837 and its language was also employed, except for one phrase, by The New York Life (Nautilus) when that company began business in 1845. Up until 1855 The Mutual Life continued to use this basic form for almost all its insurance, filling in the blank spaces to fit each case and only altering the specific terms as the regulations of the Company changed.

Several features of this policy immediately attract the attention of one who is familiar with present life insurance contracts. It will be noted that the policyholder in this case was Sarah Ayres and that she contracted to pay the premiums, while the insured was her husband Thomas. The premiums were to be paid annually on fixed dates; provision for dividends was omitted from the contract, although the rules of the Company provided for such payments; and the Company was allowed sixty days in which to pay the death claim after notice and proof of death had been received. But more striking than these features were the restrictions placed upon the insured. The Company feared that the mortality of the insureds might be greater than anticipated and desired to distribute risks among persons who encountered approximately the same hazards. Hence the contract stipulated that the policy would become null and void if the insured were to die on the seas, pass beyond the settled limits of the United States, the two Canadas, Nova Scotia, and New Brunswick, the southern boundaries of the states of Virginia or Kentucky, or enter into any military or naval service without the consent of the Company endorsed upon the policy. Furthermore, the contract was nullified if the insured died by his own hand, as a result of a duel, at the hand of justice, or in violation of any law of the land. There was no period of grace, as in more recent policies, in which to pay premiums—they had to be paid

THE MUTUAL LIFE INSURANCE COMPANY OF NEW YORK,

This Policy of Insurance WITNESSETH,

ANNUAL PREMIUM.
$108 50/100

SUM INSURED.
$5000

That THE MUTUAL LIFE INSURANCE COMPANY OF NEW YORK, in consideration of the sum of *One hundred & eight* dollars, and *fifty* cents, to them in hand paid by *Sarah C. P. Ayres* and of the annual premium of *One hundred eight dollars and fifty* cents, to be paid on or before the *first* day of *February* in every year during the continuance of this Policy, Do Assure the Life of *Thomas N. Ayres* of *the City of New York* in the County of *New York* State of *New York* for the sole use of the said *Sarah C. P. Ayres* in the amount of *Five thousand* dollars, for the term *the whole Continuance thereof*

And the said Company do hereby Promise and Agree, to and with the said assured, her executors, administrators, and assigns, well and truly to pay, or cause to be paid, the said sum insured, to the said assured, her executors, administrators, or assigns, for her sole use, within sixty days after due notice, and proof of the death of the said *Thomas N. Ayres* And in case of the death of the said *Sarah C. P. Ayres* before the decease of the said *Thomas N. Ayres* the amount of the said insurance shall be payable after her death to her children, for their use, or to their guardian, if under age, within sixty days after due notice and proof of the death of the said *Thomas N. Ayres* as aforesaid.

Provided always, and it is hereby declared to be the true intent and meaning of this Policy, and the same is accepted by the assured upon these express conditions, that in case the said *Thomas N. Ayres* shall die upon the seas, or shall, without the consent of this Company previously obtained, and endorsed upon this Policy, pass beyond the settled limits of the United States, (excepting into the settled limits of the British Provinces of the two Canadas, Nova-Scotia, or New-Brunswick,) or shall, without such previous consent thus endorsed, visit those parts of the United States, which lie south of the southern boundaries of the States of Virginia and Kentucky; or shall, without such previous consent thus endorsed, enter into any military or naval service whatsoever, (the militia not in actual service excepted;) or in case he shall die by his own hand, in, or in consequence of a duel, or by the hands of justice, or in the known violation of any law of these States, or of the United States, or of the said Provinces; this Policy shall be void, null, and of no effect

And it is also Understood and Agreed, to be the true intent and meaning hereof, that if the declaration made by the said *Sarah C. P. Ayres* and bearing date the *twenty fifth* day of *January* 1843 and upon the faith of which this agreement is made, shall be found in any respect untrue, then, and in such case, this Policy shall be null and void: or in case the said *Sarah C. P. Ayres* shall not pay the said annual premiums on or before the several days herein before mentioned for the payment thereof, then and in every such case, the said Company shall not be liable to the payment of the sum insured, or any part thereof: and this Policy shall cease and determine.

And it is further agreed, that in every case where this Policy shall cease, or become or be null or void, all previous payments made thereon shall be forfeited to the said Company.

N. B. If Assigned, notice to be given the Company.

In Witness whereof, the said Mutual Life Insurance Company of New York, have, by their President and Secretary, signed and delivered this Contract, this *first* day of *February* one thousand eight hundred and forty *three*

M. Robinson President.

Jno. H. Harney Secretary.

punctually on the stipulated dates. Nor was there any incontestable clause, as there is today, to place a limit upon the time within which the Company could contest the truth of statements in the application. In those early policies all statements were warranted to be true. If they were not accurate or if the premiums were not paid when due, the policy contract was to "cease and determine." Finally, and most harsh of all, the policy had no guaranteed cash surrender value in case the policy-holder did not faithfully perform his part of the contract. If for any reason the contract were to become null and void or were to "cease and determine," all the premiums which had been paid were automatically forfeited to the Company.[12]

The injustices which were possible under the terms of the contract are obvious, and the better companies modified the terms for the better protection of policyholders. To be sure, restrictions on travel, residence, and hazardous occupations continued beyond the period now under consideration, but they aimed to protect the persons who were insured in the Company from bearing the consequence of higher premiums which would have resulted if the Company had accepted such risks at standard rates. Such restrictions disappeared in large measure with the effecting of safe travel, improvement in conditions of health in the Southern States, and safe working conditions in dangerous industries.

Those aspects of the early policy which concern us here pertain to the truth of the statements made by the applicant for insurance, the prompt payment of premiums, and forfeitures of premiums in case of nonfulfillment of the contract. The law has always considered that insurance contracts were made in the utmost good faith (uberrimae fidei), but at first it was inclined to regard all statements made in applications for insurance and all terms of the contract as warranties. The consequence of this attitude was that the validity of the contract depended upon the absolute and literal truth, irrespective of materiality, of the applicant's statements and that unscrupulous companies could secure the forfeiture of insurance if they could discover even the most trivial or honestly un-avoidable inaccuracy in the information obtained from the insured.[13] The injustices which were perpetrated under this legal device led legislatures in about 1861 to enact laws requiring that statements made by

---

[12] It should be noted that the policy could be assigned, that is, made over to another, such as a creditor, upon notice sent to the Company. A New York court held in 1864 (*Eadie vs. Slimmon*, 26 N.Y. 9) that a policy of insurance to a married woman for her benefit or for that of her children could not be transferred so as to divest the interest of the wife and children. Such assignment was made possible by laws of 1873 and 1879.

[13] George L. Amrhein, *The Liberalization of the Life Insurance Contract* (Philadelphia, 1933), p. 140.

applicants for life insurance be considered common law representations rather than warranties, which meant that materiality was required as the basis for forfeitures.[14] The better companies also became more lenient in their treatment of policyholders,[15] trying in the interests of equity to prevent voiding policies on mere technicalities. They decided that much of this aspect of the insurance business should be included in the risk and hence began to adopt the incontestable clause—a clause, included in the contract, which stipulated that after a given length of time, usually two or three years, the company would not question the validity of the representations made by the insured or contest the contract.[16] The first company in the United States to adopt this clause was probably the Manhattan Life Insurance Company, in 1864.[17] The Mutual Life, after years of lenient treatment of its policyholders, adopted it in 1890, but state laws did not require it generally until after the New York state insurance investigation of 1905.

Misrepresentation was not, as we have seen, the only ground upon which the premiums paid to an insurance company could be lost. They might have to be entirely forfeited to the Company by a mere delay in paying premiums—a delay that might be caused by illness, negligence, or even absence from home. On this question The Mutual Life early took a liberal view in its efforts to provide equitable treatment for its policyholders, making reinstatement relatively easy, but not introducing a period of grace into its contracts until 1899.[18] The obvious hardships worked on a person who might be one day late in making his premium payments or who in some other inconsequential manner placed his entire equity in jeopardy gave rise to much discussion of forfeitures and finally to a sharp attack upon them. The question was debated at length by the representatives of various life insurance companies in their first, large-

[14] The first statute in this direction was enacted in Maine in 1861. After 1906 such legislation became general. See *The Mutual Life vs. Hilton Green*, 241 U.S. 613 (1916).

[15] In the seventies some of the fly-by-night companies, on the other hand, endeavored to remain solvent by a strict adherence to the doctrine of warranties. Henry Moir, "Liberality of Modern Policies," *Transactions Actuarial Society of America*, XII (1911), 175.

[16] Joseph B. Maclean, *Life Insurance* (New York, 1939), p. 208, writes: "The reason for such a provision is found in the character of the life insurance contract. The contract is based on information supplied by the insured, and it is undesirable that payment should be disputed many years later after the insured is dead and when it may be difficult either to prove or to disprove the truth of any of the statements in question." Even a policy obtained by fraud has been upheld by the courts after the period of contestability, even though fraud is usually considered to void contracts *ab initio*.

[17] Edwin W. Patterson, *Cases and Other Materials on the Law of Insurance* (Chicago, 1932), p. 645.

[18] In 1898, 16 of 42 companies allowed periods of grace. A letter from General Manager Gillette to the general agents, dated Nov. 25, 1895, permitted 30 days of grace with interest at 5 percent.

scale efforts to exchange ideas—in the American Life Conventions held in 1859 and 1860.

To Elizur Wright has gone most of the credit for this campaign and justly so, for as a result of his efforts the first nonforfeiture law was enacted in his state in 1861. Henceforth, policyholders in Massachusetts were to be given extended term insurance in case their insurance "ceased and determined." In 1879 New York followed the example of the Bay State, although the surrender value was to be in reduced paid up insurance, the insured had to make his claim within six months of lapse, and policies without surrender values could be issued if such provisions were entered on the contract in red ink. In 1881 Massachusetts required that cash surrender values be guaranteed by the terms of the policy—a law which through the force of competition led by the end of the century to the inclusion of such clauses in most life insurance policies.[19]

Important as legislation on this subject was, some companies early allowed policyholders a part of their equity in a policy upon surrender. There were, for example, companies which took personal notes in payment of premiums and in case of lapse rarely attempted to collect on these notes, thus granting in substance a surrender value. There were also companies which granted loans to policyholders, the security for the loan being the policy itself—a practice which permitted a person to get something out of his insurance if he had to surrender it. Finally, there were companies which paid cash surrender values under certain conditions.

The Mutual Life belonged to the last class. Although for the brief span of five years (from 1850 to 1855) the Company made policy loans,[20] it was always willing to pay a certain amount of cash for a policy on three conditions—that the insurance was not for a short term, that the policy had been in force a certain number of years, and that notice of surrender reached the Company before premium payments were in default.[21] Grad-

[19] In 1905 fifty-one representative companies had such guaranties in their policies. For Elizur Wright's arguments see *Massachusetts Insurance Reports*, 1876, Vol. 21, Part 2, p. 226. Concerning the first and second American Life Conventions consult W. S. Nichols, *Insurance Blue Book* (New York, 1877), pp. 49–50.

[20] The first policy loans appear in the statement for the year ending Jan. 31, 1850. The minutes of the Board of Trustees for Feb. 14, 1855, report that all loans on policies have been paid off or transferred to a Mr. Bunker.

[21] *First Annual Report*, p. 19: "In all cases on applications to the Company, an equitable consideration will be given on a surrender of the policies, calculated by rules established by the office for the purpose, which consideration will be more or less, as the insurances may have been of longer or shorter duration at the time of surrender. . . . We may further remark that a policy of life insurance is of no value to the party, on the supposition of surrender, unless it be made for the whole duration of life; except where the insurance is effected for a long term of years, say 15 or 20, in such a case a trifling value would be attached to it, depending on the time it had to run, and of the unexpired term of the policy at the time of surrender." In the *Second Annual Report* p. 6, it was stipulated that surrender

ually The Mutual Life made its surrender practices more lenient. In 1850 it permitted a policyholder who had paid ten annual premiums to take paid-up insurance, if he so desired; in 1862 increased surrender values were granted if the policyholder surrendered only a portion of his policy in order to keep the remainder in force; [22] in 1879 nonforfeiture clauses were written into the contract, and in 1899 a table of surrender values was inserted in the policy.

With all these provisions, however, it should not be forgotten that forfeiture of premiums to the Company took place before 1879 unless notice of surrender were given before premium payments fell due or unless the policy were reinstated. Hence, the loss by policyholders was an appreciable amount, in some companies being sufficient to pay running expenses.

---

would be granted on whole life policies only and then only after two annual premiums had been paid.

The then current method of determining the cash surrender value of a policy of two years standing is explained in the *Third Annual Report*, p. 6. The rule was, "take the premium at the age of surrender, and deduct from it the premium the party has been paying; multiply the difference by the value of an annuity at the age of surrender increased by unity; this is the value. But it would be unsafe for the Company to pay the full value, as none but the best lives would surrender; therefore, we deduct from this one-third." *The Twelfth Annual Report* (1855), p. 40, states that the policyholder may get a certificate of cash value of his policy from the Company and may thus use his policy as a security for loans.

[22] *Minutes of the Board of Trustees*, May 14, 1862, report a resolution to the effect that a sum over the regular surrender value be paid in case surrender was for the purpose of keeping a portion of the insurance in force.

IV. Mortality Tables, Premiums, Reserves, and Dividends

LTHOUGH DEEPLY INTERESTED in kinds of insurance contracts, in the possible invalidation of the policy by legal action, and in forfeitures and surrenders, the policyholder was even more concerned as to the cost of his insurance and with the provisions made for securing its fulfillment, that is, with the rate of premium, the method of distributing surplus ("dividends"), and the adequacy of the "reserves" held by the company. For the proper calculation of premiums, reserves, and dividends a suitable mortality table was necessary.

When The Mutual Life opened its doors for business, little data on the rate of mortality in the United States were available. Most American companies in the 1840's based their premiums upon the Carlisle Table of Mortality—a table that had been built upon the experience of the general population of a small town in England between the years 1779 and 1787. The Mutual Life adopted the rates and the mortality table then employed by the New York Life Insurance and Trust Company.[1] This was a combination of the Carlisle Table and another similar, but older, table based on the mortality in Northampton in England.[2] Such tables were, obviously, not representative of the mortality among insured lives in America, but they were used for want of a better. In general, they overstated the mortality and so were at least safe.

Not until the approach of 1848 was the Company confronted with a serious, intricate, and pressing actuarial problem. In that year the end of the first quinquennial period was to be reached and according to the charter a balance of the affairs of the Company had to be struck and profits distributed. Such a job required expert knowledge, and the Company had to go out and hire consultants. Some of the officers and trustees were not certain that the conclusions at which these experts arrived in 1848 were sound, and besides they felt the need of a person who could advise them on the new contracts which they proposed to

[1] *Minutes of the Board of Trustees*, May 19, 1842.
[2] S. A. Joffe, "Concerning the American Experience Table," *Transactions of the Actuarial Society of America*, 1911, XII, p. 255.

write. Thus it was that Charles Gill (1805–1855), an Englishman by birth and a professor of mathematics at St. Paul's College, Flushing, by profession, was appointed the Company's first actuary, October, 1849.[3] The duties which confronted him were legion.[4] Gill undertook the important task of preparing a new mortality table suitable for use by the Company.

In England important advances were being made in actuarial science and especially in the methods of constructing mortality tables from the experience of life insurance companies. Accordingly, the Board of Trustees sent Gill to England to become acquainted with the work which was being done—a trip that, incidentally, cost $483, including $63.10 for books. Upon his return Gill applied himself diligently to his task, and in 1852[5] he presented a new mortality table to the Board. Fortunately, we know how Gill made his table, for when he died, in 1855,[6] the Company bought his library, and in this collection is a folio volume in manuscript which explains his procedure in detail. Briefly, his method was first to plot the curves of certain mortality rates based on general population experience (the Carlisle Table and the English Life Table of Mr. Farr) and others computed from the actual experience of life insurance companies (The Old Equitable's Table and the Seventeen Officers' Table). "A curve was then run freely through the representation of the Carlisle Table as near a mean as could be determined by the eye. . . . This line below the age of 60 coincided very nearly with the representation of Equitable's experience, and was apparently a fair mean among the other representations."

From this curve he worked out his mortality rates for all ages from 10 to the age when the last person would have died—to the age of 99. Upon the basis of this table he developed new schedules of premiums for every kind of policy then issued—schedules which remained in use from February 1, 1853, to February 1, 1868. In practice such rates were

[3] The International Insurance Encyclopedia (New York, 1910) and Emory McClintock, "Charles Gill; the First Actuary in America," Transactions of the Actuarial Society of America, XIV (1913), 9, 212; XV (1914), 11, 228. Gill had earlier in 1849 done some actuarial work for The Mutual Benefit of New Jersey.

[4] The duties of the actuary were outlined by the Board at a much later date, August 13, 1862, and June 7, 1865.

[5] Minutes of the Board of Trustees, Dec. 22, 1852.

[6] Gill's early death may have been hastened by trouble which he had with the president of the Company, Frederick S. Winston—an abrupt and overbearing man. See Emory McClintock, "Charles Gill; the First Actuary in America," Transactions of the Actuarial Society of America, XV (Oct. 15–16, 1914), 253. At any rate, the Board of Trustees bought the Gill library presumably to give financial aid to Mrs. Gill and paid her his salary for six months after his death. The Gill library is housed in the office of the actuary.

THE

LIFE INSURANCE
COMPANY OF NEW YORK.

THIS POLICY OF ASSURANCE WITNESSETH, THAT

THE MUTUAL LIFE INSURANCE COMPANY OF NEW YORK,

IN CONSIDERATION of the representation made to them in the application for this Policy, and of the sum of

Premium.

$

and of the   premium of   dollars and   cents, to be paid

on or before the   days of

in every year during the continuance of this Policy, **Do Assure** the Life of

                in the County of   State of   in the amount of

dollars, payable to the said

executors, administrators or assigns, on the   day of   18   when the said

shall have attained the age of   years, or to

executors, administrators or assigns, should   die previous to attaining that age.

And the said Company do hereby **Promise and Agree** to and with the said assured, well and truly to pay, or cause to be paid, the said

sum assured, as aforesaid, in sixty days after due notice (and proof of interest, if assigned or held as security,) of the death of the said

the balance of the year's premium, if any, being first deducted therefrom.

Provided Always, and it is hereby declared to be the true intent and meaning of this Policy, and the same is accepted by the assured upon

these express conditions, that in case the said   shall without the consent of

this Company previously obtained, and endorsed upon this Policy, pass beyond the settled limits of the United States, (excepting into the settled limits

of the British Provinces of the two Canadas, Nova Scotia or New Brunswick,) or shall, without such previous consent then endorsed, visit those parts

of the United States which lie west of the 100th degree of west longitude, or between the 1st of July and the 1st of November, those parts which

lie south of the southern boundaries of the States of Virginia and Kentucky, or shall be or reside within ten miles of the Mississippi or Missouri

Rivers, between the parallels of 36th and 40 degrees of North Latitude, (except while journeying,) or shall enter upon a voyage on the high seas,

or as a Mariner, Engineer, Fireman, Conductor, or Laborer in any capacity upon service on any Sea, Sound, Inlet, River, Lake or Rail-Road,

or into any military or naval service whatsoever, (the militia not in actual service excepted;) or in case he shall die by his own hand, or by the

hands of justice, or in, or in consequence of, a duel, or of the violation of any law of these States, or of the United States, or of the said provinces,

or of any other country which he may be permitted under this Policy to visit or reside in, then this Policy shall be null, void, and of no effect.

And it is also Understood and Agreed, by the within assured to be the true intent and meaning hereof, that if the declaration made by

or for the said   in the application for this Policy or any part thereof, and

bearing date the   day of   185   and upon the faith of which this Policy

is made," shall be found in any respect untrue, then, and in such case, this Policy shall be null and void: or in case the said

shall not pay the said premiums on or before the several days hereinbefore

mentioned for the payment thereof, then, and in every such case, the said Company shall not be liable for the payment of the sum assured, or any

part thereof; and this Policy shall cease and determine.

And it is further agreed by the within assured, that in every case where this Policy shall cease, or become or be null or void, all previous

payments made thereon shall be forfeited to the said Company, and that if assigned written notice shall be given to this Company.

In Witness Whereof, the said **THE MUTUAL LIFE INSURANCE COMPANY OF NEW-YORK,**

have, by their President and Secretary, signed and delivered this contract, this

day of   one thousand eight hundred and fifty.

President.

ENDOWMENT ASSURANCE POLICY, 1858

more suitable, for they reflected to an appreciable degree mortality among the selected group which was insured.[7]

DEVELOPMENT OF THE AMERICAN EXPERIENCE TABLE OF MORTALITY

The management of The Mutual Life was, however, anxious to have a table based entirely upon mortality rates among American life insurance policyholders. Accordingly, Sheppard Homans, who succeeded Gill as The Mutual's Actuary upon the latter's death in 1855, was set at the task of preparing it. Homans, a strong-minded man, came of a well-to-do family which was socially friendly with the president of The Mutual Life, Frederick S. Winston. He had been educated at Harvard, where he had displayed a marked aptitude for mathematics, and he had been employed by the United States in certain astronomical expeditions and in the Coast Survey.[8] When he took up his duties with The Mutual Life he was woefully ignorant of life insurance, not even comprehending, according to his future assistant, David Parks Fackler, the word "premium." What he lacked in insurance training, however, he made up in industry and intelligence.

Homans hoped that he would be able to construct a mortality table upon the experience of several American life insurance companies, and he sought earnestly for information from them.[9] They were, however, loath to make known what the rate of mortality among their insured was, for fear that their record, if poorer than that of other companies, would injure them. Thus, except for a little information obtained from the Mutual Benefit of New Jersey, Homans had to rely upon the mortality experience of The Mutual Life. From the methodological point of view he was exceptionally fortunate, for he had the work of Gill on which to build. In fact, he stated that he "continued the observations begun by the late Mr. Gill."

In 1858 Homans placed before the Board of Trustees his first table and an explanation of the sources of its data. He presented the actual losses by death of persons insured in The Mutual Life.[10] Obviously life insurance could not be written upon such an uneven curve as that represented by actual experience of The Mutual Life, and so Homans smoothed the curve by a freehand drawing. Inasmuch as The Mutual's

---

[7] For the mathematical formulae see S. A. Joffe, *op. cit.*, and Emory McClintock, *op. cit.*
[8] *The International Insurance Encyclopedia.*
[9] The question came up at the first Life Convention, in 1859. *Insurance Blue Book*, p. 49, and Sheppard Homans, *Report Exhibiting the Experience of The Mutual Life Insurance Company of New York for Fifteen Years Ending February 1, 1858* (New York, 1859), p. iii.
[10] *Ibid.*, pp. 10–11. The age at which the Company insured was to the "nearest birthday."

CHART IV

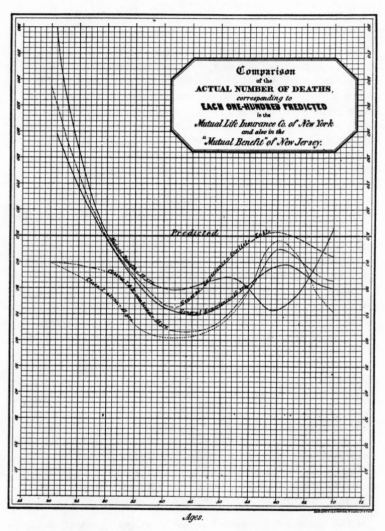

Source: Reproduced from Sheppard Homans, *Report Exhibiting the Experience of The Mutual Life Insurance Company of New York for Fifteen Years Ending February 1, 1858* (New York, 1859).

oldest policyholder was 78 years of age, the mortality rate for subsequent years was estimated.

In 1861 the Board of Trustees sent Sheppard Homans to England to consult with leading actuaries on the wisdom of establishing premium schedules upon his new table, upon methods of computing dividends, and upon other matters. The reports submitted by the English consultants are of great interest, for they give a clear idea of the status of English actuarial science at this time. The reports were published in a pamphlet and distributed privately to the Board of Trustees, the only copy at present extant being bound into the Minutes of the Insurance Committee of the Board. The English actuaries went on record as approving the table for the computation of premiums for survivorship annuities, and Homans at once composed such a schedule.

Shortly thereafter Homans began the construction of a new table, which was to become the American Experience Table; it was based on the actual experience of The Mutual Life [11] and showed the rates of death among the insured for ages from 10 to 95.[12] In 1867 he prepared rates of premiums on the basis of this table for all plans of insurance then offered to the public by The Mutual Life.[13] These premiums were adopted for new insurance in 1868. In this same year the legislature of the State of New York passed an act concerning the valuation of policies for purposes of reserves and included in the act Homans's table.[14] It was this law which christened the table the American Experience Table of Mortality and which established it as the standard for calculating reserves. Since 1868 the American Experience Table has been the standard table for all life insurance purposes (other than industrial insurance) and has been used by practically all companies. No other comparable table was constructed within a period of about fifty years. Because of

[11] The curve in the table as ultimately published had for ordinates 133.5 at age 10, that is, the number out of which one person of that age was expected to die within the year, and 16.13 at age 70. For a full mathematical interpretation of the table see S. A. Joffe, *op. cit.*

[12] Homans himself said: "The result was that after I had collated the experience of The Mutual Life I drew a curve representing the approximate rates of mortality at different ages; and then found, by a simple method of adjustment, the rates of mortality now called The American Experience Table—a name, however, that was not given by me. The table has for its basis the experience of The Mutual Life; but it is not an accurate representation of that individual Company. In other words, it is not intended to be, and never was claimed to be, an accurate interpretation of the experience of The Mutual Life." Speech delivered by Homans at the first dinner of the Actuarial Society of America, April 25, 1889, and reported in the *Transactions of the Actuarial Society of America*, I, 33–34. He stated also in this same address that the American table was prepared simply as a study and that he had made the limiting age 96 because in the records of different countries he could not find evidence that any insured person had attained the age of 100.

[13] See *Minutes of the Insurance Committee of the Board of Trustees*, Nov. 19, 1867.

[14] Act of May 6, 1868.

TABLE 8

AMERICAN EXPERIENCE TABLE OF MORTALITY

Age	Number Living	Number Dying	Number Dying per 1,000. Rate of Mortality	Average Future Lifetime ("Expectation of Life")	Age	Number Living	Number Dying	Number Dying per 1,000. Rate of Mortality	Average Future Lifetime ("Expectation of Life")
10	100,000	749	7.490	48.72	55	64,563	1,199	18.571	17.40
11	99,251	746	7.516	48.09	56	63,364	1,260	19.885	16.72
12	98,505	743	7.543	47.45	57	62,104	1,325	21.335	16.05
13	97,762	740	7.569	46.80	58	60,779	1,394	22.936	15.39
14	97,022	737	7.596	46.16	59	59,385	1,468	24.720	14.74
15	96,285	735	7.634	45.51	60	57,917	1,546	26.693	14.10
16	95,550	732	7.661	44.85	61	56,371	1,628	28.880	13.47
17	94,818	729	7.688	44.19	62	54,743	1,713	31.292	12.86
18	94,089	727	7.727	43.53	63	53,030	1,800	33.943	12.26
19	93,362	725	7.765	42.87	64	51,230	1,889	36.873	11.67
20	92,637	723	7.805	42.20	65	49,341	1,980	40.129	11.10
21	91,914	722	7.855	41.53	66	47,361	2,070	43.707	10.54
22	91,192	721	7.906	40.85	67	45,291	2,158	47.647	10.00
23	90,471	720	7.958	40.17	68	43,133	2,243	52.002	9.47
24	89,751	719	8.011	39.49	69	40,890	2,321	56.762	8.97
25	89,032	718	8.065	38.81	70	38,569	2,391	61.993	8.48
26	88,314	718	8.130	38.12	71	36,178	2,448	67.665	8.00
27	87,596	718	8.197	37.43	72	33,730	2,487	73.733	7.55
28	86,878	718	8.264	36.73	73	31,243	2,505	80.178	7.11
29	86,160	719	8.345	36.03	74	28,738	2,501	87.028	6.68
30	85,441	720	8.427	35.33	75	26,237	2,476	94.371	6.27
31	84,721	721	8.510	34.63	76	23,761	2,431	102.311	5.88
32	84,000	723	8.607	33.92	77	21,330	2,369	111.064	5.49
33	83,277	726	8.718	33.21	78	18,961	2,291	120.827	5.11
34	82,551	729	8.831	32.50	79	16,670	2,196	131.734	4.75
35	81,822	732	8.946	31.78	80	14,474	2,091	144.466	4.39
36	81,090	737	9.089	31.07	81	12,383	1,964	158.605	4.05
37	80,353	742	9.234	30.35	82	10,419	1,816	174.297	3.71
38	79,611	749	9.408	29.63	83	8,603	1,648	191.561	3.39
39	78,862	756	9.586	28.90	84	6,955	1,470	211.359	3.08
40	78,106	765	9.794	28.18	85	5,485	1,292	235.550	2.77
41	77,341	774	10.008	27.45	86	4,193	1,114	265.681	2.47
42	76,567	785	10.252	26.72	87	3,079	933	303.020	2.18
43	75,782	797	10.517	25.99	88	2,146	744	346.692	1.91
44	74,985	812	10.829	25.27	89	1,402	555	395.863	1.66
45	74,173	828	11.163	24.54	90	847	385	454.545	1.42
46	73,345	848	11.562	23.81	91	462	246	532.468	1.19
47	72,497	870	12.000	23.08	92	216	137	634.259	.98
48	71,627	896	12.509	22.35	93	79	58	734.177	.80
49	70,731	927	13.106	21.63	94	21	18	857.143	.64
50	69,804	962	13.781	20.91	95	3	3	1,090.000	.50
51	68,842	1,001	14.541	20.20	96	0			
52	67,841	1,044	15.389	19.49					
53	66,797	1,091	16.333	18.79					
54	65,706	1,143	17.396	18.09					

the general improvement in mortality rates and in methods of selecting risks, the American Experience Table substantially overstates the rates of mortality as compared with actual current experience. Consequently there has been, for some time, a trend toward the adoption of a more modern table.[15]

PREMIUMS

In order better to understand the contributions of The Mutual Life to actuarial procedures and to comprehend the operations of the Company, let us look briefly at the manner in which premiums are computed.[16] The basic element in this operation is the mortality table. If the American Experience Table is employed, examination will show, for example, that of 100,000 persons aged ten, 749 are expected to die within a year. Hence, if each of the 100,000 is insured for $1,000, $749,000 must be available during the year to pay death claims. This sum may be obtained by charging each of the 100,000 policyholders $7.49. In actual practice, however, two other elements go into premium making. The first of these is the amount of interest which the insurer estimates can be earned on the investment of premiums paid in advance. Thus, if the rate assumed is 3 percent, only $.9709, called "present value," is needed to have $1.00 at the end of the year. Consequently, interest earnings tend to reduce the sums required of policyholders. The second of the two elements mentioned above is an amount called "loading," which is added to cover the expenses of the company and to meet contingencies. All three elements combined together give the gross premium which is charged to the insured for one year. Inasmuch as the chances of death increase with age, premiums on an annual basis of this kind (yearly renewable term) would also increase with age and would ultimately become almost equal to the sum insured. To obviate this difficulty, which has been the stumbling block in the way of assessment insurance, the actuary calculates what uniform or *level* annual premium payable by each of the persons insured will be sufficient to satisfy all death claims as they occur. Such a level premium plan results in premiums in the early years which are greater than the cost on the yearly renewable term plan, but which are less in the later years. Thus is introduced the invested fund formed by the excess payments—a fund which is called the reserve and which accentuates the investment phase of life insurance business.

[15] James S. Elston, *Sources and Characteristics of the Principal Mortality Tables*, 2d ed. (New York, 1932), pp. 62–63.

[16] For a more detailed account see John H. Magee, *Life Insurance* (Chicago, 1939), pp. 199 ff. and bibliography.

When The Mutual Life began business, it adopted for its own use, as we have seen, the premium schedules used by the New York Life Insurance and Trust Company. Up to age 55, the rate of interest which it assumed would be earned on the sums invested was 4 percent and the loading was 35 percent of the "net" premium, that is, the sheer cost of insurance minus interest earnings. For ages 56 to 60, 3 percent interest and a loading of 10 percent were used.

These premium schedules remained in force until 1853. In April, 1846, the Board decided that premiums could be paid semi-annually or quarterly, "as the benefits of Life Insurance are chiefly sought by persons of limited means to whom the payment of a whole year's premium on an insurance of a considerable sum would be highly inconvenient and in many cases impracticable." To cover the increased cost of collection and the loss of interest caused by the deferred payments, the regular premiums were increased by 7 percent.

In 1853 new rates, prepared by Charles Gill upon the basis of his table, were put in force. The mortality rates at which he arrived were lower for the ages above thirty than those contained in the table previously in use, so his premiums for ages over thirty were somewhat reduced. Moreover, he assumed interest earnings of 4 percent, and his loading was a uniform 25 percent of the "net" premiums for various ages. Consequently, the new rates helped to meet growing competition.

The next change in The Mutual Life's premium making was effected by Sheppard Homans in the computation of rates on his new tables. He assumed an interest rate of 4 percent, but altered the system of loadings. He argued that if the same percentage of the "net" premium for every age and for every type of insurance was added as the loading, a relatively heavier charge was levied upon the higher ages and upon those kinds of insurance, such as endowments, that have high premiums. Thus, a 30 percent loading per $1,000 on an ordinary life policy would be $4.32 at age twenty (American Experience Table, 3 percent) and $17.48 at age sixty. Obviously the difference between the expense of writing and keeping on the books the two policies was not so great as this. Homans and other actuaries believed that a more suitable method of determining loadings should be arrived at.[17] Accordingly The Mutual's actuary decided to have two parts to his loading. The first part was to consist of 20 percent of the "net" premium, and the second part, 20 percent of the annual life rate at the same age.[18] The chief result of this method of

---

[17] See p. 32 of Homans's report *For the Private Use of the Trustees of The Mutual Life Insurance Company*, bound into the *Minutes of the Insurance Committee*, May 31, 1861.
[18] *Minutes of the Insurance Committee*, Dec. 7, 1867.

computation was to reduce rates for ages up to 45 years. These premium rates were adopted by several other companies. They were used by The Mutual Life until 1879 when premium rates were reduced. Rates were still based on the American Experience Table and have been, in fact, up to the present time. Changes have been made in the assumption as to the rate of interest, which was reduced from 4 percent to 3½ percent in 1898 and to 3 percent in 1907, and also in the "expense loadings," but the same mortality has been used since its adoption in 1868.

RESERVES

A part of the premium, called the loading, provides, as was stated earlier, for the expense of keeping a policy in force and for contingencies, which may arise from epidemics, wars, and similar calamities, and another part, for those sums which must be paid out to beneficiaries. We have also seen that on the level premium plan a "net" premium is computed which is just enough in the aggregate and under assumed conditions of rates of mortality and interest to meet claims as they become due. Again, the level premium system calls for payments by policyholders which in the earlier years of a policy are in excess of the sums needed to meet claims, but which are in the later years of a contract less than the amounts required to pay benefits. Consequently, a fund—the reserve—is created by the excess payments with interest thereon. The size of this fund has to be carefully calculated (valuation of reserves) and the sums placed in it zealously protected so that sufficient moneys are always available to satisfy claims. Finally, one should realize that life insurance reserves are not surplus, as they are considered to be in most businesses, but that they are a liability which the insurer holds as a trust for its insureds.[19]

The first calculation of the liability under existing policies, that is, of the "reserve," was made in 1848. The charter provided that at the end of every five years a balance of the affairs of the Company was to be struck and profits were to be distributed among the policyholders. To determine what the profits were, it was necessary first to establish the amount of the reserves. Just how to do this was discussed at some length and was finally placed in the hands of a special committee of the Board. It in turn sought the counsel of several persons who arrived at the following conclusion: [20]

[19] Joseph B. Maclean, *Life Insurance* (New York, 1939), chap. vi.

[20] *Minutes of the Board of Trustees*, Sept. 28, 1847. One of the consultants was George Christian Schaeffer, librarian of Columbia College. See *Actuarial Society of America*, XXI (1920), 123.

The charter directs the profits to be divided—it is necessary therefore in the first place to ascertain the increased risk on each policy. Calculation shows that the sum representing this increased risk is obtained by subtracting the premium at the time of valuation and multiplying the difference by the value of annuity at the last age, increased by unity.[21]

Upon calculation it was found that the assets in mortgages, stocks, cash, and other items amounted to $551,575.27; that the reserve should be $172,569.68, and that the net surplus was $379,005.59. To be on the safe side they added $22,000 of this surplus to the reserve for contingencies.

The method employed for establishing the reserves in 1853 is not clear, for the *Minutes of the Insurance Committee* for the years 1845–1853 are missing, and the *Minutes of the Board* do not contain the formulae employed. All we know is that the system used by Gill was approved by Professors Loomis of the University of New York and Webster of the Free Academy and that the dividends which were paid were less than in 1848.

This was the period in which Elizur Wright was waging his campaign for a sounder method of calculating reserves. At the time practically all English and most American companies computed reserves by assuming that the *gross* premiums could be counted on for claims. Elizur Wright and others insisted that only future *net* premiums (i. e., excluding the "expense loading") should be regarded, in calculating reserves, as available for payment of claims. A net premium valuation obviously meant higher reserves than a *gross* premium valuation.

From the first The Mutual Life calculated reserves on a net premium basis, but it was one of the few companies to do so.[22] That it adopted such a policy was a stroke of good fortune, for not only was its position thus

[21] The minute continues, "This principle based upon strict calculations, has been universally acknowledged as correct. The only doubt which could remain, was the particular premium to be adopted in this calculation. The premium required by the office, is the real premium as given by the Carlisle Tables, at 4%, increased by 35%. The addition of course is made to cover all extraordinary loss and to give a profit to the Company.

"As the premium increases for every year of life, the addition of 35% will of course increase the difference. Were the increased risks calculated from the office premium, the Company would be adding profits to their reserved fund, causing an unnecessary accumulation, which must be divided in future years to the injury of those who die before that period.

"The Committee, therefore, have decided to found the calculations upon the real premiums derived from the Carlisle Tables at 4%. The universal risk obtained in this manner will show the actual cost of insurance on the lives at the period of valuation and when subtracted from the amount of funds on hand will of course give the real profits.

"This mode of valuation is moreover in accordance with the system adopted by the Company in the purchase of policies, by which almost the same value is obtained."

[22] J. A. Fowler, *History of Insurance in Philadelphia for Two Centuries (1683–1882)*, (Philadelphia, 1888), p. 693.

made stronger, but it was able easily to meet the standards required by many states after 1858. In that year Massachusetts took the initiative in setting up such a standard. It placed the task of enforcing its require-ments on the capable shoulders of Elizur Wright, and he made many a company aware of its lack of adequate reserves and saved many policy-holders from being caught, as he said, in "traps baited with orphans."[23] The Mutual Life became more cognizant of the great importance of maintaining sufficient reserves, and it sought to improve the formula which it was using for making the valuations. In the valuation of 1858 The Mutual Life made an arbitrary increase of 15 percent over the amount of the reserve calculated by the net premium method. This in-crease was intended to "provide for unexpected contingencies arising from unusual mortality by reason of epidemics, decrease in the rate of interest anticipated on investments, etc., etc."[24]

TABLE 9

SUMMARY OF VALUATION OF 1858: THE MUTUAL LIFE

Class of Policy	Num-ber	Amount Assured	Present Value of Amount Assured, Co.'s Tables, 4%	Present Value of Future Premium, Co.'s Tables, 4%	Difference or Net Cost of Reinsur-ance, Co.'s Tables, 4%	Amount Actually Reserved
Life	9,478	$27,528,065	$11,328,129.38	$9,059,893.43	$2,268,235.95	$2,608,471.33
Joint life	7	13,100	5,475.56	3,670.59	1,804.97	2,075.71
Accumulative	1	287	98.75	...	98.75	113.57
Seven years	572	1,738,300	82,384.33	68,336.16	14,048.17	16,155.40
Other short terms	178	591,750	19,007.10	14,941.51	4,065.59	4,675.43
Endowment	154	609,800	352,098.84	315,634.65	36,464.19	37,375.78
Totals	10,390	$30,481,302	$11,787,193.96	$9,462,476.65	$2,324,717.62	$2,668,867.22

For the "striking of the balance" in 1863 Homans sought a still more conservative basis for reserves. He argued that if the method of valuation employed in 1853 and 1858 were continued and only the net premiums counted upon to pay death claims, there might not be enough reserve retained for the future expenses of the Company and for contingencies. Doubtless the exigencies of the Civil War led him to such a cautious position. In any case, he argued that reserves should be calculated on a new formula which would tend to make them larger—and the Board of Trustees sustained him [25] in his contention. In his calculations Homans

---

[23] See *Supplement to the Fourth Annual Report, Mass., Reports on Life Insurance*, p. 36. Wright was the author of a book called *Traps Baited with Orphans; or, What Is the Matter with Life Insurance* (Boston, 1878).

[24] *Minutes of the Insurance Committee*, February 12, 1858.

[25] *Ibid.*, May 13, 1862, and Feb. 5, 1864. This was done by arriving at the gross reserves and by setting aside only a part of the loadings for future expenses. The formula used was $nV'x = 1.20Ax + n - ax + n (.95P'x - .002)$. A and a are net American 4% values, and P' is the gross premium paid (Gill's 4%, loaded 25%).

employed the American Experience Table at 4 percent, which was an added factor in augmenting the size of the reserves.

In 1865 it was decided to go on an annual dividend basis in the next year, an amendment to the Charter having been obtained, April 2, 1862, to make this change possible. In computing the reserves for 1866 Homans used a net valuation scheme and increased the mortality ratio which he employed to arrive at them by 25 percent, thus getting larger reserves than he would have if he had used the unweighted table.[26] By 1867 the danger of an unfavorable mortality resulting from war had passed, so The Mutual Life returned to a strictly net valuation basis and has maintained it ever since. In 1870, when Sheppard Homans was having trouble with President Winston—trouble which led to the former's involuntary resignation—Homans sought the opinion of Elizur Wright concerning his method of determining the amount of reserves. Wright replied as follows: [27]

Boston, March 15, 1870

Sheppard Homans, Esq.
Actuary Mut. Life Ins. Co.

MY DEAR SIR,
  You ask my opinion of your method, stated very distinctly on the enclosed paper, for calculating the Reserves the Company should hold on each and all its outstanding policies at the close of a fiscal year. I am happy to say that I deem it not only exact, and in accordance with the fundamental assumptions of the business, but of all methods that are so, the most expeditious in practice.

DIVIDENDS

After the reserves, which are in essence the estimated liabilities on policies, have been ascertained and after all operating expenses, insurance claims, and other charges have been paid, a surplus may be left to the insurance company. This surplus may be accounted for by the fact, either that the actual mortality is less than the mortality rate of the table, or that the interest rate is higher than that assumed in the premiums, or that the operating expenses are less than the loadings, or that gains have been made from lapses and surrenders, or that capital gains have been realized on investments, or that profits have been realized in some other way. A part of the surplus obtained from one or from any combination of these sources of savings may be set aside to meet contingencies, but in a mutual company the major part is normally

26 *Minutes of the Insurance Committee,* August 10, 1865.
27 *Ibid.,* April 16, 1870.

available for distribution among policyholders in the form of "dividends." [28] The policyholders are actually getting back what they have paid in excess of the sum necessary to insure themselves.

Total surplus is ascertained automatically in striking a balance of a life insurance company's books and hence is arrived at very easily. The difficult task is to determine how much of the surplus should be distributed among policyholders and how to distribute it equitably. In the 1840's it was customary to allot the dividend which the policyholder was to receive as a percentage of the premiums which he had paid. Using this method, in 1848 The Mutual Life paid as a dividend 52 percent of the premiums which had been paid in, although it should be noted in this connection that no dividends were paid on policies which had expired before the end of the five-year period, even if the expiration had resulted from death,[29] and also that dividends were not paid in cash, but as "reversionary additions," that is, they had to be used for the purchase of additional insurance.

The large dividend which was paid in 1848 was made possible not only by the savings on mortality, loadings, and interest rate, but also by earnings on forfeitures and by too low a valuation of policy reserves. The first actuary of the Company was of the opinion that the dividends should have been 33 percent of the premiums, instead of 52 percent,[30] and Emory McClintock, another actuary of the Company, testified before the Armstrong Committee in 1905 that if The Mutual Life had continued its 1848 method of valuing reserves it would have become embarrassed.[31]

The "percentage" system of allotting surplus is a rough-and-ready one which takes no account of the sources from which the surplus has arisen. Some inkling that individual policyholders were not receiving their just proportions of the surplus came to The Mutual Life's management after the dividend of 1848 had been paid, for an amendment to the charter was sought from the New York State Legislature in 1851 to allow the Company to "credit each member with an equitable share of the profits." [32] A change was sought whereby the Company could make larger dividend payments to those who had contributed much to the surplus and smaller dividends to those who had contributed little. A step was taken in this direction in 1852, preparatory to the dividend of

[28] In a stock company this excess would go to stockholders in the form of profits.
[29] *Minutes of the Board of Trustees,* February 22, 1848.
[30] *Ibid.,* February 17, 1858.
[31] Testimony of October 24, 1905.
[32] Paragraph 2, Article 13.

1853, when it was decided that dividends on whole life policies should be in proportion to the length of time these policies had been in force. This meant that a policy that had been in force one year would get only one-fifth that of a policy in force five years and that a policy on which the premium was paid January 31, 1853, would get only 1/365 as much as a policy in force one year. No dividends were to be paid on extra premiums required for climatic risks, simply because these extras were not sufficient to cover the cost of insurance and hence did not contribute to the surplus, and only one-half the dividend rate on whole life policies was to be paid on term policies for similar reasons.[33]

This same general scheme was followed in 1858, but Homans, in his "Report Exhibiting the Experience of The Mutual Life Insurance Company of New York, for Fifteen Years Ending February 1, 1858," referred to the defects in the existing methods of distributing surplus, as follows:

The fact of charging at any age, comparative rates of premiums slightly too high or too low, is of but little consequence in a mutual company, provided we have the means of making a just compensation to the original contributors. The amount of such excess or deficiency in the rates of premiums can only be determined by tables based on actual experience; while the compensation itself may be effected, as we have already seen, by a slight modification.[34]

It was only necessary to change "compensation to the contributors" to read "contribution of the respective members," in order to get the essence of the "Contribution Plan," one of the great achievements of The Mutual Life in the actuarial realm. This plan aimed to return to each policyholder a dividend which was in proportion to the amount which he and other members of his "class" had contributed to the surplus, the classes being determined according to age, type of policy, and length of time a policy had been in force.

When Homans went to England in 1861 to get information on various aspects of actuarial problems, he at first determined to use for distributing surplus a plan prepared by an English actuary, Charles Jellicoe, which included a partial recognition of the sources from which the surplus had been derived.[35] On his return to America, however, he and

---

[33] *Minutes of the Board of Trustees*, Feb. 11, 1852.

[34] *Ibid.* Following the Aug., 1858, meeting. For Gill's views see Homans's report after his trip to England—a report, as we have indicated previously, which is bound into the *Minutes of the Insurance Committee*, at May 31, 1861.

[35] Robert Henderson, "Equity in Surplus Distribution," *Transactions of the Actuarial Society of America*, XXIV (Oct. 11–12, 1923), 292, and Joseph B. Maclean and Edward W. Marshall, *Distribution of Surplus* (New York, 1937), pp. 71 ff.

David Parks Fackler,[36] the assistant actuary, evolved a new "contribution plan." [37] As Homans described it,

The principle is that the true share of any policy-holder in a given amount of surplus is in the proportion which the excess of his payments over and above the actual cost of insurance (as determined by experience) bears to the total contributions to this surplus. In other words, each member will participate in any given surplus in proportion to the difference between his actual payments and the actual cost of insurance. [38]

By August 1, 1862, Homans had developed the "three factor system," [39] whereby savings from mortality, interest on investments, and expense loadings were to be measured separately and placed to the credit of those classes of policies in which the savings had been effected. This new system was approved by most actuaries and especially by Elizur Wright, who was consulted on the matter.[40]

[36] For a description of the contribution plan see Sheppard Homans's" On the Equitable Distribution of Surplus," *Journal of the Institute of Actuaries* (London), XI, 121 ff.

[37] *The Minutes of the Insurance Committee*, February 10, 1865, contain the following communications:

"F. S. WINSTON, *Esq.:*

I beg leave to call your attention to the service acknowledged in the accompanying note, for which—considering the large sum affected by it—I believe myself entitled to some reward.

Very respectfully,
(Signed). DAVID PARKS FACKLER."

The following note from Mr. Homans accompanied the above.

"MY DEAR MR. FACKLER:

It gives me pleasure to acknowledge to you as I did in my official Report to the Company and as I have always done verbally, that whatsoever credit may attach to the origination and successful application of entirely new principles and formulae to the distribution of the surplus of a Life Insurance Company (as in the case of the Dividend for 1858 of the 'Mutual Life') should justly be shared by yourself— Indeed the principle upon which that Dividend was based as well as some of the most important elements of the main formula were first suggested by you.

In fact I am free to acknowledge that without your valuable assistance it is probable that the work might not have been brought to such a successful completion.

You are at liberty to make such use of this communication as you may think proper.

Sincerely yours,
(Signed). SHEPPARD HOMANS."

[38] *Minutes of the Insurance Committee*, Feb. 11, 1863.

[39] *Ibid.*, Aug. 1, 1862.

"1. Each member to be *credited* with the amount reserved for his policy and additions at the last valuation and also with the full participating premiums paid since that time, both accumulated at compound interest *during the interval*, at the rate realized by the Company from investments; and *charged* with the actual cost of the risk to which the Company has been exposed, and also with the amount now reserved to meet his claim. The difference between the sum of his credits and the sum of his debits will determine his contribution to the surplus; and his equitable share of surplus bears the same proportion to the entire surplus divided as his contribution bears to the total contributions."

The three factors correspond to the three elements in the gross premium for (1) gains from medical selection, (2) surrender and lapse, and (3) miscellaneous gains.

[40] *Twenty-First Annual Report*, pp. 118–123.

The charter of your Company, in requiring the surplus to be equitably divided among the policyholders seems to me to require it to be returned to them in proportion as the excesses, whether of premiums within the quinquennial period, or of interest on premiums previously paid, have contributed to produce it; in other words, in proportion as they have been in any way overpaying the cost of insurance. . . . It may not be possible in the present distribution to make exact amends for the deficiency of previous ones. Their imperfection was due mainly to a want of certainty as to the Company's own rate of mortality, which time and experience only could remedy. . . . I have carefully examined the formulae devised by Mr. Homans for representing the equitable proportion of the general surplus which belongs to each member, and believe it combines with rigorous exactness all the elements required by the principles above stated. Its construction does great credit to both his skill and faithfulness. I have also had the pleasure to compare with it an independent original formula prepared by Mr. D. P. Fackler (Assistant Actuary) for the same purpose, which starting from hypotheses substantially the same produce results nearly identical, the one confirming the other. Either process cannot fail, after the general surplus is duly ascertained, to effect a distribution of it true to the demands of equity and of the charter.

The formulation of the contribution plan was a great step toward placing life insurance on a more scientific and equitable basis, but it did not solve all the problems concerning dividends. The Mutual Life was confronted with three other important questions: (1) What adjustment should be made in dividends paid to policyholders if a new reserve or dividend plan were adopted? (2) In what form should dividends be paid—in cash, in the form of additional insurance, or as a reduction of future premiums? (3) What time periods should be considered as those in which the policy contributed to surplus?

The first of these problems arose in 1853, when the Gill Mortality Table was first used, and again in 1863, when Homans's first table was introduced for some policies and the contribution plan was adopted. At each of these dates adjustments in the dividends were made so that policyholders who had at one time been paid too much were for subsequent periods paid less, or vice versa.[41]

The second question arose at various times and was settled in different ways. The issue at stake was whether or not the amount of insurance in force should be increased by making policyholders take their dividends in additional insurance, or whether the cost of insurance should be lessened by allowing policyholders to use dividends to pay their future premiums. Adherents of the former view maintained that the principle

41 A manuscript volume by Solomon Joffe explains these adjustments in great detail. This volume is kept in the Actuary's Office of The Mutual Life.

of insurance was one of accumulation and should be strictly adhered to, while the advocates of the latter opinion contended that the individual should be allowed to decide whether it was more advantageous for him to have a greater amount of insurance than it was to reduce the size of his future premiums. Furthermore, the proponents of the latter scheme believed that policyholders should be allowed to use their dividends for the reduction of premiums so that The Mutual Life would be able better to compete with those companies which took the personal promissory notes of their insured in payment of premiums.

The debate fluctuated back and forth. In the distribution of 1848 dividends could be used only to buy additional insurance (so-called reversionary additions); in 1853 they could be employed for additional insurance or for the payment of premiums; in 1858 they were again earmarked for additional insurance; [42] but in 1864 they could once more be used for either purpose. From 1884 to 1905 an effort was made to encourage "accumulations" of surplus by the adoption of a type of policy which deferred the payment of dividends for a period of years—but that's a story for a later page.

The third problem concerned the time-span during which a policy earned dividends for its owner. Up until 1863 a policyholder who became insured immediately after the declaration of a dividend and died before the next dividend was not allowed to share in the surplus. The injustice in this arrangement was pointed out by a group of examiners in 1856,[43] and rectification was made for the fourth quinquennial dividend. It was decided that if a person was insured subsequent to a dividend and died prior to the next dividend, his beneficiaries should receive an equitable share of the surplus due on his policies when the next dividend was declared, that is, they should be paid "post mortem" dividends.[44]

With the introduction of annual dividends (1867), which was another move better to compete with the "note-companies," [45] the question arose

---

[42] There was some criticism of the change, and to meet it the Board decided Feb. 17, 1858, that, "on application of the policyholders the Company will purchase from the assured any portion of their policies with a relative proportion of the Dividend or profits on the same." This was, however, to be discouraged.

[43] *Minutes of the Board of Trustees*, July 23, 1856. For an explanation of the examination at this time see below, pp. 114–116.

[44] *Ibid.*, May 14, 1862. "Resolved, that in the cases of persons insuring subsequent to a dividend, dying before the next dividend, that the equitable shares of surplus due on their policies be ascertained and paid to the proper representatives when the next dividend is declared." By a resolution of August 16, 1865, the Board decided to credit the dividends at the time that they were declared but that the policyholder could not enjoy them until the close of the policy year.

[45] A triennial dividend was paid to cover the years 1864, 1865, and 1866.

whether in view of the expense incurred at issue policies should receive a dividend at the end of their first year, because it was clear that a large part of the initial premium went to cover the agent's commission, the expense of the medical examination, and other overhead costs connected with placing the insurance in force. This question was resolved by fixing the dividend for the first year at a lower rate and by paying no dividend unless the second premium was paid.[46]

In spite of the remarkable contributions which Sheppard Homans made to actuarial science and to the conduct of the business of The Mutual Life, his career with the Company had an unpleasant and unfortunate ending. In 1869 the Superintendent of Insurance for the State of New York recommended that The Mutual Life change its fiscal year, which began on February 1, to coincide with the calendar year. While this change seemed desirable and was decided upon, it gave rise to the question whether or not dividends could be declared for any other period than from February 1 to February 1. President Winston and the Company's counsel were of the opinion that dividends would have to be based on the surplus earned in cash during the original fiscal period, for such seemed to be specified by the charter. Homans, on the other hand, believed that dividends should be based on the surplus earned in "policy years," that is, from the period between policy anniversary dates.

Homans refused to approve the audit of the Company (November 17, 1869), because his system was not employed. The battle was on. It became immediately complicated by the fact that W. E. C. Bartlett, a mathematician from West Point, was consulted by the president on the principles involved. He concocted extravagant and complicated formulae, which were entirely impracticable. Homans countered Bartlett's suggestions with other formulae and pleas for practicability. The dispute became acrimonious and was finally submitted to three referees, of whom Elizur Wright was the best known. They endeavored to settle the difficulties by preparing still other formulae—a procedure which was of no avail.

Matters went from bad to worse; Homans won the scientific debate, but lost his standing with the officers of the Company. A letter which he wrote to some friends about the excellent financial standing of another company was made public.[47] This was the climax. Homans "resigned"

[46] *Minutes of the Insurance Committee*, Dec. 7, 1867. See also *The Condition of the Life Insurance Companies of the State of New York Investigation by the Assembly Committee* (Albany, 1877), pp. 534 ff.
[47] For the text of this rather innocuous letter see *Minutes of the Finance Committee*, Dec. 21, 1870.

on January 25, 1871, from his position as actuary, remaining for a time consulting actuary at one-half his former salary. Professor Bartlett became his successor. That Homans had been in the right in the year-long argument soon became evident, for when Bartlett endeavored to apply his fancy formulae to the allocation of dividends for 1872, he became badly snarled. For the dividends of 1873, he resorted essentially to the methods employed by Homans. The Mutual Life had made an egregious error. It had lost the services of one of America's most capable actuaries.

V. Selecting Risks and Marketing Policies

T HE EQUITABLE TREATMENT of policyholders was the goal which
was sought by those actuaries of The Mutual Life who between
1843 and 1870 devised the methods by which the amount of
premiums and the distribution of dividends should be determined. One
aspect of the search for equity among the insureds has not yet been
touched upon—the "selection of risks." This phase of the business is,
however, of primary importance, for justice dictates, if a large number
of persons decide to share risks and to pay standard premiums, that these
risks be approximately the same. Nothing would be more inequitable
than to insure at the same cost the strong and healthy with the weak and
infirm, the residents of unhealthy regions with persons who live in
salubrious climates, or the employees in extremely dangerous occupations with those who are employed in the nonhazardous walks of life.
Insurance companies do not want the strong and long-lived to bear the
whole burden of caring for the weak, the adventurous, and the short-
lived. To pursue any other policy would be to invite insurance from such
poor risks that a company's entire standing would be jeopardized.[1]

In order to distinguish between good and poor risks, life insurance
companies had by 1843 begun the practice of requiring prospective
policyholders to provide information about their ways of life and about
their health.[2] Thus The Mutual Life, in accordance with its early policy
of borrowing the best from its predecessors, adopted at the very outset
of its existence the rule that there should be a careful selection of risks.
Selection was based upon information furnished by the applicant for
insurance, by his physician, and by a friend of long acquaintance. The
Company wanted to know not only the age of the applicant but also
whether or not he lived in a healthful climate and region, was engaged
in any hazardous occupation, had had some of the more dangerous diseases, was a person of good habits, and was at the time of making the
application in good health.

---

[1] See H. W. Dingman, *Selection of Risks* (Cincinnati, The National Life Underwriter Co.,
1933).
[2] Cornelius Walford, "History of Life Insurance," *Journal of the Institute of Actuaries*
(1886–87), XXVI, 8, and J. M. Hudnut, *Semi-Centennial History of the New York Life Insurance Company* (1895), chap. iv.

Correct answers to all the questions in the application were important, for the granting of the insurance and the rates charged were based upon them. In fact, any "untrue or fraudulent allegation, made in effecting the proposed insurance" rendered the policy void, as was made clear in Form A, question 21. By 1857 the application had become part of the contract and was so recognized by the courts,[3] although the tendency was for them to hold that the statements made were representations, requiring materiality as a ground for forfeiture, rather than warranties.[4] In 1889 The Mutual Life began the practice of attaching a copy of the application and of the medical examination to the policy—a practice which was not generally required by state law until after the Armstrong Investigation of 1905.[5]

In the application of 1844 most of the questions pertaining to health were of a very general nature and did not presuppose a special physical examination. Almost immediately, however, the insufficiency of such a check on the health of applicants became apparent, and a concerted effort was made to render the medical examination more rigorous. This task fell to Dr. Minturn Post, who was appointed physician to The Mutual Life in 1842; he remained with the Company until his death in 1869. His long tenure in office and his prominence in the medical profession gave Dr. Post an opportunity to establish standards and office procedures of medical selection which were adopted by most American insurance companies. In 1845 the Board of Trustees decided that every applicant for insurance in The Mutual Life should be examined personally by Dr. Post, but, if this were impossible, that every medical examination conducted by a family physician should be scrutinized by him. For this work, which required attendance at the Home Office at least one hour per day, Dr. Post was to receive the munificent sum of $500 and in 1849 the title Medical Examiner.

With the great increase in the Company's business and with the greater care which was exercised in examining applicants for insurance, Dr. Post's duties became more time-consuming, and consequently his salary was increased.[6] Not only did he have to prescribe the type of

---

[3] *Vose vs. Eagle Life and Health Ins. Co.* (New York, 1850), 6 Cush. (Mass.), 42, 47. Also G. L. Amrhein, *The Liberalization of the Life Insurance Contract*, p. 109.

[4] See above, pp. 53–54.

[5] Pennsylvania enacted such a requirement in 1881, and Massachusetts in 1893. See H. L. Seay, "Broadening Insurance Coverage to Meet Life's New Problems," *Proceedings of The Association of Life Insurance Presidents* (1928), XXII, p. 54.

[6] See *Transactions of the N.Y. State Medical Society for 1871* (1872), pp. 350–351. Dr. Post's salary was increased to $800 plus his regular examination fees February 15, 1854, but with a maximum of $1,500. On June 6, 1855, this salary was augmented to $3,000 for services rendered between 11 A. M. and 3 P. M.; on June 7, 1865, to $6,000 plus ½ percent of the annual dividends.

medical examination which was required, but also he had to pass on applications, study those factors in a person's history which contributed to longevity, compile mortality statistics, arrange information as to the cause of death, and maintain a staff of medical examiners in the field.[7] This last point is especially important, for the Company began to lose confidence in the reports made by the "family physician" who might be any Tom, Dick, or Harry. At first an effort was made to check the findings of these men by having those applicants whose cases suggested some flaw examined by a Company physician, but when this system did not obliterate abuse, Company examiners were appointed in various parts of the country.[8] By 1869 this corps, numbering about 3,500, was divided into regional bodies, each under the supervision of a medical referee.[9] Medical examinations were thus rendered much more reliable and were carefully checked at the Home Office by Dr. Post or by one of his two assistants.

Another factor in improving the selection of insurable risks was the requirement that persons seeking insurance should provide more detailed information about themselves than had been asked for in the early applications. Dr. Post realized early the importance of making the questions more specific and the examination more thorough, and so excellent were the forms which he devised that they were soon copied by other companies.[10] In the application which was in use in 1860 questions were asked about diseases or conditions which might leave a permanent impairment to health; special attention was paid to the effects of yellow fever; a new interest was shown in family longevity; and a questionnaire to be filled out by the Company's medical examiner was provided. The application made by Thomas A. Edison in 1874 shows that questions had been added to cover information on overweight and whether or not the applicant had ever been declined by a medical examiner of any company. Life insurance applications furnish, indeed, an interesting approach to the medical history of the United States. They indicate what diseases or physical conditions were at given periods considered the greatest curbs on longevity.

In 1876 a detailed report of The Mutual Life's mortuary experience

---

[7] His duties are specified in *The Minutes of the Board*, Aug. 13, 1862, and in the *Minutes of the Insurance Committee*, Jan. 30, 1869.

[8] See *Instructions for the Government of the Agents and Physicians of The Mutual Life Insurance Company of New York* (April, 1855), p. 4.

[9] *Minutes of the Insurance Committee*, January 30, 1869. Examination fees up to this time had been either $2 or $3. They were now raised to $5.

[10] *Minutes of the Board of Trustees*, May 17, 1865.

was published, which showed the effect of medical selection.[11] It was found that selection resulted generally in a lower death rate among the insureds during the first five years after their policies had been taken out, although for persons more than fifty years of age the selection had a

TABLE 10

THE RATIOS OF ACTUAL MORTALITY TO THAT PREDICTED BY THE AMERICAN TABLE DURING EACH QUINQUENNIUM FOLLOWING THE DATE OF INSURANCE

| Age at Entrance | RATIOS DURING | | | | | | Average for Whole Time |
	1st Five Years	2nd Five Years	3d Five Years	4th Five Years	5th Five Years	6th Five Years	
20 to 24	.775	1.003	1.143	1.066	1.229	.450	.879
25 to 29	.714	.983	.787	.848	1.055	1.000	.812
30 to 34	.716	.911	.931	.917	.806	.731	.806
35 to 39	.694	.843	1.000	.860	.938	.969	.797
40 to 44	.723	.896	.880	.977	.936	.532	.811
45 to 49	.674	.801	.730	1.126	.916	.516	.758
50 to 54	.730	.753	.741	.870	1.264	.871	.774
55 to 59	.633	.833	.869	.902	1.189	.862	.747
60 to 75	.806	.781	1.105	.582	.172	.833	.789

more lasting effect. The causes of death were also explained in this same report in great detail. A summary of the findings is provided by the chart on page 80.

HAZARDOUS RISKS

In addition to selecting its risks from among those who met certain physical standards, The Mutual Life was, from its very inception, cautious about insuring at regular rates those persons who were exposed to various extraordinary dangers. The restrictions were established in 1843 concerning the amount of insurance which could be taken with the Company by persons who resided in certain parts of the country, who were engaged in specified occupations, in extensive travel, and in military or naval service.[12] In some instances the extra risk was taken care of by extra premiums or by special permission granted by the Company, but in other cases the application was simply refused. The officials of The Mutual

---

11 *Mortuary Experience of The Mutual Life Insurance Company of New York from 1843 to 1874* (1876). The greatest losses occurred during epidemics. Thus, deaths from cholera were so numerous in 1848 and 1849 that the losses were as great as expected. *Minutes of the Board of Trustees* reported, Feb. 14, 1855, that in the preceding year deaths caused by cholera, yellow fever, and other diseases brought actual losses for the second time up to the expected number—a statement which is not, however, borne out by the report of The Mutual's mortuary experience for the years 1843–1858. Few of The Mutual's policyholders were affected by the cholera epidemic of 1866, according to the *Twenty-Fourth Annual Report*.

12 *First Annual Report*, pp. 33–35.

Life knew that it was necessary to charge premiums which were proportionate to the risk, if the Company were to succeed, and they believed that although the benefits of insurance should be widely available, the

CHART V

CAUSES OF DEATH AMONG THE MUTUAL LIFE'S POLICYHOLDERS, 1843–1873

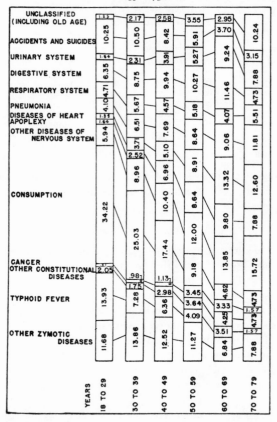

risks which were accepted should in all fairness to the insured be of a relatively equal kind.

One of the most perplexing factors concerning the early exceptional risks was that of residence. It was thought, and correctly so, that the death rate in the South was greater than it was in the North and accordingly that insurance rates for the two regions should be different. Thus, standard rates were from the outset granted only to persons who resided in the states north of the southern boundaries of Virginia and Kentucky, in the states of North Carolina and Tennessee, except in those parts bordering the Atlantic Ocean and the Mississippi River, in the settled parts of Wisconsin, Iowa, the Northwestern territories, and the British possessions in North America. Only between the first of November and the first of July was permission granted to reside south of these limits without paying an extra premium—a premium that up to 1848 varied from one-half to one percent of the sum insured.[13]

In 1854 the entire territory of the United States was divided into sections, called "classes," with specified rates for each. These extra rates, which were altered from time to time, were kept in operation until the 1880's, when a noticeable improvement had been made in conditions of health in the South.[14] They were always severely criticized by Southerners, and the Company was periodically engaged in trying to allay their fears of being treated unjustly. In 1857 a Southern physician was employed to investigate conditions and to report on his findings—findings which fully vindicated the Company.[15] The Mutual Life's experience during its first fifteen years showed conclusively that the death rate in the areas where extra premiums were charged was higher than in the others. Thus, effects of this higher rate were mitigated by the extra premiums and by the fact, as can be seen by reference to the columns of the extreme right in Table 11, on page 83, that only a small percentage of the Company's business was written on lives in unhealthy regions.[16] Furthermore, the actual number of deaths among persons insured in The Mutual

[13] *Minutes of the Board,* June 6, 1848. The rates at this time were reduced to ¼ and ½ percent of the sum insured.
"Acclimation for the purpose of Life Insurance is obtained:
   1. By birth and continued residence in the place where insurance is sought.
   2. By long continued summer residence, and during the seasons when and where epidemic and endemic diseases prevail.
   3. By having had the disease incident to the climate or locality.
   4. Acclimation against Yellow Fever is not considered complete unless the party has had it, and has continued since to reside in places where it is epidemic." *Seventeenth Annual Report,* p. 38. Standard rates applied only in the territory east of the 100th meridian of west longitude.
[14] *Minutes of the Board of Trustees,* May 15, 1878. President Winston, who had been on a trip in the South for his health, thought that insurance could be written there save in Louisiana, Alabama, Mississippi, and Florida. In the *Agents' Rate Book* for 1886 the only restriction on residence was that the insured should not reside in the torrid zone during the first two years after the policy was issued.
[15] *Report on the Vital Statistics of the United States Made to The Mutual Life Insurance Company of New York,* by James Wynne, M.D., of Baltimore.
[16] *Report Exhibiting the Experience of The Mutual Life Insurance Company of New York for Fifteen Years Ending February 1, 1858* (New York, 1859), pp. 12 and 22.

Life was so much less than the number provided for by the Gill Mortality
Table that unfavorable experience in certain areas was not a serious
danger to the Company. The mortality saving between 1843 and 1858
was nearly 18 percent—a saving which was reflected in higher dividends.

TERRITORIAL DIVISIONS OF THE UNITED STATES FOR THE
ESTABLISHMENT OF REGIONAL RATES
FROM THE REPORT OF THE MUTUAL LIFE, 1855

Another of the hazardous risks against which The Mutual Life, in
conformity with the general practice of life insurance companies,[17] tried
to guard itself was that of travel. Although Mutual policyholders were
at first allowed freely to travel inland, except to unhealthy regions between July 1 and November 1, foreign voyages were looked upon as
dangerous. In 1844 a round trip to Europe or to the Gulf of Mexico
necessitated paying an extra premium of one-half of one percent of
the sum insured, while a round trip to the West Coast or to the Far East
was subject to an extra of 1 percent of the sum insured. These rates were
subsequently reduced when travel became less dangerous, although during the Civil War no charges for travel were quoted because of the ab-

17 G. L. Amrhein, *The Liberalization of the Life Insurance Contract*, pp. 202 ff.

normal conditions. After the conclusion of that conflict the Company's rate books were silent on the subject of travel, and by 1885 there were no restrictions on voyages except on those to the torrid zone.

The Mutual Life also endeavored to avoid insuring at standard rates

TABLE 11

PERCENTAGE OF THE ACTUAL NUMBER OF DEATHS TO THE NUMBER PREDICTED BY THE GILL TABLE, 1843–1858

Ages	15–25	25–35	35–45	45–55	55–65	65–75	All Ages	Actual Amount of Claims Paid, 1853–1857
Class I alone	90	77	61	66	98	71	70.53	$782,005
Class I & II (combined)	90	86	65	67	95	83	74.07	. . .
Class II (incl. VI)	89	127	80	71	83	195	89.66	230,650
Class III alone	662	85	96	90	99	. . .	95.62	101,800
Class IV alone	595	215	156	79	44	122	136.43	208,500
Class V (incl. VII a)	431	337	159	201	. .	. . .	230.62	26,450
Whole company	145	99	73	73	89	80	82.02	. . .

a Class VII comprised risks in foreign countries, sea risks, and all not included in the other classes.

persons who were engaged in dangerous occupations. In the first annual report an extra rate of ½ percent of the amount insured was quoted for shipmasters in the regular European packet service, 1 percent for shipmasters in the "East India and China trade, whaling voyages, or in the merchant service to any port or places around the Cape of Good Hope and Cape Horn," and special rates to be obtained at the office on the lives of military and naval officers on or off duty in time of peace. By 1855 engineers and firemen on steamboats and railroads were declared uninsurable, while by 1860 all seafaring officers and men, even those engaged in coastwise and inland navigation, as well as train conductors, engineers, and firemen were simply subjected to extra premiums. In the course of time these extra payments were largely abolished, and most persons were either insured at standard rates or declared uninsurable. Thus, the rate books for 1886 stated that the Company refused to insure: "gamblers, barkeepers, hotel proprietors who attend their own bars, saloon keepers . . . keepers of billiard parlors, or any individual who may be engaged in retailing alcoholic drinks, or engaged personally in the manufacture of the same; also laborers, ordinary seamen, engineers and firemen, whether of stationary or moving engines, or men working blast furnaces."

And during the first two years that a policy was in force, it did not cover those who died by their own hand, or who "engaged in blastings, mining, submarine labor, aeronautic ascensions, Arctic explorations, the manufacture of highly explosive substances, service upon any railroad train, as in switching or in coupling cars, or on any steam or other vessel, or military or naval service in time of war." [18]

The Mutual Life Insurance Company of New-York,
Office, No. 94 Broadway.

Permission is hereby given to_____

assured under the annexed Policy, No._____ to make a voyage to Europe by Steamer or a first-class Packet Ship, to travel while there in good conveyances, and to reside in any part thereof North of Forty-two degrees North Latitude, and West of Thirty degrees East Longitude, and also to return in a like manner. It is, however, mutually understood, and agreed by the parties in interest that the said _____is not assured against death in or by any War, or by any risk, casualty, or consequence of any War, at or in any place where he may be. This agreement will not keep the above Policy in force, unless the regular premiums are duly paid, and the other covenants are observed.

And in Consideration of the extra premium of_____per cent. (being $_____) paid thereon, permission is also given to the above-named party to extend his travels, with like restrictions in regard to conveyances and a state of War, to_____

_____

_____

New-York,_____186

_____President.

TRAVEL PERMIT USED DURING THE CIVIL WAR

A curious combination of hazardous risks confronted life insurance companies during the California gold rush, for persons who sought their fortunes in the Far West were subjecting themselves to great dangers of travel and of occupation. On December 29,1848, the Board of Trustees took cognizance of the situation by resolving that The Mutual Life would take "no risk for a residence in upper California except on life policies with the addition of one percent extra," with one percent for risks of the sea voyage to California and return and a policy limit of $2,500. On January 24, 1849, however, the Board decided to refuse all new California risks because of the uncertainty of the dangers involved. This action was not rescinded until December 15, 1853, and then insurance

[18] *Agents' Rate Book*, 1886.

was granted only at extra rates [19] on selected lives of those persons living in the principal towns of California and Oregon who were engaged in some trade or occupation of a healthful character and not engaged in mining. That this caution was well founded can be seen from the following statement of October 31, 1851.[20]

TABLE 12

CALIFORNIA RISKS

Amount of risks originally taken	$505,050
Deduct forfeited, expired, and deaths	241,600
Amount at risk October 31, 1851	$263,450
Total amount of premiums received thereon	$42,500
Total losses	$42,200

The Mutual Life also exercised care in insuring certain other risks. Thus, an extra premium of one-half of one percent was charged on the lives of women between the ages of eighteen and forty-eight because of the danger of child-bearing.[21] A limit of $10,000 [22] was set upon the amount of insurance that any one person could have with The Mutual Life, because if one or two very large policies were issued and the insured died at once, the Company would sustain a loss which could not be made up by premiums from other policyholders. Furthermore, experience showed that persons who sought a large amount of insurance were in

[19] *Minutes of the Board of Trustees,* May 11, 1859. The extras for California risks were to be ½ of one percent instead of one percent, but the risks on passage to and from California were to be charged at the earlier rate of 1 percent.

[20] *Minutes of the Board.* For a curious list of deaths see *ibid.,* August 14, 1850, from the president's report for the quarter ending July 31, 1850.

"The following is a list of casualties which have occurred during the last six months by which the Company has sustained the loss of $20,500. viz—

Jas. P. McKain of Camden, S.C. Lost by burning of St. Johns Steamboat—	$5000.
F. H. Brooks of Mobile. Lost by burning of St. Johns Steamboat—	$2000.
F. G. Brown of Mobile. Fell overboard and was drowned in Mississippi—	$5000.
Sullivan Bigelow. Shot in California—	$2000.
David B. Cook. Gored by elk in California—	500.
David Colden of New York. Died in consequence of injuries received from being struck by a Racket Ball—	5000.
Benjamin Driver. Lost by burning of Steamboat Griffith on Lake Erie—	1000.
	$20500"

In the *Report Exhibiting the Experience of The Mutual Life Insurance Company of New York for Fifteen Years Ending February 1, 1858,* p. 14, Sheppard Homans wrote "while the actual number of deaths corresponding to each hundred predicted was (in California), previous to 1853, nearly four hundred and nineteen, (418.68) it was during the past five years, one hundred and one (101.22) only, owing no doubt to the increased facilities of procuring the comforts and necessaries of life in that State."

[21] See *Annual Report* for 1858, p. 61, and for 1865, p. 17, and the *Agents' Rate Book,* 1886.

[22] This limit was raised to $20,000 May 18, 1864, and to $30,000 on Nov. 20, 1872. See *Minutes of the Board of Trustees* for these dates.

general those who led such strenuous lives or encountered such dangers that their expectation of life was short. A similar problem arose from the kind of insurance which the applicant desired to have, for he frequently wanted insurance against some extra hazardous risk, known only to himself. The experience of the Company between 1853 and 1858 was that the rate of mortality was inversely proportionate to the length of term of the policy itself.

TABLE 13

MORTALITY EXPERIENCE: THE MUTUAL LIFE, 1843–1858 [a]

Term of Policy	No. of Lives Exposed to Mortality	Probable No. of Deaths, Company's Table	Actual No. of Deaths	No. of Deaths to Each 100 Predicted	Actual Rate of Mortality	Probable Rate of Mortality	Extra Annual Premium Which Should Be Charged
Life	33,222.52	460.56	341	74	1.02	1.39	...
Endowment	83.02	0.88	0	0	0.00	1.60	...
Seven years	3,255.56	44.03	56	127	1.72	1.35	1.090
Other short terms	624.64	7.74	13	168	2.08	1.24	1.878
Whole Company	37,185.74	513.21	410	80	1.10	1.38	...

[a] *Report Exhibiting the Experience of the Mutual Life Insurance Company of New York for Fifteen Years Ending Feb. 1, 1858* (New York, 1859), p. 16.

INSURANCE AND THE WAR BETWEEN THE STATES

After the outbreak of the Civil War, life insurance companies had to deal with the problem of war risks. The policies which had been issued up to this time had definitely stated that the insurance offered no protection to those actually engaged in war. But now that large numbers of insured were going off to war, it was patently inequitable to deprive them of all protection. The officers of the The Mutual Life realized this and as a preliminary step toward meeting the difficulty offered early in 1860 to pay a cash surrender value for policies presented to the Company.[23] The inadequacy of such a measure became apparent with the outbreak of hostilities in 1861, and the president of The Mutual Life took the initiative in calling together at his office the representatives of sixteen leading life insurance companies to determine, if possible, upon a common policy.[24] These persons studied the mortality rate in the Mexi-

[23] *Seventeenth Annual Report,* 1860, p. 38.

[24] William Barnes, Superintendent of Insurance for the State of New York, wrote to President Winston, April 29, 1861, as follows:

"I was glad to see the liberal and patriotic action of The Life Companies as to war risks, even if the business don't [sic] pay in a pecuniary point of view. I think you are the man who had the foresight, boldness, and patriotism to urge this policy." See *Minutes of the Board of Trustees,* April 22, 1861.

can War, the Peninsular and Crimean War, and the recent war in India —rates which were based on scanty data. They decided finally to recommend that soldiers should be charged an extra premium of 5 percent per annum of the sum insured for service north of the 34 degree of latitude and of 10 percent for service south of that line.

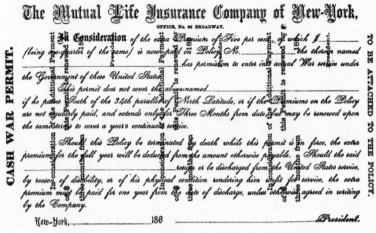

CASH WAR PERMIT USED DURING THE CIVIL WAR

The Mutual Life not only adopted this recommendation but also did not require extras from home guard volunteers unless they served away from home.[25] It allowed its policyholders to pay the extra premiums in cash as they fell due or to pay them at the time dividends were declared. The Company agreed further to deduct from the face amount of the policy any unpaid premiums, if the policy became a claim through death or surrender. All companies were not so generous in this regard as The Mutual Life,[26] and even this Company exercised great care in issuing policies with war risks. Special instructions were issued to agents and examining physicians to check upon the "constitution, health, and bodily vigor of the applicant," to ensure that if he should survive the war he would not easily be the victim of disease on account of any unusual hardship which he had endured.

In spite of the exceptional dangers to life which the War entailed and a mortality rate among the armed forces which was six times greater

---

25 *Minutes of the Board of Trustees,* August 12, 1863. A refund was given those men if they were in service less than three months.

26 Amrhein, *op. cit.,* p. 210, footnotes 65–67.

than that among the civilian population,[27] the Company did not suffer any losses on war risks.[28]

TABLE 14

REPORT ON CIVIL WAR RISKS [a]

EXPOSED TO MORTALITY FOR ONE YEAR		PROBABLE LOSSES BY GILL TABLES		ACTUAL LOSSES		PERCENTAGE OF ACTUAL LOSSES TO NUMBERS EXPOSED	
Lives	Amount	Lives	Amount	Lives	Amount	Lives	Amount
1,164.41	$2,569,261	13.34	$30,675	74	$129,300	.06	.05

Ordinary premiums on policies submitted to war risks	$64,358
Total war extras	141,000
Total	$205,358
Total losses [b]	129,300
Balance in favor of Company	76,058 [c]

[a] Minutes of the Board of Trustees, June 7, 1865.

[b] On three death claims no proof of death was provided.

[c] A high rate of mortality among veterans was expected, so some loss on the war risks was envisaged.

The Mutual Life, contrary to a policy which has been maintained fairly consistently during its entire history, made contributions from its surplus to certain war organizations. Its largest pledges were to the United States Sanitary Commission—a body that performed services similar to those of the modern Red Cross. So important did the work of the Commission seem that the Company guaranteed a sum sufficient to finance its activity.[29] President Winston also took the initiative in organizing a home guard from among the employees of "monied corporations," and The Mutual Life made the first contribution—the sum of $1,000—toward its expenses. This body was soon the famous Twenty-Second New York Regiment, or "Union Grays." Finally, The Mutual Life helped to finance the war by investing heavily in government securities—a story to which we shall return on a later page.

One of the most perplexing problems connected with the War between the States was how to handle Southern business. At the end of May, 1861, the postal service between the North and the South was discontinued, and on August 16 of the same year President Lincoln prohibited by proclamation all commercial intercourse between the two districts. Consequently, Southerners could not pay their premiums, thus invalidating their contracts, and the Company could not for the time being

[27] Minutes of the Board of Trustees, April 27, 1898.

[28] Forty-First Annual Report (1884), p. 28.

[29] The total contribution to the U.S. Sanitary Commission and to the United States Christian Commission was $20,000. See Minutes of the Board of Trustees, May 14, 1862, and February 10, 1864; and The Forty-First Annual Report (1884), p. 30.

pay death claims. Under these circumstances the Company decided to consider every Southern policy as surrendered at the date up to which the last premium was paid and to pay such surrender value whenever the policy was presented. If an earnest attempt to pay premiums was made by a Southern policyholder, the Company agreed to reinstate his policy after the war.[30] As a result of these decisions the number of surrenders and forfeitures increased greatly in 1861, and the Company withdrew from the seceded states, attempting to make up for this loss by cultivating the fertile fields of the Middle West and the Northwestern states. Not until the late 1860's and 1870's did The Mutual Life begin once again to do business in the Southern States.

TABLE 15
ANNUAL FORFEITURES AND SURRENDERS [a]

	Feb. 1, 1860	Feb. 1, 1861	Feb. 1, 1862	Feb. 1, 1863
Forfeitures	$785,000	$900,000	$2,412,400	$779,150
Surrenders	$847,345	1,089,587	$2,467,449	$973,375

[a] Annual Reports.

MARKETING LIFE INSURANCE

In avoiding many hazardous risks in their effort to get a favorable selection, life insurance companies have been to some extent dependent upon the agent in the field. He is frequently the only representative of an insurance concern who personally knows the applicant and he is in a position to decide within broad limits whether or not the prospective policyholder meets all moral and financial desiderata of the home office. In another way, too, the life insurance industry has had to rely upon its field force, for that force performs the most fundamental task of all— it gets people to share their risks in a given company. It sells insurance.

One of the most curious facts about life insurance is that it has to be *sold*. Few people, no matter how convinced they are of the wisdom of sharing risks, buy life insurance of their own free will and accord. Wherever and whenever insurance undertakings have been attempted without a sales force, a small amount of business or complete disaster has been theirs. Thus, The Old Equitable of London, operating without agents, issues but a few hundred policies a year, whereas some of its more recent English competitors write nearly that many in a single day. Similarly, savings bank insurance in Massachusetts has remained very small in spite of its low cost, and postal insurance in Great Britain was a distinct failure. The need for an agency system was realized by Elizur Wright,

[30] *Minutes of the Board of Trustees*, Feb. 12, 1862.

who expressed himself on the subject in the *Insurance Times*, 1873, as follows:

Life insurance, sweetening every night the sleep of millions of people with tired brains and troubled hearts, and saving from utter desolation and want thousands of bereaved families every year,—it is a fact which could not have existed but for the Life Insurance agents. When the world has become so good and wise as not to need a gospel preached to it, and every man is a moral law unto himself, then will there be no need of Life Insurance agents—and not much sooner.

If good work will not do itself, it must be done by somebody. And whoever does it should be paid according to his work.

The idea of having agents to sell life insurance was imported from England and employed in this country prior to 1843. Most of these early agents were, however, merchants, merchant bankers, lawyers, or commission men of one kind or another who added life insurance to their general stock in trade. They usually waited for persons to come to them to "buy" a policy of insurance and did not go out into the field to "sell" insurance to likely prospects.

With the establishment of The Mutual Life a new step forward in marketing life insurance was taken. To be sure, the agents which the Company hired in 1842 to obtain pledges for the first million dollars of insurance needed to begin business were bankers, lawyers, and merchants, who regarded life insurance as an auxiliary part of their activity. Yet both they and their early successors began to take a more aggressive attitude toward marketing, for President Robinson encouraged them— even drove them—to attempt personal solicitation. He realized that without the working capital obtained by the sale of shares, The Mutual Life would be short-lived if insurance was not written at once and in considerable volume. Consequently, to President Robinson has gone the credit of founding person-to-person solicitation—one of the most important earmarks of American life insurance.[31]

Although a sales force was part and parcel of The Mutual Life's organization from the very first, it was small and in the early days was concentrated in the large cities of the East, especially in New York State. Gradually, as the life insurance business developed, the agency system was enlarged, following the routes of trade to the South and to the West, making a living from insurance commissions a possibility. This led to the appearance of full-time agents in urban centers—men who had a

---

[31] See J. Owen Stalson, *Marketing Life Insurance in America* (Cambridge, 1942), pp. 126 ff.

contract with the Company to sell insurance in their territories and who were known as local agents.

From time to time an especially gifted person was employed on a salary as a "general traveling agent" to assist local agents in selling especially difficult cases. Thus, Henry Hazen Hyde, father of the founder of The Equitable, became a general traveling agent for The Mutual Life in 1853, before he became the Company's agent in Boston.

From the practice of having local agents and general traveling agents grew the general agency system, whereby a general agent was given jurisdiction over a large territory—part of a state or even several states—and was required to devote all his time to selling life insurance for The Mutual. He had also to select agents and examining physicians for appointment by the home office, supervise these agents, forward applications, and attend to local advertising. The first of these general agents was appointed in 1858, and he was so successful that during the Civil War, when the Company was anxious to get business to offset the losses in the South, several others were chosen to carry on similar work in other areas.[32] By 1869 the system had been widely developed in the United States, and expansion to Europe had even been considered (1863, 1868).

The remuneration of The Mutual Life's agents was provided for by commissions. From 1843 to 1853 these amounted to 5 percent of the first year's premium and, in order to keep a hold on the agent, to an additional 5 percent on all subsequent (renewal) premiums *so long as the agent sold life insurance exclusively for The Mutual*.[33] In 1853 these rates were raised to 10 percent on first year premiums, while 5 percent was paid on renewals, 1 percent for the collection of premiums on policies sold by other agents, and 2½ percent on special extras, except war extras. These rates remained in force until the introduction of the general agency system, when direct relations between the Company and the local agents ceased. Thus, from about 1863 the general agents were given 15 percent of the first premium and 7½ percent of all renewals during the existence of a policy, and from moneys thus received they had to pay the agents or solicitors who worked for them. In 1869 the basis of

---

[32] *Minutes of the Agency Committee*, May 25, 1863, and Dec. 16, 1862.

[33] A pamphlet called *Instructions to Agents* was issued in 1850, 1853, 1855, and 1857. See *Minutes of the Agency Committee*, May 21, 1859. For a short time extra inducements were offered to some agents. *Minutes of the Board of Trustees* for November 13, 1850, contain this statement: "On motion the Agency Committee was authorized in their discretion to offer gratuities in certain cases to Agents for increased efforts to obtain applications for life insurance, provided in their judgment such a step will promote the interests of the Company." These extras were criticized in 1853 and seem to have disappeared.

the commissions to general agents was altered so that the sums paid were 30 percent of the first premium, 7½ percent of renewals for four years, and, as a collection fee, 2 percent of all subsequent renewals. Finally, The Mutual Life paid a brokerage of 25 percent of the first year premiums to agents of other companies who sold policies for this Company, and in such cases it paid the general agent a fee of 10 percent of these same premiums.

That the agents played an essential role in the building up of the business of The Mutual Life is supported by an abundance of data to be found in the *Minutes of the Agency Committee of the Board of Trustees* —a committee that was established in 1853. By way of example, it was reported that of the $296,908,000 of insurance issued between 1843 and 1868, inclusive, only $17,402,000 came to the office unsolicited and was not subject to agents' commissions.[34] Moreover, during the first ten years of the Company's existence, the mortality rate on the insurance sold by agents was less than on that which was unsolicited.[35] By 1870 nearly all insurance was sold by agents, and the risks which they wrote were as good as they had been earlier. Yet the earnings of agents were on the average not large. The average annual income of The Mutual's 1,499 local agents, most of whom were on a part time basis, was in 1868 only $127.[36]

Relations between the home office and the agents were not always harmonious, for the great number of accounts which had to be kept led sometimes to misunderstandings, the agents did not always forward premiums promptly, there were peculations, and agents were frequently deserting life insurance or The Mutual Life for other callings or for other companies. When Henry B. Hyde, founder of The Equitable, opened his books for business, he made his father Henry H. a trustee, a stockholder, and presumably an agent. The Mutual Life refused adamantly to have their agent sell insurance for another company and refused any settlement of commissions on renewals which might come to him.[37] Another famous case in which an agent came into conflict with the Company concerned John C. Johnston, the schoolmate of Henry B. Hyde, who with his son built up a most successful Mutual Life agency in New York. Johnston got proxies as well as new insurance and thus became so powerful that he could do much to swing the election of Mutual's trustees and officers. In fact, he played a large role in forc-

---

[34] *Ibid.*, July 16, 1869.   [35] *Ibid.*, Oct. 20, 1853.
[36] *Ibid.*, July 11, 1869. No soliciting in the Company office was allowed by either clerks or agents where commissions or brokerage fees were claimed. *Ibid.*, Sept. 22, 1863.
[37] *Ibid.*, June 29, 1859.

ing President Joseph B. Collins out of office in 1853 and in putting Frederick S. Winston in his place.

Immediately after this election John C. Johnston decided to retire from business, and the officers of The Mutual Life paid him a lump sum settlement of his claims for renewal commissions.[38] The purchase or commutation of future commissions was, indeed, not an uncommon practice. So extensive did commutation become that in 1869 70 percent of all premiums received were free from commissions.[39]

ADVERTISING AND COMPETITION

The arguments which insurance salesmen used in the first three quarters of the nineteenth century were not unlike those used today. Inasmuch as the main purpose of life insurance was, then, as it is now, to provide for one's dependents in case of death or to combine this protection with saving for some large and expected expense, it was only logical that stress be placed upon the uncertainty of life and the necessity of savings. But life insurance advertising of these early days was, like contemporary preaching, full of fire and brimstone. Both played upon the emotions of fear—and both were effective, if rather morbid.

Many of the early appeals contained in The Mutual Life's literature were directed toward women. It was natural that this should be the case, for life insurance was most frequently taken for their protection and death benefits payable to married women were within certain limits free under New York law from their husbands' creditors. An excellent example of this kind of approach is found in the following quotation from *Consideration on Life Insurance by a Lady* (New York, 1855).

Woman's Agency

To woman, who in the main is the especial beneficiary of Life Insurance, we would say, if you are solicitous for its increasing diffusion, show it in your words and by your works. This is a work on which you may gladly smile.

Woman's influence lies in the power of properly cultivated affections.

---

[38] The value of the future commissions on policies obtained by Johnston and Son was stated by the actuary to have been $29,035.44. The Company, nevertheless, awarded him $30,000 and a paid-up insurance on his life of $5,000, but in return made both members of the firm pledge that they would never directly or indirectly enter into the "service of any other life insurance company whatever or interfere directly or indirectly with the election of Trustees except by voting as members of the Company"—a pledge that was supported by a $10,000 bond. Yet in spite of this agreement, Mr. Johnston was instrumental in the founding (1858) of The Mutual Life Insurance Company of Wisconsin, which was the future Northwestern Mutual Life Insurance Company. See *Minutes of the Board of Trustees*, Nov. 9, 1853.

[39] *Minutes of the Agency Committee*, July 16, 1869.

Her empire is the heart. Seeking no authority, insisting on no right, she for this reason is successful when the QUESTION IS RIGHT. And wherever the human mind has been regenerated, and human character elevated, in each and all the true moral reforms of the world, Providence has chosen her as a powerful auxiliary. It is the wife, the mother, the daughter, and the sister, who need to be protected when their natural protector is taken away. It is to these Life Insurance makes its appeal; and for these may not man be taught to practise prudence, sobriety, and economy, and become the possessor of a life policy? What a crush and ruin to these would it not save! What oceans of lamentation and wailing would give place to their rejoicing and permanent joy for a "heritable habitation," secured to them through this institution!

We are compelled to urge female influence and agency in this great work of the age, and ashamed to confess that she who is most interested has hitherto done nothing. Nothing! We appeal to her by all the claims of virtue, by all the sufferings of humanity, to delay no longer. The American mind is awakening to the benign influences of Life Insurance, and needs but her active persuasion to melt it on this subject into one flow of emotion.

Similarly, men were appealed to in *The Advantage of Life Insurance* (New York, 1855) by the gentle reminder that "While the aged must die, the young may—and often most unexpectedly do die."

Experience demonstrates that the possession of property is almost equally unstable with that of life. Statistics, prepared by competent and accurate persons, exhibit the astonishing fact, that of all who enter into mercantile pursuits, the merest fraction * leave any property to their surviving relations. The pangs of separation are greatly increased by the bitter reflection, that a beloved wife or children are about to lose their natural protector and friend, and be left, often worse than penniless, to the cold charities of the world.

Such arguments were rammed home by printing lists of insured who had died soon after taking out their policies, such as the following from the *Annual Report* of 1844.

A Medical gentleman whose emoluments, from a widely extended practice, averaged $1500 per annum, reflecting upon the precarious tenure of his health in the sphere of his duties, which necessarily exposed him to the constant vicissitudes of the weather, besides bringing him frequently into contact with parties affected with infectious diseases, took out a policy on his life for $5000. After being insured for four years he died from a malignant fever caught on a professional visit, and his widow thus obtained $5000.

* General Dearborn, of Boston, stated in a public address:—"After an extensive acquaintance with business men, I am satisfied that among one hundred merchants and traders, not more than three ever acquire independence."

A farmer having had his attention drawn to the subject of life insurance, made a proposal for an insurance of $2500 on his life, which after the usual enquiries had been made, insurance was effected; during the next harvest he was precipitated from one of his wagons, by the horses starting forward while loading, and killed on the spot. This family received $2500, which enabled them to carry on the farm.

Insurance for business or for savings was also advertised:

1. It is applicable to the several purposes of raising money on loans, where personal security, only, can be offered.

2. Of making and perfecting marriage settlements.

3. Of securing the eventual payment of doubtful debts, due to individuals or bodies of creditors.

4. Of enabling proprietors of real estate, charged with mortgages, or with portions or other encumbrances, payable on the termination of their own or others' lives, to answer the charges when they fall due.

5. Of securing to parents the return of moneys paid as premiums for clerkship or apprenticeship, marriage portions, capital embarked in business, or other advances made for children, in the event of their premature death.

6. Of reimbursing to the purchaser of any life-estate, or annuity, his principal, on the death of the person during whose life it was holden.

7. Of rendering contingent property nearly equal, in point of security, to absolute property; and

8. Generally as affording means of certain indemnity against any pecuniary loss, claim, or inconvenience whatsoever, to which one individual may become subject, by reason of the death of another.

Now in effecting an insurance on his life, the husband or father secures to his surviving relations, beyond the usual contingencies of human events, a certain resource against the ills of poverty: his last hours are soothed with the consciousness of having so far done his duty to his family; and while endeavoring to seek reconciliation and acceptance with his Creator, his meditations are not interrupted nor his mind harassed with the agonizing fear or knowledge that his beloved ones will at once be suffering from destitution and all its horrors after he is taken from them.

The Mutual Life also seems to have spent a great deal of energy in trying to break down a religious prejudice against life insurance. Although the oldest insurance institution in the land was devoted to providing protection for Presbyterian ministers, many persons believed that life insurance "implies a distrust in Providence, and is an impious attempt to provide or control His will." Consequently, several of the Company's pamphlets attacking this contention were written by a "Clergyman." Finally, much attention was given in the sales literature to emphasizing the scientific basis and substantial nature of life insurance.

Once the advertisements had driven home the wisdom of having life insurance protection, they went on to explain why that protection should be with The Mutual Life. In the first years after 1843, the argument most frequently employed was that the best insurance was obtained from a mutual company rather than from a stock company, because the mutual would return any profits or excess payments to the policyholders, while the stock company would pay them to stockholders. As the Company acquired experience, much was made of the Company's excellent record—the amount of insurance sold, the large dividends, the huge benefits paid, and the sound investments. Then, as now, the successful nature of the Company's operations was emphasized by pointing out that more money was paid in dividends and benefits or was held in reserve for the benefit of policyholders than was actually received in premiums. Protection, it was declared, cost nothing except the use of money.

Such arguments were carried in the Company's annual reports, in flyers, in pamphlets, and in announcements in the press. In 1855 The Mutual Life issued one of the first house organs—*The Life Insurance Advocate*—which is not to be confused with the *Insurance Advocate and Journal* published by the Connecticut Mutual.

In some of this early literature attacks were made directly or by innuendo on The Mutual Life's competitors. These attacks had to do mainly with those aspects of life insurance in which there was competition—the net cost of insurance, kinds of insurance, financial stability of the insurer, and getting to the prospect first. So far as net cost, kinds of insurance, and financial stability were concerned, The Mutual Life was in an excellent competitive position.

In order to compete with it, the Nautilus (later the New York Life), which was having difficulty in getting insurance placed and had an unfavorable mortality rate because of the insuring of negro slaves, decided to allow policyholders to pay part of their premiums in cash and part in promissory notes.[40] This practice was expected to appeal to persons who were short of cash and yet hoped to be able to carry life insurance. Against it The Mutual Life trained its guns as early as 1846. The Company contended that premiums paid in part with promissory notes, and dividends in turn paid with Company scrip were just a snare and a delusion—that a policy of life insurance would lose all its protective powers if the insured simply *promised* to pay premiums. The Mutual

[40] James M. Hudnut, *Semi-Centennial History of The New York Life* (New York, 1895), pp. 22, 25.

Life adhered strictly to cash premiums and eventually saw its policy receive the approval of the law.

Rivalry between The Mutual Life and The Equitable Life Assurance Society also became sharp in the 1860's. The founder of this company, Henry Baldwin Hyde, who was an employee of The Mutual Life, conceived the idea of establishing an institution to write the large risks which The Mutual refused. At the age of twenty-four he broached his plan to President Winston, who dismissed brusquely both him and his plan. Thereupon Hyde leased rooms in the same building as his erstwhile employer and hung out a sign that completely dwarfed The Mutual's shingle. This episode illustrates well the spirit of the man—a spirit to which was added boundless enthusiasm and energy. To meet his competition, The Mutual Life adopted the payment of annual dividends—a move which The Equitable could not duplicate—but not disheartened Hyde began to issue tontine in order to get more rapidly ahead.[41] Such competition among The Mutual Life, the New York Life, and The Equitable was profoundly to influence the course of life insurance history in subsequent years.

[41] Terence O'Donnell, *History of Life Insurance in Its Formative Years* (Chicago, 1936), pp. 540 ff.

VI. Investments and Management

AFTER A LIFE INSURANCE COMPANY has determined what kind of policies it is going to write, what premiums it is going to charge, what risks it is willing to accept, and its agents have actually sold insurance to the public, it finds itself, if operating upon the level premium plan, the recipient of moneys that must be held for the future payment of claims. These moneys constitute the assets of the life insurance business and consequently must equal or exceed reserves and other liabilities. In the course of time life insurance companies thus amass vast sums from relatively small premium payments—sums that on January 1, 1943, for three hundred and three American companies amounted to $34,931,411,348 of admitted assets.

The investment of these large accumulations has been one of the major concerns of life insurance companies. Some idea of its importance can be gleaned from the fact that in the last eighty years practically all bankruptcies of life insurance companies, which have occurred almost exclusively among small institutions, have resulted from poor judgment or mismanagement of investments rather than from excessive claims or expenses.[1]

As must be abundantly clear from what has happened, life insurance contracts are of a markedly long-range character. Moreover, they contain a specific and guaranteed interest rate that may be higher than the market rate in the distant, unpredictable future. Consequently the investments of life insurance companies tend to be of a long-term nature. Companies shy away from securities which fluctuate widely in value, because extensive changes in value might result in temporary insolvency; they seek extreme safety rather than large earnings. In general, the various qualifications for life insurance investments are most commonly found in mortgages and bonds, and for this reason these types of securities have loomed large in life insurance portfolios.

LEGAL RESTRICTIONS ON INVESTMENTS

Because the financial responsibilities of life insurance companies are

[1] Lester W. Zartman, *The Investments of Life Insurance Companies* (New York, 1906), p. 145.

of such a special, long-range character, various restrictions have been placed upon investments. The earliest of such curbs were contained in the charters of the companies. Thus, the charter of The Mutual Life provided in articles ten and eleven that:

The whole of the premiums received for insurance by said corporation, except as provided for in the following sections shall be invested in bonds and mortgages on unincumbered real estate within the state of New York, the real property to secure such investment of capital shall, in every case be worth twice the amount loaned thereon. The trustees shall have power to invest a certain portion of the premiums received, not to exceed one-half thereof, in public stocks of the United States, or of this state or of any incorporated city in this state.

Here there was no disposition to allow the investment of life insurance funds in canals, which had already reached their apogee, or in railways, which were in their infancy, or in any of the industries which were then expanding. Nor was there any indication that the founding fathers envisaged the growth of life insurance companies into great financial institutions with such large assets that satisfactory investments could only be made on a national scale. Emphasis was placed upon temporarily gilt-edge investments which were so located that they could be carefully watched. In fact, the early life insurance companies did largely a local business.

The first law to prescribe what investments should be made of the capital stock of an incorporated life insurance company or what investments a mutual company had to make before it could begin operations was enacted by New York State in 1849.[2] The provisions of this measure were similar to those of The Mutual Life's charter—that $100,000 should be invested in bonds of the cities of New York, bonds of the State of New York or of the United States, or in mortgages on real estate in New York worth double the amount loaned thereon. Furthermore, to prevent the life insurance companies from doing any business other than insurance, the law prohibited them from holding more real estate than was necessary for the conduct of their business or than fell to them from foreclosures or from the satisfaction of debts. Thus, New York endeavored not only to insure the safe investment of life insurance capital but also required that these sums be invested within the boundaries of the state.

Shortly after this legislation had been enacted, other states, taking their cues from the act, decided that part of the capital of their companies

2 Section 6, Act of April 10, 1849.

should be invested within the borders of the home state.[3] Also in line with this state protectionism was the New York law of 1857. It provided that the general funds (assets) of New York life insurance companies had to be invested according to the provisions of the 1849 act, or in the bonds or stock of any institution incorporated in New York, or in collateral loans on such securities.[4] It did permit, however, investment in the bonds of any state in the United States. By 1870 six states had laws restricting the purchase of state bonds to those of the state where the company was located. Only Illinois and Wisconsin adopted the reasonable rule that companies chartered by them could, when they wrote business in another state, invest funds in the same securities in those states in which they were permitted to invest at home.

The regional restrictions which were thus placed upon life insurance investments ultimately had a stifling effect on the companies, particularly in New York, for they evoked retaliation in kind. The New York companies thus found themselves cut out of some important fields, although these companies were allowed to purchase bonds of the states which required a deposit of their capital obligations as a prerequisite to doing business within their borders.[5] In spite of this law, however, New York companies maintained, and justly so, that they were being deprived of many lucrative opportunities for placing their funds—especially in the rapidly growing Middle West. Finally they secured action by the legislature to permit them (1868) to loan money on real estate outside New York, provided the property was located within fifty miles of New York City; [6] in 1875 to make mortgage loans in states adjacent to New York; [7] and subsequently to make such loans in all states. Thus were the laws regarding investments early changed to meet the needs of the business and of the growing economy. Life insurance companies were losing their local character.

INVESTMENTS OF THE MUTUAL LIFE

Because of the legal restrictions outlined above, the investments of The Mutual Life from 1843 to 1870 were limited largely to mortgage loans

[3] Wisconsin by Act of February 9, 1850; New Jersey by section 6, Act of March 10, 1852; Kentucky and Ohio in 1867; California, Iowa and Maryland in 1868; Georgia, Illinois, Michigan, Minnesota and Missouri in 1869; and Kansas and Tennessee in 1870.

[4] As Zartman has pointed out, *op. cit.*, p. 162n, the wording of this law of 1857 was ambiguous. "The law of 1849 regulated capital and 'funds.' The law of 1857 regulated 'surplus accumulations' above capital stock, but provided that if any permanent fund is established by a company it shall be invested as required in the law of 1849."

[5] According to provisions of the Act of 1857. Zartman, *op. cit.*, p. 163, is apparently in error on this point. He refers to the New York law of April 12, 1860, section 1.

[6] Section 1, Act of April 24, 1868.   [7] Section 2, chapter 423, acts of 1875.

in New York, to New York State bonds, to New York municipals, and to United States governments. The fortfolio of the Company clearly reflected these limitations. The authorization for The Mutual's first investment was given February 22, 1843—an investment in the "City of New York 6 percent Water Loan Stock." [8] The second placement of funds, coming after a decision of the Finance Committee to make no loans on property other than that located in the city or county of New York, was a mortgage loan on houses in Grand Street. The third investment authorization [9] was for the purchase of New York State "Stock" at 5½ or 6 percent, whichever will pay the "best interest." And then followed a long series of loans on "bond and mortgage"—so called because the borrower had to pledge not only certain property as security but also because he had to give a bond to meet his obligations.

On January 31, 1846, the assets of the Company were as follows: [10]

Stocks of the State and City of New York	$ 41,901.15
Bonds and mortgages on real estate in this City and Brooklyn	151,650.00
Deposited in Bank of New York	13,136.23
Cash on hand and at agencies	10,292.90
Total	$216,980.28

The major portion of the assets of The Mutual Life continued during the period up to 1870 to be in mortgage loans, but during the Mexican War (1846–1848) and the Civil War (1861–1865) the Company bought heavily of government securities. Although the exact amount acquired during the former conflict cannot be ascertained because of the lumping of all New York City, State, and Federal bonds under one heading, it would seem that they were increased from nothing on February 1, 1846, to about $83,000 on February 1, 1847, to $116,000 on February 1, 1848, and to $157,571.84 on February 1, 1849.[11] During the Civil War, The Mutual Life's investments in governments increased as follows: [12] for the year ending February 1, 1861, $386,000.00; for 1862, $730,550.00; for 1863, $2,016,791.00; for 1864, $4,587,599.00; for 1865, $5,413,728.25.

In both instances the motivating factors for purchasing government securities were patriotism and good interest rates. That the profit motive was well satisfied is abundantly clear. Government bonds increased in value to such an extent after the Mexican War that The Mutual Life

---

[8] The term "stock" was employed for some years in our present-day sense of "bond." *Minutes of the Finance Committee*, February 22, 1843.

[9] September 28, 1843.   [10] *Minutes of the Board of Trustees*, February 10, 1846.

[11] President's reports in *Minutes of the Board of Trustees*.

[12] *New York Insurance Reports*.

decided (1850) to sell them, as well as New York State bonds, and by 1853 it had completely emptied its portfolio of them. Similarly, the government securities marketed during the Civil War under the aegis of Secretaries of the Treasury Chase and Fessenden, who had the assistance of that super-salesman Jay Cooke, appreciated to such a degree that upon the conclusion of the conflict The Mutual Life had made a half a million dollars.[13] And as though this were not enough, United States bonds were exempt from taxes and bore interest in specie rather than in paper money —a tremendous advantage in view of the fact that there was a premium on gold in 1864 of more than 150 percent and that some premium existed for thirteen long years thereafter.

Aside from these purchases of government securities, the making of a few policy loans between 1850 and 1855, erecting the first home office building in 1864, and small holdings of New York City and State bonds, the portfolio of The Mutual Life remained steadily inclined toward mortgages. Most of them were located in New York City or its immediate vicinity, but in 1849 a decision was reached to invest in mortgages on New York country real estate—a decision that was turned into a policy in 1858.[14] At both of these dates, following as they did the bottom of a business cycle, money was plentiful and the Company was having difficulty in placing its funds at interest—a phenomenon which was repeated again in 1868, when permission was granted to invest on property located within fifty miles of New York City. But there were other extenuating circumstances for the adoption of this policy. Interest rates on country mortgages were high; the security was considered good; and people outside metropolitan New York insisted that the funds which they put into life insurance should be available to them for borrowing purposes.[15] In 1862 the geographical distribution of The Mutual Life's mortgage loans was as follows in the counties of New York:

Albany	$30,681.22	Lewis	1,000.00	Rensselaer	25,900.00
Alleghany	135,400.00	Livingston	104,300.00	Richmond	307,000.00
Cayuga	13,000.00	Monroe	143,671.20	Rockland	10,000.00
Chautauqua	11,700.00	New York	3,954,718.99	St. Lawrence	66,967.00
Cattaraugus	69,800.00	Niagara	38,600.00	Saratoga	15,000.00
Chemung	55,300.00	Oneida	11,000.00	Schuyler	2,000.00
Columbia	4,000.00	Onondaga	160,750.00	Seneca	30,000.00
Dutchess	52,000.00	Ontario	6,000.00	Tioga	2,500.00
Erie	78,000.00	Orange	10,000.00	Ulster	8,000.00
Greene	10,000.00	Oswego	30,900.00	Wayne	3,000.00
Genesee	31,700.00	Otsego	10,500.00	Westchester	419,800.00
Jefferson	15,200.00	Putnam	6,000.00	Wyoming	115,374.00
Kings	482,842.00	Queens	66,000.00	Total	$6,538,604.41

13 *Minutes of the Board of Trustees,* November 21, 1877.
14 *Minutes of the Board of Trustees,* February 14, 1849.
15 *Minutes of the Finance Committee,* June 30, 1858, and May 31, 1860. See Appendix.

In general, The Mutual Life pursued an ultra-conservative policy in making its investments, a fact which stands out clearly from an analysis of the portfolio and a comparison of it with those of other companies. But none of the companies in this period played a large role in financing directly either industry or transportation. There was little indication of the heavy placements which were to come later in railroads, manufacturing, and public utilities.

TABLE 16

ASSETS OF THE MUTUAL LIFE INSURANCE COMPANY[a]

	May 1, 1851	Feb. 1, 1861	Dec. 31, 1870
Real estate owned by company	$ ...	$ 40,239.14 (.6%)	$ 945,383.07 (2.1%)
Loans on bond and mortgage	1,188,231.22 (88.2%)	6,422,320.39 (88.4%)	33,960,521.62 (76.4%)
Interest due on said mortgages	...	17,498.57 (.2%)	41,322.15 (.1%)
Interest accrued on said mortgages	...	80,000.00 (1.1%)	324,542.00 (.7%)
Loans on bond and mortgage, with more than 1 year's interest due	...	...	38,900.00 (.1%)
Cash on hand and in banks	32,829.66 (2.4%)	120,050.39 (1.7%)	2,608,910.74 (5.9%)
Agents' balances	5,631.84 (.4%)	20,005.60 (.3%)	55,593.38 (.1%)
Premiums due and unpaid	...	33,132.38 (.5%)	281,408.67 (.6%)
Deferred premiums	...	135,000.00 (1.9%)	1,007,616.39 (2.3%)
Suspense account	4,067.38 (.3%)	...	...
Stocks, bonds, etc., owned by the Company	117,919.09 (8.7%)[b]	386,000.00 (5.3%)[c]	5,201,732.75 (11.7%)[d]
Totals	$1,348,679.19 (100%)	$7,254,246.47 (100%)	$44,465,930.77 (100%)

[a] New York Insurance Reports.

[b] U.S. stocks (par value $109,941.02) cost	$115,684.34
N.Y. city corporation stocks (par value $2,000)	2,234.75
Total	$117,919.09

[c] Account of stocks of the State of New York and the United States, and of all other stocks and bonds absolutely owned by the company:

	Par Value	Market Value
86 shares, $1,000 each, of U.S. 6 percent stock	$ 86,000	...
300 shares, $1,000 each, of U.S. 5 percent stock	300,000	...
Total	$386,000	...

	Par Value	Market Value
[d] U.S. 6 percent bonds, 1881 registered	$2,100,550.00	$2,321,107.75
U.S. 5–20 bonds, registered	2,000,000.00	2,165,000.00
U.S. 10–40 bonds, registered	50,000.00	53,125.00
U.S. 5 percent bonds, 1874	50,000.00	52,500.00
New York State Bounty Loan 7 percent bonds	500,000.00	540,000.00
Cherry Valley Town bonds	50,000.00	50,000.00
Yonkers Town bonds	20,000.00	20,000.00
	$4,770,550.00	$5,201,732.75

Among the many questions which arose in placing the assets of the Company at interest were, first, how closely could funds be invested, that is, how much could be invested and how much must be kept on

TABLE 17

DISTRIBUTION OF ASSETS OF SELECTED COMPANIES [a]

(Percentage)

Kind of Assets	1860	1870
Cash items	2.4	4.3
Deferred and outstanding premiums	3.1	5.3
Accrued interest	1.4	1.2
Total uninvested assets	6.9	10.8
Premium notes	20.5	21.5
Policy loans	.0	.1
Total notes and loans	20.5	21.6
Mortgage loans	59.2	44.4
Real estate	2.7	3.5
Collateral loans	1.6	1.2
U.S. Bonds	3.1	9.1
Foreign public bonds	. . .	. . .
State bonds	.6	1.5
County and municipal bonds	2.2	5.5
Total public bonds	5.9	16.1
Railroad bonds	.8	1.2
Light and water bonds	. . .	.0
Miscellaneous bonds	.1	.2
Total corporation bonds	.9	1.4
Railroad stocks	.5	.4
Bank and trust company stock	1.6	1.1
Light and water company stock	.1	.0
Miscellaneous stock	.1	.0
Total stock	2.3	1.5
Total corporation bonds and stocks	3.2	2.9

[a] Lester W. Zartman, *The Investments of Life Insurance Companies* (New York, 1906), p. 14.

hand to pay death claims, and, secondly, to what extent should moneys be used to improve public health. Concerning the former question, it is curious to note that the Company had to borrow money to make its first investment [16]—in New York City Water Stock—and that it had again

[16] *Minutes of the Finance Committee,* February 22, 1843.

to resort to borrowing to pay the first death claim in April, 1844.[17] Investing as closely as this did not, however, turn out to be a wise procedure, and although it was continued until 1849,[18] after the latter date the Company aimed to have enough liquid capital to pay claims. Concerning the investment of funds in public health enterprises, it should be remarked that the first loan was in a movement destined to improve the health of the people in the City of New York, where most of the early policyholders of the Company lived. In fact, the early management seems to have been interested in such causes, for in 1864 it not only gave money to the United States Sanitary Commission but also devoted $2,000 to the Citizen Association of New York to study sewage disposal, drainage, tenement houses, and other sources of epidemic diseases.[19]

Much more important than these considerations were, however, safety of investments and rate of earnings. Safety was sought not only by placing funds in high grade classes of securities, as provided by law, but also by scrutinizing individual investment with care. Authorization for each investment had to be approved by the Finance Committee and subsequently to be ratified by the Board of Trustees—and members of this Committee or its agents had personal knowledge of every piece of property mortgaged to the Company. Usually no loan was made before title papers, bonds, and mortgages had been presented to the Company; mortgage loans were granted only up to 50 percent of the value of city property and to 40 percent of farms (exclusive of buildings); and reappraisals were made periodically to assure these margins of safety.[20] The only criticism to which investments were subject was that loans were made to members of the Board of Trustees,[21] but such cases were infrequent. From 1843 to 1865 losses of principal were insignificant, for only $827 out of total investments of upwards of $20,000,000 was written off as irretrievable.[22]

To estimate the rate of earnings of The Mutual Life's investments during the period of 1843–1870 is an extremely difficult task, for not only do depreciation and appreciation of values have to be considered, along with the cost of handling the investments, but the Company made

---

[17] *Fifty-fifth Annual Report*, p. 15.

[18] *Minutes of the Finance Committee*, Oct. 1, 1849.   [19] *Ibid.*, July 14, 1864.

[20] In the reappraisal of 1849–1851 only three properties did not meet the requirements. Other revaluations were made, for example, in 1854 (*Minutes of the Finance Committee*, Sept. 17, 1854) and in 1867 (*Minutes of the Finance Committee*, December 5, 1867).

[21] *Examination of Witnesses before George W. Miller, Superintendent of Insurance in Relation to Certain Charges against the Trustees and Officers of The Mutual Life Insurance Company* (1870), pp. 82–83. This work, which is very rare, may be found in the Library of Congress.

[22] *Minutes of the Board of Trustees*, February 15, 1865.

no careful contemporary study to serve as a guide. We do know, however, that the rate of earnings in 1849 was 6½ percent, that in 1860 mortgage loans brought 7 percent, that the net interest on investments for the five years 1858–1862 was 6½ percent, and that the interest rate on all loans

TABLE 18

RATE OF EARNINGS OF THE MUTUAL LIFE

(Based on market values; includes capital gains and losses)

Years	Rate of Earnings of Total Assets	Rate of Earnings of Real Estate	Rate of Earnings of Mortgage Loans	Rate of Earnings of Bonds and Stocks
1860	6.8	...	...	...
1861	5.7	...	...	...
1862	7.7	...	...	...
1863	9.7	...	7.3	12.3
1864	10.7	...	4.1	15.3
1865	3.6	3.5	6.5	−4.2
1866	8.0	6.4	7.3	...
1867	7.5	7.4	9.8	13.4
1868	3.4	6.7	...	...
1869	7.1	7.4	7.1	...
1870	6.0	4.0	7.3	...

TABLE 19

AMERICAN RAILROAD BOND YIELDS [a]

January Index Numbers

1860	8.788	1866	8.108
1861	8.662	1867	7.786
1862	8.412	1868	7.822
1863	6.136	1869	7.992
1864	6.658	1870	8.215
1865	6.867		

[a] From Frederick R. Macaulay, *The Movements of Interest Rates, Bond Yields, and Stock Prices in the United States since 1856* (New York, 1938), p. A108.

with satisfactory security was reduced from 7 to 6 percent in 1863.[23] Perhaps the most complete study of The Mutual Life's rate of return was made by Professor Lester W. Zartman, who used market values for his calculations and omitted managerial expenses, but included in income capital gains and losses.[24] When his findings are compared with an index of the yield on railroad bonds, The Mutual's earnings seem to have fluctuated unduly and yet to have followed in a rough way the general curve of yields. In any case, it is clear that the earnings were far more than the 4 percent which the Company assumed would be made when the premium schedules were drawn up and that consequently The Mutual Life had in these years an appreciable gain from investments— a gain which went to swell dividend payments.

[23] See *Annual Reports* for 1849, 1860, and 1864.
[24] Lester W. Zartman, *The Investments of Life Insurance Companies*, pp. 75, 84, 90, 98.

ORGANIZATION OF THE MUTUAL LIFE

The investing of the assets of The Mutual Life, the selection of risks, the marketing of policies, the fixing of premiums, the paying of mortuary claims, and the performance of the hundred and one other duties connected with a large life insurance business involved a tremendous amount of labor, required a highly-trained office force, and demanded great managerial skill. Thus, as The Mutual Life grew in size and complexity, its executive and administrative organization became more complex, its personnel more numerous, and its departmental chiefs more highly specialized. In 1849 the Company appointed its first actuary; in 1862, its first full-time attorney, Richard A. McCurdy, a future president of The Mutual Life; and in the sixties, new physicians to assist Dr. Post. In 1870 the internal structure of the Company's Home Office was completely revised, a "division of labor" being effected by the creation of bureaus to handle special aspects of the business.

The Board of Trustees also became more highly organized in order adequately to supervise the work of the employees. Thus, to the standing Committee on Finance and the Committee on Insurance, which were established in 1842, were added the Agency Committee (1853), the Committee on Audit (1858), the Committee on Mortuary Claims (1870), and the Committee on Expenditure (1870). Each of these committees corresponded to some administrative bureau, as can be seen from the organizational chart, and each had the duty with the aid of the president, to determine policies and to oversee the activities of these bureaus. For example, the By-Laws of the Company stipulated that the Insurance Committee should "determine the rates of premium and the principles upon which policies and other obligations may be issued or purchased by the Company" and should have "supervision of all questions relating to the distribution of surplus." But as we have seen in earlier chapters, the actuary and his assistants furnished the technical information necessary for the fixing of premiums and dividends, and the entire Board passed upon the Committee's recommendations, if the questions involved were of sufficient importance.[25] Consequently a method of carefully scrutinizing every action was provided by this system and yet the responsibilities of management fell most heavily upon the executive officers, especially upon the president. The main organizational lines thus laid down by 1870 have been followed up to the present time with remarkably few changes.

[25] *Minutes of the Board of Trustees*, Nov. 17, 1870.

CHART VI

THE MUTUAL LIFE INSURANCE COMPANY OF NEW YORK ORGANIZATION CHART, 1870 [a]

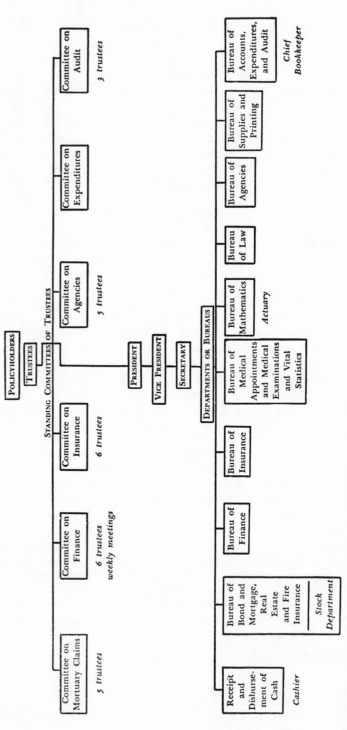

[a] Minutes of the Board of Trustees, September 2 and November 17, 1870.

MANAGEMENT

To the men who were the life blood in the organization of the Company almost no attention has been paid in the preceding pages, for it seemed preferable to describe the historical evolution of The Mutual Life in functional rather than in personal terms—to try to explain what life insurance was, how it came to be, and how the Company operated rather than to concentrate upon the role of individuals. Important, however, as is that part of our story which has already been told, it must not be overlooked that men made the wheels of this business go 'round.

We left our discussion of early management at the point where the Company had just been organized and its affairs were being directed by Morris Robinson, the first president, Samuel Hannay, the secretary, Minturn Post, the physician, and a rather indifferent Board of Trustees. As the business of The Mutual Life grew in size and complexity, the staff was greatly increased and its salaries were enlarged.[26]

In 1848 the staff consisted of six members:

	Salary		Salary
Morris Robinson, president	$4,000	Henry V. Gahagan, clerk	600
Samuel Hannay, secretary	2,500	Henry B. Robinson, corresponding clerk	1,250
Isaac Abbatt, bookkeeper	1,750		
Minturn Post, physician	750–1,500		

By 1868 it had grown as follows:

	Salary		Salary
F. S. Winston, president	$20,000	J. Stephens, Actuary's Dept.	2,200
R. A. McCurdy, vice president	10,000	B. Griffen, Actuary's Dept.	2,000
S. Homans, actuary	10,000	J. M. Easton, premium tickler	2,000
M. Post, M.D., medical examiner	9,000	W. G. Davies, bond & mortgage clerk	2,000
J. M. Stuart, secretary	6,000	J. C. Winston, corresponding clerk	2,000
I. L. Kip, M.D., medical examiner	6,000	R. B. Browne, physician's register	1,800
L. C. Lawton, assistant actuary	4,000	W. V. Woodworth, office tickler & policy examiner	1,800
I. F. Lloyd, bookkeeper	3,000	W. J. Easton, policy register clerk	1,750
G. Waterhouse, Agent's Register Dept. (chief)	2,750	T. E. Brown, policy clerk	1,750
F. Schroeder, Secretary's Dept.	2,500	A. K. Hobby, permit & general clerk	2,000
C. A. Hopkins, acting cashier	2,500	J. C. Perrin, Jr., assistant bookkeeper	1,600
W. P. Sands, bond & mortgage clerk	2,500	F. S. Vulte, Jr., policy clerk	1,700
R. T. Shannon, agent's register	2,250		
G. H. Elliott	2,250		

[26] *Ibid.*, June 3, 1863.

	Salary		*Salary*
E. H. Shannon, receipt clerk	1,500	C. G. Child	1,000
C. Johnson, Jr., alphabetical register	1,300	J. J. Hunter	1,000
		J. C. Rosknecht	900
J. M. Stuart, Jr., premium tickler	1,250	W. H. Wallace, receipt clerk	900
		A. T. Greene, policy clerk	900
O. W. Mauriac, assistant corresponding clerk	1,200	F. M. Arenguren, Actuary's Dept.	800
B. B. Bicknell, Actuary's Dept.	1,200	S. M. Hankins	800
W. B. Seton, copyist, etc.	1,200	F. Elliman	800
C. F. Ulrich	1,200	A. S. Cass, messenger, etc.	750
J. S. G. Strong	1,200	R. G. Dickson, receipt clerk	750
R. H. Jackson	1,100	E. A. Benjamin	600
M. R. Hibbard, porter & messenger	1,100	A, N. Waterhouse, Agency Dept.	600
C. J. Hartt, Actuary's Dept.	1,000	D. H. Hopkins, Messenger, etc.	600
R. D. Bronson, Actuary's Dept.	1,000	W. E. Miller	350
W. N. Ely	1,000	W. Franklin	300
C. C. Haskins, Actuary's Dept.	900		

This rise in salaries between 1848 and 1868 must be attributed largely to the added responsibilities which were placed on employees as the business grew and to the increased ability of the Company to pay adequate compensation. Yet there were other reasons for this augmentation of salaries which ought to be mentioned. In the first place, the cost of living rose rapidly during the Civil War, and the income tax which was then levied caused especial hardships among salaried persons. This situation led the clerks to demand that the Company pay their income taxes, to the serving of free-lunches to the home office staff—a practice which has been continued to the present day [27]—and to the payment of bonuses based on dividends or upon a percentage of the existing salary. The first salary increases had usually followed a period of successful operations or of extra work involved in making the quinquennial reports, but in 1865 we find that the actuary was to receive $8,000 plus ½ percent of the dividends paid to policyholders; that the medical examiner was to get $6,000 plus ½ percent of dividends; that the assistant medical examiner was to be paid an extra of ¼ percent of the dividends, and so forth. In 1866 we learn that employees who did not get a percentage of the dividends in addition to their regular salaries were given a bonus of 20 percent of their salaries.[28]

[27] The first mention of these lunches in the *Minutes of the Board* is to be found in the report of the meeting held May 20, 1868, when it was decided that wines and liquors should not be served.

[28] *Minutes of the Board of Trustees*, November 11, 1865, and February 21, 1866.

The arguments in favor of such bonuses were that they "incite to greater efficiency and economy" and that "it is a recognized principle among practical men that business is most successfully conducted when the managing and executive departments are in the hands of those who are compensated directly from the profits of the business itself." The "profits" in a mutual company were, however, overpayments and hence were not a good basis for fixing compensation. This was ultimately realized and sharply commented upon, whereupon the trustees decided that such bonuses should be stopped (1869). Nevertheless, by 1869 substantial increases in salaries had been effected, and the executive positions in life insurance companies were highly coveted.

The trustees also began to receive some remuneration for their services. In 1853 a committee which had been appointed to look into this question recommended that the members of the Board receive $5.00 for attending each of the regular monthly meetings, and it seems that such sums were soon thereafter paid. With the election of trustees living at some distance from New York and with the building of railways, which made feasible their coming to New York at regular intervals, moneys on the following scale were allotted to cover their traveling expenses—from Rochester $15.00, from Elmira $15.00, from Albany $10.00, and from Buffalo $20.00. In 1866 the fee for regular meetings was raised to $10.00, a fee of $5.00 was paid for attending committee meetings, and a little later a sum of $25.00 per day was given to trustees for services rendered outside New York City.[29]

Such fees were not sufficient in themselves to attract business leaders to serve on the Board of Trustees, but there were other inducements which made a position on the Board much desired. In the first place, such an office brought with it a considerable amount of prestige, and the Board counted among its members many distinguished men—Lucius Robinson, a governor of the State of New York; Robert H. McCurdy, a prominent businessman and the father of the future president of the Company, Richard A. McCurdy; John V. L. Pruyn, a lawyer and educator; George S. Coe, president of the American Exchange National Bank; W. E. Dodge, of the Phelps-Dodge Company; Millard Fillmore, President of the United States, and many others.[30] Then, in the second place, trustees served for the good which they could render in administering an institution that performed a useful social function.

[29] *Ibid.*, February 8, 1860, November 21, 1866, and June 5, 1872. Meetings were held monthly until January 2, 1844; then quarterly.
[30] See the Appendix for a complete list.

During most of the history of The Mutual Life, policyholders have not taken much interest in the election of the trustees—not enough even to exercise their right to vote. The result has been that in the annual elections to the Board,[31] candidates making up the Company or official list have been nominated by the trustees, and they have run for office unopposed by candidates which might have been selected by groups of policyholders. They have been elected by a very few voters—frequently by a corporal's guard composed largely of home office workers. Although greater interest on the part of policyholders in elections is desirable, the practical difficulties in the way of securing a wide exercise of the franchise are almost insurmountable. Moreover, care has to be used to prevent management from falling into the hands of unscrupulous persons. So important is this point that laws in most states are framed to ward against it.

The trustees usually reëlect the incumbents in the presidency, vice presidencies, and other major offices. Such action allows much needed continuity of management, but the almost automatic reelection of the existing officers has the danger of leading to managerial dictatorship or to inefficiency. It would appear that the vast majority of persons who put their money into life insurance also put their trust in the companies' management. They desire either to be free from the worry involved in helping to select trustees and officers, or they do not feel qualified to make wise selections of directorial personnel. They believe, and not unjustly, that managerial errors will be uncovered by some member of the Board or by the state insurance department.

In spite of what might seem like the perennial lethargy of policyholders and the tradition-bound manner of perpetuating a given regime, persons insured in The Mutual Life have in two periods had recourse to the power of the ballot box. But in each, the initiative to effect a change was taken by members of the Board of Trustees. The second and most important uprising against the existing management took place in 1905–1906 as a concomitant of the Armstrong Investigation into the insurance companies of New York—an uprising which will be treated at length in a later chapter; the first took place in 1853 and was largely in the nature of a palace revolution.

This last-named episode revolved around the defeat of Joseph B. Collins for the presidency of the Company and the election in his place

---

31 The trustees were divided at first into four classes of nine each, one class being elected every year. From 1906 to 1937 one-half of the Board stood for election every year. In the latter year provision was made for the division of the Board into three classes of twelve each. See p. 327n.

of Frederick S. Winston. Collins, who had been a trustee since 1843 and came from an important family of publishers, succeeded Morris Robinson as head of The Mutual Life after the latter's death in 1849. Almost immediately the new business of the Company fell off, and Collins was held responsible for the decline. It was asserted that he was devoting himself assiduously not to the affairs of life insurance, but to the invention of an apple corer,[32] that he was undiplomatic in his handling of agents and clients, and that he was not efficient in the conduct of The Mutual's affairs. Consequently a group of trustees sought to unseat him by getting enough proxies to elect a Board favorable to their candidate, Mr. Winston, a dry-goods merchant. The chief solicitor of these opposition proxies was John C. Johnston, to whom we have referred above as one of The Mutual's most successful agents. Enough proxies were thus obtained so that the opposition slate of trustees was elected by a vote of 342 to 330. The new Board then chose Winston as president by a vote of 15 to 9. Feelings were highly aroused by this result. The Collins forces sent a memorial to the New York State legislature criticizing the use of proxies. The Winston supporters printed two pamphlets and several advertisements to explain their actions.[33] And the controversy found expression subsequently in sharp criticism of the Winston regime.

Whatever the respective merits of Mr. Collins and of Mr. Winston may have been, it should be noted that a few months after his defeat Mr. Collins was chosen president of the United States Life Insurance Company and for many years served that Company with success. Mr. Winston, on the other hand, reported in October, 1853, that his mer-

[32] The story of the apple corer does not appear in the literature of the time. Richard A. McCurdy reported it in his address on the occasion of the fiftieth anniversary of the Company, printed in the *Independent*, Feb. 2, 1893, in the following manner:

"A member of the Finance Committee one day entered the office of the Company and found the President intently occupied in some manual occupation, which he put aside at the approach of his visitor. Some questions were asked about business, amount of insurance, condition of his finances, etc., which the President appeared unable or indisposed to answer. His manner was preoccupied, and he seemed bored. At last, as if he could command his attention no longer, he lifted the cover of his desk and brought out a small combination of springs and cogs and some hand tools, and proceeded to explain the principles and working of a mechanical apple-corer, which he was perfecting. His visitor gazed at him, and then coldly took his departure. He was a man of brains, and emphatically a man of action. He thought The Mutual Life required for its president a different kind of a man from the inventor of an apple-corer, and was not long in impressing his views upon his associates. At the next general election a change was effected."

[33] *A Statement of Facts to the Policyholders in The Mutual Life Insurance Company of New York* (1853) and *A Card to the Policyholders of The Mutual Life Insurance Company of New York* (1853). A bill to prevent voting by proxy in mutual life insurance companies was before the New York State Senate in 1851. The Company sent a petition to the Senate against its adoption.

cantile house had gone into bankruptcy—a predicament which he attributed to the calumny directed against him. Under the circumstances, he believed it wise to offer his resignation to the Board. The trustees, however, gave him a vote of confidence, and he agreed to continue in the presidency—a position which he held until his death in 1885.

CHECKS ON MANAGEMENT

The belief that management could follow its own dictates and run rough-shod over all opposition—a belief that grew up as a result of the disclosures in the Armstrong Investigation of 1905—was not well founded. Management was subjected to many checks aside from the necessity of standing for annual election. It was directly responsible to the Board of Trustees and had to give a periodic account of its stewardship. Brief reports were made at first every month and beginning in 1844 every quarter, while full reports were made quinquennially and after 1866, annually. Thus, not only were many of the individual decisions of the management approved by the Board or its committees before any action was taken, but also the over-all operations were presented to the trustees, audited by them,[34] and in abbreviated form published in the annual reports for the scrutiny of policyholders.

The trustees might also appoint special committees to examine the conditions and management of the Company. The first such examination[35] was in 1856 and was an outgrowth of the feud between the Collins and Winston groups. Several charges were made against the existing regime by some of the policyholders, led by Joseph Blunt, who was the chief supporter of Collins among the members of the Board of Trustees and had resigned as counsel of the Company in 1856. His bill of complaints was presented in the form of a Memorial to the Legislature —an act which led the Board to invite that body "to cause a rigid scrutiny to be made into the management and affairs of the Company."[36] In

[34] The accounts were first examined and certified by the actuary and were then audited by committees of the trustees. These audits took place quarterly and after 1858 were in the hands of the Auditing Committee, save that the annual reports were usually checked by a special committee. *Minutes of the Board of Trustees,* November 16, 1864. Meetings of the Board of Trustees were held monthly until 1844, when they began to be held quarterly. In 1870 a return to monthly meetings was made.

[35] An examination was held in 1848 in conjunction with the first five-year reports—an examination conducted by a committee of the Board and decidedly different in character and purpose from these later examinations. A careful examination of the accounts was also made in 1855. *Minutes of the Board of Trustees,* February 14, 1855.

[36] *Ibid.,* March 5, 1856.
"The undersigned Trustees of The Mutual Life Insurance Company of New York respectfully represent that they have learned that a certain Memorial has been presented to the Senate purporting to be signed by Ten Policyholders in this Company inferring charges

fact, the officers proposed a bill to require the Company to make an annual report to the Supreme Court of the first judicial district "in such form and verified in such manner as the Court may direct" and to pay for an examination of the Company by a referee appointed by the Court.

Owing to lack of time, this bill did not receive its third reading before the Legislature adjourned, and consequently the Board decided to invite three persons not connected with The Mutual Life to make an investigation of the Company for the period since Winston's election. Three experts were accordingly selected—one upon the demand of Joseph Blunt; and for three months they delved into the intricacies of life insurance, taking testimony from the disgruntled and poring through Company records.

These gentlemen began their final report by lauding life insurance,

---

alike injurious to the Company and dishonorable to those who are entrusted with its management. It must doubtlessly have been observed by your Honorable body that these charges are based upon no fact pretended to be known by the Memorialists but upon the mere alleged rumor in a vague 'it is said.' On such grounds alone it is insinuated that the Funds of the Company were paid to an Agent for obtaining proxies and that they have been otherwise unlawfully used by the present Trustees. We deem it unnecessary to take any further notice of these insinuations than to pronounce them in every particular destitute of even the shadow of truth and to invite the most thorough and searching investigation which it may please your Honorable body to institute.

"The undersigned are well aware of the sacred character of the Funds entrusted to them, and being personally and largely interested in its safety and wise management have endeavored to rescue it from the rule of incapacity and negligence and to place the Institution where it now unquestionably stands in advance of all others of a similar character in this country. To this end, during the last 13 years the By Laws have been made more restrictive and the business details of the Company more systematic, and the most effective checks have been imposed on all receipts and payments of money. The Bonds and Mortgages and Titles held by the Company have all been thoroughly and rigidly re-examined and all errors corrected; the Mortgaged property has all been reappraised by careful and competent appraisers and in every instance where it was found to be less than twice the amount of the loan enough has been called in to bring it within that rule. No loans whatever are made upon personal security. The loans to Trustees do not amount to more than about Four and one-half per cent of the whole invested fund and are made under the same rigid rules and secured in the same manner as all others. More than three-fourths of the Trustees never had or applied for any loans.

"Our efforts to improve the condition and management of the Company have been crowned with gratifying success. Its annual business has been nearly doubled in three years. Its accumulated Fund has increased from $1,907,381.22 in 1853 to $3,084,233.26 in 1856 and whilst we have been making this large increase we have been accomplishing the humane and beneficent objects of the Institution by paying out to the Widows and Orphans of our Country nearly a Million of dollars. We respectfully suggest that the facts thus briefly alluded to are sufficient to show that the position and character and objects of this Institution are such that it ought not to be lightly or wantonly assailed. The number of its Policyholders is nearly 9,000. Ten of these have chosen to present to your Honorable body the Memorial above referred to, the effect of which may be to excite the fears or shake the confidence of others. We therefore not only invite again a thorough investigation pledging ourselves to afford every possible facility for conducting it; but we respectfully submit that under the circumstances we are entitled to have such examination either by a Committee or otherwise as your Honorable body should deem proper.   N.Y. March 5, 1856" praising the actuarial basis of The Mutual Life's business, and surveying the investment policies of the Company.[37] They criticized, however, three practices of the institution:—(1) the refusal to pay dividends on polices which became claims before the end of a quinquennial dividend period, (2) the inability of the policyholder to decide whether or not his dividends should be used to buy more insurance or to reduce future premiums, and (3) the insufficiency of the charge made on the surrender of policies.[38] The examiners answered all the complaints made by Joseph Blunt and the other memorialists and concluded their report with this peroration:

It is believed, therefore, after careful and full examination that this Institution in the method of administration was never so judicious; in the principles of its transactions never so sound; or in the general condition of its affairs, so prosperous and safe as at the present time.[39]

[37] *Ibid.*, July 23, 1856.

"It appears that in the cases of the early loans outstanding, the Titles were originally examined, approved, and certified as valid by the former legal Counsel of the Company, Joseph Blunt, Esq., and in the case of Loans more recently made, the Titles were approved, examined, and certified by one of the present three legal Counsel of the Company. They are now generally in each case, accompanied by an Abstract of Title, and Searches showing the Estate to have been, at the time they were mortgaged to the Company free and unincumbered."

It should be added in this connection that on February 23, 1856 the Board resolved that "No Trustee shall be eligible for re-election as a member of the [Finance] Committee for more than three years in succession." On May 13, 1857 it was voted that no trustee should be eligible for re-election to this committee. These rules were not adhered to for very long. An attempt by Mr. Blunt to get a resolution passed forbidding any Trustee who was indebted to the Company from being a member of the Finance Committee failed.

[38] *Ibid.*, July 23, 1856.

"The deduction of one-seventh from the calculated value of a surrendered policy is certainly not adequate protection, for a careful calculation will show that even then the Company will be discounting its own Bonds at a rate less by one per cent per annum than they are realizing now by the ordinary employment of funds."

[39] This summation continued (*ibid.*) with this advice:

"So far as the Policyholders of the Company are individually and directly concerned we might rest here, but the responsibilities of such an Institution as this have a double aspect. They regard not more a just performance of its contracts, with the holders of its Policies, than they do the faithful execution of a great Public trust. The Public not less than individuals, are deeply interested in the due administration of the affairs of Associations like this. Life Insurance Companies are among the most interesting Institutions of the time. As public Institutions, & important Agencies for general good it is fitting and proper, that enlightened Public opinion, should exercise in regard to them a vigilant observation & controlling influence. But these should be constructive, not destructive in their character and exercise. It should be to guard, build up, and sustain; not to embarrass, weaken and destroy. While unsoundness of fundamental Principle, or abuse in administration should be fearlessly disclosed, and firmly rebuked, the utmost delicacy and care should be observed in abstaining from all unjust reproach, and groundless, or careless insinuation.

"The usefulness of these Institutions depends upon the entire confidence reposed in them, by those, whose all is embarked in their success. Nothing is more sensitive than that confidence. Although a breath cannot create it, yet a breath may destroy.

"Whatever then tends to disturb that confidence, or unnecessarily to excite the fears, or

This type of examination won great favor with Mr. Winston, for he asked in 1864 and again in 1869 that new investigations be made by groups of policyholders and trustees.[40] The first committee to look into the "integrity, fidelity and efficiency of the officers" found nothing "to condemn and much to praise." The second group, which secured the technical assistance of Professor Bartlett, the future actuary of the Company, and Church of West Point, also gave The Mutual Life a clean bill of health. In fact, they elicited from the Superintendent of Insurance of the State of New York, William Barnes, the opinion that the "general management of the affairs of The Mutual Life Insurance Company of New York [is] sound, discreet, and judicious. Indeed no such institution as that which now surprises the actuaries and statisticians of two continents could have been built up under any other auspices." [41]

Yet criticism of the Company was not all allayed by these findings. A group of discontented policyholders presented opposition candidates, one of whom was Sheppard Homans, in the election to the Board in 1869, and although they met with defeat because of the proxies which were marshaled against them, their action indicated their hostility to the existing administration.[42] Voice was given to their position in the press and in public meetings, James W. McCulloh of the New York State assembly leading the way. These attacks against Mr. Winston's regime finally led George W. Miller, the new Superintendent of Insurance, to examine the Company (1870). Thus was The Mutual Life subjected to its first investigation by public authorities.

For three months Mr. Miller heard witnesses, checked the books of the Company, and ran rumors to the ground. Finally he presented his report in the form of answers to specific charges. To the complaint that elections had been rigged by the solicitation of proxies, Mr. Miller replied that so far as he could discover the choice of trustees had been conducted fairly and honorably. To the charge that loans had been made contrary to the terms of the charter, he replied that this was not so except during the Civil War, when the state, having voted money to care for sick and wounded soldiers, needed advances and got them for short periods from The Mutual Life. To the accusation that bonuses and gratuities had been given officers, Miller answered that these had

---

doubts of those who repose in it, is in the highest degree cruel to them and unjust to others. "It impairs the usefulness, and defeats the objects of these beneficent Institutions, and should be carefully avoided by all." It should be added that at the conclusion of the investigation each of the examiners was paid $1,000 for his services.

[40] *Minutes of the Board of Trustees,* November 16, 1864, and June 9, 1869.
[41] *Ibid.,* July 21, 1869.   [42] *Ibid.,* May 18, 1870.

been approved by the Board and that no bad faith or fraud was involved. To the complaint that fees had been paid to certain persons and had been entered on the books as taxes, the Superintendent replied that these expenditures had gone, as frankly admitted by the officers, to secure the services of men "in behalf of the Company in appearing before Committees of the Legislature and Congress, to oppose the passage of measures which would, if enacted, have largely increased the taxes of the Company and in other ways have been prejudicial to its interests."

In short Miller concluded that the general charges were not sustained. To the contrary he held:

It is a fact worthy of remark that the strictest scrutiny into the management of this Company during the past sixteen or seventeen years, during which such a vast amount of business has been done and such immense sums of money have been received and invested, not one dollar is discovered to have been lost by embezzlement, defalcation, or breach of trust of any officer or trustee.

It is to be regretted that in any case the officers or agents of one Company should resort to a vilification of another Company or its officers, with a view to advancing the interests of their own Company or themselves.[43]

A state examination of this kind was, as has already been remarked, a new thing, and yet from early in the nineteenth century the law had required that publicity be given to the operations of life insurance companies.[44] A New York statute of 1827 required the companies to make annual reports to the comptroller of the state.[45] As time went on the information required in these reports became more detailed and searching. A step was taken in this direction in 1849 and another much more forward one in 1859, when the insurance department of the state was created.

The publicity which was thus given to the operations of life insurance

[43] *Examination of Witnesses before George W. Miller, Esq., Superintendent of the Insurance Department of the State of New York, in relation to certain charges against the officers and trustees of The Mutual Life Insurance Company of New York; entered, according to Act of Congress, in the year 1870, by The Mutual Life Insurance Company of New York, in the clerk's office of the District Court of the United States for the Southern District of New York.* See the *Reports of the New York Insurance Commissioner* (Albany, 1870), pp. 82–83, 237; *Report on the Committee on Grievances, Relative to the Petition of Stephen English* (1873), New York Assembly Document 155. The entire incident has been played up by Burton J. Hendrick, *The Story of Life Insurance* (New York, 1907), pp. 83 ff. and pp. 180 ff.—a muck-raking book; and by Terence O'Donnell, *History of Life Insurance* (Chicago, 1936), pp. 535 ff. See also the testimony in *The Condition of the Life Insurance Companies of the State of New York* (Albany, 1877), pp. 32 ff., and *The Insurance Times, passim.*

[44] E. W. Patterson, *The Insurance Commissioner in the United States* (Cambridge, Mass., 1927), p. 527. Citing N.Y.L., 1827–1828, Pt. 1, ch. 18, Titles 11, 19, 20, 51.

[45] See Appendix, pp. 354 ff.

companies undoubtedly helped to prevent abuses, but, as we shall see later, it did not prove to be sufficiently effective. Periodic state examinations and legal restrictions were to become the order of the day. Yet in this period from 1843 to 1870 legal restraints were not wanting. Charters prescribed the way in which companies were to be administered and the kind of investments which were to be made, while statutes and judicial decisions regulated the nature of the insurance contract and the amount of reserves to be held on policies. The states, like the better companies, were endeavoring to establish life insurance upon a sound basis.

THE EXPENSES OF MANAGEMENT AND BENEFITS OF INSURANCE

Whatever the criticisms may have been which were leveled against The Mutual Life in the decades of the fifties and sixties, the fact remains that the percentage of total receipts which were expended for management did not increase. This percentage was 11.1 for the first two years of the Company's operations; [46] 10.54 for the first five years; 10 for the years 1848–1853; 10.125 for the first three years of Winston's regime (1853–1856); [47] and 7.8 for the year 1871. For the entire period 1843–1871, the percentage of expenses to total receipts was 10, of which 5.68 went for the payment of commissions to agents.[48] How these moneys were expended can be seen from the following table.

Although most of the items of expense are self-explanatory and the increases in overhead are clear, two matters deserve brief mention. The first of these is taxation. New York was one of the first states to impose a tax specifically on life insurance companies. In 1851 the mutual companies were required to deposit $100,000 with the comptroller of the state,[49] and in 1855 to pay a tax on this amount of personal property.[50] An attempt was made, however, to collect taxes on all The Mutual Life's accumulated funds. As this bill was enormous, the president secured the passage of an act in 1857 [51] which limited the sum taxed to the amount

[46] *Minutes of the Board of Trustees*, April 15, 1845.
[47] *Ibid.*, July 23, 1856.
[48] *Ibid.*, October 16, 1872. According to the *Thirtieth Annual Report*, pp. 16–17, the annual ratios of expenses to gross receipts were:

1843	16.1	1849	9.6	1855	9.3	1861	9.8	1867	13.6
1844	9.2	1850	8.6	1856	9.5	1862	8.4	1868	12.6
1845	10.4	1851	8.5	1857	9.4	1863	9.5	1869	10.6
1846	10.5	1852	7.3	1858	9.5	1864	10.0	1870	9.2
1847	9.9	1853	13.5	1859	10.6	1865	12.6	1871	7.1
1848	9.2	1854	10.6	1860	8.3	1866	16.1	1872	6.98

[49] Act of April 8, 1851.
[50] Chapter 83, Laws of 1855.
[51] Act of April 16, 1857. See *Minutes of the Board of Trustees*, May 13, 1857.

provided for in the law of 1855. Yet there were other taxes which had to be met. In 1853 New York imposed a tax of 2 percent upon the annual gross premiums on the business done within the state by companies organized outside its boundaries.[52] This measure led other states to take

TABLE 20

EXPENDITURES OF THE MUTUAL LIFE

	1844 [a]	*1872* [b]
Commissions	$2,020.86	$335,015.29
Advertising	658.58	55,600.07
Salaries & office expenses	4,740.97	268,702.90
Exchange	136.25	
Postage	354.27	54,584.23
State tax by agent in Baltimore	18.98	
Taxes (on business in other states)		90,489.47
Medical examinations		38,506.80
Law		28,965.38
Printing and stationery		54,214.50
Sundry expenses		66,925.66
Total	$7,929.91	$993,004.30 [c]

[a] *Minutes of the Board of Trustees*, April 15, 1845.
[b] *Ibid.*, January 15, 1873.
[c] To which might be added $332,448.46 for the commutation of future commissions.

similar steps, especially those in the Middle West, which had no insurance companies of their own and resented the draining of capital to the East. Kentucky was one of the initiators of this move, in 1864 levying a 5 percent tax on gross premiums collected in Kentucky by companies organized in other states.[53] By 1870 twenty-two states were collecting taxes on gross premiums—were taxing the provisions which a great body of policyholders were making to prevent dependents from becoming charges of the states. The lack of wisdom in such taxes was heralded far and wide, but to little avail. Premium taxes had come to stay.

The second item of expense which needs clarification is that which went toward providing a home office. As we have already seen, The Mutual Life began operations as a tenant in the offices of The Mutual Safety Insurance Company at the present 56 Wall Street. In 1848 the Company's address was 35 Wall Street, but its quarters soon proved to be inadequate, and in 1851 it was looking for a site upon which to erect a building. The trustees decided, however, in 1852 to take a five-year lease on the first floor of the Trinity Building, "on the side next to the church yard," at 111 Broadway.[54] Here difficulties arose with the proprietors over the question of a suitable vault, and The Mutual Life again

[52] Section 15, chapter 463, Laws of 1853.   [53] Section 5, chapter 478, Laws of 1864.
[54] Rent was not to exceed $5,000 a year.

began to cast about for a building of its own. It finally purchased a site on the corner of Broadway and Liberty Street,[55] nearly opposite its offices, and there erected a building, which was occupied in 1864, at the cost of $708,917.85.[56] Thus, the expense of office space, which had appeared as rent in office expenses, was in 1864 placed in the investment account under real estate.[57] This type of investment did not usually prove to be particularly remunerative, but it was one in which life insurance companies were to indulge heavily.

TABLE 21

ACCUMULATIVE RECORD OF RECEIPTS, DISBURSEMENTS, AND
LEDGER ASSETS FROM ORGANIZATION TO DECEMBER 31, 1870

Receipts	*Total 28 Years*
Insurance premiums	$77,239,184.09
Annuity premiums	375,127.01
Total premiums	77,614,311.10
Interest & rents	13,854,054.07
Profit & other receipts	850,096.01
Total receipts	92,318,461.18
Disbursements	
Death benefits	13,986,073.58
Matured endowments	202,593.21
Annuities	259,903.71
Surrenders	9,296,537.79
Dividends	16,756,068.39
Total policy payments	40,501,176.68
Expenses	9,327,838.64
Loss & other payments	107,028.30
Total disbursements	49,936,043.62
Ledger assets	42,382,417.56

These overhead costs, management, investments, state regulation, mortality tables, and the other subjects so far discussed were simply means toward an end—toward providing safe and cheap insurance for the American public. As every institution should be measured by the service which it renders to society, so should a life insurance company be judged by the attainment of socially desirable goals. By this criterion The Mutual Life Insurance Company was an acknowledged success. As we have already seen, it had drawn together from small savings large amounts of capital which might not otherwise have been made available

[55] The cost of the site, which included numbers 140, 142, 144, and 146 Broadway, was $210,000. *Minutes of the Board of Trustees,* April 22, 1863.

[56] *Minutes of the Building Committee,* I, 83.

[57] Up to February 17, 1869, office rent was charged as a sinking fund to diminish the book value of the building. This was discontinued on that date because "the value of the Company's property was largely in excess of its cost."

for concerted use, and these sums were employed chiefly up to 1870 to finance the development of Metropolitan New York. We have also mentioned the effect of life insurance in improving sanitary conditions in some areas and in investigating the causes of longevity. Most important of all, however, The Mutual Life furnished people a method of saving and of providing for their dependents in case of death. During the first twenty-eight years of its existence it received in premium payments $77,614,311.10, it disbursed to policyholders or their beneficiaries $40,-501,176.68, and it had as ledger assets to the credit of its more than 68,000 members $42,382,417.56. The Mutual Life thus provided part of the security which modern man so earnestly seeks at less expense than the interest obtained on policyholders' money.

PART THREE
1871-1906

VII. The Development of Life Insurance

BETWEEN THE YEARS 1843 AND 1870 the foundations of American life insurance were, as we have seen in preceding chapters, laid down. In this period the leading companies of the present day were established and, inasmuch as most of those organized before 1859 [1] adopted the principle of mutuality, the greatest body of financial co-operatives which the world has ever seen came into existence. By 1870 most phases of the life insurance business had been developed to a point of workability. A mortality table had been drawn up to provide a safe gauge of the rate at which insured people in America were expected to die and had permitted the establishment of adequate premium and reserve schedules. The contributory plan for the distribution of dividends had been formulated and adopted in an attempt to treat policyholders more equitably. The basic kinds of ordinary life insurance—whole life, endowment, term, and limited payment life—had been made available to the public. The selection of risks had reached a state of development in which persons with relatively equal chances of survival paid the same rates. The marketing of insurance had been entrusted to a body of salesmen working on a commission basis. The investment of assets had been regulated by charter or state statutes. A large corpus of insurance law had been built up. State insurance departments had come into being to oversee the entire industry. Management of the larger companies had become subdivided so that much of the work was in the hands of specialists. Severe competition had put in an appearance and had threatened to lead to cut-throat practices. And finally life insurance companies had begun to provide on a large scale the services for which they had been founded—to allow persons to share the risks of death. In 1870 they had in force nearly 750,000 policies and more than $2,000,000,000 of insurance,[2] and this accomplishment gave credence to the assertion that the institution of life insurance had become an integral part of the

---

[1] The New York Law of 1859 which required a deposit of $100,000 with the state made the establishment of mutuals practically impossible.

[2] Figures are for sixty-eight companies. See Frederick L. Hoffman, "Fifty Years of American Life Insurance," *Quarterly Publications of the American Statistical Association*, XII (1911), 717.

American scene and would in the future keep pace with the entire economy.

The role which The Mutual Life had played in these developments was a leading one, especially in actuarial science, the selection of risks, company management, marketing, and services rendered. But in the next thirty-six years, although the Company retained for the most part its position of primacy from the point of view of size, it tended to be a follower rather than an initiator of current practices. This fact should, however, redound to its credit rather than to its discredit, for many of the new developments in life insurance were not of a substantially constructive character.

As was pointed out in Chapter I, life insurance history between the years 1870 and 1906 was characterized by (1) severe competition, (2) managerial control, (3) increasing state supervision, climaxed by the Armstrong Investigation of 1905, and (4) the great growth of the amount of insurance in force. Each one of these phases of the evolution of life insurance and the part played therein by The Mutual Life will be discussed in the following chapters, but before that detailed account has been attempted it may be well briefly to scan the highlights of the period.

Competition in the life insurance business was not new in 1870, but in the years after that date it increased in degree—and quantitative changes frequently result in qualitative changes. The increase in competition came about from the speed with which Henry B. Hyde, who had founded The Equitable in 1859, pushed his company forward and from the fact that Hyde's prototype, William H. Beers, upon assuming the active management of the New York Life in 1868,[3] strove to rehabilitate an institution which had suffered from poor management and the influence of Pliny Freeman.[4] Both Hyde and Beers were almost abnormally energetic and scored resounding successes. To meet their competition, The Mutual Life began in 1866 to pay dividends annually, in the belief that the other companies would not be able to follow suit —a belief which proved to be well founded. Yet Hyde was not disheartened, and, while searching for a solution to his problem, stumbled upon the tontine principle, which he decided to revive.

The original tontine scheme used by the French state provided for

---

[3] James M. Hudnut, *Semi-Centennial History of the New York Life Insurance Company, 1845–1895* (New York, 1895), p. 232.

[4] *Ibid.*, p. 40. Freeman was charged with buying at a discount the scrip issued by the company for dividends and getting it redeemed at its face value. He held the office of actuary in the New York Life from 1845 to 1864, but he knew little of the actuarial science. See Burton J. Hendrick, *The Story of Life Insurance* (New York, 1907), p. 126 and footnote.

the sale of interest bearing bonds or annuities upon the understanding that in the case of the death of any of the owners of these annuities the principal should be surrendered to the state, while the interest should be continued to the surviving annuitants on a pro rata scale. Hyde adopted a variation on this theme. In 1868, and more successfully in 1871, he offered to the public insurance policies, the dividends on which were to be paid only to survivors after periods of five, ten, fifteen, or twenty years. Thus, survivors were apparently to receive enormous dividends; those who died before the fixed number of years had elapsed were to receive no return of overpayments; and in the meantime Hyde was to have the use of a large amount of capital. The fund thus amassed was not hamstrung by contractual obligations to pay any dividends whatsoever and was augmented by a refusal to give a cash surrender value on these policies—a fact of vital importance when it is realized that about 50 percent of the tontine policies issued by The Equitable were forfeited.[5]

The success which attended Hyde's tontine project put such a strong temptation in the way of other life insurance companies that the majority of them could not resist it. The New York Life made tontines available to its clients in 1871, and, although The Mutual Life at first fought the idea bitterly, the Company gave way to it between 1870 and 1873. President Winston was, however, opposed to such "an aberration of life insurance," preferring to do battle with rebates and low premiums, as we shall see in more detail later. But President McCurdy believed that semi-tontines, or, as they were called by The Mutual Life, deferred dividend policies, would increase the size of the Company, and he made them part of The Mutual's wares from 1885 to his resignation in 1906. In fact, all but three of the more important companies—the Mutual Benefit of New Jersey, the Connecticut Mutual, and the Provident Life and Trust—yielded to tontine temptation.

Competition among the life insurance companies brought strong leaders to the fore. Perhaps it is not unfair to say that the "managerial revolution" [6]—the control of business by paid executives rather than by owners or investors—appeared on a large scale in life insurance only very shortly after it had become apparent in banking. Hyde was the dictator of The Equitable; Beers made of the New York Life a one-man concern; and Richard A. McCurdy dominated the affairs of The Mutual Life. They received large salaries, indulged in a certain number of

5 Hendrick, op. cit., p. 148.
6 See James Burnham, The Managerial Revolution (New York, 1941).

extravagances, and did not do all that might have been done to reduce the cost of insurance. They were the counterparts in life insurance of John D. Rockefeller in the petroleum industry, Jay Gould in railroads, J. Pierpont Morgan in banking, Jim Fisk in finance, and Armour in meat packing. Such men, although at times employing business ethics which would not be condoned today, must be credited with the organization of great and useful enterprises.

In spite of the introduction of deferred dividend policies, large expenditures, and the control of large companies by domineering men, life insurance registered certain distinct gains between 1870 and 1906. Reserve requirements were raised and in general kept at a high level. Insurance contracts were liberalized for the benefit of the insured, especially by the adoption of the incontestable clause, and by dropping extra premiums for most regional, climatic, and many occupational risks. Premium rates were lowered. Insurance was made available to the poorer classes under the name of "industrial insurance," which was a step forward, even though costs were high. Cash surrender values were made part of insurance contracts; granting policy loans became a not uncommon practice; state insurance departments increased their vigil over the operation of life insurance companies; and insurance funds were employed to help finance America's economic expansion.

From time to time life insurance companies were the object of attack, usually by discontented cliques within a company's management. Such attacks led to the introduction of assessment insurance projects, which aimed to lower costs, and to state investigations. The most penetrating of the legislative searchings into life insurance was conducted by the Armstrong Committee in New York State in 1905. Its findings resulted in such a drastic reformation of life insurance that the ethics of this industry became and have remained to the present time as high, if not higher, than that of any other.

LIFE INSURANCE AND ITS ECONOMIC SETTING, 1870–1906

Whatever criticisms may have been leveled at the managements of life insurance companies during the period now under consideration, one dominant fact remains—life insurance attained new heights of importance and social usefulness between 1870 and 1906. In this growth The Mutual Life played a large part. As can be seen in the accompanying chart, the aggregate amount of insurance in force for all reporting companies increased by 577 percent between 1870 and 1906; that of The Mutual Life increased by 527 percent; the amount of insurance per

CHART VII

GROWTH OF ORDINARY LIFE INSURANCE, 1870–1906

*Peaks in business are indicated by broken vertical
lines; troughs by solid vertical lines*

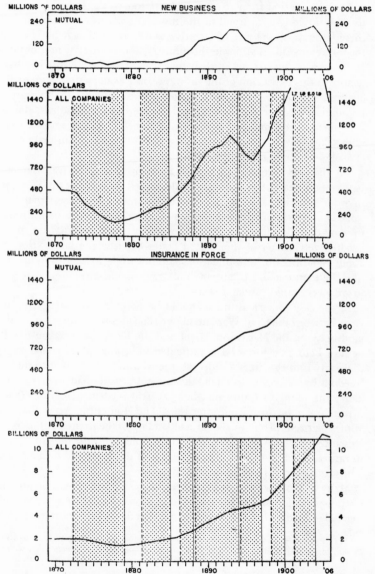

Sources: Stalson, *Marketing Life Insurance* (Cambridge, 1942), pp. 813, 820–821; the turning points of the business cycle are those made public by the National Bureau of Economic Research (1941).

capita rose from $55.11 to $160.61; and total admitted assets, by 958 per-cent.

As in the period from 1843 to 1870, so, too, in the period from 1870 to 1906 the long-term trend in life insurance was upward, although in these latter years the rate of growth was not so rapid as it had been in the former and fluctuations in the industry, as measured by new business in force, were more marked than they had been previously. The basic factors in this expansion of life insurance, as was suggested in an earlier chapter, have been the general growth of the economy, the increase in population, greater economic interdependence of individuals, the de-velopment of economic relationship of a monetary nature, and the trend toward urbanization, with everything which that entails in making the care of dependents more difficult.

To give any complete picture of the growth of American economy between the years 1870 and 1906 would exceed the scope of this work, yet in order to understand the history of life insurance it is necessary to have some conception of American economic development. Statistical meas-ures of that development indicate a great long-term increase in the productive capacity of the United States between the late sixties and about 1907. Because of foundations laid in this period newer industries, like the manufacture of automobiles, radios, and airplanes, were able to grow very rapidly in later years.

In the case of agriculture it should be pointed out that during the years between the Civil War and about 1890 almost all the easily arable land between the Mississippi River and the Rockies was taken up. To be sure, before the former date cattlemen and cotton planters had forged their way into the great Southwest, the Mormons had sought religious freedom by migrating to Utah, and the gold rushes had strewn people along the paths to California, but the real settlement of the Trans-Mississippian territory came after 1862. The Homestead Act of that year allowed citizens to obtain 160 acres of land upon the payment of nominal fees and upon five years' residence on the holding, while the land grants to railroads led to advertising the virtues of the West and to the sale of lands to Easterners and to immigrants.[7]

Many of those who went West became heavily indebted, for the cost of transportation and of stocking and equipping a farm was large. Dur-ing and immediately following the Civil War debts were contracted when

[7] F. L. Paxson, *History of the American Frontier* (Boston, 1924); W. P. Webb, *The Great Plains* (Boston, 1931); and B. H. Hibbard, *A History of the Public Land Policies* (New York, 1924).

prices were very high. Then when prices fell because of the dear-money policy of the government, which reached a climax with the demonetization of silver in 1873, and when in the seventies agricultural goods were overproduced, the settlers of the West found the payment of their obligations almost impossible. To get out of their difficulties they agitated for cheap money; they fought the railways in an effort to reduce transportation rates, and they also bought large quantities of agricultural machinery in an attempt to reduce costs of production. With the coming of high prices in the nineties, the predicament in which farmers had found themselves was largely removed, and much of their special pleading ceased. But before that time was reached, as well as after it, the opening of the West had offered many opportunities to life insurance companies. The uncertainties of the future made the security of life insurance attractive, while the building of the Western railroads, the growth of agricultural implement companies, and the financing of the farms themselves provided many outlets for the investment of insurance funds.

Perhaps even more phenomenal than the settling of the West was the development of mechanized industry upon a large scale during the forty years after the close of the Civil War. In fact, one of the most remarkable aspects of the history of the last one hundred and fifty years has been the coming together of certain forces for the first time in man's recorded past to create the so-called industrial revolution. No country in the world possessed all the prerequisites for an industrial revolution—a demand for goods, capital, and capitalist spirit, techniques of production, raw materials, an available labor supply, and transportation facilities—in the same measure as the United States in the fifty years prior to 1914. Nor at the turn of the century did any country have as great an industrial production as America. In 1900 the value of goods manufactured in the United States was twice as large as that of those turned out in England and half as large as that of all those produced in Continental Europe. Most of the important American industries—milling, textiles, lumber, meat packing, and leather—were based upon the products of the farm or forest, but giant enterprises were taking shape in metallurgy, mining, machinery, petroleum, and power. The years from 1865 to 1906 witnessed the formation of the Carnegie steel trust, the development of Standard Oil, the founding of the electrical industry, the coking of coal on a large scale, the production of large quantities of copper, lead, zinc, and aluminum, the refrigeration of meat, grinding grain with steel rollers, making of shoes by mechanical sewing, the speeding up of spinning machines and looms, and countless other changes. From 1850 to

1900 the value of agricultural products tripled, while that of manufactured goods increased eleven times; and in 1890 the output of factories and mines far exceeded the value of farm and forest produce.

The great expansion of both agricultural and industrial production provided a material basis for a substantial increase in the population. With the possibility of making a living, large families were the rule, and immigration was encouraged.

TABLE 22

POPULATION OF THE UNITED STATES

Year	Number	Percentage of Increase over Preceding Census	Percentage of Foreign Born Increase over Preceding Census
1870	38,558,371	22.6	34.5
1880	50,155,783	30.1	20.0
1890	62,947,714	25.5	38.5
1900	75,994,575	20.7	11.8
1910	91,972,266	21.0	30.7

With more people in the United States, there were more applicants for life insurance, and with a high birth rate there was a large proportion of younger risks seeking insurance. Furthermore, the greatest population increases were registered in the cities, and urban dwellers proved to have more need for life insurance than did the inhabitants of rural areas.

The trend of the population toward urban centers, the growth of industry, and the settling of the West were accompanied by a remarkable division of labor—the performing of specialized tasks. The farmer tended to concentrate on one crop rather than upon diversification; factory workers made parts of finished products or assembled those parts; and the individual everywhere found to an increasing degree that he had to supply his wants from the market place. In order to do this he had to obtain money either by the sale of his labor or by the sale of goods. The exchange of goods by the medium of money became the order of the day. How important this development of a money economy was is witnessed by a variety of quantitative data. Banks increased in number, in size of deposits, and in lending activity.[8] A greater percentage of the population became employed in trade, services, and transportation. The proportion of realized private income obtained by persons in distribution grew tremendously. Finally the exchange of goods was made possible by, and in turn gave impetus to, railroads, steam shipping, the telegraph, the telephone, the automobile, and the airplane—all of which

[8] See U.S. Comptroller of the Currency, *Annual Reports.*

TABLE 23

REALIZED PRIVATE PRODUCTION INCOME, BY INDUSTRIES [a]

(In millions of dollars)

Year	Agriculture	Mining and Quarrying	Electric Light & Power & Gas	Manufacturing	Construction	Transportation & Communication	Trade	Service	Finance	Misc. [b] Other	Total Private Production Income
1839	545	5	1	162	95	277	135	222		135	1,577
1849	737	16	2	291	133	398	196	355		198	2,326
1859	1,264	44	6	495	184	694	494	572		345	4,098
1869	1,517	102	23	1,000	387	718	1,039	968		534	6,288
1879	1,371	153	33	960	360	896	1,166	1,099		579	6,617
1889	1,517	232	44	2,022	631	1,154	1,803	1,341		834	9,578
1899	2,933	416	58	2,714	655	1,528	2,578	1,745	196	1,013	13,836
1900	3,934	453	65	2,941	627	1,626	2,720	1,774	233	1,077	14,550
1910	5,563	949	168	5,447	1,136	2,853	4,496	2,557	544	1,856	25,569
1920	10,559	2,628	480	16,811	2,224	7,474	10,048	5,436	1,488	3,837	60,995
1930	6,761	1,918	1,559	15,958	2,910	7,012	10,628	7,889	2,963	4,371	61,968
1938	6,117	1,248	1,262	11,883	1,650	5,225	7,770	6,880	1,753	3,680	47,468
1940	5,309	1,816	...	18,055	...	...	...	...	...	...	59,600
1942	11,041	2,497	...	33,267	...	...	...	...	...	...	93,300

[a] National Industrial Conference Board.

[b] Miscellaneous, including finance, prior to 1899.

offered new means for employment. The industrial revolution was, indeed, accompanied by a profound and far-reaching social and commercial revolution. By 1940 the average consumer spent about $571 [9] per year—a sum which went almost entirely for things which he did not produce or process to the point of use.

In this economic order, which was quantitatively very new, money or easily negotiable wealth became a *sine qua non* to living. To obtain sustenance during nonproductive old age or to provide in case of death for one's dependents required the saving of large amounts of money. For many this proved to be impossible, for either their incomes were too low to permit saving, or the standard of living to which their dependents had become accustomed was so high that adequate sums could not be set aside to maintain it, or all available capital was needed in their business enterprises.[10] Hence rich and poor alike looked to life insurance as a boon. Here was an institution which would provide ready money for dependents in case of early death or which would promote savings in case of a long life.

LIFE INSURANCE AND THE BUSINESS CYCLE

Although the long-term trend of all the statistical data which have thus far been presented was markedly upward, it should not be thought that business in general and life insurance in particular did not experience temporary setbacks or sudden forward bursts. The business cycle had been experienced in the United States before the Civil War, as we have seen in an earlier chapter, but it took on a new aspect with the more complete industrialization of the country, with the greater development of a money economy, and with increasing economic interdependence.

Inasmuch as the business cycle has been an important phase of modern economy, it may be well to mention briefly some of its main characteristics. If the cycle be broken into at the beginning of an expansion, it will be seen that there is an augmentation in the physical volume of production, fuller employment, an increase in wage rates, larger profits, and greater consumption. These conditions usually, but not always, tend to push prices up; businessmen become optimistic, investment is encouraged, and plants are expanded. As these various factors expose them-

9 Mutual Life Research Division. Based on Department of Commerce data.

10 According to an estimate of savings made by the Brookings Institution, nearly $18 billions was saved in 1929. Two-thirds of the family savings were effected by those with incomes of $10,000 or more. See also Simon Kuznets, *National Income and Capital Formation, 1919–1935* (New York, 1937).

selves more and more intensely, interacting upon each other, business reaches a point in the upward spiral where it has as much to do as it can handle profitably. Costs of production per unit increase, management has a tendency to become less efficient, and prices or the demand for goods reach a limit beyond which they cannot be pushed. Expansion of plant ceases, and makers of producers' goods especially begin to close their shops. Purchasing power decreases, unemployment sets in, wages decline, and banks begin to withdraw or withhold credits. A recession then gets under way which may turn into a period of contraction or depression as optimism turns to pessimism, prices fall, production declines, profits are reduced, bank loans shrink, and unemployment increases. When this phase in the cycle is entered, less money is needed for the conduct of business and interest rates fall. Moreover, management becomes more efficient, and prices are so low that persons who have purchasing power can start to improve their standard of living. Retailers have to begin to replenish their stocks and manufacturers to renew their equipment. Bankruptcies grow fewer, prices are stabilized or show a slight tendency to go up, and confidence commences to return. A revival is thus inaugurated which may develop into a period of expansion.

Although modern business cycles follow roughly this pattern, each individual cycle is somewhat different from every other, for myriads of factors are at work conditioning the course of our economy. In the period from 1870 to 1906 there was a tremendous extension of bank credit, which tended to aggravate the cyclical movement. The development of industry and means of transportation, as well as the settling of the West, offered irresistible opportunities for overexpansion, while ultimately the productive capacity of large-scale, mechanized industry made possible a fluctuating output with no great extension of plant. Furthermore, the many new inventions of the period had a tendency to give a "lift" to business and the Civil War to delay the satisfaction of many wants. Finally the business cycle operated from 1864 to 1897 against a long-term fall in prices, which was a depressive factor, and from 1897 to 1920, against a secular price rise, which was a buoyant force.

Immediately after the Civil War, between the years 1865 and 1867, business experienced a recession, but from 1868 to 1870 it enjoyed a revival, and in the next two years, a boom. In 1873 a panic hit the country—a panic which was given a dramatic impetus by the failure of Jay Cooke and Co. A deflationary price movement brought prices in 1879 back to their prewar level, and this fall in prices, accompanied by the resumption of specie payment in 1879, helped to depress business to such an extent that 20 percent of the railway investment was sold under foreclosure between 1876 and 1880. The indebted South and West suffered extensively, and many industries, especially steel and coal, were forced drastically to curtail production.

Thus, business wallowed in despondency until about 1878, when a recovery began to be noticeable. Poor European crops in 1879 and 1880 gave American agriculture an outlet for its products and attracted gold, which facilitated specie payments. Manufacturing increased, railroad construction revived, and prices tended upward to 1882. The spring of 1884 witnessed a sharp financial panic, but because the basic economic factors in this situation were not so unfavorable as they had been after 1873, the depression was short-lived. In 1885 there was a revival, which by 1887 had reached the prosperity stage and which, except for a brief reaction following the Baring crisis in 1890, lasted until 1893.

In the first half of 1893 the stock market collapsed; runs on Southern and Western banks began; and these institutions in turn started to withdraw funds from New York. Bank loans were contracted, and business activity declined. The total number of commercial failures was three times greater than that of 1873, but the total liabilities involved was only one-half greater. As after the panics of 1837 and 1873, so after that of 1893 recovery was slow, in part because of the stringency of money, low prices, especially of grains, and overexpansion of railroads and industry. In 1896 interest rates reached the lowest level which the nation had thus far experienced.

With the defeat of Bryan in 1896 and the fear of cheap money dispelled, business began to revive in 1897 and continued its upward trend to 1920, with only minor setbacks marked by the years 1903, 1907, and 1914. An increase in gold production, beginning about 1893, helped to save mankind for being "crucified on a cross of gold" and initiated a secular upward trend in prices. A better market for agricultural goods rescued indebted farmers, transportation costs went up more slowly than prices, and the export trade increased more rapidly than that of imports. In 1903 the feverish formation of trusts led to the failure of a few combinations, although general business activity declined only slightly. Finally, in 1907, financial stringency again hit the economic system, but again the depression factors had a short run.

Some connection between the curve of the business cycle and life insurance can be observed in the statistical tables. In the boom which preceded 1870 many new companies were founded—in fact, the number doing business in New York State increased from 17 in 1860 to 71 in

1870, while many companies passed out of existence in the depression following 1870—the number remaining in 1879 being 32. There was a rapid increase in life insurance companies in 1879; then a level was reached which was fairly maintained until 1886, and thenceforth a fairly steady augmentation was registered, the most notable increases

CHART VIII

SURRENDERS AND LAPSES, 1870–1906

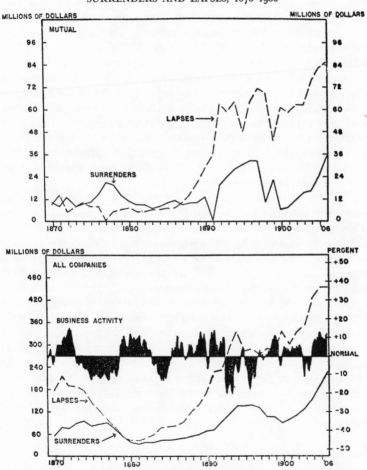

Sources: New York (State) Insurance Department, *Reports* (Albany, 1871–1907); The Cleveland Trust Company, *American Business Activity since 1790* (Cleveland, 1944).

being in 1899, 1903, 1905, and 1906. The amount of life insurance in force followed a similar curve. A marked decrease began in 1873 and attained the bottom of the trough in 1879. Then an increase took place at uneven pace until 1896, when the rise became rapid. New insurance issued had a much closer correlation to the business cycle, however, than did these other series. The decline began in 1870 and continued until 1878. Then a rise took place to 1894, a fall to 1896, an upward trend to 1904, and a downward tendency to 1907. Yet the life insurance statistical series which show the closest correlation to the business cycle are those for surrenders and lapses, as can be seen in Tables 52 and 53, of the Appendix and in Chart VIII, page 137.

Data showing the activity of The Mutual Life coincides with the business cycle much less well than the data for all life insurance companies. The Mutual's insurance in force dropped slightly in 1871, but then rose until 1875, fell in 1878, and then climbed steadily to 1905. New business was low in 1870, increased to 1873, fell far down by 1877, went up slowly to 1883, was low again in 1884, rose rapidly to 1893, was low but stable from 1896 to 1898, went up to 1904, and again back down to 1907. Surrenders in The Mutual Life, as in all companies, show the best correlation with the general cyclical trend.

This analysis indicates that for the most part life insurance is not so susceptible to the short-term vagaries of business as are most branches of the economy. Such sluggish reaction of life insurance to the business cycle is to be explained by the long-term nature of most of the contracts made in the industry. Furthermore, the experience of one company tends to deviate more widely from any cyclical curve than that of the whole industry because of special circumstances usually pertaining to managerial policy. On the other hand, life insurance does react very strongly to long-term trends, as we have seen in outlining the growth of the industry from 1870 to 1906. Insurance grew with the population and the general economy. Perhaps the only retarding long-term influence was the yield on investments—a yield that for about twenty-five companies fell from 6.81 percent of mean ledger assets in 1875 to 4.57 percent in 1905. Just how life insurance, as reflected in the history of The Mutual, was conditioned by these long-term trends is the subject of the next four chapters.

VIII. The Coming of Deferred Dividend Policies

COMPETITION OF THE SEVEREST KIND was, as we have seen, one of the main characteristics of life insurance history between the years 1870 and 1906. So strong was it, in fact, that it influenced all aspects of the business—selling, investments, management, and the kinds of contracts offered to prospective policyholders. In this last respect rivalry led to the introduction of the deferred dividend policy—a contract which was also known as the semi-tontine and in slightly altered form by a variety of other names. The distinctive feature of the deferred dividend contract was that dividends were paid only at the end of specified periods and to those policyholders whose policies were still in force. If the insured died prior to the end of a dividend period, his beneficiary received the face amount of the policy, but no share of the surplus. This arrangement naturally results in larger dividends to those who survive. This, it was argued, is only just, for those who live long ought to enjoy a greater share of the excess earnings than those who die early and whose beneficiaries profit largely from a financial standpoint.

The deferred dividend plan was applied to all the principal forms of insurance contracts and proved exceptionally popular in the thirty-five years after 1870. Within three years after deferred dividend policies were made available by The Mutual Life only one-half of one percent of the Company's new business was written on an annual dividend basis.[1] This was largely owing to the fact that deferred dividend business was encouraged by the payment of higher agents' commissions. Throughout the period now under consideration all but three American companies included deferred dividend contracts in their stock in trade.

The deferred dividend system, when properly understood by the policyholder, was perfectly sound and had obviously attractive features. In operation, however, it became subject to two serious abuses. The undistributed surplus was not a legal liability and was not so treated by the companies in their financial statements. This lack of responsibility

[1] *Minutes of the Board of Trustees,* April 25, 1888.

for an accounting of surplus funds held for future distribution led eventually to extravagance in the conduct of the business which increased the cost of insurance for all. Moreover, the practice grew up of making "estimates" and issuing "illustrations" of the expected results. Unfortunately, owing to changes in conditions and increased liberalities in the contracts, as well as to extravagance, these "illustrations" proved, as a rule, to be greatly overstated and led to serious dissatisfaction and to criticism of the whole deferred dividend system. In New York the deferred dividend system was prohibited by legislation enacted subsequent to the Armstrong Investigation.

Some of the problems connected with deferred dividend policies had already been encountered by The Mutual Life and certain other companies prior to 1870, for they had paid dividends at the end of every three or five years and at first had not paid post mortem dividends, that is, dividends on policies which had become claims prior to the end of the distribution period.[2] When in 1866 The Mutual Life decided upon the payment of annual dividends as a competitive measure against companies which took promissory notes as partial payment of premiums, the earlier system, with all that accompanied it, went temporarily out of existence. It was not, however, easy for other and younger companies, with their relatively higher expenses and smaller surplus funds, to adopt the annual dividend plan. It was this situation which led The Equitable, in 1868, to devise the "Tontine" plan out of which the deferred dividend plan developed.[3] Under the tontine plan not only were dividends to be paid solely at the end of specified periods to surviving policyholders but also no cash or other surrender value was allowed in case of lapse.

The reception of the tontine policy by life insurance authorities varied widely. Sheppard Homans, who was retained by the New York Life after he left The Mutual, heartily endorsed the plan by stating that

The benefits you [the New York Life] propose to extend to those selecting this class of policy are more varied in their character and advantages than are afforded by any plan of insurance now in use by any company within my knowledge, and are such as cannot fail to render the Tontine Investment Policy a safe, popular, and highly remunerative form of insurance.[4]

Elizur Wright, on the other hand, clearly saw that the tontine system was, in effect, the antithesis of the basic principle of insurance and damned tontines as "life insurance cannibalism."

[2] See above, pp. 69–70.

[3] William Alexander, *Seventy-Five Years of Progress and Public Service; a Brief Record of the Equitable Life Assurance Society of the United States* (New York, 1934), p. 11.

[4] Hudnut, *History of the New York Life*, pp. 158–159n.

Its sole and only function is [he maintained], to make the richer part of the company richer by making the poorer part poorer. It is as if a temperance society should endeavor to promote its cause by establishing a liquor saloon under its lectureroom, or a church should support its minister by a lottery.

With these latter views President Winston of The Mutual Life was inclined to agree, and yet he was sorely tempted. In 1868 new business issued by The Mutual fell off, and in 1869 The Equitable surpassed The Mutual in new insurance written, taking first place among all companies of the country. Moreover, in 1868 Jay Cooke had founded the National Life Insurance Company of the United States and had adopted very low premiums; by 1870 Winston was having trouble with his actuary Sheppard Homans, and investigations of various kinds were endlessly badgering him. Under such circumstances, but without conviction, Winston decided in 1870 to sell tontine policies.[5]

Winston's heart was, however, never in the tontine scheme. Only 382 such policies were sold by The Mutual Life, and they were dropped in 1872. The *Annual Report* issued at the close of that year explained the reasons for this action in the following words: [6]

No effort was made, however, by the Company, to press this form of policy before the public, since the executive officers were never entirely satisfied of the wisdom and equity of the plan; and the whole amount assured in it upon tontine policies was comparatively small. But several cases of great hardship were soon forced upon the notice of the Company. The plan made it obligatory upon us to forfeit every such policy absolutely and finally, if the premium were not paid upon a certain day, and left us no discretion to consider a claim for a surrender value. This experience satisfied the trustees that the plan, in its nature, is wholly outside of the proper range of legitimate life insurance; being little else than a contract by which the Company binds itself to execute an unequal wager, securing the stakes to the winner. In such a wager as this, the most needy, whom life assurance is especially designed to protect, are pretty sure to prove the losers. Besides, the large accumulations which tontine insurance gathers in the hands of a company, at the expense of those who die, or are unable to maintain their policies, during the tontine period, offers a strong temptation to wasteful expenditure, which, if indulged, must sooner or later bring disappointment even to the survivors of those who play at tontine hazard.

For these reasons, the trustees of the company have decided to discontinue the issue of tontine policies.

THE MUTUAL LIFE'S REDUCTION OF PREMIUMS

The decision to discontinue the issuing of tontine policies seemed to deprive The Mutual Life of a formidable competitive weapon; but the

---

[5] See Appendix, p. 358. [6] *Thirtieth Annual Report* (1872), pp. 24-25.

Company had another arrow in its quiver. At the very meeting of the Board when action was taken against tontines, the trustees voted to reduce premiums.[7] The reception which the anouncement of this move received was decidedly hostile. Old policyholders claimed that they were being discriminated against, although provision had been made for paying them correspondingly higher dividends, and the officials of competing companies banded together to oppose this "attack on the institution of life insurance." In fact, twenty-two companies united to combat the move, because only two were in a position to compete with such low rates.[8] They elicited from Elizur Wright, Sheppard Homans, and David Parks Fackler the opinion that the proposed reduction was "a virtual abandonment of those cardinal principles of security and equity upon which the claims of The Mutual Life Insurance Company to the confidence of its policyholders and of the Community have rested," and they requested President Winston and the Board to reconsider its action. Their entreaties and perhaps also their arguments were effective, and The Mutual Life decided to postpone indefinitely the execution of its reduced premium plan.

This action appeared to disarm the Company at a time when instruments of war were becoming more imperative. For a while President Winston and the Board of Trustees seemed willing to surrender their aggressive program and to adopt a defensive attitude. In fact, the president proposed that the Company limit its size to 100,000 members. He argued that, although it would take several years to attain this maximum, the annual decrement in membership would provide ample room for new policyholders, that 100,000 members "will be as large and as extensive a trust as can be well managed by the executive officers and trustees of any one corporate institution, and probably as large as state authority and public policy will permit it to hold," that a definite limit would make the work of agents easier and improve the selection of risks, and that a limit on growth might better be established voluntarily "instead of incurring the hazard of having it rudely done by acts of the Legislature or the courts of law." [9] Strangely enough this discourse on optimum size, especially that part of it which aimed to allay criticism of the Company's power, seemed to impress the trustees. A special committee of the Board reported that if the president's proposal were adopted

---

[7] *Minutes of the Board of Trustees*, November 20, 1872. Existing policyholders were given the option of leaving their policies undisturbed or of taking out new policies at the new rates, if they met the requirements of a new medical examination.

[8] Hudnut, *Semi-Centennial History of the New York Life Insurance Company*, p. 160.

[9] *Minutes of the Board of Trustees*, Dec. 13, 1873.

"we should no longer hear the alarming cry that within a generation this great corporation will hold New York City under mortgage, and that within a century it will own Albany, and the City Hall." [10] Furthermore, the committee believed that 100,000 members would be sufficient to allow the Company to obtain all the advantages to be derived from sheer size—the working of laws of average and low overhead costs. Such arguments carried the day, and the proposed limitation was adopted January 9, 1874.

The defensive frame of mind of the management indicated by such a limitation on the Company's size was, however, only temporary. The years of depression and severe competition not only precluded the possibility of excessive growth but also greatly reduced the amount of new business which was being written. Consequently, a more aggressive program was looked for, and ways of selling more insurance were keenly sought. Among the more persistent plans for attaining the desired end was the scheme for reducing premiums. Professor Bartlett, the actuary, indicated from time to time that the reduction proposed in 1872 would have been feasible,[11] while President Winston's antipathy for tontine policies prevented, in the meantime, the adoption of the tontine, semi-tontine, or deferred dividend systems.

Thus it was that in 1878 the Company turned definitely toward lower rates. In September of that year a rebate of 30 percent of the first two premiums on whole life policies and of 15 percent of the first two premiums on other policies was allowed to new insurants.[12] At once a hue and cry was raised by old Mutual Life policyholders against this move. Protest committees were formed in New York and other cities, and complaints rained upon the Company. It was contended that these rebates worked an injustice upon existing policyholders, that the first two premiums were reduced below the actual cost of insurance, and that the agent's remuneration was greatly reduced. So loud was the clamor against the rebate plan that the Board of Trustees had to take cognizance of it. Although the rebates had contributed, as it was hoped that they would, to a marked increase in new business, the Company deemed the criticism of them so well founded that a decision was reached early in 1879 to abolish them. Yet lower premiums seemed to be so advantageous that the Board decided to substitute for the rebates a modification of its 1872 plan—a general reduction of premiums amounting to 15 percent

10 *Ibid.*, Jan. 9, 1874.
11 *Ibid.*, Jan. 19, 1876, Nov. 21, 1877.
12 *Ibid.*, Feb. 19, 1879. See, *Brief Summary of the Arguments of the Committee of The Mutual Life Insurance Company against the Rebate Plan* (1879).

on whole life policies and to a "proportionate amount" on all other contracts.[13] In the actual application of this scheme, premiums on endowments and children's endowments were not reduced, because they had proved to be low, but the rates on all other insurance contracts were cut substantially.[14] Furthermore, an option was given to existing policyholders to accept the new rates or to have the difference between the old and new rates added to dividends.

THE ADOPTION OF DEFERRED DIVIDEND POLICIES

By this reduction of premium rates The Mutual Life hoped to improve its competitive position, but its hopes were only partially realized. Although the new rates proved to be safe,[15] they were criticized as being too low, and they failed to bring in new business on the scale desired. President Winston was loath to take the action which seemed to be necessary to meet competition, that is, to issue tontine or semi-tontine policies, and he watched The Equitable and the New York Life creep ahead of The Mutual Life. To him this was not a pleasing sight, and to others in the Company it was sheer anathema. From agents and from Vice President Richard A. McCurdy pleas arose for the adoption of deferred dividend policies and for more aggressive action.

[13] *Ibid.* and *Minutes of the Insurance Committee,* Feb. 21, 1879.

[14] Rates on annuities were unchanged. These rates were increased in 1878 although the age limit at which annuities would be offered was raised from 75 to 90, because the annuity account had shown a loss. The unfavorable experience with annuities had resulted not only from cheap rates but also from an adverse selection and from such a small number of annuitants that the laws of average did not operate. See *Minutes of the Insurance Committee,* May 17, 1878. In 1886 the rates on annuities were raised again. *Minutes of the Insurance Committee,* July 27, 1886. They were reduced in 1888. *Minutes of the Insurance Committee,* May 22, 1888. In collaboration with The Equitable and the New York Life, The Mutual Life increased annuity rates in 1892. *Minutes of the Insurance Committee,* Apr. 25, 1892. Each schedule was based on the Carlisle Mortality Table and 4 percent interest, except the last. The McClintock Table had 5 percent loadings and 4 percent interest.

[15] About this the *Minutes of the Board* for Oct. 20, 1880, contained the following: "1. It appears, then, that on the general run of all kinds of Insurance, the habit of the Company was to overcharge under its old rates, thirty-four and a quarter per cent on all cash premium receipts: That is to say that for every one hundred dollars ($100) of premiums required to pay death claims, furnish an ample reserve, defray the expenses of business including commissions, salaries, fees, taxes, rents and office necessities, the Company under its old rates made an overcharge of $34.25 which had to be returned to the insured either in cash or its equivalent in additional insurance. 2. That under the old rates the overcharge was nearly $60 on every $100 on ordinary life Policies. 3. That under old rates the overcharge for 10 year life Policies was $31. 4. That under the old rates the overcharge for 10 year Endowments was $24. 5. That under our reduced rates, the overcharge would have been $35 for ordinary life policies. 6. That under the new rates for 10 year life it would have been $19. 7. That under the new rates for 10 year Endowments it would have been $16. 8. And finally that our reduced rates exceed by nearly $8 in every $100 the non-participating rates (which have been in operation for years) of other companies, and therefore judged by this standard, reduced rates are safe beyond question." The reduction of premium was declared by the Legislature to be within the bounds of the Company's Charter.

To the pressure thus generated President Winston and several of the trustees yielded with reluctance in 1884.[16] The Company prepared and offered to the public in September, 1885, a deferred dividend policy sometimes called a "distribution policy." This new contract was, as has

FIVE-YEAR DISTRIBUTION POLICY, 1885

already been stated, a modification of the tontine scheme. The insured was to receive no dividends until a stipulated number of years had elapsed—a period which was at first five years, but which was soon extended to ten, fifteen, or twenty years—and then the surplus earned on all the policies was to be distributed among the survivors. Also, as in the case of tontines, the accumulated surplus on these policies was not considered as a legal liability, although The Mutual Life, unlike its largest rivals, set aside every year sums earmarked for distribution at the end of the deferred period, but was treated as surplus in the annual statements. Unlike the tontine policies, the deferred dividend policies had a provision for surrender values either in paid-up insurance after the third annual premium had been paid, as required by law, or in cash at the end of dividend periods. Cash values were, in fact, allowed after three years, although not guaranteed in the contract. This was the main distinction between deferred dividend, or semi-tontine, policies and the "straight" tontines. Premiums on these new contracts were higher than the rates established in 1879, because of the "greater liberality of this form of policy." The deferred dividend principle was applied to all types of contracts—whole life, endowments, and limited payment life.

During the interval between the preparation of the new policies and the actual sale of them to the public, President Winston died (1885) and was succeeded in the chief office of the Company by the vice president, Richard A. McCurdy. McCurdy was a "go-getter" in every sense of the

16 *Minutes of the Insurance Committee*, June 18, 1884; *Minutes of the Board of Trustees*, July 16, 1884; and *Testimony Taken before the Joint Committee of the Senate and Assembly of the State of New York* (Albany, 1906), p. 1836.

word and immediately served notice on all and sundry that The Mutual
Life was going to strain every muscle to regain its position of primacy
in the insurance world. Of a like mind was the president's chief assistant
and kindred spirit, Robert A. Granniss—a man who had had insurance
experience with the New York Life, the Widows and Orphans Benefit
Life, and with the Metropolitan. These men made a strong and fiery
pair, and in their hands they held an effective weapon—the new deferred
dividend policies—and they intended to use it as extensively as possible.

McCurdy had an almost blind worship of size, and to this fetish he
brought an emotional zeal. He argued that The Mutual Life had been
converted by the past administration "into a loan and trust institution
with a life insurance branch, instead of remaining a life insurance company" and that the Company should be restored to a "life insurance company with its loan and trust department as part of its management." [17]
He maintained that a grievous error had been committed in allowing
what he called the "dispersion of funds" by lower premiums, cash surrender values, and cash dividends, for efforts to reduce the cost of insurance had resulted in diminishing the surplus, in the loss of the best
salesmen, and in a decline of business. He insisted (1) upon a return to
the "accumulative principle," so that the miraculous force of compound
interest would operate, (2) upon a large amount of new business, especially upon young lives, in order that the mortality rate among the
insured would be reduced, and (3) upon The Mutual Life's becoming
again America's largest insurance institution.[18]

To attain the goals thus set, McCurdy was to extend the territory
covered by the Company throughout the United States, to Europe, to
Africa, and to Australia, Cuba, and Mexico; he was to instill new energy
into the sales force and increase commissions; and he was to pursue an
ambitious investment program. But in his race for size and for the
accumulation of large sums the president was to find the deferred dividend policies of the greatest value. From the moment of their introduction the new business written by The Mutual Life rose rapidly, aided
by an upward swing of the business cycle. From 1885 to 1888 new insurance more than doubled, and from the latter date to 1904 it more than
doubled again. By 1889 the Company had surpassed the New York Life
in new business, and in 1893 it also passed The Equitable. As we have
seen, within three years after the introduction of deferred dividend
policies less than one-half of one percent of new business written was on

17 *Minutes of the Board of Trustees*, June 3, 1885.
18 *Ibid.*, Dec. 28, 1887; April 25, 1888; Jan. 27, 1892; and Nov. 23, 1892.

the annual dividend plan. About half the insurance issued provided for a twenty-year "distribution period," and the remainder for shorter periods. This preponderance of deferred dividend business continued until deferred dividend policies were eliminated by legislation following the Armstrong Investigation. The result was that in 1907 about 80 percent of the entire existing business was on the deferred dividend plan.[19] Only an insignificant part of that business remains in force today.

During the period we have been discussing (1884–1906) the emphasis on size and on new business led to the devising of many new types of life insurance contracts. Only a few of these had real merit.[20] One was the Continuous Installment Policy, which was first issued in 1893 on the occasion of the Company's semi-centennial. Devised by Emory McClintock, who had succeeded Bartlett as The Mutual's actuary in 1888, it was a development of the installment policy which had been first written in 1866 and was described on page 49. The Continuous Installment Policy was a combination of life insurance with a "deferred survivorship annuity," and, instead of a lump sum, it provided an income to the beneficiary for life with the guarantee of payment for not less than 20 years.

Another of the semi-centennial contracts issued in 1893 was the Five Per Cent Debenture Policy. Written on either the life or the limited payment plan, it provided that the Company would pay upon the death of the insured 5 percent of the face amount of the policy, then dividends for twenty years, and the principal sum at the expiration of these twenty years. Then there was a combination of the endowment and annuity principles which was called the "Consol," first issued in 1896. This policy required the payment of premiums during a fixed number of years, provided insurance for this period, and upon maturity paid the insured the face amount of the policy, accumulated dividends, and an annuity for life.

A feature of many contracts issued in this period was the provision for payment of claims in gold. This provision was introduced toward the end of the period in which agitation for the free coinage of silver was strong, but their special attractiveness waned after the defeat of William Jennings Bryan and the increase in the supply of gold. In 1896,

---

[19] *Ibid.*, Apr. 25, 1888, and *Annual Report of the Superintendent of Insurance of the State of New York* (Albany, 1908), p. 184.
[20] *Minutes of the Board of Trustees*, Dec. 28, 1898.

for example, The Mutual Life offered the public a Five Per Cent Twenty Year Gold Bond Policy which stipulated that at the death of the insured or at the maturity of the policy the face amount of the contract should be paid in coupon bonds of the Company, redeemable in gold coin at the end of twenty years and bearing 5 percent interest, which was also payable in gold.[21] In 1899 the Guaranteed Compound Interest Gold Bond Policy was placed on the market. According to its terms, there was credited to this policy, whenever a premium fell due, 3 percent of all premiums previously paid. Thus, 3 percent of the first premium was credited when the second premium became payable; 6 per cent of a single premium when the third premium was due; 9 percent when the fourth premium was paid; and so forth. These credits bore interest at $3\frac{1}{2}$ percent, compounded annually, could be drawn upon to pay premiums in case of necessity, and were, like the principal sum, payable in gold coin.

In addition to the policies described there were others—some of doubtful merit—mostly designed to attract new customers. One of these was the semi-endowment of 1881, which simply reduced the endowment feature by one-half in order to show lower premiums.[22] Another of this group was the Expectation Term Policy of 1899, which provided insurance for the period of the insured's "expectation of life." This period was divided into two equal parts, and a "deferred dividend" was payable on survival to the end of each part. The first of these dividends was applied in reduction of the premiums payable during the second half. Then there was the Selected Benefit Policy (1903), which allowed the insured to determine the amount of income and the number of years, not to exceed thirty, which he desired for a beneficiary.[23] There was also the consol-double settlement, which permitted the insured upon the maturity of his policy to take the principal sum due him either in cash or to use it for paid-up insurance. Finally, there was a system of "contingent additions," which provided for payment at death, if that occurred before the end of the period, of a certain sum, in addition to the face amount of the policy, for each premium that had been paid.

Some of these special contracts, which were subject to misrepresentation and were sometimes misleading in character, were abolished in New York State in 1906 and subsequently in other jurisdictions. The

21 The Company agreed to pay at death or maturity $1,305 in cash for each $1,000 bond it might have to issue. Another variety of this policy was the Yearly Bond Contract (1903), which provided for a face amount of $20,000 over a term of 20 years, but allowed to the insured a thousand dollar bond each year. *Minutes of the Insurance Committee,* May 28, 1903.

22 *Ibid.,* Apr. 19, 1881.

23 For details concerning these policies see the *Rate Books of The Mutual Life Insurance Company,* especially for 1899 and 1903.

most popular contracts continued to be the standard forms of policies which had been established in the earlier period and to which the deferred dividend principle had been applied—straight life, endowments, and limited payment life. The amounts of insurance written give full proof of this fact.

Of other forms of sharing risks which made notable strides forward during the period 1870–1906, the most important were assessment and industrial insurance. Both of them stemmed from attempts of fraternal organizations and assessment societies to furnish some kind of security to their members, and both of them aimed to serve the poorer classes who could afford only small coverage. These organizations frequently operated on the basis of assessing their members on a pro rata basis for sums needed to pay claims and operating expenses rather than by providing for contractual premium payments. Such a scheme had a special appeal at about the beginning of the 1880's, for many of the companies writing legal reserve premium insurance had failed after the business crisis in 1873, and the insurance written by the ordinary life companies was not geared to the small saver. Thus, the amount of insurance in force in fraternal orders reached the impressive figures of $2,625,192,842 in 1890 and of $8,136,201,919 in 1906, while that of assessment associations of a non-fraternal character was $1,172,747,954 in 1890, but only $582,099,387 in 1906. The assessment societies were, for the most part, unsound financially. In particular, the plan of "pro-rata" assessment of claims was impracticable and was fore-doomed to failure. Most of these societies survived only a short time. For a time, nevertheless, the assessment principle had such a vogue that The Mutual Life attacked it with vigor and permitted the payment of premiums on a monthly basis (1885) in order to attract the patronage of the working classes.[24]

The most severe competition for small policies was to come, not from assessment association or fraternal orders, but from companies writing industrial insurance. The type of insurance in which they specialized had its beginnings in the practices of fraternal organizations in England, where small weekly premiums could buy enough insurance to cover burial expenses. In 1875 the Prudential Insurance Company of America began to issue small policies which required no medical examination and called for the weekly payment of premiums amounting to a few cents. The John Hancock Company soon followed this example, and in 1879

---

[24] These attacks may be found in the *Thirty-Ninth, Forty-First,* and *Forty-Second Annual Reports,* pp. 24, 18, 11, respectively. See also M. M. Dawson, "Assessment Life Insurance," in L. W. Zartman and W. H. Price, *Yale Readings in Insurance* (New Haven, 1923).

TABLE 24

EXHIBIT OF POLICIES: PAID-FOR BUSINESS ONLY

December 31, 1906

CLASSIFICATION	WHOLE LIFE POLICIES		ENDOWMENT POLICIES		TERM AND OTHER POLICIES, INCLUDING RETURN PREMIUM ADDITIONS		ADDITIONS TO POLICIES BY DIVIDENDS	TOTAL NUMBERS AND AMOUNTS	
	Number	*Amount*	*Number*	*Amount*	*Number*	*Amount*	*Amount*	*Number*	*Amount*
Totals	585,717	$1,349,752,499	137,947	$281,817,974	7,324	$24,125,297	$21,404,590	730,988	$1,680,100,360
Outstanding at end of year *a*	534,406	$1,224,271,258	124,426	$255,166,485	6,093	$19,465,493	$18,353,944	664,925	$1,517,257,180

a Paid-up insurance included in the final total (including additions to policies), number of policies 84,773; amount, $164,287,936. The annuities in force December 31 last were in number 10,355, representing in annual payments $2,901,865.02.

the Metropolitan entered the field. The popularity of this form of insurance soon spread, and the amount of industrial insurance in force was greatly increased.

TABLE 25

INDUSTRIAL INSURANCE IN FORCE WITH AMERICAN LIFE INSURANCE COMPANIES, 1876–1906 [a]

Average Amount of Policies on All Plans Combined

Year	Amount of Insurance in Force	Average Amount of Policy in Force	Year	Amount of Insurance in Force	Average Amount of Policy in Force
1876	$ 443,072	$ 92	1892	$ 583,533,745	$114
1877	1,030,655	92	1893	662,647,364	115
1878	2,027,888	89	1894	803,067,595	117
1879	5,763,867	95	1895	820,746,562	118
1880	20,533,469	87	1896	888,267,912	120
1881	33,501,740	91	1897	996,144,739	124
1882	56,564,682	96	1898	1,110,078,702	126
1883	87,793,650	100	1899	1,293,329,995	129
1884	111,115,252	102	1900	1,468,928,342	131
1885	145,938,241	106	1901	1,640,827,454	133
1886	198,431,170	111	1902	1,806,894,473	134
1887	255,533,472	111	1903	1,978,241,009	135
1888	304,673,004	109	1904	2,135,859,103	136
1889	365,841,267	109	1905	2,309,754,235	137
1890	428,789,342	110	1906	2,453,616,207	138
1891	481,925,977	112			

[a] Industrial Insurance was begun in the United States in 1875; the first policy was issued on November 10 of that year. See *History of The Prudential Insurance Company of America* (Newark, N.J., 1900); and John F. Dryden, *Addresses and Papers on Life Insurance and Other Subjects* (Newark, N.J., 1910).

The potentialities of industrial insurance were not at first clear, and the management of The Mutual Life seems never to have discussed them in an official manner until 1909, and then a decision against entering this field was reached. Yet the industrial companies tapped an exceedingly large market, and their rates were maintained at such a high level that they had funds for expansion. Finally, they developed an enormous sales force which was ultimately put to work selling not only the very small policies, but also those of intermediate size and eventually those which were in direct competition with ordinary life companies. Thus, two of the concerns which began early to write industrial insurance are today the largest life insurance institutions in the world.[25]

25 For bibliography see Magee, *Life Insurance* (Chicago, 1939), pp. 507–509. See especially J. F. Dryden, "Burial or Industrial Insurance," in L. W. Zartman and W. H. Price, eds., *Yale Readings in Insurance* (New Haven, 1923); W. S. Myers, *Fifty Years of the Prudential* (Newark, 1927); *The Metropolitan Life Insurance Company, Its History*, etc. (New York, 1908); Frederick L. Hoffman, *History of The Prudential Insurance Company* (Newark, 1900), M. E. Davis, *Industrial Life Insurance in the United States* (New York, 1944), and Louis I. Dublin, *A Family of Thirty Million* (New York, 1943).

LIBERALIZING THE INSURANCE CONTRACT

The insurance contract became definitely more liberal between 1870 and 1906. Nonforfeiture laws were passed, and minimum surrender values established; provisions were added for a period of "grace" in payment of premiums, for incontestability after a stated period, and for reinstatement in event of lapse. The literal truth of statements made by the insured (i. e., legal "guaranty") was not required or enforced, and many restrictions as to travel, residence, and occupation were removed or modified.

Of the various changes which were thus made in life insurance contracts, none was of greater importance to the policyholder than the nonforfeiture and surrender-value provisions. Prior to the 1860's, as we have seen, the entire equity in a life insurance contract might be forfeited to the insurance company for some minor breach of the contract, such as tardiness in paying premiums. The campaign conducted by Elizur Wright against this practice resulted in laws requiring surrender values in paid-up insurance—like the Massachusetts nonforfeiture law of 1861, the New York law of 1879, and similar legislation by other states—and in a more earnest attempt on the part of insurance companies to send out premium notices—an effort that was clear in the case of The Mutual Life in 1875. The mailing of premium notices and the enactment of nonforfeiture laws were definite advances, but room was left for further progress in the matter of providing guaranteed cash surrender values. By the end of the century much had been achieved along these lines, for it came to be recognized that the reasons which motivated a person to insure his life might cease to exist and that in that case he should be allowed an equitable cash value, the amount of which should be a matter of contract to be determined in advance. So cogent was this reasoning and so strong was competition in securing clients by attractive policy terms that by 1905 the policies of fifty-one representative companies guaranteed a cash surrender value.[26]

The Mutual Life had from its inception been willing to purchase the policies which it had issued provided application was made to the Company before premiums had gone into default. By 1873 this practice had become so well established that attention was focused more especially upon the amount of the surrender value rather than upon the practice itself, although the granting of any cash surrender value was considered to be a favor rather than an obligation. The principle which had been

[26] Amrhein, *The Liberalization of the Life Insurance Contract* (Philadelphia, 1933), p. 254.

followed in determining the amount of the surrender value was to allow the policyholder one-half of the reserve on his policy and the whole of the cash value of his reversionary credits from dividends. This principle was, however, attacked in 1873 as working an injustice upon the Company, for (1) those who surrendered their policies were usually good risks, and their retirement meant an adverse selection of risks among the members, and (2) surrenders deprived the insurer of expected income from loadings with which to defray future expenses—a fact which resulted frequently in a net loss on policies that did not remain in force long enough to pay initial costs of commissions, medical examination, and issue. Consequently the Company decided to allow surrender values only on policies for which two annual premiums had been paid and to give the policyholder only a portion of his policy reserve, an arrangement which Professor Bartlett expressed in detailed formulae for all types of insurance.[27]

Bartlett's calculation of surrender values was a liberal one, especially for policies that remained in force only a few years. It was responsible, in part, for a "run" upon The Mutual Life in those years of deep depression which followed its adoption, although values found by his formulae were reduced in 1875 by 20 percent and in 1877 by 50 percent. From 1874 to 1878, both inclusive, the Company paid $6,927,284 in cash surrenders on $24,201,169 of insurance. The average age of policies thus surrendered was well under ten years.[28] There was a tendency to give a surrender value on new policies only in paid-up or extended insurance and to prolong the period before any surrender value would be given to three years from the date of original issue.[29] But as this was all that the New York nonforfeiture legislation of 1879 required, the Company was ready to and did comply with the law before it went into effect in 1880.

Contemporaneously with the effort to establish legal provisions for nonforfeiture, a plea was made for large surrender values and for a guarantee of them. Against the guaranteeing of fixed sums the actuary of The Mutual Life took a strong stand, because the experience of the middle seventies had impressed upon his mind the possibility of wide fluctuations in the fortunes of America's economy and the dangers which surrender values of definite amounts might have in case of a run upon his Company. However, in an effort to appease those who were making an appeal for such contractual provisions, the Company increased its surrender values in 1879, and, as business conditions improved, it re-

27 *Minutes of the Insurance Committee*, Dec. 2, 1873.   28 *Ibid.*, Feb. 18, 1880.
29 *Ibid.*, Feb. 10, 1877; Nov. 14, 1879; July 13, 1885.

duced its opposition to both guaranteed and cash surrender values. When Massachusetts passed a law (1880) requiring guaranteed surrender values in the form of reduced paid-up insurance, the extension of the practice to other states became an almost foregone conclusion. The deferred dividend policies issued by The Mutual all contained provision for a guaranteed cash surrender value at the end of the dividend period and, in some cases, at other times (such as at the end of five-year intervals thereafter) as well.[30]

Not long after the inauguration of this practice the Company began to make policy loans.[31] In 1899 new policies provided that in case premiums were not paid after three annual payments had been made, the policy would be automatically surrendered for paid-up insurance. The insured was then freed from the necessity of notifying the Company of a desire to surrender and of possible loss. In 1895 policyholders were allowed a thirty-day period of grace in the payment of premiums, although they were charged 5 percent interest on the amount which was overdue, and in 1899 these concessions were written into new contracts.[32] Also, in 1899 a table of loan values and of guaranteed surrender values was made a part of the life insurance contract.[33] Throughout the years the reinstatement of lapsed policies was permitted under certain conditions. Thus, by the end of the period now being surveyed, because of reforms made mostly under the stress of competition, new policyholders in The Mutual Life were thoroughly protected from forfeiture because of their inability or negligence in meeting premium payments.

The more liberal treatment of policyholders by The Mutual Life in the matter of surrender values in the period between the years 1870 and 1906 was not an isolated phenomenon. It was only part of a general trend to make the insurance contract more attractive to the public and to free it from petty or semi-petty provisions which were proved to be impracticable or nonessential. The form and language of the contract became clearer, simpler, and more precise, especially in 1875 and 1883.[34] Many of the restrictions on travel, residence, and occupation were gradu-

---

[30] Ibid., July 13, 1885.   [31] The rate of interest charged on these loans was 5 percent.

[32] Letter of the General Manager to general agents, dated Nov. 25, 1895.

[33] The only precedent of this kind in The Mutual's history was a table of guaranteed surrender values for paid-up insurance issued in conjunction with Limited Payment Life Policies in 1864 and for a short time thereafter.

[34] The second United States Chamber of Life Insurance, founded in 1873, had as one of its projects this particular reform and the adoption of standard policies by all member companies. See Insurance Blue Book (New York, 1877), p. 60, and The Mutual's Thirty-Second Annual Report, p. 25. Standard forms for fire insurance were required by law in Massachusetts in 1873. In life insurance they were tried after the Armstrong Investigation, but were shortly abandoned. Standardized clauses do, however, exist generally today.

ally eliminated, for the dangers which they aimed to reduce were greatly minimized. Then, when the courts and the legislators took the position that statements made in life insurance applications were not warranties, but only representations, and that the insurance company was not relieved of its obligations even if a false statement were made that was immaterial to the risk, the life insurance companies began to be less ready to fly to court to contest the veracity of data about the insured.[35] Finally, these companies decided that a kind of self-imposed statute of limitations should be made to apply to the insurance contract and began to introduce into their policies a clause whereby they agreed not to use as a legal defense any error, concealment, or even fraud by the insured after the contract had been in force a certain length of time. The Equitable adopted such a clause in 1879,[36] and The Mutual Life made their contracts incontestable after a period of two years in 1890.[37] By 1905 this principle was to be found in the policies of fifty-one American life insurance companies, and in 1906 it was required by New York State Law.[38] The amount of litigation over the details of the application was henceforth greatly reduced.

PREMIUMS, RESERVES, AND DIVIDENDS

In the preceding pages reference was made to the reduction of premiums by The Mutual Life in 1879 and to the increase in premiums to a point above the rates in force prior to 1879 in the deferred dividend policies.[39] During this period the American Experience Table of Mortality continued to be used in the computation of all premium rates except for annuities, for which the famous and widely employed McClintock An-

[35] The great number of cases which would have been involved and the abolition of forfeiture contributed also to this tendency. See Edwin W. Patterson, *Cases and Other Materials on the Law of Insurance* (New York, 1932), pp. 412 ff. Ohio passed a law in 1872 which declared that the life insurance contract should be incontestable after three years.

[36] The Manhattan Life Insurance Company had been the leader in this move, introducing incontestability in 1864.

[37] The terms of the contract were: "It is hereby further promised and agreed that after two years from the date hereof the only conditions which shall be binding upon the holder of this policy are, that he shall pay the premiums at the times and place and in the manner stipulated in said policy and that the requirements of the Company as to age and Military and Naval Service in time of war shall be observed and that in all other respects if this policy matures after the expiration of the said two years, the payment of the sum insured by this policy shall not be disputed."

[38] Amrhein, *op. cit.*, p. 150.

[39] It should be noted that the trend in premium rates was downward from 1860 to 1870, and then upward. The average premium rate of several companies for $1,000 at age 25 on the whole life participating plan was $19.89 in 1860, $19.62 in 1870, $19.69 in 1880, $19.93 in 1890, $20.29 in 1900, and $20.80 in 1910. For further statistical information on this question see F. L. Hoffman, "Fifty Years of American Life Insurance Progress," *Quarterly Publications of the American Statistical Association* (Boston, 1911), p. 747.

nuity Table was adopted in 1892. Loadings on insurance premiums were increased,[40] and the interest rate was decreased—both increasing the premiums payable. The reduction in the interest assumption is of especial significance, for it reflected declining earnings on investments—a subject which will be dealt with more in detail in Chapter X. Up to 1898 the rate of interest which was employed in the calculations of premiums was 4 percent, from 1898 to 1906 it was 3½ percent, and from 1907 to the present it has been 3 percent. The net level premium method of establishing the reserve was used consistently throughout this period.

A reduction in the assumed rate of interest results in increasing both premiums and reserves.[41] It might be well to note here that the larger statistical series in this study are based on data obtained directly or indirectly from the *New York Insurance Reports* and that the state's basis for the valuation of policies has fluctuated more widely than that of The Mutual Life. Differences between Company and New York State figures are, therefore, to be accounted for by different reserve valuation bases as well as by the correction of errors and other minor differences. No attempts have been made in this study to effect a reconciliation between these different sets of statistics or to adjust either set to a single base which would be impossible at this time. Nevertheless, it should be pointed out that the reserve basis adopted by the state in 1866 was the English Life Table No. 3, for males, and 5 percent interest; in 1868, the American Experience Table and 4½ percent interest; in 1884, the Combined Experience Table and 4 percent—a higher standard; in 1892, the basis used by the company being examined; and in 1901, as a minimum, the American Experience Table and 3½ percent interest.[42] Thus, the general trend was to establish higher reserve standards, but not until 1901 was the same basis used by both the state and The Mutual Life, although after 1896 the Company employed the state's system for its public statements.[43]

The premium and reserve basis was not the only part of The Mutual's

[40] From 1879 to 1884 the loading basis was 19 percent of the net premium for all forms of insurance; from 1884 to 1897 it was for all plans 22 percent of the net premium for ordinary life plus 22 percent of the net premium of the specific plan; and from 1898 to 1906 it was 20 percent of the net premium for ordinary life plus 16 percent of the net premium for the individual plan plus $.80. For annuities see footnote (14).

[41] Maclean, *Life Insurance,* p. 132. On an ordinary life policy taken out at age 25, in force 5 years, the reserve, using the American Experience Table is at 3 percent $45.76; at 4 percent $36.59.

[42] For issues prior to Jan. 1, 1901, the Combined Experience Table and 4 percent could be used and for issues after that date the American Experience and 3½ percent. In 1906 the select and ultimate method was applied to the American Experience Table. See for more details Rainard B. Robbins, "Reserve Standards for Life Insurance," *Actuarial Society of America Transactions,* XXIV (1923), 312 ff.

[43] See Appendix, p. 357.

actuarial structure to be remodeled during the years between 1870 and 1906—the method of distributing surplus was also changed. As was seen in Chapter IV, the Company began in 1867 to pay dividends annually, and it endeavored to allot them equitably by employing the three-factor contribution plan. In 1872 dividends began to be paid on the anniversaries of policies rather than on a specified date, and a sum of $2,204,627.51 had to be used to make the adjustment.[44] Thus was settled a question which had been a hornet's nest for Sheppard Homans.

When deferred dividend policies were introduced, an entirely new problem concerning the distribution of surplus arose, for, as we have seen, dividends on such policies were to be paid only at the end of specified periods. The system adopted by The Mutual Life was to compute for each such policy a hypothetical annual dividend and to accumulate these hypothetical dividends at interest, including those which had been allotted to policies terminated by death or otherwise during the dividend period. The "deferred dividend fund" formed in this way was the basis of the actual distribution to survivors at the end of the period.

In determining how much surplus was available for dividends, it was customary for the actuary to get the Insurance Committee and the Board to approve in the month of November a certain sum for this purpose, a sum that was based on estimates of the Company's assets and liabilities at December 31. The amount actually distributed did not always reflect the actual surplus earnings of any one year. In fact, a definite attempt was made to keep dividends uniform or at any rate to avoid wide fluctuations and the complaints which would arise at the end of lean years if dividends were low.[45]

In 1895 Emory McClintock adopted in place of the three factors the two-factor system—the two factors being (1) excess interest and (2) loading plus mortality gains. This new method of computing dividends simplified the numerous operations necessary in allotting dividends. It combined two of the three factors on the assumption that mortality savings were an offset to initial excess expenses. This method was employed by the Company until 1925, when a return was made to three factors because of the increased relative importance of mortality gains.

[44] *Thirtieth Annual Report* (1873), pp. 9–10. This was made possible by a New York Law of March 9, 1872. See also law of 1892, section 83.

[45] Testimony of Emory McClintock in *Testimony before the Joint Committee of the Senate and Assembly of the State of New York to Investigate and Examine into the Business Affairs of Life Insurance Companies Doing Business in the State of New York* (Albany, 1906), pp. 1875 ff.

IX. Extension of The Mutual's Market

IMPORTANT AS WAS THE PREPARATION of new and more attractive contracts in the developments of life insurance from 1870 to 1906, it was only one phase of the tremendous growth of the business during those thirty-six years and, compared with the extension of the market, was perhaps not the major phase. The westward expansion of the United States and the rapid industrialization of urban areas provided new opportunities for life insurance, and the building of an agency force commensurate with these opportunities was one of the great achievements of President Winston and President McCurdy. Agents of The Mutual Life followed in the footsteps of the early settlers, multiplied in the large centers of population, and finally went abroad in the wake of commercial and financial interests. Toward the end of this period the Company had salesmen, or "underwriters," in all parts of the United States and in most of the leading business centers of the entire world.

To present in detail the annals of The Mutual's expanding agency system from 1870 to 1906 would require more space than can be allotted to it here, but some of the highlights of that story are essential to an understanding of the Company's history. One of those highlights concerns the extension of business to the South. As was pointed out in Chapter V, all The Mutual's operations below the Mason-Dixon line had to cease during the War between the States, and most of the insurance in force there was ultimately surrendered to the Company. Upon the conclusion of the conflict agencies were reëstablished in Baltimore, Maryland, and Louisville, Kentucky, to do business in the more northernly areas of the South, but the Company showed great hesitancy in pushing activity in these regions and generally shied away from the deep South. The death rate in these areas was high, problems of reconstruction were upsetting, and so much new insurance was being written in the North that expansion in the South was not urgent.

With the hard times which followed 1873 and with more severe competition from The Equitable and the New York Life, hostility toward Southern business began to wane. In 1878 President Winston made an extensive tour of the South and reported that in his opinion [1] insurance

1 *Minutes of the Board of Trustees,* May 15, 1878.

could be written safely in Western Arkansas, Texas, Georgia, South Carolina, and North Carolina, except near the sea coast, as well as in Kentucky and Tennessee. He urged caution only in the swampy parts of Louisiana, Alabama, Mississippi, and Florida. Consequently the approved areas were soon brought within the confines of The Mutual's market or were worked more vigorously than ever, and in the ten ensuing years all the South was placed under the jurisdiction of general agents or of their subordinates—Florida in 1881, Arizona in 1886, Louisiana and Mississippi in 1888, and Alabama in 1889.

Another highlight of the territorial expansion of The Mutual's agency activities was its coverage of the West. During the Civil War, when compensation for loss of Southern business was being sought, the area between the Appalachians and the Mississippi was cultivated more assiduously than it had been previously, but it was not until after peace between the states had been restored that the trans-Mississippi region was seriously opened up by the Company. In 1867 the St. Louis agency covered the states or territories of Missouri, Kansas, Nebraska, and Colorado, but shortly thereafter new areas were allotted to it. In the annual reports we find that business was begun in Minnesota in 1868, in North and South Dakota and Wyoming in 1874, in Utah in 1881, in New Mexico and Oklahoma in 1891, in Montana in 1893, in Nevada in 1895, and in several places in Canada at intermittent dates. Then, in an effort to tap potential markets which might otherwise be poorly served, an Army and Navy Bureau was established (1887) to sell insurance to members of the Nation's armed forces, and in the following year the system of employing special executive agents to coöperate with the general agents in writing large risks was revitalized and enlarged.

Accompanying this expansion of The Mutual's market was the attempt to work that market more effectively. After 1878 a careful record of the territory allotted to a general agent and of his success in it were kept,[2] and in 1881 a definite policy was adopted of breaking up certain large and unwieldy agency territories, which had grown like Topsy, into smaller and more easily worked units. Thus, the number of domestic general agencies increased from fourteen in 1878 to fifty-six in 1900. Some idea of the territorial expansion of the Company's sales force may be gleaned from the accompanying maps.[3]

[2] *Minutes of the Agency Committee*, Aug. 23, 1878.

[3] *The Mutual Life Insurance Company of New York, Exhibit, Paris Exposition, 1900.* It might be added that The Mutual Life ceased doing business in Texas following the passage of the Robertson Law of 1907. This law provided that life companies loan 75 percent of the reserves on policies written on Texan lives in Texas. With this condition The Mutual Life decided it could not comply.

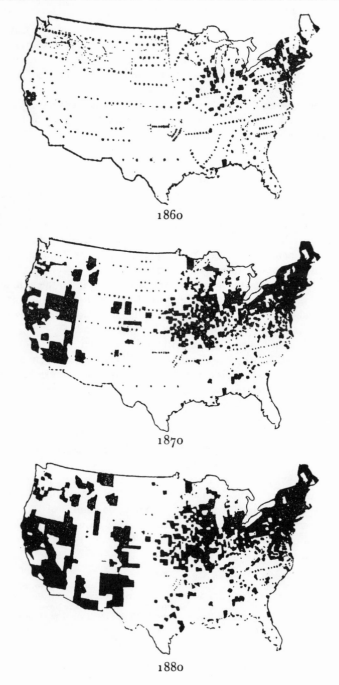

1860

1870

1880

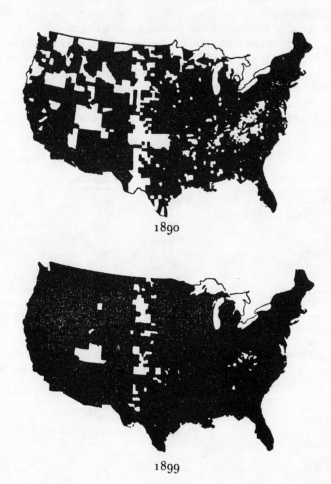

1890

1899

Great as were the business opportunities resulting from the extension and deepening of the home market, they did not entirely satisfy some of the more ambitious souls in The Mutual Life's management. As early as 1868 these men had cast wistful eyes in the direction of overseas markets, and, although the Board of Trustees disapproved at first of their vision, their dream of doing business abroad was ultimately to be realized. When McCurdy became president of the Company and began his great drive for more insurance, he became the champion of their cause. He pointed out that from one-fourth to one-third of the new insurance written by The Equitable and the New York Life had for several years come from their foreign agencies,[4] and he saw no reason why The Mutual should not reap some of this harvest. He believed that with the Company's effective sales methods the cost of obtaining foreign business would not be great, that in most overseas markets mortality rates would be as low as in America, and that when this was not the case higher

TABLE 26

PRINCIPAL FOREIGN AGENCIES

Agency	Date of Inception	Discontinuance of New Business	New Business 1904
Mexico	1886	1911	$2,327,725
Hamburg	1886	1904	145,317
Berlin	1886	1904	112,558
Sydney	1886	1917	1,696,497
London	1886	1917	6,030,769
Porto Rico	1886	1905 [a]	120,518
Paris	1888	1906	8,312,275
Brussels	1889	1914	957,592
Copenhagen	1889	1905	512,917
Genoa	1889	1907	2,377,087
Budapest	1890	1913	1,512,465
Vienna	1890	1913	2,440,109
Cape Town	1890	1917	2,949,740
Amsterdam	1890	1914	334,136
Bermuda	1891	1893	. . .
Madrid	1892	1907	1,096,598
Stockholm	1893	1914	433,418
Glasgow	1894	1900	. . .
Havana	1899	1917	1,097,490
Levant	1899	1906	1,599,954
Shanghai	1900	1904	41,255
Yokohama	1902	1903	221,400
Lisbon	1903	1908	2,477,882
Helsingfors	1906	1914	. . .
Oslo (formerly Christiania)	1906	1912	. . .

[a] Later reopened as a domestic agency.

premiums could be charged without losing a competitive position. These arguments finally won the day, and in 1886 the first foreign agencies were established under the general management of President McCurdy's son, Robert H. These initial undertakings were so remarkably success-

[4] *Minutes of the Board of Trustees,* July 25, 1888.

ful that others were soon begun, and in the home office enthusiasts boasted that the sun never set on The Mutual's flag.

In the course of time, however, the foreign agencies proved to be more troublesome than had been imagined possible. Peculation occurred because of the difficulty of keeping close tabs on the far-flung empire.[5] Hostile governments, especially in their protectionist moments, made life for the Company miserable. Prussia actually prohibited The Mutual from conducting business within its borders in 1900, and the German Empire, in 1904. Other nations harassed the Company in a number of ways, the most common one being to require the investment of large sums in government bonds. By this method The Mutual Life was virtually forced out of Japan, France, Denmark, and Mexico. Finally the outbreak of the Balkan Wars and the World War wrote "finis" to the Company's imperial adventure. The bulk of the business which had been so laboriously put on the books was transferred to local companies, the last arrangement of this kind having been made in 1940. But while the overseas agencies existed, they were a source of pride and income for the Company.

FROM THE GENERAL AGENCY TO THE MANAGERIAL SYSTEM

Closely allied to the enormous undertaking of extending the sales force of The Mutual Life to all parts of the United States and to four overseas continents were the organization and administration of that force. The mere declaration that some new territory had been added to the Company's empire and that a general agent had been placed in charge of it was only the beginning of the work. A plan of campaign had to be devised; an army of agents had to be organized; effective occupation had to take place; and headquarters in New York had to keep the soldiers constantly on the alert. This work was extremely important, for as time went on less and less insurance was sold directly by the home office and more and more by agents.

The system of organizing the field forces, which The Mutual Life had adopted in the late fifties and early sixties,[6] was that of the general agency. Although a few local agents continued to write insurance for the Company and room was made for brokers who placed business with several insurers, the standard practice became the allotting of territory to a general agent for his exclusive cultivation. He himself employed sub-agents and solicitors and determined the amount of their remuneration. With the Company these salesmen had no legal relationship, and

[5] See, for example, *ibid.*, Nov. 24, 1897.
[6] See p. 91.

they were not recognized as representing it in any respect. Neither the general or local agents were allowed to make, alter, or discharge contracts, to make pledges or promises, to bind the Company in any way, or to sign receipts for premiums. Their duties were simply the solicitation and transmission of applications for policies and of premiums. They were middlemen without authority.[7]

Upon the general agents fell the responsibility for the insurance activities of The Mutual Life within their districts. Not only did they have to hire and supervise solicitors, but also they had to maintain appropriate offices, transmit applications for insurance to New York, return the policies to the insured, oversee the collection of premiums and the forwarding of them to the home office, advertise locally, and perform a hundred-and-one other duties involved in the insurance business. Under their contracts they were held entirely accountable for the actions of sub-agents and agents and for the moneys which these men handled. Finally, and most important of all, they had to "produce," as it is called in the trade, substantial amounts of new business or their contracts would not be renewed.[8]

The general agents were placed under such heavy responsibilities that the course of affection between them and the Company did not always run smoothly. Sometimes the general agents lost their loyalty to The Mutual Life, at times they did not write new business enough to satisfy the home office or to earn a good income for themselves, and frequently matters of commissions, to which we shall turn presently, were irritating. In other instances the general agent did not have enough capital to launch his enterprise and asked for advances. In still others that part of the commissions which were aimed to cover operating expenses of the general agency was not used for that purpose. Then, there were general agents who did not, in spite of periodic inspections by representatives from New York, keep their records accurately. Finally, and most important of all, the general agents had difficulty in making their field workers toe prescribed marks.

A combination of these problems led gradually to a complete overhauling of the agency system. When the European field was opened in 1886, persons could not be found who had enough capital and were willing to assume the burdens usually shouldered by domestic general agents. Hence the Company hired salaried managers to take charge of

---

[7] *Thirty-First Annual Report* (1874), pp. 34 ff.

[8] For rules governing the general agencies in 1872 see *Minutes of the Agency Committee,* May 14, 1872. For some years an attempt was made to collect premiums through local banks. *Minutes of the Insurance Committee,* Feb. 14, 1893.

what amounted to branch offices. It had to provide the initial investment in offices and equipment, to direct the foreign agencies, and to assume most of the financial responsibilities. But it did retain in its own hands complete control of all phases of the business from the appointment of the manager to the conduct of the solicitor, and this control had definite advantages.

With the Company providing the working capital, the branch offices were able rapidly to develop new markets. Business came in at such a rate from the overseas agencies that especial virtues were at once attributed to the organization of the sales force. The new system seemed more efficient and more effective than the general agency arrangement and appeared, in fact, to be so good that it was soon being introduced into America. In 1890 [9] and, more especially, in 1898 the Company started to appoint salaried managers in place of general agents, to make contracts directly with sub-agents and local agents, and to assume the responsibilities of handling moneys through agency cashiers. The transition to this system took time because of existing contracts, but by 1905 the changes had been largely accomplished. Henceforth the Company was to have complete control of its agency force.

COMMISSIONS AND QUOTAS

Next to the extension of the market and the reorganization of the agency system, no question concerning selling insurance loomed larger between 1870 and 1906 than how to remunerate agents. At the beginning of this period the general agent received as his commission 30 percent of the first premium, and 7½ percent on four renewals premiums, and a collection fee of 1 or 2 percent on subsequent premiums, but out of the sums thus received he had to pay his agents and agency expenses. With the coming of hard times in 1873 and a more rigid check upon the work of the general agents, these rates were somewhat increased, 7½ percent being allowed on six instead of four renewals, a collection fee of 2 or 3 percent thereafter on renewals, and an additional 2½ percent on the first premium for miscellaneous expenses.[10] Yet these increases did not prove entirely satisfactory, either to the Company or to the agents. The latter pointed out that the depression had caused a large number of surrenders, which cut their commissions on renewals and yet resulted in a gain to the Company, and they felt that they should be paid one large commission on the first premium. Against this proposal the Company took a strong

[9] *Minutes of the Insurance Committee,* Jan. 25, 1892.
[10] *Minutes of the Agency Committee,* Dec. 21, 1872, Nov. 29, 1873, and March 18, 1879.

stand. It argued first, that the abolition of commissions on renewals would lead to a relaxation of solicitors' efforts to keep policies in force and hence to a larger percentage of surrenders [11]—and surrenders, even though they might produce a gain, were not to be desired—and, secondly, it contended that agents were already inclined to work hardest to insure older persons because of the high premiums required at advanced ages and that to pay a single commission would only accentuate this adverse age selection.[12]

In view of these arguments the 1873 commission schedule stood unchanged and was not seriously attacked again until 1879. In that year a reduction in premiums threatened to reduce commissions—a decrease which amounted to 4½ percent on life policies. From this danger general agents immediately tried to protect themselves, pointing out that a diminution of income would make it impossible for them to hold their sales forces together, that the selling costs of The Mutual Life were lower than those of any of the other leading life insurance institutions,[13] and that in the Company the ratio of commissions to assets had greatly declined.[14] Proposals for an increase in the percentages of premiums for commissions were, however, turned down by the Board of Trustees on the ground that agents would be able to maintain their present real income under existing conditions. It was held that the return to specie payment and the decline in prices had so increased the purchasing power of the dollar that a decrease in money income would not be burdensome. Furthermore, the Board reminded the sales force that in 1878 it had authorized the giving of rebates to prospective clients up to 30 percent of the first year's premium—a practice which was, however, abolished after it had been in force a few months [15] —and that this advantage, coupled with a reduction in the size of premiums, would enable the field workers to sell much more insurance.

[11] *Ibid.*, March 18, 1879.
[12] The actuary reported that "at present the Company is paying for a policy of $10,000 having but twenty-five years to run $928.95 and for another, of same amount, having 70 years to run, $212.60. The latter is greatly more valuable to the Company and the absurdity is manifest." *Minutes of the Agency Committee*, March 13, 1879.
[13] According to the *Minutes of the Agency Committee*, Jan. 17, 1876, and March 18, 1879, the average ratios of commissions paid to assets were:

Equitable	.0332	New England Mutual	.0160
Connecticut Mutual	.0168	Mutual Benefit	.0150
New York Life	.0160	Mutual Life	.0117

[14] *Ibid.*, March 17, 1879.
[15] *Ibid.*, Sept. 27, 1878. The rebate was to be 30 percent of the first and second annual premiums on life policies and 15 percent on the first two annual premiums on all other types of policies. See also *Minutes of the Board of Trustees*, July 16, 1879.

In spite of the position taken by the Company at this time, commissions were to rise fairly steadily from the early eighties to the Armstrong Investigation of 1905. When deferred dividend policies were introduced in 1886, 10 percent extra commission on the first premium and renewal commissions for ten instead of six years were allowed with the hope that agents would push this type of contract with more vigor than other forms of insurance.[16] In 1890 the number of renewals on which commissions were allowed was reduced, although this was compensated for in part by increasing the commission on the first premium, and at about the same date differences between the commissions on various types of policies were greatly enlarged. The trend which was taking place can be seen from the following table of commissions paid to and by the

TABLE 27

COMMISSIONS: THE RAYMOND AGENCY, 1888–1903

	COMMISSIONS PAID TO RAYMOND AGENCY			COMMISSIONS PAID BY RAYMOND AGENCY TO ITS SOLICITORS		
Year	Percentage of First Premium	Number of Renewals	Percentage Paid on Renewals	Percentage of First Premium	Number of Renewals	Percentage Paid on Renewals
1888	45–65	5–10	10	30	5–10	5–50
1889	45–65	5–10	10	35	6–10	5–45
1890	45–65	5–10	10	35	4–10	5–45 or 35 flat to 65 flat
1891	30–70	6	10	35	4–6	5–55 or 25–65 flat
1892	25–60	1–5	10–25	25	1–6	5–55
1893	35–80	1–6	7½–10	40	6	5–60 or 45 flat to 70 flat
1894	40–65	1–5	7½–25	50	1–6	5–70
1895	35–80	1–6	7½–10	50	1–6	5–70
1896	45–80	6	10	50	1–6	5–70
1897	45–80	6	10	50	1–6	5–70
1898	45–80	6	10	50	1–6	5–70
1899	45–80	6	10	50	1–6	5–70
1900	45–80	6	10	65	1–6	5–75
1901	45–80	6	10	65	1–6	5–75
1902	45–80	6	10	65	1–6	5–75
1903	45–80	6	10	65	1–6	5–75

[16] The commissions in 1881 were as follows:

Type of Insurance	Percentage of First Year Premium	Percentage on Six Annual Renewals
Children's endowment	10	5
Five year	10	5
Single premium	5	..
All others	30	7½

Flat brokerage fee 35 percent of first annual premium. Extra for advertising 10 percent of first annual premium. Extra for expenses on 1st year 2½ percent. Collection fee 3 percent after expiry of commissions.

Raymond Agency in New York—an agency which had a somewhat favorable position.[17]

The periodic rearrangement of the commission schedule was not, however, the only stimulus given to agents to produce more business. As has been mentioned earlier, executive specials, those supersalesmen who coöperated with the field forces in "cracking" large and difficult cases, were employed extensively after 1888, and, although they were transferred from the executive to the agencies department in 1902, they continued to exert a powerful influence. Up to 1902 they were paid a base salary of about $3,000 and usually received from the general agents all of the commission on the first premium and shared with the solicitors the renewal commissions, as a rule getting half. They were thus well paid, and to improve their record they indulged in rebating, upon which the Company frowned.[18] Indeed, The Mutual Life entered a formal agreement against rebating with other companies, and the New York law of 1889 prohibited it.[19]

Another stimulus to agents was the adoption of the quota system and bonuses for exceeding prescribed requirements. In 1888 John W. Guiteau was appointed to the position of statistician of The Mutual Life, and one of his tasks was to investigate the potentialities of the insurance market within each general agency in order to determine whether or not the territory was being satisfactorily worked. Rough guesses had been attempted previously, but Guiteau endeavored to make them precise and thus became the first analyst of the life insurance market. His work so impressed his superiors that quotas for each agency were soon established and bonuses for meeting the requirements were granted. In 1893, for example, the Raymond Agency was given a quota of $4,000,000 of new business.[20] On anything in excess of this sum, an additional 5 percent commission on the first year's premium was granted, and still another 5 percent on amounts in excess of $8,000,000.[21]

To facilitate the labors of the sales force, The Mutual Life, like all similar institutions, endeavored to establish in the public mind not only its name but also a favorable impression of its operations. Its chief ve-

---

[17] Armstrong Investigation, *Exhibits*, No. 255. A few agencies had overriding commissions to cover extra expenses. Armstrong Investigation, *Testimony*, p. 1310. See Appendix, p. 359.

[18] *Minutes of the Insurance Committee*, Nov. 23, 1905.

[19] *Minutes of the Board of Trustees*, Dec. 28, 1898, and the Armstrong Investigation, *Testimony*, pp. 1086–1087.

[20] Armstrong Investigation, *Exhibits*, No. 260. Those bonuses were not given on "Class D and E" business. See above, footnote 18.

[21] Prizes were also given for production. In 1896 there were "President's Cups" for the most successful agents.

hicles of advertising were the insurance press and pamphlet literature. In the former the Company not only inserted bona fide advertisements, but it also paid editors to run its messages as news articles or editorials. For the campaign against Jacob L. Greene of the Connecticut Mutual, The Mutual, along with The Equitable and the New York Life, hired the services of C. C. Hine, editor of the *Insurance Monitor,* Stephen English of the *Insurance Times,* and Charles J. ("Dollar-a-Line") Smith of the *Insurance Record.* The editor of the *Insurance Monitor* had a fixed price for his Connecticut Mutual extras of $50 a thousand and boasted that he sold them "by the ton." The use of such methods had, however, serious disadvantages, for not only was the practice expensive, but it sustained a group of mercenaries who could be employed for retaliation in kind or who could make a living out of blackmail. English, in fact, served The Equitable's Hyde so successfully in a campaign against The Mutual that McCurdy finally hired him.[22] And a certain Joe Howard, Jr., who worked for both The Mutual and The Equitable, was not above holding up either company.[23] Finally the bitter attacks evoked so much public interest that replies became "news stories" and could be run without charge in the large dailies—a practice used by President Greene of the Connecticut Mutual.

Although the campaigns waged by various companies upon their rivals did not prove to be advantageous, threatened to undermine public confidence in all insurance institutions, and led directly to many state investigations, they continued with more or less vigor throughout this period of managerial domination, being especially evident after the turn of the century in the advertisements of general agents. Nevertheless, there was some indication that advertising was becoming more genteel. The Mutual Life began in 1885 a publication, *The Weekly Statement,* for the enlightenment and encouragement of its agents, and when the managerial system went into operation, it founded a series of advertising pamphlets, *Points,* for the use of its salesmen.[24] Both these papers were relatively free from aspersions on other companies, and the same could be said of The Mutual's advertisements in magazines and newspapers. At the Paris Exposition of 1900 the Company had an elaborate display of wall charts, which were later reduced and arranged in

---

[22] *New York Insurance Investigation* (Albany, 1877), p. 315.

[23] Trustees' investigation of the New York Life (1887).

[24] *The Weekly Statement* became known as *The Statement* in 1901, as *Mutual Interests* in 1907, as *The Mutual Life Quarterly* in 1916, and as *Best Assets* in 1920. *Points* has continued to appear ever since its beginning in 1901. Another house publication was *Applied Salesmanship,* begun in 1922.

book form, portraying the growth and operations of the institution without mention of competitors. And along with this improved tone of The Mutual Life's publicity came a friendlier attitude toward its rivals. James W. Alexander, president of The Equitable, was invited to a meeting of the Board of Trustees to see the unveiling of the Paris Exposition display, and a telegram of greeting was sent to John A. McCall when he became president of the New York Life.[25]

LIBERALIZING THE SELECTION OF RISKS

Although the management of The Mutual Life exerted every effort to increase its sales, it had at the same time to limit its market to good risks. As was explained in Chapter V, the Company had charged from its inception extra premiums for such hazards as travel, war, dangerous occupations, and residence in regions where mortality rates were high and had refused insurance to persons whose health had been impaired. It selected risks for the purpose of establishing a degree of equality among its insured and of keeping its mortality rate below that of the tables which it was using.

As time wore on, many of the dangers against which the Company had endeavored to protect itself were so minimized that it was felt safe to abolish the extras for them. Thus, although restrictions on residence were found in the tontine policies of 1870 and of the nonforfeiture clause contract of 1879, they were absent from the deferred dividend forms of 1886. Only in the foreign business was a kind of residence extra charged, and that was done by requiring high premiums in certain countries such as Mexico and Japan.[26] Likewise, the requirement of permits or of extra premiums for travel did not appear in the rate books after 1885 or in the distribution policies, for ocean and railway transportation had become relatively safe. The only restriction on travel at this time was that no trip could be taken to the torrid zone during the first two years in which a policy was in force. So far as occupational hazards were concerned, the Company stated in 1886 that it would not insure bartenders, ordinary seamen, engineers, firemen, and operators of blast furnaces and that its contracts did not cover during the first two years death from suicide, mining, blasting, aeronautic ascensions, service upon trains or vessels, war, and submarine labor. Curbs of this kind were maintained by The Mutual Life even after 1900, although dispensation from them could be obtained by permission or by the payment of extras. By 1905

---

25 *Minutes of the Board of Trustees,* Feb. 15, 1892, and Feb. 21, 1900.

26 For Mexico the premiums averaged 37 percent higher than home rates, and for Japan 8 percent higher. See *Minutes of the Insurance Committee,* July 27, 1886, and Apr. 24, 1888.

only eight of fifty-one representative companies imposed occupational restrictions after a policy had been in force one or two years.[27]

Among other special risks against which The Mutual Life endeavored to protect its policyholders, those arising from suicide, alcoholic drink, large policies, and war were the most important. In 1884 New York State legislated against refusing a benefit in case of suicide committed by an insane person and subsequently some of the companies dropped all restrictions on self-inflicted death. The Mutual Life was, however, reluctant to follow suit, for suicides had been numerous during the depression of 1873 and were to loom important in the crisis of 1893. Nevertheless, by 1905 this Company, along with all but one other, agreed to pay claims in case of suicide if a policy had been in force one or two years.[28] Poor risks caused by alcoholic drink were, on the other hand, weeded out insofar as possible by refusing insurance to those who were not of temperate habits. The policy of 1875 with the following anti-alcoholic provision was thus the exception rather than the rule.

If the said person, upon whose death this policy matures shall die by disease, violence, or accident brought about by intoxication, or shall impair his health by narcotic or alcoholic stimulants, or shall have delirium tremens, the Company shall be released from all liability on account of this contract.

War clauses were, however, regularly a part of The Mutual's contract, but a difficulty arose over how much to charge in case of military service. In Germany in 1888 The Mutual increased the rates for those who were liable to military service from between 15.1 percent and 1.3 percent of its normal premiums and levied an extra $3 per thousand on combatants. During the Spanish American War and the Boer War, on the other hand, the Company returned premiums in the case of the death of a person who had no war permit, but on policies for which a war permit was given an extra was charged with the understanding that a refund would be made of that part of it not needed to cover increased mortality. Thus, in the case of Americans who fought in the Spanish American War the extra actually necessary for those who did not go to the Philippines was 1 ⅔ percent of the amount insured.[29]

[27] In this connection it should be noted that in 1886 and more especially in 1888, The Mutual's restrictive clauses appeared in the applications rather than in the policy forms— a change that was of little importance because by 1888 the application was recognized as part of the contract and was attached to the policy itself. The last contract which did not cover death from hostile Indians seems to have been the Tontines of 1870. See also L. G. Fouse, "Policy Contracts in Life Insurance," *Annals of the American Academy of Political and Social Science* (Philadelphia, 1905), pp. 39–40.

[28] *Ibid.*

[29] *Minutes of the Insurance Committee,* Apr. 24, 1888, and *Fifty-Sixth Annual Report,* p. 15.

The least troublesome of all these special risks in the period from 1870 to 1906 was the large policy. Although the limit of insurance on one life was increased from $20,000 to $30,000 in 1872 and a few years later to $50,000, a careful examination of the Company's experience with cases in excess of $20,000 showed that mortality among them was about two-thirds as high as among all policyholders. This finding provided Mc-Curdy with a way of increasing insurance in force. He argued that inasmuch as holders of large amounts of insurance had a low death rate, there was no danger in issuing large policies. Consequently he got the limits on one life extended to $100,000 in 1887 [30] and in 1895 the right to determine what the maximum amounts should be. Thus, in 1899 one of the most successful life insurance salesmen of the period, C. F. Troupe, who wrote $21,000,000 of insurance in twenty years, placed a million dollar policy with The Mutual—the largest single policy that had ever been issued.[31] The hazard in such cases was real, and at the time some hesitancy was felt in accepting risks of this kind. To protect itself, the Company required the applicant to meet high standards of health and probity and reinsured part of the risk in other companies.

THE DEPARTMENT OF REVISION

Measuring the integrity of prospective policyholders has always been one of the most puzzling problems of selection, and yet it is one of the most important. False information in the application may upset the expected rate of mortality, financial inability to pay premiums leads to early surrenders, and general dishonesty may result in attempts to make false claims upon the insurer. These dangers were realized from the first, but the responsibility of meeting them was placed largely on the agent, who was supposed to "know" his client.

To prevent the perpetration of all frauds against insurance companies was impossible, and from time to time The Mutual Life was the victim of dishonest claims. Perhaps the most famous instance of this kind was the conspiracy of John W. Hillmon of Medicine Lodge, Kansas, his wife, and two other relatives to cheat not only The Mutual, but also the New York Life and the Connecticut Mutual. Shortly after a large amount of insurance had been placed upon the life of Hillmon, he was declared by his wife to be dead. An investigation showed, however, that the body which was supposed to be that of Hillmon was not his. Although the head of the murdered man had been partially burned, dentists proved that the teeth were not the same as Hillmon's, and physi-

---

[30] *Minutes of the Insurance Committee*, Dec. 22, 1887.   [31] *Leslie's Weekly*, Sept. 9, 1899.

cians testified that the stature of the dead man was several inches in excess of the conspirator's. Confronted with this evidence, the plotters confessed their guilt, but for twenty years the case was fought in the courts, because of disagreements by juries, until the insurance companies finally won. The litigation was expensive, costing many times the amount of the insurance, but the defendants stuck tenaciously to their guns on the ground that policyholders' money should not be sacrificed in the payment of such claims.[32]

To protect itself against such unscrupulous persons as the Hillmons, The Mutual Life urged its agents to be more wary in writing insurance on persons of questionable character and checked more carefully on documents submitted in proof of death. From the early 1850's to the 1920's the Company required as evidence of the decease of an insured sworn statements from the attending physician, a friend, and the undertakers, but in the 1880's it demanded more frequently reports from one of its agents or investigators.

In 1876 Dan Gillette, brother of the Company's medical examiner, was employed to solve a fraudulent claim and was so successful that he was given a regular position as special detective. When the Hillmon case appeared on the docket, Gillette began to realize more clearly than ever before that to wait until a policy became a claim before investigating the moral hazard involved was like calling the fire department after one's house had burned down. He proposed that a Department of Revision be created not only to check death claims and the insurability of policyholders but also to scrutinize the integrity of and to secure other information about applicants before insurance on their lives was issued. So logical did this plan seem that in 1884 it was adopted—the first thing of its kind in American life insurance.[33]

Although the new department was not equipped at first to handle every case, it was expanded in 1890 by bringing Charles B. Holmes, owner of a credit service bureau, into The Mutual Life. His list of correspondents and his credit files formed the basis for the organization within the

[32] *Thirty-Seventh Annual Report*, p. 18; *Minutes of the Board of Trustees*, Oct. 27, 1897, and John B. Lewis and Charles C. Bombaugh, *Stratagems and Conspiracies to Defraud Life Insurance Companies* (Baltimore, 1896), pp. 173 ff. There was some discussion about the claim on Boss Tweed's endowment policy. It was, however, ordered paid, Sept. 30, 1878. *Minutes of the Board of Trustees*, Jan. 15, 1879. The Committee on Mortuary Claims submitted 65 cases to the Law Department during 1878. It was found that twenty-six of these claims were just. Hence they were ordered paid. Of the other cases eighteen concerned intemperance, fourteen suicide, three forfeiture, three misrepresentations in applications, and eight suits by policyholders.

[33] The American Service Bureau, Inc., owned and controlled by the American Life Convention, was set up in 1921 to perform these services for many of the companies.

Company of The National Commercial Agency which was capable of checking about one-fifth of prospective risks.[34] In the year 1894, when $211,000,000 of new insurance was applied for, the National Commercial Agency sent out blanks for reports on $43,300,100, made unfavorable returns on $2,964,000, and classified as questionable $4,743,500. In the same year the Department of Revision tracked down an absconding agent, uncovered some fraudulent death claims, and investigated 2,471 of the Company's medical examiners.

MEDICAL SELECTION

Valuable as were the services of the Department of Revision, the medical examination remained the most important basis for determining what risks should be accepted and what should be refused. Every effort was made to have a corps of trustworthy examiners scattered throughout the areas in which The Mutual Life did business and to have them probe deeply into the physical conditions of applicants. The application form of 1889, which was the first attached to a policy, demanded, like its predecessor, a great amount of detail about the illnesses of the prospective policyholders. By 1899, when the application was printed in the policy itself, more attention was being placed upon the health record of the applicant's family and upon degenerative diseases than had formerly been the case.[35] Logically enough, specific questions about certain diseases which were being brought under control, such as yellow fever, were entirely dropped.

Medical selection reduced decidedly the number of those who died from tuberculosis, heart diseases, Bright's disease, or brain diseases soon after taking out life insurance, but had apparently little effect in improving the rate of mortality from other causes.[36] For this reason medical examiners concentrated their efforts on preventing those who showed tendencies toward the former diseases from becoming insured. They realized that a lower mortality rate from pneumonia, influenza, typhoid fever, malaria, and certain other diseases could be effected only by advances in medicine and public health.

---

[34] Correspondents usually received $.25 for a report. This was subsequently increased to $.50. See the *Minutes of the Insurance Committee*, Feb. 12, 1895.

[35] See above, p. 78.

[36] Elias J. Marsh and Granville M. White, *Mortality Records of The Mutual Life Insurance Company of New York for Fifty-six Years, from 1843 to 1898* (New York, The Mutual Life, 1900). The only important measures taken by The Mutual Life, which might be classified under the rubric "preventive medicine," were sporadic efforts to improve sanitary conditions in certain areas and the distribution to policyholders about 1900 of pamphlets describing how to care for patients suffering from disease or accident.

The ultimate purpose of medical selection is to eliminate the poor risks and to reduce in so far as possible the death rate among policy-holders. The lower that rate is, the cheaper life insurance becomes. To get a low ratio of actual to expected mortality, it has been necessary constantly to insure a number of young lives as well as to select good physical risks, for among the young there is the greatest possibility of lengthening the expected span of life. The Mutual Life's ratio of actual to expected mortality from 1875 to 1906 shows only a slight improvement, for by the former date the Company had already a wide distribution of ages among its members, and improvements in public health had not been extensive enough to make much of an impression on the rate.

TABLE 28

RATIO OF ACTUAL TO EXPECTED MORTALITY: THE MUTUAL LIFE [a]

1875	93.1	1882–87	Unavail-	1893	86.4	1900	73.9
1876	84.4		able	1894	78.0	1901	74.2
1877	73.2	1888	82.9	1895	78.0	1902	69.8
1878	74.3	1889	75.4	1896	78.2 [b]	1903	78.6
1879	79.7	1890	79.9	1897	76.6	1904	81.9
1880	84.8	1891	79.0	1898	79.0	1905	80.4
1881	78.3	1892	82.9	1899	92.9	1906	75.0

[a] From manuscript volume in Actuary's Library, *Mortality Experience, 1875–1903*, and manuscript volume entitled *Abstract of Annual Statements*.

[b] Change in method of computation.

X. Broadening the Investment Portfolio

THE CHANGES in American life insurance which set off the period 1843–1870 from the period 1870–1906 were not limited to the introduction of deferred dividend policies, the liberalization of the contract, the extension of the agency force, the appearance of managerial domination, improvement in the selection of risks, or even the great growth of insurance itself. Indeed, one of the most important differences between life insurance as it was practiced in the thirty years prior to 1870 and as it was conducted in the thirty years prior to 1906 concerned investments. In the latter three decades the assets of life insurance companies grew to such proportions that they completely dwarfed the earlier accumulations. So large did they become, in fact, that they were not able to find employment in the local fields where such funds had previously been used, and they had of necessity to seek a broader range. The most attractive new outlet seemed to be that of securities, especially railroad securities, and by 1900 life companies had more than 31 percent of their assets in these stocks and bonds and 37.7 percent in corporate holdings.[1] This shift in the character of life insurance investments was far reaching, as we shall see, but it was not the only one which took place. There was a very marked falling off in the proportion of mortgage loans made by the life insurance companies, an increase in policy loans, and a slight augmentation of real estate held. Finally, there was a breakdown of state protectionism, which had required the holding of assets within certain political jurisdictions, and there was the very important fact that the secular trend in interest rates from the 1870's to 1906 was downward.

LOOSENING THE STRAIT JACKET OF INVESTMENT LAW

When The Mutual Life began business in 1843, its investments were limited by the terms of its charter to mortgage loans on New York real estate and to the bonds of the United States, New York State, and incorporated municipalities of New York State. Following the depression of 1848 restrictions on life insurance investments were tightened

[1] Zartman, *The Investments of Life Insurance Companies*, p. 14.

by New York's first general insurance law (April 10, 1849). Henceforth life insurance companies of the state could not buy or make collateral loans on New York State municipal bonds which were selling below par, could not deal in any commodities or engage in any business except life insurance, could possess only that real estate which was necessary for the conduct of their business or which came to them in the settlement of debts, and had to sell all real estate, except home office buildings, within five years—a provision that was added because of English experience with large accumulations of land under the rule of mortmain.[2] During the depression of 1857, however, when life insurance companies were experiencing difficulties with investments, the investment laws of incorporated life companies were somewhat extended so as to permit the purchase of stocks or bonds of any corporation domiciled in the State of New York and to make loans on such securities if the market value was 10 per cent more than the sum loaned thereon.[3] Then, in 1868, the privilege of making mortgage loans outside the state, but within a radius of fifty miles from New York City, was granted.[4]

The objectives which such curbs were expected to attain were, first, the safeguarding of life insurance funds and, secondly and less laudatorily, the keeping of moneys within the borders of New York State. The actual results of such policies were not, however, so satisfactory as had been originally expected, for not only did the very small-gauge outlets for insurance funds force New York companies to make loans on undesirable security or to accept low rates of interest but also the attempt to prevent capital from going outside the state evoked retaliation in kind from other states. Just how important this latter development was can be seen from the fact that of the nine states in 1870 having general laws regarding the investment of life insurance assets, only three went so far as to permit their companies to purchase even the bonds of other states.[5]

Although new legislation to protect life insurance funds was passed in the 1870's because of the plethora of failures among life insurance companies—the total loss to policyholders in this decade was about $35,000,000—,[6] the strait jacket into which investments had been placed was considerably loosened from 1870 to 1905. The severe depression of 1873 made clear the inadequacy of existing statutes to achieve safety and remunerative employment of life insurance accumulations. New York State attempted to meet this situation by its very important law of 1875.

[2] Laws of the State of New York, 1849, Chapter 308.
[3] *Ibid.*, 1857, Chapter 469.   [4] *Ibid.*, 1868, Chapter 318.   [5] Zartman, *op. cit.*, pp. 162–164.
[6] John A. McCall, *A Review of Life Insurance* (New York, 1898), pp. 15–17.

This act opened a new field to New York companies, for, although it allowed mortgage loans only within those states adjacent to New York, it permitted New York companies to invest their funds in or to make collateral loans on the state, county, and municipal bonds of any state or on the stocks and bonds of any corporation within any state where the companies were transacting business.[7] It was this law, therefore, which led to widescale investment in the stocks and bonds of private corporations and was to lead life insurance companies ultimately to entrepreneurial practices that were condemned in 1905.

This law of 1875 was soon followed by others which aimed to extend the legal boundaries within which life insurance companies might place their funds. In 1876 New York permitted its companies to purchase real estate beyond that required for offices,[8] in 1883, to buy foreign or out-of-state real estate property necessary for the conduct of its business,[9] and in 1896, if approval was obtained from the supreme court of the state, to invest moneys obtained from the sale of real estate in new real estate, though none of these assets could be held for more than five years.[10] In 1886 the Empire State allowed its life insurance companies to make mortgage loans in any state or foreign country where they were doing business.[11] In 1892 it granted its statutory permission to make loans on policies up to their full legal reserve, required that investments must be income-bearing or dividend-paying, and placed no limits on the amount of cash which could be deposited in banks.[12]

This extension of the fields open to New York companies for the investment of their funds was accompanied by similar action by other states. By 1905 the twenty-two states which did most of the life insurance business had laws regulating investments. Of these, eighteen allowed their companies to buy the bonds of any state, and fourteen, the bonds of any county or municipality. Only four—Georgia, Nebraska, Pennsylvania, and Texas—confined mortgage loans to property of the home state of the Company. Nearly all allowed the purchase of corporate securities, although a few ostracized bonds and stocks in mining and some other types of companies. Nine states made definite provisions for policy loans up to a certain percentage of the reserve. A majority permitted collateral loans on securities which the companies had a legal right to own. And Massachusetts did away in 1888 with all restrictions on life insurance investments. Only in foreign countries was there a trend toward keeping life insurance money at home, and in

---

[7] Laws of the State of New York, 1875, Chapter 423.
[8] *Ibid.*, 1876, Chapter 357.   [9] *Ibid.*, 1883, Chapter 361 and 1885, Chapter 394.
[10] *Ibid.*, 1896, Chapter 35.   [11] *Ibid.*, 1886, Chapter 394.   [12] *Ibid.*, 1892, Chapter 690.

these lands legislation usually took the form of requiring the purchase of government securities.[13]

BROADENING THE INVESTMENT PORTFOLIO

Greater freedom in the investment of life insurance funds was an absolute necessity, for not only did the assets of life companies increase from $269,520,441 in 1870 to $2,924,253,848 in 1906 but also most of the large companies were in the East, and they needed to invest in other areas almost as much as other areas needed to have the use of their capital.

Furthermore, the economic expansion of the United States created such a large demand for capital over such wide expanses of territory that the earlier restrictions on life insurance investments became obsolete. The building of railways and of great industrial establishments brought a tremendous quantity of rail and industrial bonds into the market. The settling of the West and the mechanization of agriculture gave an impetus to farm mortgages for new buildings, land, and implements. Greater city and state enterprises resulted in an increase in municipal and state financing. From these new opportunities for the use of capital life insurance companies were not to be kept by outmoded regional jealousies.

Financing the industrial, commercial, and to some extent agricultural expansion of the United States was made relatively easy for investment institutions by the development of the corporation and by the centralized marketing of corporate stocks and bonds. Although the corporate form of business organization was centuries old, it was only after the panic of 1873 that it began to be, as Thorstein Veblen extravagantly said, "the master institution of civilized life." [14] Corporate financing was furthered by bond issues secured by corporate mortgages with provisions for foreclosing on property in case of default, by corporate trust companies which began to replace individual trustees, and by the appearance of holding companies, which by the Pennsylvania statutes of 1868 and 1872 and by the famous New Jersey law of 1889 allowed cor-

13 Zartman, op. cit., chap. vi, and R. L. Cox, "Statutory Direction of Life Insurance Investments," Proceedings Association of Life Insurance Presidents (New York, 1924), XVIII, p. 133.

14 Absentee Ownership and Business Enterprise (New York, 1923), p. 86. See also Thomas C. Cochran and William Miller, The Age of Enterprise; a Social History of Industrial America (New York, 1942); Adolph A. Berle, Jr., and Gardiner C. Means, The Modern Corporation and Private Property (New York and Chicago, 1932); George W. Edwards, The Evolution of Finance Capitalism (London and New York, 1938); and George Heberton Evans, Jr., "Business Incorporations: Their Nature and Significance," Journal of Economic History (New York, Dec., 1941), pp. 67 ff.

porations to hold the stocks of other companies. In 1869 the New York Stock Exchange was established by the amalgamation of three existing bodies in the Exchange, the Open Board, and the Government Bond Department—and other exchanges were soon created in New York, Baltimore, Boston, Chicago, Philadelphia, and San Francisco. From 1870 to 1910 the number of stocks listed in the New York Stock Exchange increased from 143 to 426, and the number of bonds from 200 to 1,013.[15] On November 28, 1879, the New York Stock Exchange attained a peak turnover of 700,000 shares; in December, 1886, the million-share-a-day mark was set; and on April 30, 1913, the high, up to that time, of 3,281,-226 shares was reached. In this corporate growth railroads played a leading role. From 1873 to 1879 about $1,000,000,000 of new railroad securities were put on the market, and between 1880 and 1890 the par value of railroad securities was increased by $4,000,000,000. Yet industrial securities were not completely overshadowed, for the number listed on the New York Stock Exchange went up from 20 in 1898 to 86 in 1905. John Moody stated in 1904 that there were 445 "trusts" with a total capital of $20,000,000,000 in the industrial, railroad, and public utility fields. The United States Steel Corporation was capitalized for $1,370,000,000—the first billion dollar corporation; nine other incorporated companies were capitalized at over $100,000,000, and more than one hundred exceeded the $10,000,000 mark. The great flood of securities thus placed on the market was further swollen by a small increase in the Federal funded debt as a result of the Spanish American War, by an increase in municipal indebtedness between 1890 and 1902 of $587,000,000, and by the augmentation of all state and other local debts of about $85,000,000 within the same period.[16]

If life insurance companies had been prevented from investing their funds in the securities of private corporations, they would have been deprived of an enormous market and of relatively high yields. The companies realized the opportunities created by corporate securities and, as soon as laws allowed, began to buy them in large amounts, particularly railroad bonds and stocks. Although there was still some financial manipulation of rails, state regulation, begun by Massachusetts in 1869, Federal intervention, initiated by the Interstate Commerce Act of 1887, and the pumping of some water out of railroad stocks in the depression of 1873 indicated that investments in the new arteries of commerce

15 New York Stock Exchange Bulletin, Feb., 1932, p. 1.

16 William J. Shultz and M. R. Caine, Financial Development of the United States (New York, 1937), pp. 388, 433, 441, and 456, and George Edwards, op. cit., p. 167. See Table 57, Appendix.

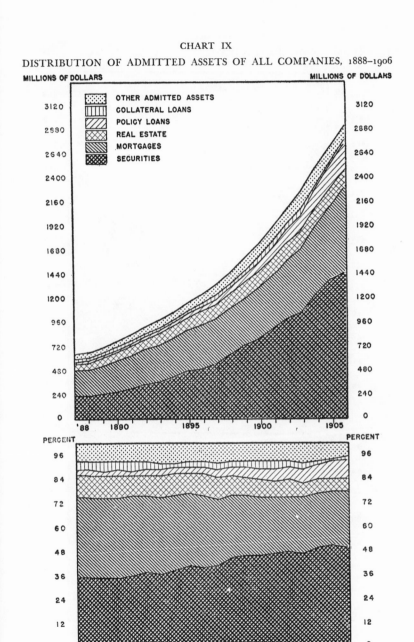

CHART IX

DISTRIBUTION OF ADMITTED ASSETS OF ALL COMPANIES, 1888–1906

MILLIONS OF DOLLARS   MILLIONS OF DOLLARS

- OTHER ADMITTED ASSETS
- COLLATERAL LOANS
- POLICY LOANS
- REAL ESTATE
- MORTGAGES
- SECURITIES

Source: *Spectator Insurance Yearbook* (Philadelphia, 1889–1907).

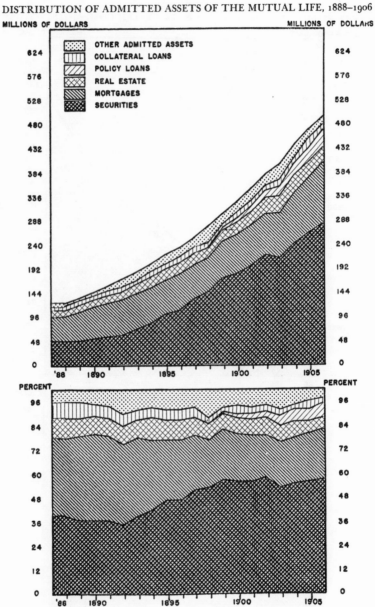

CHART X

DISTRIBUTION OF ADMITTED ASSETS OF THE MUTUAL LIFE, 1888–1906

MILLIONS OF DOLLARS   MILLIONS OF DOLLARS

OTHER ADMITTED ASSETS
COLLATERAL LOANS
POLICY LOANS
REAL ESTATE
MORTGAGES
SECURITIES

were going to be less speculative than they had been previously. Gradually, then, life insurance companies began to purchase securities, especially of railroads, to reduce drastically the proportion of mortgage loans.[17]

Like other life insurance companies, The Mutual Life began to alter the composition of its portfolio in the late 1870's and more particularly in the 1880's. The Company acquired its first railroad bonds and made its first collateral loans on securities in 1880 and obtained its first railroad stock in 1883. Total securities rose from 11.3 percent of admitted assets in 1871 to 57 percent in 1906. Of these securities, railroad stocks and bonds increased from 4.8 percent of admitted assets in 1881 to 41.4 percent in 1906. Real estate—mostly in the form of office buildings at home and abroad—collateral loans, policy loans, public utility securities, and, in the 1890's, bank stocks gained in favor. Mortgage loans, which had accounted for 76.8 percent of admitted assets in 1871, declined to 24.6 percent in 1906.

INVESTMENT EARNINGS

To ascertain the absolute net interest earned on these investments, that is, the gross interest less investment expenses and investment losses, is extremely difficult, if not impossible, because of the nature of life insurance accounting. It may be well, indeed, before any such attempt at estimating rate of earnings is made, to glance briefly at the idiosyncrasies of life insurance accountancy. In 1874 the National Convention of Insurance Commissioners, which had been founded in 1871 and which came to include most of the state insurance superintendents, adopted the so-called Convention Form in order to standardize the financial reports of all life companies.[18] In all essential details this form of 1874 has remained in use to the present date and consequently does not reflect the tremendous progress that has been made in the accountancy field.

The Convention Form begins with an itemized statement of receipts for a given year, which are added to the ledger assets as of the closing of the books of the preceding year. This is followed by itemized disbursements for the year, the sum of which is subtracted from the total attained above to give the new ledger assets, which in turn are itemized. Ledger assets (values on the company's books) are followed by non-ledger assets, which include chiefly due and accrued interest and rents,

17 *Proceedings Association of Life Insurance Presidents* XIII (1919), 128.
18 Consult C. O. Shepherd, "The Convention Statement," *The Record*, American Institute of Actuaries (Vol. XXVI, Part 1, No. 53) (May, 1937), pp. 103 ff.

excess of market value of stocks and nonamortizable bonds over book values, and net amount of uncollected and deferred premiums. From this total are subtracted the assets not admitted, which include the excess of book values over market value of nonamortizable bonds and stocks, any interest due and accrued not admitted, and other miscellaneous items. The balance gives the admitted assets. The liabilities consist chiefly of policy reserves, amounts held on deposit for policyholders and beneficiaries, policy claims outstanding, unpaid expenses, amounts held for dividends payable, and special reserve funds. The balancing item to equal the admitted assets is the company's surplus.

TABLE 29

RATE OF INTEREST EARNED ON LEDGER ASSETS [a]

(Twenty-five companies to 1893; Twenty-eight companies after 1893)

Year	Full Mean Rates	Bonds and Stocks	Loans on Mortgages	Real Estate	All Other Securities
1875	6.81	...	...	...	...
1876	6.66	...	...	...	...
1877	6.38	...	...	...	...
1878	5.90	...	...	...	...
1879	5.85	...	...	...	...
1880	5.46	...	...	...	...
1881	5.49	...	...	...	...
1882	5.54	...	...	...	...
1883	5.51	...	...	...	...
1884	5.44	...	...	...	...
1885	5.41	...	...	...	...
1886	5.36	...	...	...	...
1887	5.44	...	...	...	...
1888	5.40	...	...	...	...
1889	5.22	...	...	...	...
1890	5.14	...	...	...	...
1891	5.19	...	...	...	...
1892	5.07	...	...	...	...
1893	5.06	...	...	...	...
1894	4.99	4.88	5.66	4.21	3.88
1895	4.99	4.75	5.48	4.18	5.04
1896	4.90	4.69	5.44	4.27	4.52
1897	4.85	4.70	5.32	4.47	4.36
1898	4.87	4.75	5.29	4.83	4.18
1899	4.80	4.68	5.10	5.02	4.34
1900	4.70	4.51	4.99	5.27	4.25
1901	4.63	4.50	4.87	5.46	4.05
1902	4.59	4.34	4.81	5.69	4.35
1903	4.61	4.36	4.78	5.82	4.43
1904	4.59	4.34	4.84	5.79	4.39
1905	4.57	4.34	4.83	6.12	4.25
1906	4.63	4.27	4.82	6.48	4.77

[a] Frederick L. Hoffman, "Fifty years of American Life Insurance Progress," *Quarterly Publications* of the American Statistical Association, 1911, pp. 744–745.

The Convention Form has been criticized because it does not follow those accounting practices and terms which are employed in other businesses and because it is not easily understood by a person unfamiliar with life insurance. Yet, criticism of the Convention Form should not be too harsh, because company books tell a fuller story than the statement made in the Form. Nevertheless, life insurance accountancy creates many difficulties in computing accurate yields on investments. In gross yields, no allowance is made for investment expenses, while in net yields, "investment expenses," which are determined according to a formula that includes an item for overhead, are deducted, but losses of principal are, as is usually the case in accounting, excluded from the computation. This fact tends to make investing seem more remunerative than it actually is. In spite of deficiencies in the statistics, however, some idea of rates of interest can be and is arrived at for practical purposes.

From these tables, a declining rate of earning on life insurance investments can be observed. In November, 1898, The Mutual Life began to lend on mortgages under 5 percent.[19] On January 1, 1905, the Company had $19,143,100 on mortgages at 4 percent, $2,000,000 at 4⅛ percent, $51,001,475 at 4½ percent, $27,457,377.45 at 5 percent, $140,000 at 5½ percent, and $2,285,940.97 at 6 percent.[20] The earning power of railroad bonds was also declining.

To obtain a more accurate picture of yield than is given by these tables, some estimate of the ratio of investment expenses to assets is necessary. In the period from 1896 to 1904, when statistics are available, such ratios for some companies ran as high as 2.77 percent of mean assets and some as low as .06 percent. On real estate the percentages were much higher, ranging from 1.6 to 29.9, while they were relatively low on security investments and mortgage loans. Investment expenses thus explain in part why life insurance companies tended to shift their portfolios to stocks and bonds.[21]

Important as it was to secure a satisfactory yield from investments, it was by no means so necessary as to protect principal from loss. President McCurdy was clear on this point. "The practice of this Company has been, in seeking for investments, to look firstly for entire security, and secondly for productiveness."[22] To determine what class of securities was the safest was not an easy task. In periods of severe depression, especially after 1873 and 1893, the Company had to take over

19 *Minutes of the Finance Committee*, Jan. 25, 1899.   20 *Ibid.*, Jan. 11, 1905.
21 Zartman, *op. cit.*, pp. 116, 119, 121.   22 *Fifty-Ninth Annual Report* (1902), p. 19.

large blocks of real estate on foreclosure proceedings, and some loss
was experienced. In 1893 a list of one hundred and ninety-six stocks
shrank 14.57 percent, and a list of three hundred and forty-three bonds

TABLE 30

THE MUTUAL LIFE; RATE OF EARNINGS [a]

(Figures in last four columns based on market values; include capital gains and losses)

Years	Gross Interest Rates on Mean Admitted Assets	Net Interest Rates on Mean Admitted Assets	Rate of Earnings of Total Assets	Rate of Earnings of Real Estate	Rate of Earnings of Mortgage Loans	Rate of Earnings of Bonds and Stocks
1871	6.58	...	6.2	...	...	...
1872	6.67	...	6.8	4.6	6.8	6.0
1873	6.70	...	6.7	2.7	6.9	6.2
1874	6.56	...	6.8	1.7	7.2	8.1
1875	6.47	...	6.8	1.6	7.1	11.6
1876	6.41	...	5.6	1.8	7.0	−5.7
1877	6.15	...	5.3	1.2	6.9	3.8
1878	5.75	...	6.8	1.2	6.6	7.3
1879	5.70	...	5.2	2.3	6.9	4.4
1880	5.55	...	6.6	2.9	6.7	15.2
1881	5.40	...	5.9	3.2	6.6	8.6
1882	5.44	...	5.4	3.1	6.2	5.2
1883	5.29	...	5.7	2.8	6.0	7.1
1884	5.22	...	4.5	2.7	5.8	4.3
1885	5.23	...	7.2	3.4	5.8	11.2
1886	5.03	...	5.3	3.7	5.7	6.2
1887	5.04	...	4.5	3.9	5.5	3.9
1888	5.03	...	6.0	3.5	5.9	7.8
1889	4.87	...	3.4	3.5	4.0	1.5
1890	5.07	...	5.4	5.2	5.2	5.9
1891	5.06	...	3.8	5.1	5.5	5.2
1892	4.86	...	6.1	4.9	5.4	8.0
1893	4.88	...	4.5	4.6	4.6	2.9
1894	4.80	...	6.9	4.4	5.5	3.3
1895	5.13	...	8.9	3.4	5.5	3.4
1896	4.55	...	1.7	−2.7	5.3	5.0
1897	4.40	4.05	5.1	−6.2	5.2	7.7
1898	4.40	4.05	6.3	−2.4	5.3	8.8
1899	4.46	4.11	6.3	5.6	5.0	7.4
1900	4.23	3.86	5.1	4.6	4.8	5.7
1901	4.08	3.73	5.5	4.5	4.7	6.5
1902	4.06	3.67	4.5	4.7	4.6	4.7
1903	4.33	3.96	2.3	4.9	4.6	0.5
1904	4.33	3.98	6.7	4.8	4.7	8.5

[a] All columns except one and two are taken from Lester W. Zartman, *The Investments of Life Insurance Companies* (New York, 1906). Columns one and two are from Company figures.

shrank 6.76 percent, but the shrinkage in the market value of the stocks
and bonds owned by The Mutual Life was only 1.136 percent.[23] Fluctuations in the value of securities was greater than that of other parts

[23] *Minutes of the Finance Committee*, Jan. 31, 1894.

of the portfolio, because there was an active market for stocks and bonds, but within the years under discussion actual losses were small. Collateral loans were usually made with a margin of about 40 percent, which practically precluded loss, and were approved because of their safety and flexibility. In them, however, competition with commercial banks was very keen and interest rates were usually low. In 1894 demand loans were at 2.54 percent and time loans at 5.25 percent.[24] Table 30 gives some idea of the security of various investments. The small returns or losses on real estate should, however, be set against the apparently

TABLE 31

GEOGRAPHICAL DISTRIBUTION OF MORTGAGE LOANS AND REAL ESTATE: THE MUTUAL LIFE [a]

MORTGAGE LOANS		FORECLOSED REAL ESTATE		
Place	Amount	Place	Pieces	Assets
1878		1904		
New York City	$26,446,482	New York City		
New York State	14,372,311	Manhattan	3	$497,166.40
Brooklyn	4,666,500	Brooklyn	1	100,000.00
New Jersey	10,321,624	Richmond	4	67,850.73
Pennsylvania	1,224,050	Rochester	28	251,717.39
Massachusetts	214,000	Elmira	2	128,138.24
Connecticut	53,000	Syracuse	17	230,639.78
		Buffalo	3	113,000.00
1904		Lockport	3	30,791.44
New York City (Man-		Jamestown	3	5,317.67
hattan)	$74,388,750.46	Balance of State	22	114,245.57
Temporary Loans	410,000.00	Pennsylvania	5	117,775.78
Brooklyn, N.Y.	5,280,628.00	New Jersey	35	172,972.34
Rochester, N.Y.	2,170,405.10			
New York State	5,950,081.82			
New Jersey	10,494,090.54			
Pennsylvania	2,258,527.50			
California	500,000.00			
Massachusetts	460,410.00			
Maryland	100,000.00			
Connecticut	15,000.00			

[a] Minutes of the Finance Committee, Jan. 15, 1879, and Jan. 18, 1905. See also William W. McClinch, "Life Insurance Investments in National Developments," Proceedings Association of Life Insurance Presidents, 1922, pp. 41 ff.

stable character of mortgage loans, for most of the real estate was obtained through foreclosure proceedings.

In this connection, reference should be made to the fact that The Mutual Life endeavored to distribute its investments geographically in

[24] Ibid., Jan. 30, 1895. Collateral loans were not made on industrials, and only on securities which had paid interest or dividends in the preceding five years. Armstrong Investigation, Testimony, pp. 461–462.

order to satisfy its policyholders in various regions that their capital was not being drained off. To give for years prior to 1905 an accurate picture of the territorial spread of the Company's investments is practically impossible because of complications arising from allocating to individual states the correct proportion of funds in interstate investments. Not until the Association of Life Insurance Presidents (now the Life Insurance Association of America) was founded (1907) were formulae worked out for solving this problem and the association's data on the subject do not precede 1906.[25] Under the circumstances the only really informative geographical distribution of life insurance assets which is available is limited to mortgage loans.

FORMULATING INVESTMENT POLICIES

From the very beginning of The Mutual Life much of the burden of investing funds fell upon the chief executive officer or officers and upon the Finance Committee of the Board of Trustees. With the mounting sums available for investment, with the broadening of the portfolio to include corporate securities, and with the geographical spread of mortgage loans, the task of formulating investment policies assumed new proportions. A large office staff was necessary to handle the details, and men of wide business knowledge and keen, decisive judgment were required to determine what investments should be made.

Investing became such an important phase of the Company's business that new executives were appointed in 1884 to relieve the president and the vice president of much of the work. A treasurer was named to have general oversight of all stocks, bonds, and Company office buildings, and a comptroller, to take charge of all mortgages, collateral loans, and real estate.[26] In the course of time the personnel of both the Bureau of Finance, which came to be known as the Financial Department, and of the Bureau of Bonds and Mortgages, which became the Real Estate Department in 1875, greatly increased in size and importance.

Investments were planned by these officers, the president, and vice presidents and then were submitted for approval, recommendation, or rejection to the Finance Committee of the Board of Trustees of which the president, vice presidents, and treasurer were ex officio members. As the number and size of financial transactions increased, the work of

25 Railroad investments were allocated to states according to mileage within states, securities in other corporations, on the basis of property in various states, and Federal bonds on the basis of population.
26 *Minutes of the Finance Committee,* May 28 and June 18, 1884.

this committee became enormous. About 1887 a subcommittee of the Finance Committee was formed to lighten the burdens of the larger body, and in 1906 the labor was somewhat divided by creating a Real Estate Committee. Sometimes the pressure to reach a decision was so great that action was taken prior to the receipt of authorization by the Finance Committee. In fact, the Finance Committee and the subcommittee tended generally to follow the advice of the officers in the fifteen years prior to the Armstrong Investigation.[27]

The persons mainly charged with the investments of The Mutual Life were extremely capable. Aside from the president, the officers who were chiefly responsible for decisions regarding investments were Frederic Cromwell, who became the first treasurer in 1884 and acted briefly as president of the Company after McCurdy's resignation in 1905, James Timpson, who became assistant treasurer in 1893 and was instructed in 1897 to relieve Cromwell of much of his work, and William W. Richards, comptroller of the Company from 1885 to 1906. Among the members of the trustees who served on the Finance Committee, the most prominent and the one to serve the longest was George F. Baker, president of the First National Bank of N.Y. As a member of the committee during almost all his trusteeship, 1879 to 1931, he did more than any other trustee to shape the financial destinies of the Company. Samuel D. Babcock, banker, financier and trustee from 1853 to 1902, was also a member of the committee for many years. Seymour L. Husted, president of the Dime Savings Bank, Frederick H. Cossitt, vice president of the Central Trust Co., George G. Haven, vice president of the National Union Bank, Augustus D. Juilliard, merchant, Adrian Iselin, Jr., vice president of the Guaranty Trust Co., Lewis May, banker, Charles R. Henderson, banker, John H. Sherwood, vice president of the Fifth Avenue Bank, and William Rockefeller were among the other prominent men who served the longest terms. As a rule the membership of the Finance Committee remained much the same year after year, the principal changes being occasioned by death.

The fact that the president, vice presidents, and treasurer of The Mutual Life were wealthy New Yorkers and that the majority of the Finance Committee were New York City bankers explains, in part, the character of The Mutual's investment program. In the portfolio were to be found such items as $873,205 of Metropolitan Opera bonds [28] and

---

27 Armstrong Investigation, *Testimony*, pp. 200–201.

28 See the portfolio as detailed in the *New York Insurance Report* (Albany, 1897) for the year 1896, p. 55. For the year 1906 the holdings of Metropolitan Opera and Real Estate Company, 1908, 4's amounted to $950,000.

$250,000 of Columbia College 3 percent bonds,[29] which reflected the interest of The Mutual's trustees and officers in both these local institutions. Of a more important nature was the relation of those responsible for the Company's investments with other businesses. All the senior officers, all the members of the Finance Committee, and nearly all the members of the Board of Trustees were directors of corporations and had important financial interests. It was only logical, therefore, that they should suggest or even decide that The Mutual Life should invest its funds in enterprises with which they were familiar and which personally they believed to be safe.

Two extreme cases will illustrate the problem of interlocking directorates and interests. George F. Baker was a director of the following railroads: Central R.R. of New Jersey, Chicago, Burlington and Quincy, Colorado and Southern, Delaware, Lackawanna, and Western, Erie, Lake Erie and Western, Lehigh Valley, New York Central, New York, Chicago, and St. Louis, New York, New Haven, and Hartford, Northern Pacific, Pere Marquette, Pittsburgh and Lake Erie, Reading, and Rutland. In 1900 he was in addition president and director of the First National Bank of New York, the Astor National Bank, the Long Branch Water Supply Co., and New York and Long Branch R.R. Co., vice president and director of the Bankers' Safe Deposit Co., a director of the Atlas Cement Co., Car Trust Investment Co. of London, the Citizens' Insurance Co., the Continental Insurance Company, the East Jersey Trust Co., the Farmers' Loan and Trust Co., the Guaranty Trust Co., the Liberty National Bank, Metropolitan Opera and Real Estate Co., the Montclair Water Co., Navesink Park Co., the Spring Brook Water Supply Co., trustee of the Consolidated Gas Co., Provident Loan Society, and the Bowery Savings Bank. In the same year Richard A. McCurdy was director of the Bank of New Amsterdam, Continental Insurance Company, Guaranty Trust Co., International Bell Telephone Co., Lawyers' Surety Co., National Union Bank, United States Mortgage and Trust Co., Morton Trust Co., Morristown (N.J.) Trust Co., and National Bank of Commerce.[30]

In the twenty years prior to 1905 The Mutual Life created a number of subsidiaries and extended its entrepreneurial functions outside the field of life insurance. Sometimes the Company had to go into business to try to safeguard some investment which had appeared to be endangered; more frequently it created subsidiaries to provide an outlet for investments, and on occasion it engaged in speculative enterprises.

29 *New York Insurance Report* (Albany, 1907), for 1906, p. 179
30 Armstrong Investigation, *Exhibits*, No. 283.

The influence of the bankers on the Finance Committee seems to have been important in leading The Mutual Life into banking, especially investment banking. The purchase of stocks was sometimes a step toward control of companies.

THE MUTUAL LIFE BECOMES AN ENTREPRENEUR

The earliest entrepreneurial activity of The Mutual Life, except its insurance business, was in the erection of, for that time, large and imposing office buildings and in the renting of excess space to others. By the early eighties the Company had outgrown its quarters on the corner of Broadway and Liberty Street, and in 1884 it moved into the main part of its present home office at 34 Nassau Street. In 1888 an addition was built at 59 Cedar Street; in 1892 a fifteen-story structure was added at 32 Liberty Street; in 1902 another connected fifteen-story building was erected, which ran from 18 to 26 Liberty Street and through to 51–55 Cedar Street. A little later the Company acquired the Stokes Building, at 45–49 Cedar Street, and a building on the corner of William Street. Other buildings were owned in Boston, Philadelphia, San Francisco, Little Rock, Seattle, Buffalo, Berlin, Paris, London, Sydney, Capetown, and Mexico City. In 1906 all these structures were valued at $29,355,000, which amounted to 5.9 percent of the Company's assets, and they earned, including the charges made to the Company for rent, 2.77 percent. Apparently they were not a particularly good investment, and except for the home office they were ultimately sold off. But while they were in the possession of the Company, they made The Mutual Life an important lessor.

The Company also got into business by taking an interest in the management of concerns in which its investments were large when these concerns failed or were about to fail. In the depression of 1893 railroads were hit so hard that by 1895 one-fifth of the total mileage of the country was in the hands of receivers. Inasmuch as The Mutual Life's holdings in railroad securities amounted to $56,151,898 in 1896, the depression was bound to impair some of the investment. Consequently, the Company played an active role in bankruptcy proceedings, on bondholders' protective committees, and in reorganization plans. The policy usually pursued in such cases was established in 1890; it consisted of getting a member of the Finance Committee to represent the Company's interests.[31]

31 This was done, for example, in the case of the South Carolina Railway Company and the Indianapolis, Decatur, and Springfield. See *Minutes of the Finance Committee*, Jan. 22, 1890.

Sometimes the Company had to cut deeper than this. A considerable sum was loaned to David C. Robinson, who was a trustee from 1891 to 1893, on the security of mortgages and bonds of the Elmira Municipal Improvement Society. This society was a holding company for the Elmira Gas and Illuminating Company, The Elmira Illuminating Company, and the Elmira Waterworks, and had a controlling interest in the Elmira and Horseheads Railroad Company. When these companies reached the verge of insolvency, The Mutual Life stepped in, appointed new managers, and for years nursed the entire enterprise until the holdings could be sold.

Foreclosures on mortgage loans likewise placed going concerns and properties in the lap of The Mutual Life, and they had to be mothered until some disposition could be made of them. In 1905 the Company had, for example, the Universal Building in Brooklyn, a building on West Broadway, and the old Grosvenor Hotel. The last-named property had been acquired in about 1889 and had been run by a manager employed by the Company.[32]

In the field of banking the entrepreneurial activity of The Mutual Life resulted from a definite and aggressive policy. About 1890 the executive officers and the members of the Finance Committee came to believe that new outlets were necessary for the investment of funds. They decided that if they got control of a number of banks they would have a better chance of purchasing desirable stocks, bonds, and debenture bonds and at the same time would have good bank securities. Accordingly, in 1891 The Mutual Life began to buy bank stock, beginning with the New York Guaranty and Indemnity Company—the future Guaranty Trust Co.[33] On December 31, 1906, the Company owned $4,248,000 of United States Mortgage and Trust Company debenture bonds and considerable amounts of stock in other banks.[34]

To illustrate the procedure employed in getting control and making use of these subsidiary banks, let us consider the case of the New York Guaranty and Indemnity Company. For some time this institution had not been very active, yet it had a charter containing valuable privileges for doing a trust business. The bank was reorganized with a capital of $2,000,000 and a surplus of $500,000 which was obtained by the sale of stock. The Mutual Life acquired in 1891 about half of this stock, and the rest went to directors and former stockholders. Among the directors were to be found many of Mutual's trustees—Samuel D. Babcock,

32 Armstrong Investigation, *Testimony*, pp. 1539–1540, 1673, 1681–1695.
33 *Minutes of the Board of Trustees*, Oct. 28, 1891.
34 Armstrong Investigation, *Exhibits*, No. 64.

Henry W. Smith, Augustus D. Juilliard, Oliver Harriman, George G. Haven, Richard A. McCurdy, Frederic Cromwell, Henry H. Rogers, Adrian Iselin, Jr., and Walter R. Gillette—a total of ten out of fifteen.[35] Therefore, these individuals had a voice in formulating the policies of two institutions in which they had a personal financial interest. They hoped that the bank would assist the insurance company in obtaining new issues of securities, for the former would be in a better position than the latter to underwrite large issues and to participate in or to form investors' syndicates.[36] An effort was made to adjust investment practices to the exigencies of the times.

In many ways The Mutual Life fostered its adopted child. It caused the word "indemnity" to be dropped from the bank's title and the name Guaranty Trust Co. to be used, because "indemnity" implied the transaction of a kind of business done by other Mutual subsidiaries. The Company also kept large sums at about 2 percent on deposit with the bank—deposits which ranged from $1,500,000 to $3,350,000 in the year beginning May 1, 1903—and it stood ready to provide money by deposit to cover exceptional needs.[37] This combination, that gave the bank large financial support and placed at The Mutual's disposal large banking facilities, proved successful, and the stock of the Guaranty increased in value from a par of $125 in 1891 to $555 a share in 1905.[38]

Another bank which The Mutual Life took under its wing was the United States Mortgage and Trust Co. The Company's first large block of stock in this institution was acquired in 1893, and by the time of the Armstrong Investigation their holdings totaled 10,736 shares at a par value of $1,073,600, or a market value of $1,665,191.04, the total capitalization being $2,000,000.[39] Here, too, several of The Mutual's trustees were directors and stockholders—among others there were Richard A. McCurdy, Frederic Cromwell, Charles R. Henderson, George F. Baker, and Robert A. Granniss. Through this institution The Mutual Life hoped to make investments in mortgage loans in Western states, where there was a steady clamor for the placement of the funds of Eastern life insurance companies, and to avoid setting up a special staff for this purpose within its own organization.[40] The Mutual purchased debentures of the United States Mortgage and Trust Company, and although

---

[35] As of 1893. George F. Baker later became a director of the Guaranty Trust.
[36] Armstrong Investigation, *Testimony*, pp. 157 ff.
[37] *Ibid.*, pp. 495–496, 4548.   [38] *Ibid.*, pp. 161.
[39] *Ibid.*, p. 206, and *Minutes of the Finance Committee*, Jan. 18, 1893.
[40] Armstrong Investigation, *Testimony*, pp. 503 ff., 1600, and 1607–1609.

these securities brought less than the mortgage loans which stood behind them, the belief was that the difference was a fair charge for services which, if performed by the Company, would have cost much more.[41]

The Mutual Life's interests in other banks were essentially for the same purpose as its control of the Guaranty Trust Co. and the United States Mortgage and Trust Co. So profitable did operations resulting from such connections seem that in 1894 a standing order for the purchase of stock in New York City banks was approved by the Finance Committee.[42] The Company helped to organize the Mutual Alliance Trust Co. (liquidated in 1915) in the Grand Street area in order to further investments on the Lower East Side, appointed Trustees as directors of the bank, and kept about $250,000 on deposit there to assist operations. In the Morristown Trust Company, a bank in which Richard A. McCurdy was interested, as a stockholder, director, and a citizen of Morristown, The Mutual Life bought 1,750 shares in 1905, kept on deposit $200,000 at 2 percent, and had several of its trustees on the board of directors.[43] In the Morton Trust Company, later merged into the State Trust Company and eventually into the Guaranty Trust Co. in 1910,[44] The Mutual Life bought 2,000 shares in 1899, appointed trustees as stockholders and directors, and maintained a steady deposit of $500,000 at 2 percent. A large interest was bought in the Bank of California, in which Trustee William Babcock was a director, to further The Mutual's investments on the Pacific Coast. The large interest and deposits in the National Bank of Commerce, merged with the Guaranty Trust in 1929, were established, on the other hand, because this bank provided The Mutual with current banking services.[45]

Close affiliation with these and other banks provided, so the officers of the Company believed, not only necessary outlets for insurance funds but also, through the purchase of bank stock, excellent investments. The large deposits in these banks were not, however, remunerative, usually bringing only 2 percent. Yet it was thought that the deposits provided in most cases working capital which allowed the banks to make a profit and in turn raised earnings on or the value of the stock.[46]

Syndicate operations of The Mutual Life were particularly important during this period, for new issues were becoming so very large

[41] *Ibid.*, pp. 473 ff.   [42] *Minutes of the Finance Committee*, Jan. 17, 1894.
[43] Shares were bought at $300, but the market value in 1905 was $525.
[44] For this and other data on bank mergers or failures see *Moody's Manual of Investments.*
[45] Armstrong Investigation, *Testimony*, pp. 459 ff.
[46] Armstrong Investigation, *Exhibit*, No. 64.

that few individual investment banks could handle them. This rapid increase in size was owing in part to railroad consolidations in which a main road would issue collateral trust bonds, backed by the stock of their new subsidiaries, in order to get capital to pay for the acquisitions. Inasmuch as new issues were so large, especially in railroads in which The Mutual Life was so interested, and inasmuch as the sums of the Company available for investment were great enough to allow it to engage in underwriting, it began to enter syndicates. If the syndicate were awarded an issue, the investment bankers in it would usually want to sell the securities at an advance in price and distribute the profits thus obtained among syndicate members. Under such conditions The Mutual Life would have to pay the higher price, if it wanted any of the securities, but it stood to make something as a member of the syndicate and ran only the risk of having to take stocks or bonds for which there was no market. Inasmuch as it did not often enter into syndicate arrangements for securities which it did not want to hold, it was in frequent disagreement with investment bankers on the question of whether or not it would get securities at the inside price or only a share of the syndicate profit. Consequently, subsidiary banks were of assistance to the Company, for they could take and market securities which The Mutual did not desire and would allow the Company to retain at the syndicate price that proportion of an issue which the Company wanted for permanent investment.[47]

Although such operations were perfectly legitimate, they led to certain complications. In the first place, officers of The Mutual frequently participated on their own accounts in syndicates in which the Company was a partner, for they knew that there was little danger of loss.[48] In the second place, underwriting issues brought The Mutual Life into the speculative field of investment banking. And in the third place, the Company became a competitor of investment bankers, which had its dangerous and sometimes its ludicrous aspects. On one famous occasion The Mutual outbid J. P. Morgan and Company for an issue of New England R.R. Co's. Mortgage 4's of 1945. Whereupon Richard A. McCurdy wrote to the assistant treasurer:

Twenty years ago I used to hammer it into Mr. Cromwell that the time would come, if I lived, when The Mutual Life would be the power to be reckoned with in Wall Street and Corsair and Co. would have to ask "what

---

[47] Armstrong Investigation, *Testimony*, pp. 384 ff.
[48] For the participation of Frederic Cromwell in such arrangements see Armstrong Investigation, *Exhibit*, No. 55. For Richard A. McCurdy's participation see *Exhibit*, No. 284.

are they going to do about it up at the corner of Cedar and Nassau Street?"
For us the situation is beautiful.[49]

In addition to such underwriting practices, The Mutual Life also
showed its entrepreneurial bent by speculative promotional schemes,
the most prominent of which concerned the Brooklyn Wharf and Warehouse Company. The Mutual had mortgages on and actually owned a
large amount of dock and adjoining property in Brooklyn and believed
that if these holdings were amalgamated their value would be enhanced.
Through its subsidiaries, the Brooklyn Wharf and Warehouse Company
was organized, and The Mutual received and bought bonds in the
concern to the amount of $3,500,000. In 1901 the Brooklyn Wharf and
Warehouse Company was reorganized in order to scale down the securities so that they could show an earning, and The Mutual Life got
for its former bonds $1,787,500 in bonds of the new Company—The
New York Dock Company—and a like amount in preferred stock.[50] In
short, this particular enterprise was not a great success, and in the future The Mutual tended to steer clear of promotional schemes in which
it bore the largest responsibilities.

Business ventures outside the pale of strictly life insurance business
were prevented by legislation enacted in New York State in 1906. Enterprises of the kind mentioned proved generally profitable, but it was
thought that policyholders' money should not be used in such ways.
In any case, we shall return to these matters in our consideration of
the Armstrong Report and see how strongly opposed to them Charles
Evans Hughes was.

[49] The details of the case were as follows: The New York, New Haven and Hartford R.R.
Co. asked for bids for $10,000,000 of bonds, the bids to be in at noon August 1, 1904. The
Mutual was not advised promptly of the offer and asked President C. S. Mellen of the New
Haven if the bids could be put in later. Mellen replied that if they got to his office early
on the morning of Aug. 2 they would be acceptable, because they would not be considered
until noon. Mutual acted accordingly and in conjunction with the Guaranty Trust Co.
bid $107.52. The next highest bidder was J. P. Morgan and Co., with $106.777. The bonds
were at first awarded to Morgan, who was a member of the special committee of the New
Haven to pass on the bids, on the grounds that The Mutual's offer was late. McCurdy was
furious, because he was a director, along with other Mutual trustees of the New Haven, and
because The Mutual was the largest single stockholder in the road. He threatened suit on
Morgan and tried to retain Elihu Root, who refused to take the case, because he was already
tied to Morgan as counsel in the Northern Securities case. McCurdy also attacked Mellen,
who appealed for leniency. Morgan proposed to take the bonds at his price and sell them to
The Mutual at the Company's price, thus netting $75,000 for himself. This compromise was
turned down, Morgan finally agreed to take the issue at The Mutual's price and to sell half
of it to the Company at its price.
[50] Armstrong Investigation, *Testimony*, pp. 564–565.

XI. Managerial Control

IN THE PRECEDING PAGES several references have been made to the domination of American life insurance companies by strong executives during the period 1870–1905, and some of the effects of their powerful leadership, especially in the case of The Mutual Life, have been pointed out. Certainly Henry Baldwin Hyde and James W. Alexander of The Equitable, William H. Beers and John A. McCall of the New York Life, and Frederick S. Winston and Richard A. McCurdy of The Mutual Life put a definite stamp on the life insurance of their day.[1] They and their immediate supporters took authority into their own hands, selected trustees, determined all the major policies of their companies, and made a cult out of sheer size.

To appreciate the mentality of the men who "controlled" The Mutual Life prior to the Armstrong Investigation, it is necessary to look briefly at their biographies. With Frederick M. Winston we have already dealt, but it should be recalled that he had come to the presidency of The Mutual Life from the dry goods business, that he had been a trustee of the Company prior to his election to the chief executive office, and that he had waged a bitter war against the "Collins forces" during the first part of his administration. When Henry B. Hyde, then a young man and a Mutual employee, had proposed to Winston the founding of a company to write the large risks refused by The Mutual Life, Winston had thrown the ambitious young man out of his office, discharged him, and then carried into execution (1860) a plan that had been brewing for some time—the establishment of the Washington Life Insurance Company to handle Mutual's applications for large policies. Winston fought bitterly with Sheppard Homans and had several tiffs with policyholders in the 1870's. He worshiped size, and when the Company did not grow to suit his tastes, he momentarily issued tontines, of which he did not approve, offered large rebates for a few months, greatly expanded the agency force, and finally consented to the idea of writing deferred-dividend policies.

[1] Amzi Dodd, president of The Mutual Benefit of New Jersey, and Jacob L. Greene, president of the Connecticut Mutual, were also great leaders, but because of the policies which they pursued they should not be classed with the officers of the "big three" companies.

When President Winston died, in 1885, Richard A. McCurdy (1835–1916) was definitely the heir apparent. McCurdy came of a wealthy family (his father, a banker, had been a Mutual trustee from 1843 to 1880), and he enjoyed all the privileges of upbringing which wealth could furnish. He studied law at Harvard University and entered into a partnership with Lucius Robinson, later governor of New York. In 1862 he became attorney for The Mutual Life, having previously served the Company successfully as counsel, and in 1865 he was elected vice president. When he became president, in 1885, he immediately took steps to restore The Mutual Life to that position of primacy in the field of life insurance which it had formerly held and had lost in the last years of Winston's regime. He pushed deferred-dividend policies with all his might, opened new agencies, extended the Company's activity abroad, and, as we have seen, gloated over the possibility of bearding the lion of investment bankers in his den. He ruled the Company with an iron hand. He himself selected most of the trustees; he got their approval for his policies, or ignored them entirely; and he lorded it over the home office. His personality, although of the blustering type, was very powerful. He was a stickler for details and the story is told that as he walked through the halls of the home building, he would drag his finger along a molding, and if it turned up dust, he would call the janitor and dress him down on the spot. When he left his office to go home, a lackey blew a whistle to stop the elevator, and the elevator operator signaled the doorman to call up McCurdy's coach—all in order that the president could catch a ferry which made connections with a train that got him into Morristown in time for dinner.

McCurdy flanked himself by similarly strong and somewhat imperious men. Robert A. Granniss (1840–1917) began his business career as a clerk in a wholesale dry goods establishment and received his first life insurance experience as a clerk in the office of the New York Life. Later he served as secretary of the Mutual Benefit Life Insurance Company and of the Metropolitan Life Insurance Company, entered the employment of The Mutual Life in 1877 as second vice president, and became first vice president and a member of the Board of Trustees in 1885. He shared Richard A. McCurdy's ambitions to make The Mutual Life the largest American life insurance company, and he labored tirelessly and vigorously to that end.

The other first vice president at the time of the Armstrong Investigation was Dr. Walter R. Gillette (1840–1908). He was educated at Colgate University (then Madison University) and at the College of

Physicians and Surgeons in New York. He served as an army surgeon during the Civil War, upon the conclusion of that conflict became surgeon to the New York Post Office Department, and in 1869 was named adjunct professor in the medical department of New York University. In 1871 he joined The Mutual Life; in 1875 he became Medical Director of the Company; in 1890, General Manager and a member of the Board; and in 1903, vice president. Thus, as medical director he played an important part in liberalizing the rules for the selection of risks; as general manager he reorganized the domestic agencies into branch offices; and as vice president he was McCurdy's right-hand man, as we shall see in more detail later, in overseeing expenditures.

The second vice president was Isaac F. Lloyd (1835–1921), who in 1865 became a clerk and chief accountant in The Mutual Life—a position which was changed to auditor in 1870. In 1876 he became secretary, and in 1885, second vice president. In the latter position his duties consisted in signing many of the official documents and in checking various aspects of the business for the president. The treasurer was Frederic Cromwell, who was appointed to that office in 1884 and to whom reference has been made above. The third vice president was John A. Fonda (1841–1914), who rose in the ranks of the Company to be cashier in 1875, assistant treasurer in 1885, and to his highest office in 1902. The secretary from 1885 to 1918 was William J. Easton, who had been in the employment of The Mutual Life since 1865. The actuary was Emory McClintock, who was one of the most distinguished members of his profession in America and had come from The Northwestern to The Mutual Life in 1889; he remained the actuary of the Company until 1911.

Finally, among the leaders in The Mutual Life should be included Robert H. McCurdy (1859–1931), son of the president. He was educated in European schools and at Harvard, being graduated from the latter institution in 1881. In that year he became a clerk at a salary of $1,000 a year in the office of Charles H. Raymond, then general agent of The Mutual Life for New York City. After one year in this position, Colonel Raymond, a close friend of The Mutual's president, took young McCurdy into partnership. When the Company decided to extend its operations abroad, Robert H. was put in charge of the foreign department, where he did such an excellent job that he began to be considered comparable to his father in executive ability. In 1903 he became a trustee and general manager of the Company—positions from which he resigned in 1905 and 1906, respectively.

These executives of The Mutual Life constituted a remarkable group of men. They had almost without exception strong personalities, and from long experience in the business had a wide knowledge of life insurance. Yet, they were no more remarkable than the Board of Trustees of the period 1870–1905. As has already been pointed out, many of the prominent bankers of New York were represented on the Board—the dean of them all being George F. Baker. In addition to this group, the Board had among its members leaders from other fields—Henry E. Davies, chief justice of the Court of Appeals, his son Julien T. Davies of the law firm of Davies, Stone and Auerbach,[2] Alexander H. Rice. governor of Massachusetts, Thomas Dickson, president of the Delaware-Hudson Canal Company, S. Van Rensselaer Cruger, comptroller of the Trinity Church Corporation, Rufus W. Peckham, justice of the U.S. Supreme Court, John W. Auchincloss, merchant, Stuyvesant Fish, president of the Illinois Central Railroad, H. Walter Webb, vice president of the New York Central, Cornelius Vanderbilt, financier, and A. N. Waterhouse, one of the two or three agents of the Company to have been trustees.

EXECUTIVES IN CONTROL

Part of the strength of the executives rested upon the fact that they knew what they were doing and what ends they desired to achieve. By 1870 the main technical phases of life insurance had reached a point of development at which no serious uncertainty existed. A satisfactory mortality table was in use, premiums had been computed on a basis adequate to take care of the expenses of a well-managed company, sufficient reserves were established to cover expected claims, and marketing organizations had been created. Thus executives of successful companies in the period from 1870 to 1905 were relatively free from having to solve basic technical problems—the only new development of great importance was the deferred-dividend policy—and could bend most of their energies to problems of growth. This is exactly what the leaders of The Mutual Life did. Bigness became the goal toward which they all worked—and with success.

The placing of new business upon the books of the Company had certain very favorable results. Insuring a number of young lives meant for a time, at least, a lower average mortality rate among The Mutual's policyholders, while the use of the deferred-dividend contract resulted

---

2 For tributes to both of these men see Joseph S. Auerbach, *The Bar of Other Days* (New York, 1940), *passim*.

in the accumulation of great sums that could, if necessary, be employed as a safeguard against any eventualities. The rapid growth of a life insurance company gives it temporary advantages, yet a point must be reached, according to marginal analysis, beyond which the cost of getting more new insurance exceeds the gains to be derived from it. By 1904 this point was in danger of being attained, for expenses were 109.34 percent of loadings, and $9,830,753.46 was spent in getting new business, while only $2,140,700 was obtained from loadings on the first year's premiums.[3]

President McCurdy understood this problem, and in 1892 he agreed to a suggestion made by Emory McClintock that the amount of new insurance should be limited to $100,000,000. As we have seen in an earlier chapter, a limit of 100,000 members was set up in 1874 as a bromide to public opinion, but this limitation was abolished in 1886. The new maximum aimed to avoid increasing or excessive costs, the new business written in 1892 largely exceeding $100,000,000.

The rapid growth and the accumulation of funds had other effects upon The Mutual Life than those already mentioned. They tended greatly to enhance the reputation and prestige of the executive officers and thus to make easier the domination of the Company by the chief officers. The trustees and the policyholders for years placed implicit faith in the management and made little use of those democratic controls which had been provided in the charter. During the entire period from 1880 to 1905 there was never a contested election to the Board of Trustees, but to assure victory in case of opposition the president and vice president had a large number of proxies at their command, about 25,000 in 1905.[4]

Even the trustees placed utmost confidence in the executive officers. The many members of the Board who were picked by President Mc-Curdy presumably had a great amount of personal loyalty to him. This fact accounts, in part, for their sometimes apathetic attitude toward the affairs of the Company, although most of the men were of high business ability and of strong personality. The trustees tended to approve, without careful analysis, the policies presented to them. The personnel of the standing committees of the Board remained much the same year after year, and these committees came to act more and more automatically. Sometimes subcommittees with power to make important decisions were given authority over certain matters, and the whole

---

[3] Armstrong Investigation, *Testimony*, pp. 1391, 1902; *Minutes of the Insurance Committee*, Jan. 25, 1892.

[4] Armstrong Investigation, *Testimony*, p. 22.

Board did not know what steps were taken. Thus a subcommittee on salaries was appointed with power from the Finance Committee in 1893,[5] and salaries were increased without the knowledge of all the trustees or even of the entire Finance Committee.[6]

McCurdy himself stated to the Board in 1905 that:

No ripple of dissension has occurred during my administration among the Trustees as a body, nor have any policyholders organized to protest against or demand anything in the administration of the Company. The Trustees as a Board and the Committees have always been unanimous and the Executive Officers have worked absolutely in accord and in sympathy with the Company's administration. . . .

Now what are the reasons which have during this long period of twenty years mainly conduced to the quiet and repose as well as to the progress of the Company? One reason was this: my predecessor showed extreme sagacity when forty years or more ago he established the rule that no vote should be taken upon any question of the investment of the funds of this Company in the Finance Committee. The result has been that necessarily the action of the Committee has been unanimous, and if differences of opinion have occurred in regard to any particular subject, those differences were modified by amicable discussion or harmonized until the result in either case was unanimous, but if still a single number failed to be convinced, the President withdrew the proposition and the subject was dropped. . . . All this contributed largely to the speedy disposition of questions under consideration, for even if a member was somewhat doubtful in his mind, he yielded courteously and good temperedly to the opinions of the other members of the Committee.

To contend, however, that the Board of Trustees played no role in the affairs of The Mutual Life would be erroneous. The mere presence of this body acted as a restraint upon the unlicensed action of executives; its members did help in some degree to formulate policies or to check on those proposed by the officers. When the Armstrong Investigation uncovered practices which did not seem to be legitimate, the Board was willing to accept part of the blame. Julien T. Davies stated: [7]

It is impossible for any member of this Board to be relieved from responsibility in the present situation. The responsibility varies in degree, but not in kind. . . . This is not the time and place to discuss the questions of errors and of degrees of responsibility. It is, however, the time and place for us to take courage and gird ourselves to perform our obvious duty. This is not to attempt to defend the indefensible, but manfully and courageously to shoulder what responsibility belongs to us, to endeavor to correct such mistakes as have been made, to reform what has to be reformed, and to

5 *Minutes of the Finance Committee*, Jan. 18, 1893.

6 Armstrong Investigation, *Testimony*, pp. 1393–1394, 4546, and *Minutes of the Board of Trustees*, Nov. 16, 1905.

7 *Minutes of the Board of Trustees*, Oct. 25, 1905.

examine into the affairs of the Company, with the strength that accompanies purity of motive and the intention that all should be done in connection with this great corporation that is right and proper, so far as we, the custodians and guardians of the interests of the policyholders, can see it and carry it out.

It is a curious fact that this statement was prompted by Richard A. McCurdy himself, for he moved that the Board should appoint a committee "to examine into the organization and management of the affairs of the Company and to report 'from time to time to this Board their recommendations in respect thereto." This committee, under the chairmanship of William H. Truesdale, president of the Delaware, Lackawanna, and Western Railroad, set about to put The Mutual's house in order. Its work showed clearly, as we shall see later, that the Board of Trustees could play an important role in a mutual company once its members were aware of the need for action.

ADMINISTRATIVE ORGANIZATION AND EXPENSE

One of the reasons why the trustees did not, for a long number of years, maintain a closer vigil over all the operations of The Mutual Life was simply because they placed too much reliance upon the employees of the Company to handle many of the questions which arose and too much faith in the completeness and accuracy of reports made to them. They committed the error of believing that their duties were fulfilled when they approved fundamental policies and checked the accounts rendered.

The increasing complexities of the activities of The Mutual Life have been referred to above in various connections, but attention should be called to the machinery which was created to deal with them. Although the main lines of organization which had been laid down earlier were followed, new departments were added, old ones reorganized, and several new executives appointed to relieve the president of many of his onerous duties.[8]

The home office force was, during the period 1870–1906, greatly enlarged. In 1868, when $59,022,136 new business was written and $199,818,578 insurance was in force, the staff had numbered fifty-five and the annual pay roll had amounted to $132,550. In 1906, with new insurance for the previous five years averaging about $206,000,000 a year and with $1,517,257,180 insurance in force, the home office employees numbered 645 and the annual pay roll amounted to $1,060,992.[9] If the figures for 1904 be taken, that is, before salary reductions which

---

[8] For the by-laws of this date see *ibid.*, May 29, 1903.   [9] See above, p. 109.

CHART XI

THE MUTUAL LIFE INSURANCE COMPANY OF NEW YORK ORGANIZATION CHART, 1903

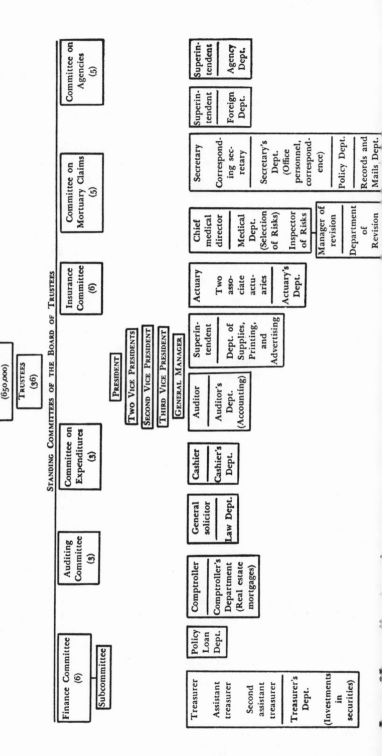

resulted from the Armstrong Investigation were made, salaries will be found to have been considerably higher.

The largest proportionate increases in salary were effected in the higher brackets. Thus the president's salary was increased from $30,000 in 1877 to $50,000 in 1886,[10] after McCurdy had been in office a short time, to $75,000 in 1893, to $90,000 in 1895, to $100,000 in 1896, and to $150,000 on June 1, 1901—this last augmentation having been made by the subcommittee of the Finance Committee without the knowledge of the full Board.[11] The first vice president received $20,000 in 1877 and $50,000 in 1902.[12]

TABLE 32

HOME OFFICE PAY ROLL, 1906 [a]

	Number of Employees	Amount		Number of Employees	Amount
Officers' pay roll	6	$105,000	Inspector of risks	7	$12,774
Executive	19	31,710	Insurance loan	21	19,708
Actuary's	100	124,436	Law	32	63,322
Advertising	7	4,194	Medical	55	86,632
Auditor's	56	74,702	Policy	54	51,462
Cashier's	16	36,686	Records and mail	12	12,450
Comptroller's	22	64,450	Dept. of Revision	31	47,182
Dept. of Correspond-			Supply	14	24,315
ence	31	28,218	Treasurer's	11	45,474
Domestic agency	40	85,512	Employees in reserve	12	18,925
Foreign	99	123,840	Total	645	$1,060,992

[a] Minutes of the Finance Committee, March 30, 1906.

So far as the salaries of clerks were concerned, a policy was pursued in the years prior to 1886 to effect a "rude kind of justice by marking up, every one, two, or three years, nearly every clerk in the office." [13] This system was abolished at the latter date, and for it was substituted what was thought to be a merit system. Then, in 1901 a "system of regular civil service gradation" was introduced for the purpose of saving the president from "importunities for increase of pay." [14] In 1906 office boys received annual salaries of about $400, clerks, from about $500 to the rare top of $5,000, and stenographers, in the neighborhood of $1,000.[15] Furthermore, a pension plan was adopted in 1902 which provided that employees of the Company, who had been in service a stipulated number of years, could retire on half-pay.[16]

[10] Minutes of the Board of Trustees, July 28, 1886. In 1879 the salary was $25,000.
[11] Armstrong Investigation, Introductory, p. 11; Testimony, p. 1393; and Exhibit, 264.
[12] Armstrong Investigation, Testimony, p. 27, and Exhibit, No. 264.
[13] Minutes of the Finance Committee, Jan. 19, 1886.
[14] Armstrong Investigation, Testimony, p. 1819.
[15] Minutes of the Finance Committee, Mar. 30, 1906.
[16] Minutes of the Board of Trustees, Jan. 29, 1902, and Armstrong Investigation, Testimony, p. 1365.

Salaries, which came to be about one-seventh of annual expenses, were only one of the increases in operating costs during McCurdy's tenure of office.[17] Many of the increases in expenses can be accounted for by the larger amount of business transacted by the Company, but some of the items need explanation. Commissions were proportionately much larger in 1901 than in 1871 because of the higher rates paid to agents, as described in Chapter IX. The entry "Exchange" was occasioned by foreign exchange losses resulting from arbitrary rates established by the Company to facilitate its bookkeeping when business overseas was begun. Advertising, legal work, printing, and stationery were all greatly increased, in part because of more activity in these fields, but also because of the lobbying which was being done by the Company and from which the smaller companies benefited.

The amounts paid out in "taxes" require special mention, for the taxation of insurance funds came to be a well-established practice. A levy on insurance companies was inaugurated in 1853 by New York when 2 percent was charged on the annual gross premiums collected by companies organized outside the state. The law which provided for this tax was aimed to keep the insurance business of New York State for New York State companies, but it had the same effect as did the investment legislation—it evoked retaliation from other states. Thus, one state after another began to tax the premiums collected by outside companies operating within their borders until in 1904 two-thirds of all the states had such taxes and some taxed for purposes of revenue the premiums collected by their own companies.

Another tax which was tried was a tax on assets. This impost did not prove to be practicable, for it made rates high and drove many companies out of business.[18] Yet, seven states had such taxes in 1904 and

---

[17] *Abstract of Annual Statements*, a manuscript volume, Table IX.

[18] Kentucky practically forced its insurance companies out of business with a tax on assets. New York passed a law in 1880 taxing income from investments at 1 percent. Because of a technicality this law was not enforced. Connecticut had a tax on assets which from 1872 to 1881 was ½ percent. In 1883 it was dropped to ¼ percent. This tax tended to make the rates of Connecticut companies high.

TOTAL INSURANCE TAXES PAID, 1871–1880

Company	Rate per $1,000 of Mean Annual Assets	Company	Rate per $1,000 of Mean Annual Assets
Aetna	$5.26	Mutual Life	$2.05
Phoenix	5.59	Equitable	2.67
Connecticut Mutual	7.22	Mutual Benefit	2.72
Northwestern	2.01	New York Life	2.05

For further details consult Zartman, *The Investments of Life Insurance Companies*, chap. viii, and P. L. Gamble, *Taxation of Insurance Companies* (Albany, 1937).

three charged a fee for the valuation of policies—a fee that amounted to large sums.

Thus, taxation of life insurance funds was greatly augmented between 1870 and 1905, and it evoked a great amount of criticism. The main argument against it was that moneys saved to provide against misfortune and to alleviate the state of social responsibilities should be free from levies. In support of this contention, life insurance companies pointed to the tax-free savings banks. Furthermore, life insurance taxation resulted in "double taxation," and this was held to be inequitable. In spite of such arguments, however, life insurance taxation had come to stay, for collections on such large masses of capital as had been accumulated were relatively easy, and one of the principles of public finance seems to be to levy taxes that are most readily obtained. The amounts of money which had to go into taxes and to other expenses at times frightened the management of The Mutual Life and induced it to attempt economy. One such period was in the late seventies, when depression and competition had greatly reduced the amount of new insurance written, and, as we have seen, the Company was trying desperately to regain lost ground. On February 19, 1879, the trustees ordered a 20 percent reduction in expenses "because of the return to specie payment." [19] A special committee was appointed to carry out this

TABLE 33

PERCENTAGE OF EXPENSES TO MEAN AMOUNT INSURED

(.00 omitted)

Name of Company	1870	1871	1872	1873	1874	1875	1876	1877	1878	1879
The Mutual Life Ins. Co. of N.Y.	57	52	47	69	54	48	46	55	46	58
N.Y. Life Ins. Co.	97	76	78	68	60	58	59	81	74	81
Equitable Life Assur. Soc.	78	79	84	85	98	72	75	73	75	79
Northwestern Mutual	87	81	79	73	87	71	81	73	67	72

"The above ratios copied from the report of The Massachusetts Insurance Department." *Minutes of the Board of Trustees*, Oct. 20, 1880.

recommendation, and it slashed drastically into various items. Salaries were cut, advertising was reduced 40 percent below the figure for 1878, printing and stationery were to be purchased only on competitive bids, per diem allowance to trustees who were traveling on Company busi-

[19] See *Minutes of the Board of Trustees*, Feb. 19, 1879, April 16, 1879, and May 21, 1879.

REDUCTION OF SALARIES BY DEPARTMENTS

Executive Dept.	$13,050	Auditing Dept.	$3,350
Law Dept.	6,040	Real Estate Dept.	1,000
Actuarial Dept.	8,510	Dept. of Printing & Stationery	1,600
Medical Dept.	6,740	General office	11,320
Bond & Mortgage Dept.	2,900	Janitor	600

ness were cut 20 percent, the luncheons were fixed at $.50 per person, and an order went out that no one in the Company should receive any fee aside from his salary. Accounts of the agents were to be examined in the future by the Committee on Agencies, and no medical fees were to be paid for examinations in New York or Brooklyn—applicants were to come to the home office and be examined by the Company's physicians. Finally, and most important of all, a budget system for the various departments was initiated—a budget being required every six months.

President McCurdy became worried about expenses in 1897, when business was again falling off and the so-called "Silver Campaign Depression" was showing its effects in the business world. In 1896 an outsider was asked to make an investigation of expenses, but when he reported that close supervision of expenditures should be established, McCurdy's feathers were ruffled, and he appointed a committee of officers to look into the matter.[20] To them he stated:

While some progress was made in 1897 in the desired direction, a comparison of our expenditures in that year with those of other companies doing approximately an equal amount of business shows that the cost of our work is still excessive. I do not regard either one of the two companies in question as models of economical management, yet it would appear as to 1897, after making due allowances, that as compared with the N.Y. Life Insurance Co. our expenses were decidedly heavier, and that in addition our future premiums have been burdened with a greater liability for renewal commissions; and that the like holds good, on the whole, in comparison with the Equitable, except as regards renewal commissions.

I am aware that our scale of commissions to General Agents is greater than those of the other companies in question, and I particularly ask you to take into consideration this subject. Our General Agency system is intended to cover all the costs of the Agency work. For this reason, our expenditures on other accounts connected with the active prosecution of business should be very considerably smaller than the corresponding accounts in the other companies, whose custom is to assist their agents by additional allowances of various kinds. I am not satisfied that we succeeded in carrying out our theory.

In addition to the agency expense, the president pointed out that The Mutual spent $188,000 for advertising against the New York Life's $137,000, that it paid out $413,000 for printing and stationery against The Equitable's $106,000—a difference which was accounted for in part by printing new policy forms and rates—and that The Mutual had

20 *Ibid.*, Oct. 28, 1896, Nov. 25, 1896, and April 27, 1898. For the cost of new business see Armstrong Investigation, *Report*, p. 308.

an item for "Sundries," amounting to $271,000, which was "trifling in the Equitable and disguised in the New York Life." Into all these and other matters of expense the president wanted the committee to look and to report. As a result, expenses showed a decline in 1901, but for that year only. Business was improving, and while new insurance was being placed upon the books, less interest was shown in cutting costs.

In this connection two sources of expense should be explained briefly. One had to do with contingency reserves, and the other with the home office building. In 1875 The Mutual Life established its first contingency fund, because the depression resulted in shrinking values. In that year $1,080,000 was put aside to meet possible losses, and in 1876 $900,000 was earmarked for the same purpose, in addition to $250,000 as a real estate sinking fund.[21] Up to 1880 the amounts thus employed to cover losses were charged to "expense of management"—a fact that was severely criticized by the State Superintendent of Insurance and proved difficult to explain to policyholders.[22] Consequently, when severe depression came again, a special reserve was set aside for contingencies. Thus, in 1897 $1,000,000 was used to write down the value of office buildings, $1,000,000 to safeguard foreclosed mortgages, and $1,000,000 to protect stocks and bonds.[23] This method of setting aside funds to meet the contingency of a decline in the value of assets has been followed ever since.

The second item of expense, that of erecting and maintaining an impressive home office, badgered The Mutual Life Insurance Company as it bothered every life insurance institution. Every company thought that it had to have an "architectural masterpiece" for its offices in order to give outward evidence of success, and many spent enormous sums to this end. In the early 1880's The Mutual Life purchased a site at 34 Nassau Street for its home office—a site that was to become and to remain for many years the center of the insurance industry in the city. This plot had certain historical interest, for on it had been built in 1727 the famous Middle Dutch Church, from the towers of which Benjamin Franklin had conducted many of his experiments and within which the British had imprisoned several New York patriots during the Revolutionary War. From 1790 to 1840 the church was used again for religious purposes, but at the latter date it was purchased by the Government as a location for the city's central post office. It was from the Govern-

---

[21] *Minutes of the Board of Trustees,* Jan. 19, 1876 and June 8, 1881.
[22] *Ibid.,* June 8, 1880. [23] *Ibid.,* Nov. 24, 1897.

ment, then, that The Mutual Life purchased the land at a cost of $650,000.

The building which was erected at 34 Nassau was considered a marvel of the period, both for its architectural and its engineering features.[24] It was supposed to be fireproof, and it made use of the latest developments in steel framework, elevators, and heating. It was Italian Renaissance in style, with impressive doorways and porticoes. Its interior was adorned with colored Italian marble and had many architectural gems, of which the spiral staircase was the most precious. This building, with its additions, has remained the home office of The Mutual Life to the present date. Although its exterior has been darkened by age and dwarfed by its towering neighbors, the interior has still a solid appearance and a certain charm.

CHECKS AND BALANCES

Strong as the executive branch of The Mutual Life may have been before 1905, the "checks and balances" of the Company's organization were not completely inoperative. The trustees, although somewhat uncritical and lethargic, were there to forestall any gross malfeasance of office. They had at least to go through the motions of approving managerial policies, and they had to audit the Company's books. In this latter work they were assisted, beginning in 1897, by outside accountants, who unfortunately concentrated more on ascertaining the accuracy of the books than upon the general conduct and condition of the Company.[25] The trustees also had annually to elect the president, and although McCurdy was returned year after year without opposition, unbridled action on his part would have led to his defeat.

The policyholders and also the general public exerted some control, even though it was indirect, upon the management. Events had proved that an unsuccessful management would eventually have the policyholders down on its head and have the public doing business with competitors. McCurdy and his cohorts were fully aware of this fact, and according to their lights they tried to provide life insurance on favorable competitive terms. Nor is their record of achievement to be minimized. From 1871 to 1905 The Mutual Life received in premium pay-

---

[24] See Appendix, p. 362.

[25] The first so-called professional accountants, W. A. Harding and Charles E. Townsend, were employed in 1893. *Minutes of the Board of Trustees,* December 27, 1893. In 1897 the Audit Company was employed to investigate all the foreign agencies where some speculation had been going on. It did such a good job that it was engaged to report on some of the domestic agencies, and finally on the accounts of the home office. *Minutes of the Board of Trustees,* Nov. 24, 1897, and December 22, 1897.

ments $934,403,478.16, it disbursed to policyholders or their bene-
ficiaries $625,222,289.12, and it had at the beginning of 1905 as ledger
assets for approximately 650,000 members $408,293,315.73. Thus, dur-
ing the period under consideration the sums actually paid to or held
to the credit of the policyholders or their beneficiaries exceeded premium receipts by $56,729,709.13. From 1885 to 1905, that is, during
McCurdy's regime, premium receipts were $737,356,649.29, total policy
payments were $445,960,478.15, and ledger assets were built up by $311,-
283,502.65. Thus under his management sums paid to policyholders
or their beneficiaries or held to their credit exceeded premium payments by $19,887,331.51. Insurance protection cost Mutual Life's mem-
bers less than the interest on their money.

TABLE 34

ACCUMULATIVE RECORD OF RECEIPTS, DISBURSEMENTS, AND
LEDGER ASSETS FROM ORGANIZATION, FEB. 1, 1843

	Total 62 Years
Receipts	
Insurance premiums	$975,091,708.05
Annuity premiums	36,926,081.21
Total premiums	1,012,017,789.26
Interest and rents	274,992,866.85
Profit and other receipts	18,268,011.77
Total receipts	1,305,278,667.88
Disbursements	
Death losses	310,193,672.88
Matured endowments	68,206,605.53
Annuities	15,709,435.65
Surrenders	158,918,837.85
Dividends	112,694,913.89
Total policy payments	665,723,465.80
Expenses	221,773,170.36
Loss and other payments	9,488,715.99
Total disbursements	896,985,352.15
Net receipts (ledger assets)	$408,293,315.73

This record of accomplishment would have been impossible if management, with all its power, had worked exclusively for selfish ends. The
public had to be pleased, not damned. Furthermore, management could
not ignore the inquisitorial eye of state insurance commissioners. Annual financial reports had to be rendered to state insurance departments—after 1874 on the Convention Form—and these documents
were made available to the public. When experience showed that unscrupulous managers were not above falsifying such documents, periodic examinations of life insurance companies became the rule, being
conducted every three or four or five years toward the close of the cen-

tury.[26] Unfortunately, the state commissioners, like contemporary accountants, were more interested in accurate bookkeeping and solvency of companies than in managerial efficiency and seldom probed deeply. The investigating committees of state legislative bodies really went to the root of things, but such committees were extraordinarily rare.

In 1870 The Mutual Life was examined, as we have seen, by the Superintendent of Insurance for the State of New York, George W. Miller, and received a favorable report.[27] Henry B. Hyde kept sniping, however, at The Mutual, and through Stephen English of the *Insurance Times* maintained a running fire. Ultimately these shots aroused the ire of President Winston, who charged English with criminal libel, sued him on a multitude of counts, and got him held in $80,000 bail, which was not furnished. For six months English remained in jail waiting for a trial, and this incarceration attracted the attention of all New York. Finally the New York State Assembly appointed, in 1873, a committee to investigate life insurance companies—a committee that was favorably disposed toward English.[28] Its report led to a temporary truce between Winston and Hyde and to the employment of English by The Mutual.[29]

This was not, however, the end of the affair, and in 1877 a policyholder succeeded in getting the state assembly again to investigate life insurance companies. The new committee went back into the old fight between Homans and Winston, into the question of post mortem dividends, into competitive practices, and into other matters. Finally its members issued a mild reprimand in the hope that it would serve as a cure.[30]

26 Armstrong Investigation, *Testimony*, p. 4272; Frederick L. Hoffman, *Insurance, Science and Economics* (New York, 1911), pp. 199 ff.; and E. W. Patterson, *The Insurance Commissioner in the United States* (Cambridge, Mass., 1927), pp. 519 ff. Efforts to secure Federal in place of state supervision were made by John Patten, president of the Union Central Life Insurance Co., in 1892, and by John F. Dryden, president of the Prudential, in 1905. No general interest in this change was evident.

27 See above, pp. 117–118.   28 *New York Assembly Document*, No. 155 (1873).

29 *The Condition of the Life Insurance Companies of the State of New York* (Albany, 1877), p. 437.

30 This period was rife with pamphlet and periodical literature: George H. Andrews, *Address . . . to the Policyholders of The Mutual Life Insurance Co. of N.Y. Represented at a Meeting Held at . . . Providence, R.I., Jan. 10, 1879* (New York, 1879), a speech in favor of the Company; "The Best of Investments, Life Insurance as a Matter of Fact," *Harper's Weekly*, XXIII (Aug., 1879), 634; *Facts and Observations as to the Financial and Business Affairs Generally and Their Influence on the Investments and Conditions of This Company* (New York, 1876); articles in *The Insurance Times* and *The Insurance Monitor;* and Sheppard Homans, *Circular Letter to Messrs. Alexander H. Rice, William E. Dodge, and Others—Special Committee of Trustees of The Mutual Life Insurance Company of N.Y.* (New York, 1879).

Thenceforth, until 1905, there were no penetrating investigations of New York insurance companies, although New York companies had by 1897 to satisfy commissioners in forty-four states. Examinations of individual companies by all these officials would, of course, have been very burdensome to the companies, for the companies had to pay the costs. Consequently, the practice of placing the responsibility of examining a company in the hands of a certain number of commissioners and of exchanging certificates of approval grew up under the aegis of the National Convention of Insurance Commissioners.[31] To be sure, some states refused to coöperate in this development, and not until 1909 was the present zoning system of examinations adopted; but in 1898 we find The Mutual being examined jointly by the commissioners of seven states.[32]

These examinations were, as has already been stated, usually limited to determining the solvency of a company and the accuracy of its computations, and were not extended, notwithstanding denials of the fact, into the realm of managerial policies. Some idea of the scope of the work was indicated in the report of the examination of 1903—an examination which, incidentally, President McCurdy had requested.[33]

This examination, just concluded, has occupied the entire time of the examining force of the Insurance Department since January second last, and during this period of nearly nine months every detail of the Company's transactions has been subjected to the closest scrutiny. The prompt closing of all accounts by the Company permitted the work to be commenced immediately after December 31, 1902, to which date its condition is herewith given. The counting of bonds and stocks owned, call loans on the collateral security of the former, loans on bond and mortgage, loans of policyholders, examination of deeds representing real estate owned, and finally confirming the title to these various assets by tracing their acquirements to the cash disbursed on account thereof, necessitated the expenditure of considerable time and labor. The great bulk of the examination work, however, involved the checking in detail of receipts and disbursements from the date of a prior examination by the Insurance Department in 1898 to the close of business December 31, 1902. This checking, with that made in 1898, now covers an investigation of receipts and disbursements for a period of eight years, as in 1898 these items were examined from December 31, 1894.

In an examination of a life insurance corporation whose transactions are as extensive as those of The Mutual Life, it is made necessary to formulate a line of procedure as to the general scheme of the work, which will result in ultimately arriving at a comprehensive result. If the scope of the investi-

---

31 Patterson, *op. cit.*, pp. 368 ff.   32 *Minutes of the Board of Trustees*, Nov. 23, 1898.
33 *Ibid.*, Oct. 27, 1903. The expense of state examinations to the Company in 1903 was $20,661.54.

gation were confined solely to ascertaining the fact that the corporation was solvent under the law, that is, that its assets were properly invested thereunder and equal to or in excess of liabilities, the time occupied in determining this question would be relatively limited compared to that required to determine likewise whether the Company had been managed in the best interest of policyholders, the cost of whose insurance to them, in a purely mutual company, depends largely upon an intelligent administration of its affairs.

An examination therefore of receipts and disbursements for a series of years becomes necessary, if we are to arrive at any idea of the conduct of a company's business, with the view of confirming the belief that the welfare of all policyholders has been conserved by the character of its management in the past. I believe the time occupied in establishing this fact was amply warranted. It necessitated among other things inspecting and reviewing in specific detail as to items contained therein, the monthly reports of all agencies since December 31, 1897. Thus agency receipts from new and renewal premiums with corresponding commission disbursements and all expenses of every nature pertaining to the procuring of new business or the renewing of old, have been thoroughly examined both as to domestic agencies and agencies under the supervision of the Company's Foreign Department. So also have all disbursements for expenses properly chargeable to home office been exhaustively reviewed. Every facility was afforded by the Company's officers and the heads of its several departments, thoroughly to accomplish the work, which has been materially expedited by the admirable methods in vogue at the home office in the handling of accounts and keeping of books of initial or final entry. A summation of this work follows, with a brief indication of the manner in which it was done.

That there was some extravagance in the life insurance business was by 1903 becoming apparent and was to lead in 1905 to the most thorough legislative investigation of the industry that has ever been conducted. The Armstrong Investigation of that year was, indeed, to influence life insurance so profoundly that 1905 has come to be recognized as a great landmark in the history of the business. To that investigation we now turn.

XII. The Armstrong Investigation

THE ARMSTRONG INVESTIGATION of 1905 was not, strictly speaking, a "bolt from the blue." For some time the weather forecasters in the insurance business had been watching the storm clouds gather. They had heard rumblings from the insurance press, insurance officers, and policyholders, and some of them had predicted the coming of far-reaching reforms. So when the storm broke, the perspicacious were not surprised—they were only astonished at the size of the tempest.

Among the signs of the approaching disturbance were the large losses to policyholders resulting from lapses. In 1890 93 percent of policy terminations in fifty-five companies were from lapse, and only 4.9 percent were from death.[1] During the ten years prior to 1895 twenty-six companies reporting to the New York Insurance Department issued more than six billions of dollars of new insurance, excluding that not taken by applicants, but they had at the end of that period an addition to insurance in force of only 45 percent of the total or $2,736,-000,000. Fourteen percent of the six billions was terminated by death, maturity, expiry, or change of policy, while 41 percent, or $2,507,000,000, was lapsed or surrendered. For this face amount of insurance, $140,-000,000 was paid out in surrender values, but the sum forfeited to life insurance companies far exceeded this figure. The operation of the deferred-dividend policy was largely responsible for this record.[2]

Another of the warning signals prior to 1905 was the violent fluctuation in addition to insurance in force. In 1890 $403,000,000 of insurance was added by twenty-six companies to their insurance in force, while in 1895 the increase was only $154,000,000. Such a situation meant that overhead costs were greatly augmented in the fat year and could not be cut proportionately in the lean. In extremities of this kind insurance officials, in at least some of the smaller companies, did not hesitate to falsify their statements to insurance departments in order to make better showings.[3]

1 Frederick L. Hoffman, "Fifty Years of American Life Insurance Progress," *American Statistical Association* (Boston, 1911), XII, p. 739.

2 Terence O'Donnell, *History of Life Insurance* (Chicago, 1936), pp. 568, 574.

3 *The Spectator*, LV (Aug. 1, 1895), 53.

Within certain companies there was also evidence of bad weather brewing. In The Mutual Life the total amounts paid in dividends remained almost stable from 1897 to 1904 in spite of the greater amount of insurance which had been and was being placed in force—an amount that totaled $577,000,000 for the period just mentioned. Emory McClintock, the distinguished actuary of the Company, was fully aware of the situation, but was not able to remedy it.[4] Furthermore, in 1902 one of The Mutual's agents, T. H. Bowles of Milwaukee, was dismissed for "insubordination." He at once began to make charges against the Company, to circularize policyholders in an effort to get proxies, and to stir up trouble generally. He did succeed in getting several persons to complain to the management about dividends, but he was ultimately silenced by a commutation of his renewal commissions.[5]

Criticism of The Mutual's management was, however, of minor significance compared with the row which was raging in The Equitable. In 1899 Henry Baldwin Hyde, founder of the company, died, and he was succeeded in the presidency by James W. Alexander, a nephew of the first president. High in the councils of The Equitable and owner of the controlling capital stock stood the son of Henry B.—Vice President James Hazen Hyde. Hereditary successions are fraught with the danger of weak heirs, and this case was to be no exception. Henry B. had feared as much and had tried to avert trouble by naming James W. Alexander as the guardian of his son. Such a position was extremely embarrassing to the president of The Equitable, and it became progressively worse, as James Hazen assumed a dictatorial attitude, organized with other directors of his company investment syndicates, and set the heads of New Yorkers wagging with his capers in private life. Finally, the situation became so unbearable that Gage E. Tarbell, head of The Equitable's Agency Department, led a campaign to oust Hyde from the company's management. Two camps were immediately formed within The Equitable, and they loosed their heavy artillery on each other. Blast followed blast, and what was at first but a family squabble soon became a public battle. The upshot of the whole affair was that Hyde finally withdrew from The Equitable, but the insurance industry generally was subjected to a vast deal of unfavorable publicity.[6] It was

4 Armstrong Investigation, *Testimony*, pp. 1731 ff., 1829 ff.   5 *Ibid.*, pp. 1323 ff., 1495 ff.
6 In June, 1905, the directors of The Equitable appointed a committee—the Frick Investigating Committee—to sift the mass of information produced. Hyde sold his interest in the society to Thomas F. Ryan, once the stage manager for Jay Gould, the organizer of traction systems in New York City, partner of Leopold II of Belgium in Congo mines and rubber plantations, and the power behind the throne in Tammany Hall. Ryan placed the stock, for which he paid $2,250,000, in the hands of Grover Cleveland, Morgan J. O'Brien,

this publicity which led directly to a comprehensive legislative survey of American life insurance.

The Armstrong Investigation was not an isolated or exceptional episode in American economic history. In fact, between 1897 and 1912 criticism of business was one of the favorite national sports. Legislators, muckrakers, and scandalmongers reveled in disclosing the shady, the profitable, and the monopolistic features of "frenzied finance." Inasmuch as no way to fame was shorter than the route of business inquisitions, innumerable politicians and publicists danced gaily along it.

This movement may arbitrarily be said to have begun with the passage of the Sherman Anti-Trust Act of 1890 and with the publication of Henry D. Lloyd's *Wealth against Commonwealth* in 1894. Theodore Roosevelt took up the cudgels against big business when he became President in 1901, earning thereby the appellation of "trust-buster," and the more conservative William Howard Taft carried on the campaign during his administration. The Northern Securities Company was ordered dissolved in 1904, the Standard Oil in 1911, and the American Tobacco Company in the same year.[7] Legislative investigations by the states or by the Federal Government were the order of the day—the most important one against the money trust being conducted by the Pujo Committee in 1912–1913. Only with the coming of Wilson's New Freedom, which was an attempt to preserve small enterprises, and with the outbreak of World War I did trust-busting come to a halt.

While the campaign against the trusts was on, passions ran high. The New York *Sun* greeted Theodore Roosevelt with "Hail Caesar, we who are about to bust salute thee." [8] Between 1902 and 1908 *McClure's Magazine* published Ida M. Tarbell's muckraking *History of the Standard Oil Company*, Ray Stannard Baker's *The Railroads on Trial*, Lincoln Steffens' *The Shame of the Cities* and *Enemies of the Public,* and at the time of the Armstrong Investigation Burton J. Hendrick's *The Story of Life Insurance*. In the same period the *Cosmopolitan* ran David Graham Phillips's *The Treason of the Senate*, Louis D. Brandeis made his

---

and George Westinghouse in the form of a trust deed, renewable at the option of the trustees. See Terence O'Donnell, *op. cit.*, pp. 575 ff.; G. A. Henderson, "History of the Insurance Investigation," reprinted in the *Insurance Examiner*, IV (Jan., 1936), pp. 14 ff.; and William J. Graham, *The Romance of Life Insurance* (Chicago, 1909).

7 Prior to these dates there had been a considerable agitation of the Populists against big business, the Granger Cases, and the regulation of public utilities. Henry George published his *Progress and Poverty* in 1879, and Edward Bellamy his *Looking Backward, 2000–1887* in 1888.

8 From "Topics of the Day," *Literary Digest*, XXXV (Nov. 9, 1907), 671.

famous speech on "Life Insurance; the Abuses and Remedies" before the Commercial Club of Boston, *Colliers* conducted a campaign against the patent medicine racket, and Upton Sinclair published his diatribe against the meat packers in *The Jungle*.[9]

Of all the attacks upon American business society, none hit life insurance more heavily than Thomas W. Lawson's *Frenzied Finance,* which began to appear in *Everybody's Magazine* in July, 1904. The author of this series of articles was a Boston financier, who, because of his social and business status, was in a position to know the inside workings of business and to command more respect and attention than professional muckrakers. With the deft skill of a trained publicity agent, he gave only enough information in his first article to arrest attention and to whet appetites. In subsequent installments, he opened his guns on the "Big Three"—The Equitable, the New York Life, and The Mutual Life. He pilloried them unmercifully in *Everybody's*, in newspapers, and in letters to policyholders. He damned a system of life insurance which resulted in heavy lapses, condemned marketing methods, and exposed many of the investment syndicates which had resulted in profits to insurance officers. When the insurance companies attempted to counterattack, Lawson began to deal in personalities and then to harass the smaller companies. He threw consternation into their camps, aroused lethargic policyholders, and awakened legislators to the need for action.[10]

THE ARMSTRONG INVESTIGATION GETS UNDER WAY

An investigation of life insurance in the first decade of the twentieth century was definitely in keeping with the times. In fact, life insurance could hardly have expected to escape the inquisitorial power of the state when holding companies, trusts, public utilities, the money market, and political machines were being hauled over the coals. Nor could the state remain blind to the practices which were thrown into painful visibility by the searchlights of the journalists and the floodlights of The Equitable's officers. An investigation was needed, and the state did not hesitate long in making provision for it.

On July 20, 1905, the assembly and the senate of the State of New York concurred in a resolution which stated the reasons for an investigation, pointed out those aspects of life insurance upon which information was sought, called for remedial legislation, and appointed a com-

9 See Cornelius C. Regier, *The Era of the Muckrakers* (Chapel Hill, N. Carolina, 1932).
10 Terence O'Donnell, *op. cit.,* pp. 778 ff,

mittee to conduct the investigation. This resolution is important and should be read with care. It directed the committee

to investigate and examine into the business and affairs of life insurance companies doing business in the State of New York, with reference to the investments of said companies, the relation of the officers thereof to such investments, the relation of such companies to subsidiary corporations, the government and control of said companies, the contractual relations of said companies to their policy holders, the cost of life insurance, the expenses of said companies and any other phase of the life insurance business deemed by the Committee to be proper, for the purpose of drafting and reporting to the next session of the Legislature such a revision of the laws regulating and relating to life insurance in this State as said Committee may deem proper.

The resolution thus made clear the following facts (1) that public criticism of life insurance had led directly to action by the legislature; (2) that the Superintendent of Insurance did not have the necessary powers to handle the situation; (3) that the investment practices of life insurance companies had aroused the most criticism; (4) that new laws were to be forthcoming; and (5) that the committee was to have but little time or money for its work. The order was thus a tall one, and the handicaps were obvious.

That the Armstrong Investigation bore fruit was owing to three main factors—first, to the personnel of the committee, secondly, to its counsel, and, thirdly, to the temper of the times. To this last point attention has already been drawn, but the first two points deserve a word of explanation. The committee, composed of five assemblymen and three senators, consisted of clear-thinking and fair-minded men, who had no axes to grind and no personal interests to protect. Chairmaned by William W. Armstrong, they conducted themselves admirably throughout the long days of tiring hearings.[11]

Just as important, if indeed not more important, to the success of the enterprise were the counsel and his assistants. The counsel was Charles Evans Hughes, a man but forty-three years of age. He had only recently brought himself into the public eye by investigating the cost of gas in New York City and by showing in the face of stiff opposition from the gas companies that the price of gas to consumers could equitably be reduced by 20 percent.[12] He was flanked by James McKeen, a lawyer experienced in the field of corporations, by Matthew Fleming, also a

11 The members of the committee were: senators, William W. Armstrong, chairman, William J. Tully, Daniel J. Riordan; assemblymen, James T. Rogers, Robert Lynn Cox, William W. Wemple, Ezra P. Prentice, secretary, and John McKeown.
12 Clark S. Northup, "Mr. Hughes' Career," Phi Beta Kappa Key, V (Mar., 1925), 683–690.

lawyer, by Marvyn Scudder, a financial statistician, and by Miles M. Dawson, an eminent actuary.

The Armstrong Committee was organized on August 1, 1905 and began its hearings on September 6 of the same year. At the first public session, held in the City Hall in New York, Senator Armstrong outlined the purpose of the committee, presented the committee's counsel, and then asked which of the companies interested were represented by counsel in order that their presence might be noted. This last move did not grant formal rights, which an appearance would ordinarily confer, "because the Committee's time is too limited to permit of more than the proper courtesy as we go along. We will for the present assume, if I may speak frankly, that counsel who are here, other than our own counsel, have no rights, but are entitled to every courtesy." Curt as this statement may now seem, it was not misunderstood by the counsel of the companies, for they realized that the committee's time was short, that the investigation was not a trial, and that all they could expect would be to assist their clients in avoiding incriminating testimony and in clarifying the practices of life insurance companies. James M. Beck, former Assistant Attorney General of the United States and counsel for The Mutual Life, made this clear in noting his presence.

Mr. Chairman, I appear for The Mutual Life Insurance Company of New York, and desire in its behalf to express its appreciation of the action of the Committee in permitting the counsel by courtesy to be here. We are very glad to be here and want to facilitate the labors of the Committee in every way in our power.[13]

Only The Equitable's counsel, ex-Governor Frank S. Black, expressed a desire "to offer some explanation"—a desire that was very sparingly gratified.

Counsel for the committee then reviewed briefly previous legislative investigations conducted in New York State. He pointed out that since 1877 no comprehensive investigation had been made of life insurance companies, for the assembly's investigations of 1882 and 1885 had been limited, respectively, to insolvency and to The Equitable's tontine policies. The findings of 1877 he summarized very briefly, thus striking the first really ominous note.

THE HEARINGS AND THE FINDINGS

With these preliminaries out of the way, Mr. Hughes began to interrogate witnesses. The testimony which he elicited from the persons

13 Armstrong Investigation, *Testimony*, p. 9.

who took the stand fills nearly five thousand closely printed pages, plus fourteen hundred pages of exhibits, plus many pages of written statements from companies not examined. This mass of material was obtained almost entirely by a man whose remarkable patience never failed, whose keen and logical mind was able to follow witnesses as they took sidetracks and to bring them eventually back to the main line, whose rapidly acquired knowledge of the technical aspects of life insurance will astound anyone who in an equal space of time has endeavored to master the subject, whose ability to sense the importance of clues casually dropped in the course of questioning bordered on genius, whose courtesy and tact won the respect of all, and whose determination to overcome obstacles drew the well-deserved admiration of the committee and the public. If Mr. Hughes seemed to pillory the large companies and to let the smaller ones off scot free, this was only because the practices which he was investigating were more apparent and easier to disclose when in bulk. Indeed, most of the small companies which did come into his purview appeared to be engaging in all the practices of the large ones.[14]

The reactions of witnesses to the investigation was in accordance with their personalities and their temperaments. Some were urbane and apologetic; others were confused; still others were openly hostile. Richard A. McCurdy was at the outset rebellious, and at one of his early appearances he refused to answer questions, and continually referred Mr. Hughes to those officers of the Company who were specialists in various branches of life insurance,[15] objected to the methods employed by Mr. Hughes, and criticized the course which the investigation was taking.[16] Robert A. Granniss, the first witness to be examined, proved to be a mine of information. Walter R. Gillette seemed to be muddled and uncertain of his ground. George F. Baker was somewhat abashed and uninformative. Frederic Cromwell was candid and proud of the

---

[14] This is also the opinion of one of the most recent and scholarly historians of life insurance, J. Owen Stalson, *Marketing Life Insurance* (Cambridge, 1942), p. 551.

[15] Armstrong Investigation, *Testimony*, p. 1450.

[16] *Ibid.*, pp. 1432–1433. Mr. McCurdy stated: "If you had been good enough to let me know a day before the nature of the investigation, the line of the investigation you were going to follow, and what I might be expected to answer, I should have been very glad indeed to have prepared myself to answer you as well as I could. But witnesses are brought here without any knowledge of the line of examination that is to be followed, and they are taken entirely unprepared, and I must say that I do not think it is fair treatment. On the other hand, if the Committee will pardon me for stating, and will allow me to state my views on the subject, I think the whole course of this investigation, as it is called, is entirely outside of what was in contemplation of the Legislature when the Committee was constituted. It was an investigation into the conditions of life insurance, and not what it is commonly called in the newspapers, an inquisition. And Mr. Hughes, himself, with all due respect, has been generally designated the Chief Inquisitor."

Company's investment record. Robert H. McCurdy attempted to be plausible, reading a long prepared statement. Finally, Emory McClintock, the Company's best witness, was clear, precise, and helpful. He tried to defend practices which he believed to be just and to avoid being put in positions which he knew were untenable. He made a distinctly good impression upon the committee, and his testimony is even now an excellent source of information concerning actuarial practice in the preceding period.

The reception by the press of the testimony furnished by these men varied widely. Trade papers were at first inclined to applaud insurance officials, and only toward the end of the hearings began to take a defensive position. Some articles favorable to the companies appeared in daily newspapers, but many of them were paid releases.[17] Leading magazines, as we have already seen, were markedly hostile, and most dailies adopted critical attitudes. The New York *Herald* was perhaps the least sensational, but the conservative New York *Times* did not pull its punches.

The support which the press and the public gave to the investigation not only facilitated the work of Mr. Hughes but also actually prevented the committee from failing to delve into all aspects of the life insurance business. Most of what was discussed, at least so far as The Mutual Life was concerned, has been dealt with in previous chapters—high salaries, managerial control, high pressure selling, rebating, organizing subsidiary companies, underwriting new security issues, investing in common stocks, making deposits in favored banks, the role of trustees, and deferred dividend policies. The general impression which the testimony gives is, first, that fundamentally the insurance companies were providing important services, secondly, that certain practices, of which extravagance was the most important, needed correction, and, thirdly, that The Mutual Life was no worse an offender than most other companies.

Other phases of life insurance, to which very slight attention has thus far been given in this book, were likewise treated by the committee.

17 *Ibid.*, p. 1741. One of these articles read as follows:

"The examination of Richard A. McCurdy, President of The Mutual Life Insurance Company, was resumed yesterday and proved of great interest. He called attention to the fact that the investigation had drifted into an inquisition, vague in its character and dealing with no issues. Witnesses were called without notice being given of what information was required, and the inquisitor at once began to impeach their testimony. Instead of information being sought on which to base remedial legislation, witnesses were put upon the rack, as the newspapers have it."

Such documents came within the purview of the Investigation, and witnesses were questioned about them. In the case of The Mutual Life, these articles emanated from the Company's publicity man, Charles J. Smith, who used the Telegraphic News Bureau at a cost of one dollar a line to place his dispatches.

One of these was industrial insurance, for testimony showed that two of the prominent industrial companies, the Metropolitan and the Prudential, had much larger percentages of expenses to premium receipts in 1904 than the "Big Three"—a fact which was to have been expected because of the nature of industrial insurance premium collections. A second object of Mr. Hughes's shafts was the State Insurance Department. Apparently much to the counsel's surprise, the Superintendent of Insurance frankly admitted that he was concerned in his examinations only with determining the bookkeeping accuracy and solvency of companies. In the third place, the committee sharpened its focus on nepotism and on the relationship of the companies to politics. These questions, in so far as The Mutual Life was concerned, are worthy of brief consideration.

Nepotism is not necessarily an evil and is so natural that it is bound to appear in all walks of life. It is only to be condemned when it leads to undeserved rewards or to inefficiency. In The Mutual Life there were certain favored relatives, but they were capable men, who were criticized only for the rather high remuneration which they received. Louis A. Thebaud, Richard A. McCurdy's son-in-law, was advanced from a position in the general agency for New Jersey, to a three-quarter interest in the Raymond Agency in New York—an interest which provided him with an income of $147,687.74 in 1904.[18] George Raymond, a brother of Charles H. Raymond of the Metropolitan Agency in New York, was for a time agent in New Jersey. Dan Gillette, the organizer of the Department of Revision and brother of Dr. Walter Gillette, was placed in a partnership agency in Texas. And Robert H. McCurdy, the most favored of all, was promoted from a partnership with Colonel Raymond to the superintendency of the Foreign Department (1885) and to the office of General Manager (1903).[19]

In the realm of politics testimony presented to the Armstrong Com-

---

[18] Armstrong Investigation, *Testimony*, p. 1230, and *Exhibits*, No. 259.

[19] At the end of 1882 young McCurdy had a one-fourth interest in the profits of the Raymond Agency in New York. From 1886 to 1892 this interest was one-half. *Ibid.*, p. 1226. As superintendent of the Foreign Department, he received a commission on premiums collected. At his own suggestion his commission rates were steadily decreased as the foreign business became more profitable. *Ibid.*, pp. 1204 ff. In 1904 Robert H. received $99,531.79 from the foreign business and $30,000 as general manager. *Testimony*, pp. 1205–1218, 1224–1227, and *Exhibits*, Nos. 256–257. There seems to have been some favoritism shown to certain concerns from which supplies were ordered. This seems to have been the case with L. W. Lawrence & Co. and the Globe Printing Co., from whom The Mutual Life obtained most of its printing and stationery. L. W. Lawrence, who was the owner of both companies, could not be found so no subpoena could be served upon him. The details, therefore, remained cloudy, except that printing and stationery were not purchased as a rule by competitive bids.

mittee showed that The Mutual Life had played an active role. It made contributions to the National Republican Committee in 1896 and 1900 because of a belief that William Jennings Bryan's free-silver platform would work to the disadvantage of policyholders by reducing the purchasing power of the dollar.[20] In 1904 the Company contributed money to defeat Alton B. Parker, the Democratic Presidential candidate, and made a gift to the Republican Congressional Committee in order to get a Republican Congress. And from time to time it supported the Republican State Committee in the hope of getting legislators favorable to life insurance.[21]

Moreover, The Mutual Life, in coöperation with The Equitable and the New York Life, kept watch over insurance bills introduced into state legislatures. "Strike bills," which aimed to provide lobbying jobs for sponsors or for their friends, were forever being aimed at life insurance companies, and frequently ill-advised insurance legislation was proposed by persons ignorant of the subject. That the companies should have defended themselves and their policyholders against inimical laws was not only necessary and just—a fact that was acknowledged by the Armstrong Committee[22]—but the burden of this task fell upon the "Big Three," whereas it ought to have been more evenly distributed, as it has been in recent years, among all companies. During sessions of the legislature in Albany the New York Life was represented by Alexander Hamilton, while The Mutual Life had as its agent Andrew C. Fields, who sometimes acted also for The Equitable. Criticism was leveled particularly at the latter, for he had been active in Democratic circles and maintained an establishment in the capital city as a lobbying headquarters.[23]

THE COMMITTEE'S RECOMMENDATIONS AND RESULTING LEGISLATION

The Armstrong Committee completed its public hearings on December 30, 1905, and submitted its report to the legislature on February 22, 1906. This report was an extremely important document, for it summarized the findings of the investigators and provided a basis for an extensive revision of insurance law. Nor was the new insurance legislation restricted solely to New York, for on February 1, 1906, a conference of governors, attorney generals, and insurance commissioners, who formed the Committee on Uniform Legislation or the "Committee of Fifteen,"

20 Armstrong Investigation, *Testimony*, pp. 1333–1356, and *Report of the Committee*, p. 21.
21 Armstrong Investigation, *Testimony*, pp. 2576–2579.
22 *Ibid.*, pp. 1200 ff., and *Report of the Committee*.
23 *Testimony*, pp. 1575–2011, and *Report of the Committee*, pp. 15–20.

was held in Chicago to secure the general adoption of the proposed New York statutes.[24]

The committee expressed itself in favor of mutual life insurance on the level premium plan with full statutory reserves and accordingly secured the enactment of a law to prohibit the creation of new assessment companies in New York State and to facilitate the mutualization of stock companies.[25] The committee also took a stand against the managerial control of the mutuals and to break it got through a law to liberalize elections. The terms of this statute required that lists of policyholders and their addresses be filed with the Superintendent of Insurance and be made available at the home offices at least five months before election. The boards of trustees or directors were annually to nominate candidates for vacancies, but any group of one hundred members had the same privilege. Voting could be by mail, by proxy, or in person, but all existing proxies were to be canceled, and new ones were to be valid for only one election. Finally, each company was to send ballots to all qualified voters with the names of all candidates on them at least two months before the election.[26]

Laws concerning the investment of life insurance funds were radically altered in view of the committee's findings. Because some companies had purchased land and erected buildings far in excess of their office needs and because these buildings had not proved to be good investments, the purchase of real property was no longer allowed without the approval of the Superintendent of Insurance. The exchange of such holdings was prohibited, and all unnecessary property was to be sold within five years. Prohibitions were also placed on the holding of common stock and collateral trust bonds, and restrictions on collateral loans were established, because these securities led either to a proprietory interest in other businesses or placed insurance funds at the mercy of majority stockholders. Within five years the insurance companies of New York State were to dispose of all such holdings. Furthermore, laws were passed outlawing subsidiaries, syndicates, the underwriting of new issues, and the pecuniary participation of officers in company investments.[27]

The committee also paid particular attention to the costs of getting new business, for its members had been startled at the moneys expended

[24] The Armstrong Investigation led to independent investigations in New Jersey and Wisconsin, but most states took the findings in New York as their guide to new legislation.

[25] New York Insurance Law, 1906, sections 52, 95, and 200.

[26] New York Laws of 1906, Chapters 123 and 354. New York State Insurance Law, section 94.

[27] New York Laws, 1906, sections 16, 20, 36, 100.

largely to enhance the prestige of various companies without thought of ultimate costs to the policyholders. "Not only has the rivalry of the three companies [the Big Three] proved detrimental to themselves, but it has acted as a spur to the smaller companies, which to keep their footing have been compelled to make outlays disproportionate to their abilities." [28] Accordingly a law was passed which limited the amount of new insurance which any company could issue in a given year, in the following manner:

Amount of Insurance in Force	Annual Limits of New Insurance
$ 50,000,000–$100,000,000	30% of insurance in force
$100,000,000–$300,000,000	25% of insurance in force
$300,000,000–$600,000,000	20% of insurance in force
$600,000,000–$1,000,000,000	15% of insurance in force
More than $1,000,000,000	$150,000,000 new insurance

Although this law did not prove to be practical in the long run, for the moment it served as a check upon the "Big Three." Industrial insurance was excluded from these restrictions because of the large lapse rate.[29]

As a further curtailment of expenses, corporations were prohibited from making contributions to political campaigns and were to have their lobbying practices out in the open.[30] Moreover, new laws provided that every salary of more than $5,000 paid by a life insurance company be approved by the board of trustees, that employment contracts be for one year only, that no salaries be paid after an employee's death, and that every expenditure of $100 or more be evidenced by a voucher. Commissions to agents had to be limited to prearranged rates, renewal commissions could not exceed 7½ percent for nine years, premium collection charges were to be held down to 2 percent after the tenth year, advances or loans to agents were prohibited unless proper collateral was provided, and all bonuses, prizes and rewards for a large volume of new business were outlawed. Finally, certain insurance expenses of a company were not to exceed the loadings on premiums received in any one year, plus the gains from mortality resulting from selection, nor was the annual cost of new business to be greater than a fixed amount of loadings on the premiums for the first year of insurance, plus the present values of the assumed mortality gains for the first five years during which the new policies were in force.[31]

28 Armstrong Investigation, *Report of the Committee*, p. 297.
29 New York Insurance Law, section 96. The New York Life was the only company in 1904 to exceed the quota thus established.
30 New York General Corporation Law, 1906, section 41, and Armstrong Investigation, *Report*, pp. 301 ff.
31 New York Insurance Law, 1906, section 98, and Armstrong Investigation, *Report*, pp. 304 ff.

To facilitate compliance with this last condition the valuation of policies on a *select* and *ultimate* system was proposed. The American Experience Table was an ultimate table, that is, its rates of mortality were those expected after the effects of medical selection had disappeared. The select and ultimate system took into consideration the assumed mortality savings resulting from medical selection. This was a pet idea of the Armstrong Committee's actuary, M. M. Dawson, for he was interested in providing a system of valuation which would require a smaller reserve on a policy during its first five years and which would provide adequate funds from the premiums for initial expenses.[32] In practice, the select and ultimate system did not work well and is of little actual importance. The purpose which it was intended to accomplish is largely achieved now by the modified preliminary term plan of valuation, whereby only part of the net premium is placed in the reserve fund during the first year a policy is in force.[33] Inasmuch as the adoption of these plans was optional, the larger companies, including The Mutual Life, did not employ them, but retained the more conservative, full, level-premium reserve system.

As regards rebating, the belief of the Armstrong Committee was that existing statutes were sufficiently stringent to cover all cases of life insurance officers and agents, but it proposed and saw enacted an amendment to the penal code making the recipient of a rebate guilty of a misdemeanor.[34] As regards surrender values, the opinion of the committee was that in the future a policy which had been in force three full years should have a surrender value, that the surrender charge should not be more than 20 percent of the reserve, or $25 for $1,000 of insurance, and that in the case of lapse, when no notice was received from the policyholder, the policy should be maintained as extended insurance so long as four-fifths of the reserve was great enough for the purpose.[35] As regards dividends, the conviction of the committee was, and a law was passed to this effect, that dividends on all future policies should be paid annually and that definite limits should be put on the proportion of surplus which could be placed in a contingency reserve. Thus, deferred-dividend policies were outlawed for the future; dividends on existing

---

[32] Inasmuch as the American Experience Table, which was so widely used, was an ultimate table, the select rates of mortality during the first five years were assumed to be 50, 65, 75, 85, and 95 percent of the full ultimate rates at the same attained ages. Maclean, *Life Insurance*, p. 160. See also New York Insurance Law, 1906, section 84.

[33] Maclean, *op. cit.*, pp. 149 ff., 537.

[34] Armstrong Investigation, *Report*, p. 318. New York State Penal Code, 1906, section 577K.

[35] Armstrong Investigation, *Report*, pp. 318–319. New York Insurance Law, 1906, section 88.

deferred-dividend contracts had to be declared and set aside each year; and large amounts of surplus could not be applied to the depreciation of investments without the consent of the Superintendent of Insurance.[36]

In order to alleviate the confusion which had grown up in the multiplication of policy forms to attract customers by catchy titles or supposedly liberal terms the Armstrong Committee got a law enacted which took the radical step of requiring all companies to use standard forms for insurance contracts.[37] In order to prevent some policyholders from profiting at the expense of others, mutual companies were forbidden to write nonparticipating contracts, and stock companies were required to issue either participating or nonparticipating policies, but not both.[38]

Finally, the committee got action on improving state supervision and on the kinds of information which the life insurance companies had to make public.[39] Examinations of every New York State company were to be made at least every three years or when the need was proved by a creditor, policyholder, or stockholder. Moreover, the Superintendent of Insurance was given the power to subpoena and examine under oath the officers of a company or any person believed to possess material information regarding its affairs and to obtain all books and papers relating to the business of the company being examined. A full report was to be made, and, if deemed advisable, published in the press of the state.[40]

THE MUTUAL'S CHANGE IN MANAGEMENT

The Armstrong Investigation and the insurance legislation of 1906 changed profoundly the operations of life insurance companies, although they left the fundamental concept of life insurance unchallenged and intact. Some of the laws which were passed proved to be inoperative and had to be altered, but those which remained on the statute books had three long-term effects: (1) life insurance companies were henceforth to restrict their activities definitely to the life insurance business, that is, were to stop other entrepreneurial functions; (2) life insurance was after 1906 to be conducted in all its branches on a conservative basis; and (3) a new code of business ethics was to be adopted by the industry. In future chapters these matters will be discussed in detail,

[36] Armstrong Investigation, *Report*, pp. 319-327. New York Insurance Law, 1906, sections 83, 87.

[37] Armstrong Investigation, *Report*, pp. 331-332. New York Insurance Law, 1906, sections 101-102.

[38] Section 56 of the insurance law was thus repealed. See articles of the Code of Civil Procedure. Armstrong Investigation, *Report*, pp. 328-331.

[39] Armstrong Investigation, *Report*, pp. 333-337.

[40] New York Insurance Law, 1906, sections 2, 7, 11, 39, 40. See Appendix, pp. 360-361.

but before leaving the Armstrong Investigation mention should be made of one of the immediate effects of the disclosures—the change in managerial personnel.

Before 1907 had ended most of the dominant leaders in the "Big Three" had resigned and the boards of trustees and directors had been reconstituted. John A. McCall resigned as president of the New York Life and died in 1906, a broken man. The good which he had done was completely overshadowed in the public mind by the practices which he had condoned. George W. Perkins, vice president of the New York Life and one of the initiators of the managerial system of agencies, also resigned and retired from the life insurance business. James W. Alexander withdrew from The Equitable Society and embarked on travels from which he did not return until 1909, while his former ward, James Hazen Hyde, went to reside in France, where he remained until 1941. The Board of the New York Life was reconstituted, and that of The Equitable, profoundly altered.[41]

The immediate effect of the Armstrong Investigation upon The Mutual Life was similar to that on the other large companies. On October 25, 1905, the Board of Trustees appointed [42] an investigating committee from among its members, composed of William H. Truesdale, president of the D. L. and W. Railroad, chairman, John W. Auchincloss, a merchant, and Stuyvesant Fish, president of the Illinois Central Railroad, to make recommendations concerning "organization, management, and affairs of the Company." This committee, assisted by counsel and public accountants, made a thorough examination of all aspects of the business and particularly of those "revelations of the past few months involving several of the leading insurance companies of this City, among them this Company, [which] have deeply impressed the people of the whole country." [43]

A spirit of reform swept over the Company and affected through contagion even Richard A. McCurdy. Early in 1905 he seemed to have a premonition of what was coming, for when some friends suggested a public testimonial to celebrate the twentieth anniversary of his election to the presidency, he remarked that any recognition of his service which the trustees desired to make in view of the forthcoming investigation better be "confined to this building and this room." [44] Subsequently he

---

[41] Lawrence F. Abbott, *The Story of NYLIC—a History of the Origin and Development of the New York Life Insurance Company from 1845 to 1929* (New York, 1930), pp. 180 ff., and William Alexander, *Seventy-five Years of Progress and Public Service, a Brief Record of the Equitable Assurance Society of the United States* (New York, 1934).

[42] *Minutes of the Board of Trustees,* Oct. 25, 1905.

[43] *Ibid.,* Nov. 16, 1905.   [44] *Ibid.,* April 26, 1905.

appealed to the Board of Trustees for harmony in face of the Armstrong disclosures, suggested the appointment of the Truesdale Committee, and began to institute reforms before this committee could make its report. He expressed himself as being "aware that the management of this Company has been the subject of severe criticism and that as a consequence its business to a great extent has suffered." He was, however, far from admitting that all the criticism which had been made was "just or deserved," but he was not "so blind as not to know that a public opinion" had been created and "that its persistence must continue to work harm for the business of the Company." Accordingly, he asked that his salary be cut in half, to $75,000, a request which was granted; he reported that the salaries of other executives had been reduced to effect a saving of $145,000 a year; he recommended that the general agents still on commissions be made managers of branch offices; he proposed that all lobbying be left to policyholders' protective committees; he opposed future contributions to political parties; he took steps to reorganize the Supply Department so that all materials would be obtained after competitive bids had been submitted; he recommended vouchers for all expenditures; and he defended syndicate participations by officers, maintaining that no executive or trustee of the Company had made any unlawful profit from them.[45]

These belated steps were in the right direction, but they were not to forestall the Truesdale Committee. In fact, as soon as President Mc-Curdy had taken them, the committee reported that it would make no recommendations at that time on salary changes, for such questions involved committing the Company "to the continuance of the present management." On the other hand, the committee made suggestions for a number of alterations in the Company's administration and got these suggestions adopted by the Board. It proposed that in the future all salaries should be fixed by the "whole Finance Committee, when not determined by the Board, the President, or other appropriate committee." [46] It asked that all legislative matters be handled by salaried members of the Law Department. It requested that the Supply Department be reorganized, both as to personnel and methods of operation. It wanted all contracts with general agents to be canceled, the Agency Committee, rather than the Executive Department, to approve all agency contracts, and the remaining general agencies changed to managerial agencies—a move which was designed especially to break up the Raymond Agency. It recommended that no officer, trustee, or other employee should be a party to any of the Company's business transactions in which he has a financial interest.[47] It demanded that the Committee on Expenditures should meet weekly and require appropriate vouchers for every expenditure. And it advised that only the president and first vice president should in the future be members of the Board of Trustees.

The similarity between reforms proposed by McCurdy and those put forth by the Truesdale Committee is striking and indicates that the weak spots in The Mutual Life had been found and were going to be strengthened. But one point of difference between the committee and Mr. McCurdy was apparent—the personnel of the future. When McCurdy became aware of the feeling against him, he resigned from the presidency on November 28, 1905, pleading ill health, and from the Board of Trustees on January 3, 1906.[48] These moves were followed by the resignation of Robert McCurdy as general manager, to be effective December 31, 1905, and as trustee, January 3, 1906. Frederic Cromwell, who served as acting president from November 29, 1905, to January 1, 1906, surrendered his position as treasurer, January 31, 1906; Robert A. Granniss, his position as vice president on March 28, 1906; Walter R. Gillette, his vice presidency on the same day; [49] Dr. E. J. Marsh, his post as medical director on May 14, 1906; and several others, their respective posts at subsequent dates. Thebaud and Raymond were dismissed as general agents, and several of the trustees withdrew from the Board.[50]

After the departure of McCurdy and his close associates [51] The Mutual Life had to appoint almost a completely new staff of officers, for only Emory McClintock, the actuary and first vice president, and W. W. Richards, the manager of the Real Estate Department, were retained from the old group of leading executives. Some of the new officers were promoted from the ranks, but one newcomer ought to be especially noted—Charles A. Peabody (1849–1931), president. Peabody came to the Company from the law, where he had had considerable experience with real estate investments. He was a man of high ethical principles, who was to fight shy of all those measures that had been condemned by the Armstrong Investigation. Although new to life insurance, he steered the

---

[47] *Ibid.*, Nov. 16, 1905, and May 14, 1906; also Article 25 of By-Laws.
[48] *Minutes of the Board of Trustees*, Nov. 29, 1905, and Jan. 3, 1906.
[49] *Ibid.*, Dec. 6, 1905, and Jan. 3, 1906.   [50] *Ibid.*, March 28, 1906.
[51] A settlement was made in 1909 with McCurdy and certain others of the resigned employees. See *New York Insurance Report (Miscellaneous)*, 1910, pp. 731 ff. The Company had certain claims against them, and they had renewal commissions and salary claims against the Company. The portrait of President McCurdy by John Singer Sargent was disposed of in 1907. See *Minutes of the General Committee*, Jan. 9, 1907.

Company successfully through its reorganization and the hard years which immediately followed 1905. He did not worship size, as had Mc-Curdy, but rather economical management. Nevertheless, The Mutual Life more than doubled its amount of insurance in force during his administration, as we shall see in more detail in a later chapter.

With the almost complete recasting of the executive branch of The Mutual Life, there was also a recomposition of the Board of Trustees, for many of the former members resigned, refused to run again, or were not renominated.[52] Because of the new laws governing the election of trustees, which required the establishment of lists of policyholders, the filing of nominations, and the mailing of ballots to those entitled to vote, the elections of 1906 were not held until December 18. Prior to this date, an organization known as the International Policyholders' Committee, endeavored to lead a movement against the new Peabody regime, as it led agitation against the new officers of the New York Life and of certain other companies. The counsel for this committee was Samuel Untermeyer, who became the stormy petrel of the life insurance industry. He was instrumental in securing the nomination of candidates to run against the administration ticket. Among the opposition list were the names of such prominent men as Samuel S. McClure, the publisher, John Wanamaker, the merchant, Cyrus L. Sulzberger, the importer, and finally none other than Charles Evans Hughes. The administration ticket was, however, overwhelmingly successful, securing about 185,000 votes, while the leading opposition candidate got 68,176, and Hughes received 4,592.

Incidentally, this election of 1906 cost The Mutual Life $150,781.86, and similar contests in other companies proved to be even more expensive—facts which led soon to a change in the laws so that lists of policyholders did not have to be made available in uncontested elections. The Investigation had resulted, however, in such a change of personnel and business morals that no danger was seen in relaxing theoretically desirable legislation if it proved to be unnecessarily expensive.

[52] The law required that all trustees be elected in 1906, not just the classes which would normally retire in that year. New York Laws, 1906, Chapter 354.

PART FOUR
1907-1943

XIII. A New Era in Life Insurance

FROM TIME TO TIME in the history of man, the occurrence of some great event has profoundly altered the course of institutional development—has interrupted the trends of the past and has inaugurated a new period of evolution. In the history of American life insurance this has been the case. The founding of The Mutual Life in 1843 marked the end of more or less feeble but persistent efforts to launch a life insurance industry in this country and the beginning of a period in which the basic principles and practices of the business were developed to a point where the risk of death could be shared advantageously and successfully with others. The coming of severe competition in about 1870 and of deep economic depression in 1873 denoted the termination of the early proliferation of life insurance institutions and the inception of an era characterized by managerial control and the extensive use of the deferred-dividend policy. Finally, the findings of the Armstrong Investigation and the resulting legislation introduced a period in which business morals have been high and more and better insurance has been made available to the American people.

One of the chief features of the history of life insurance since 1907 has been the extension of protection to large numbers of the low-income-earning classes. Industrial insurance, with its small policies, small weekly premiums, relatively high costs, and high lapse ratio, increased from $2,576,511,425 in force in 1907 to $23,345,412,020 in 1942.[1] In 1911 group insurance,[2] a form of life insurance aimed to cover the employees

---

[1] *Spectator Insurance Year Book*, 1943, p. 318b. Except for 1932 and 1933 the upward march of industrial insurance has been uninterrupted.

[2] Group insurance is wholesale life insurance. A master policy is issued to an employer, and a certificate is given to employees, showing that they are covered. The insurance company receives the premiums from the employer, thus reducing the costs of collections. The employer may pay the premiums or may work out some scheme by which both employer and employees contribute. Usually the insured group must number at least 50, and a certain percentage of employees must participate so that the insurance company will not be subjected to adverse selection. The insurance is actually term insurance which may be renewed annually. No medical examinations are required. Coverage for the individual runs from $500 up to $30,000, depending upon salary, years of service, size of the group, and terms of the contract. If a worker ceases to work for the employer, he may turn his certificate into some other form of insurance. The wholesale features of the policy allow low rates of

in a single business establishment, was introduced; it grew to $19,862,-098,178 in 1942.[3] Savings bank insurance, championed by Louis D. Brandeis as a way of cutting out the cost of selling insurance and instituted in Massachusetts in 1904,[4] in New York in 1938,[5] and in Connecticut in 1941,[6] grew slowly, until Massachusetts had $239,895,570 in force December, 1943. Government insurance,[7] issued by the Bureau of War Risk Insurance, was inaugurated during World War I for soldiers and sailors. It amounted to $40,285,000,000 in 1919, and although it dropped to $2,561,712,000 by June, 1939,[8] it was revived during World War II.[9] In August, 1944, about sixteen million National Service Life Insurance policies were in force, providing protection of $121,000,000,-000. Old age, but not life, insurance for the masses was begun in this period. It was furnished by the Government under the terms of the Social Security Act of August 14, 1935, as amended in August, 1939,

---

premium. So-called "wholesale insurance" is nearly the same as group insurance, but there is no master policy, each of the 10 to 50 insureds making a separate contract with the insurer.

[3] *Spectator Insurance Year Book*, 1943, p. 137A. At this date 30,633 policies were in force—an average of $648,389 a policy.

[4] The Massachusetts law providing for savings bank life insurance dates from June 26, 1907. See A. T. Mason, *The Brandeis Way; a Case Study in the Workings of Democracy* (Princeton, 1938); Clyde Casady, *Massachusetts Savings Bank Life Insurance* (Springfield, Mass., 1935); and Edward Berman, *The Massachusetts System of Savings Bank Life Insurance* (Washington, D.C., 1935).

[5] Law of April 6, 1938. In these schemes, the insurance department of a bank is separated financially from the banking departments, so that one cannot be held liable for the obligations of the other. The allocation of overhead has, perhaps, been made to favor the insurance branch, but efforts have been made to do justice in this regard.

[6] In this connection, attention should be called to the Wisconsin State Insurance Fund, established in 1911. This institution may be described roughly as a state operated life insurance company. On Dec. 31, 1938, the Fund had only $2,122,090 of insurance in force.

[7] Law of Oct. 6, 1917. This was the so-called "soldiers' and sailors' insurance law." It provided for the automatic free insurance of men in the armed forces for $4,500 against death and total disability. This provision of the law ceased on April 12, 1918. But from October 6, 1917, men in the service could make application within 120 days, or later date of enlistment for annual renewable term contracts up to $10,000, on which they would pay the premiums monthly. Each policy could be renewed up to five years after the conclusion of the war, but provision was made whereby each contract could be converted into ordinary life, endowment, or limited-payment life. The first policies of this kind were issued on May 1, 1920.

[8] See *Annual Reports of the Secretary of the Treasury on State of Finances*. Mention should also be made of the World War Adjusted Compensation Act of May 19, 1924, whereby in certain cases the credit to veterans could be used for 20-year endowment insurance.

[9] National Service Life Insurance Act, Oct. 8, 1940. Applications must be made within 120 days of entrance into active service. Benefits are payable only in event of death; premiums are paid monthly by the insured. Premiums are waived in the event of total disability. Under the Soldiers' and Sailors' Civil Relief Act, Oct. 17, 1940, the Government guarantees to pay the premiums on policies up to $5,000 held by service men in commercial companies. Any moneys thus paid are considered to be loans. Later the sum was raised to $10,000.

and covered 41,600,000 people in 1941.[10] Finally, assessment insurance,[11] with all its many pitfalls for the unwary, and fraternal insurance,[12] with its danger of poor management, were strengthened by reserve requirements, although the total amounts borne by these carriers did not increase.

A second important characteristic of life insurance history during the years between 1907 and 1943 was an attempt to grade applicants for insurance into various classes of risks and to charge them accordingly. In the preceding period, as we have seen, extra premiums for many climatic, regional, and occupational risks were abolished and the proportion of people who might be insured at standard rates was increased. Joint investigations by the Actuarial Society of America and the Association of Life Insurance Medical Directors (the so-called Medico-Actuarial Investigations), published between 1912 and 1914 and added to at various subsequent dates, provided so much information about mortality rates among the physically and the occupationally impaired that insurance in "substandard" risks was made safe and was placed among the contracts offered by a large number of companies.[13] Even nonmedical insurance, that is, insurance without medical examination, was made practicable by these investigations and by experience with industrial policies, for which medical examinations had never been required. Issued after 1922,[14] nonmedical policies facilitated the placing of insurance in those districts where medical service was difficult to obtain. Finally, increased knowledge about the correlation between mortality and physical condi-

[10] See *Statistical Abstract of the United States.* The Social Security Act provides for Old Age and Survivors Insurance and through the states for unemployment insurance and public assistance of various kinds.

[11] The amount of assessment insurance in force in 1905 was $633,353,087 and in 1941, $206,731,962. *Spectator Insurance Year Book,* 1906, p. 633, 1942, p. 413b.

[12] Fraternal insurance in force amounted to $8,079,743,281 in 1907 and to $6,337,281,825 in 1942. *Ibid.,* 1942, p. 426b. On Jan. 1, 1926, assessment insurance companies in New York State had to have reserves based on the American Experience Table and 4 percent interest. In 1910 a national conference was held at Mobile, Alabama, at which representatives of the fraternal societies and insurance commissioners participated. Recommendations were made for the passage of a bill (the Mobile Bill) looking toward the actuarial solvency of fraternal societies. In 1912 a new plan (the New York Bill) was proposed, in order to eliminate differences between the insurance of fraternal societies and that of ordinary companies.

[13] R. Henderson, "Insurance on Substandard Lives," *Annals of the American Academy of Political and Social Science,* CXXX (1927), and Franklin S. Mead, "Substandard Insurance: Its Evolution and a Review of Some of Its Principles," *The Record* (June, 1922), XI, 158. It should be noted in passing that the New York Life Insurance Co. wrote substandard business in 1896, but the big development of this business did not take place until after the Medico-Actuarial Investigations had been made.

[14] The Travelers was probably the first to issue this insurance; the Prudential was the second. See James S. Elston, "The Development of Life Insurance in the United States During the Last Ten Years," *Transactions of the Actuarial Society of America,* XXVII, Part 2 (1926), 330.

tions led to the adoption of a new principle—"preferred risk" contracts, that is, policies with low premiums for persons who could meet high physical standards.[15]

A third feature of the history of life insurance since 1907 has been the selling of insurance to meet specific needs of the insured. Although the fundamental concept of this development was as old as life insurance itself and was loudly proclaimed in the early publicity of The Mutual Life, new meaning was given it in the twentieth century by the conscious efforts of life insurance companies and their agents. Thus, "business" insurance was given a new lease on life about 1910 by campaigns to get members of partnerships to take insurance against the loss of associates, corporations, against the death of gifted managers, or anyone, against indebtedness or for capital needs.[16] Life insurance for inheritance tax purposes began to be important about 1917, and trust companies were sometimes named as the beneficiaries of large policies after the early twenties in order to permit more flexibility in the details of settlement.[17] Protection against special risks, such as waiver of premium or income benefits in case of total and permanent disability or of sickness,[18] and the payment of twice the face amount of the policy (double indemnity) in case of death by accident,[19] were also introduced. Furthermore, policies were gotten up specifically to meet such exigencies as retirement, the education of children, the loss of salary through disability, and even Christmas expenditures.

Attempts to provide insurance plans to meet specific needs have led (1) to contracts with larger elements of savings, (2) to a greater use of term insurance in order to provide protection at very low premiums, and (3) to a combination of these two principles. The modified life contract, which provides for a redistribution of premium payments so that

15 The Washington Life had in 1905 a "preferred class policy." The Metropolitan, in 1909, issued a special whole life policy in amounts of $5,000 or more. The Continental American claims to have written in 1922 the first preferred risk on which there was no reduction of commission rates to the agent. See J. Owen Stalson, Marketing Life Insurance; Its History in America (Cambridge, 1942), p. 646.

16 Ibid., pp. 636 ff.

17 A trust company will also assume discretionary powers in the settlement, whereas the life insurance company will not. The term "unfunded trust" has been applied to a trust instrument which has been executed in advance of the maturity of the policy by the death of the insured. The trust company is named the beneficiary and the details of settlement are specified in a trust deed. The term "funded trust" means a trust fund created to pay premiums on a policy.

18 Stalson, op. cit., pp. 640–641, and Elston, op. cit., pp. 45–46. The Equitable offered a health and accident contract along with its regular policies in 1919 and 1920 and other companies experimented briefly with this plan.

19 The Sun Life of Maryland added an extra payment to its industrial policies in case death was accidental. The Minnesota Mutual included a similar provision in ordinary policies in 1902. The New York Life gave real popularity to this clause in 1918.

the premiums are low during an initial period and higher thereafter, was launched by the Prudential and the Aetna in 1924 and achieved success.[20] The life income policy, the family protection plan, and the family income contract [21] were designed to secure regular incomes for beneficiaries. The life expectancy policy, issued by The Mutual Life in 1899, which is basically "long-term" term insurance, "convertible term," which is term insurance with the privilege of converting without a new medical examination one contract to another form of policy, and "renewable term," a term contract with an option to renew, have all aimed to provide protection without a large outlay of money. Furthermore, certain clauses, called optional modes of settlement, were added to most contracts to permit the accomplishment of different purposes as the conditions of the insured were altered.[22]

Another distinguishing mark of life insurance since 1907 has been the training of agents for the technical aspects of their profession. This trend toward "informed selling" and sales management has, in the opinion of some observers, been the outstanding development in life insurance of the last thirty-five years.[23] Strong as this statement may be, much can be said in its support. The old notion that the "person who has failed at everything else can sell life insurance" has not held true in recent times. Life insurance to meet all kinds of needs has required of life insurance agents a wide enough knowledge and experience to allow them intelligently to fit a life insurance plan into an estate and to harmonize insurance and financial programs for their prospects.

That agents might have the requisite information, life insurance companies started at the beginning of this century to give training courses to

[20] There were also half premium policies. See *Eastern Underwriter*, 25th yr., No. 48 (Nov. 7, 1924), p. 1.

[21] Stalson, *op. cit.*, p. 645, attributes the origin of this policy to the Continental American.

[22] Life insurance benefits were at first paid in lump sums, for settlement of obligations by lump sum payments was the usual practice when life insurance got under way. Gradually, provision was made for installment settlements, as we have seen in earlier chapters, but lump-sum settlements are still the rule. The optional settlements may provide: (1) leaving the sum insured with the insurance company at a specified rate of interest for a specified length of time or upon call; (2) payment of the sum insured plus interest in equal installments for a fixed number of years; (3) payment of the sum insured in installments during the lifetime of the beneficiary; (4) payment in installments of a fixed amount until the principle is exhausted; and (5) the application of the sum insured to the purchase of an annuity for the beneficiary at favorable rates.

Perhaps attention should be called in this place to the fact that prior to World War I German companies did much of the reinsurance business on large risks. Upon the withdrawal of the Germans from this country, American companies rapidly assumed the reinsurance business, so that there was no decline in the handling of large policies.

[23] See the excellent study on selling life insurance by Stalson, *Marketing Life Insurance; Its History in America*, p. 576.

their salesmen. Schools of salesmanship cropped up, and institutions of higher learning established courses in life insurance and life insurance selling. The National Association of Life Underwriters, founded in 1890, endeavored to place life insurance salesmanship on a new and higher plane. It created the American College of Life Underwriters in 1927 and thereby gave impetus to a movement which designated qualified agents as Chartered Life Underwriters—a title in the selling field comparable to Certified Public Accountant in the field of accountancy. Finally, the Life Insurance Sales Research Bureau, founded in 1920, was set up to make, as its title implies, specialized studies in the problems of life insurance marketing.

Still another important aspect of recent life insurance history is the high ethical standard of the business. The Armstrong Investigation brought to a jolting stop most of the undesirable practices of the period from 1870 to 1905, and no widespread abuses have since been disclosed. The Pujo Committee of 1912,[24] appointed to look into the alleged money trust, took a great amount of testimony on the subject of life insurance, and so, too, did the Temporary National Economic Committee of 1938, but neither one of these bodies discovered any managerial evils except in extremely isolated instances.[25] Even the size of life insurance companies, which the inquisitors were expected to condemn, escaped serious assault. Furthermore, life insurance officers, although paid less than executives in industrial and banking establishments of equal size, have been distinguished business leaders, trustees have looked upon their duties as real trusts rather than as entrepreneurial opportunities, and state insurance departments have extended their supervision to include all phases of the business in order the better to safeguard the interests of policyholders.

Life insurance history since 1907 has further been characterized by the nature of its investments. Investment banking, the formation of syndicates, and the operation of subsidiaries of every kind have been almost entirely abolished, and investments have been restricted largely to mortgage loans, bonds, and within limits to real estate. Although such holdings have tended to protect life insurance funds, the course of economic developments has had a disturbing effect upon investments. The long and severe depression which began in 1929 caused profound changes in the portfolios of life insurance companies. The hard times which befell railroads and which caused their securities to decline in

---

[24] See *Money Trust Investigation* (Washington, D.C., 1912).

[25] See *Temporary National Economic Committee, Investigation of Concentration of Economic Power* (1941), Monographs 28, 28A.

value led life companies to reduce their holdings of railroad bonds. At the same time, companies had to foreclose many of their loans on real property, thus reducing their mortgages and increasing their real estate. Losses were large, and new investment outlets were limited. Surpluses were reduced, policy loans increased for a time, and large amounts of money were placed in low interest-bearing government bonds. The gross rate of interest earned on mean invested funds by one hundred companies fell in this period from a high of 5.33 percent in 1929 to 3.96 percent in 1942.[26]

THE GROWTH OF LIFE INSURANCE

Another remarkable feature of the history of life insurance since 1907 is its enormous growth. Although the total of ordinary insurance fell off in 1906 because of the disclosures made by the Armstrong Investigation—the first retrogression since the depression of the 1870's—a slight recovery was made in 1907 in spite of the economic recession of that year and the peak of 1905 was passed in 1908. By 1917, when the United States entered World War I, ordinary insurance in force was nearly twice what it had been in 1907, and about half of the increase had been registered after 1913. From 1918 to 1931 both ordinary and industrial insurance trebled in amount, while from 1919 to 1931 the youngest member of the insurance family—group insurance—increased nine times. In 1932 the severe economic depression began to have the effect of reducing the total amount of all insurance in force—the second time this had occurred in American history. In 1934 industrial and group insurance began to recover, and in 1935 they passed their former high points, but ordinary insurance did not begin to go up until 1935 and did not exceed its previous high until 1940.

Several aspects of the growth of life insurance from 1907 to 1943 deserve special mention. In the first place, the number of companies in the field was greatly increased after the Armstrong Investigation, for entrepreneurs were led to believe in the lucrativeness of the business and to think that the charges leveled at the largest companies would allow them to enter the market. Whereas the annual average of new companies from 1895 to 1904 had been 7.2, the annual average from 1905 to 1914 was 28.8, the high point being reached in 1909, with 48. In the twenties there was another splurge of new companies, 47 being established in 1928, but the annual average was not so great as in the earlier period.

26 *Spectator Yearbook* (1942), p. 343b.

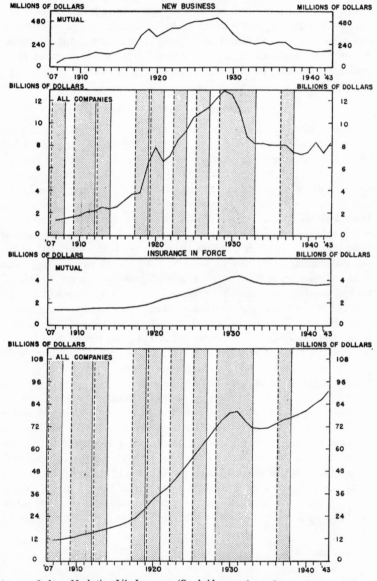

CHART XII

GROWTH OF ORDINARY LIFE INSURANCE, 1907–1943

*Peaks in business are indicated by broken vertical
lines; troughs by solid vertical lines*

Sources: Stalson, *Marketing Life Insurance* (Cambridge, 1942), pp. 821–22; *Spectator Insurance Yearbook* (Philadelphia, 1939 and 1943); the turning points of the business cycle are those made public by the National Bureau of Economic Research (1941).

As there were periods when the number of new insurance carriers increased, so, too, there were times of contraction. From 1912 to 1917, inclusive, the annual average of companies discontinuing business was 15.3, and from 1928 to 1933 it was 28.2.[27] Yet most of the companies that discontinued business were merged with stronger companies to the benefit of the policyholders of the terminating institutions. The total increase in the number of companies from 1906 to 1937 was 205; 368 were in operation at the later date. The tendency was for the newcomers to spring up in the Middle West and South. Yet the seventeen largest companies in the country, having 78 percent of the total insurance in force in 1935, were founded prior to 1876, while six of the largest companies in the New York area had 56.9 percent of the insurance in force in 1938, and ten New England companies had 19.5 percent of the total of the same date. Thus, although the older and Eastern companies have retained the lion's share of life insurance business, the relative position of the largest institutions has been somewhat altered, for those companies writing industrial, group, and health insurance have pushed ahead.

TABLE 35

LARGEST COMPANIES, RANKED ACCORDING TO AMOUNT OF
INSURANCE IN FORCE [a]

Company	KIND OF INSURANCE WRITTEN		RELATIVE POSITION	
	1905	1942	1905	1942
The Mutual Life	Ordinary	Ordinary	3	9
Metropolitan	Industrial	Industrial	2	1
	Ordinary	Ordinary		
		Group		
New York Life	Ordinary	Ordinary	1	4
The Equitable	Ordinary	Ordinary	4	3
		Group		
Prudential	Industrial	Ordinary	5	2
	Ordinary	Industrial		
		Group		
Northwestern Mutual	Ordinary	Ordinary	6	8
John Hancock	Industrial	Industrial	7	6
	Ordinary	Ordinary		
Mutual Benefit	Ordinary	Ordinary	8	10
Penn Mutual	Ordinary	Ordinary	9	12
Aetna	Ordinary	Ordinary	10	7
		Group		
Travelers	Ordinary	Ordinary	16	5
		Group		
Mass. Mutual	Ordinary	Ordinary	12	11

[a] Spectator Yearbook 1906 and 1943.

Companies writing industrial and group insurance, as well as ordinary, have profited from having large agency forces, a large number of

[27] For more detailed figures see Stalson, *op. cit.*, pp. 752-753.

small policyholders who are potential purchasers of ordinary insurance, and from the fact that neither industrial nor group insurance has been so adversely affected by depressions as has ordinary insurance. Furthermore, it should be noted that the idea of mutuality has prospered, as can be seen from the fact that the Metropolitan, Equitable, and Prudential have been mutualized, that only the Aetna and Travelers of the first ten largest institutions are stock companies, and that in 1937 eighty-eight mutuals had 74 percent of the insurance in force, while two hundred and forty-four proprietary companies had 26 percent of the total. Finally, attention should be called to the fact that the average size of ordinary policies was $1,954 in 1907 and $2,067 in 1942, while the average size of industrial policies was $137 in 1907 and $254 in 1942.

The Mutual Life's share in the general growth of life insurance since 1907 has been large in view of the fact that the Company has never written group or industrial insurance and that the transfer of its foreign business to other companies reduced the field of its activity. Only two companies which have restricted their business to ordinary insurance have surpassed The Mutual in amount of insurance in force, and one of these, by a very narrow margin. Yet the management of The Mutual Life in the last thirty-five years has never made a fetish of size. Charles A. Peabody, president of the Company from 1905 to 1927, was, in truth, opposed to rapid growth, and for ten years after 1907 supported the idea that new business should be strictly limited. Even in 1909–1910,[28] when the curbs of the Armstrong legislation on size were made so lenient as to be almost noneffective,[29] Peabody secured the establishment of a voluntary maximum, which remained in force until the end of 1916.[30] Moreover, David F. Houston, president of the Company from 1927 to 1940, pursued extremely cautious and conservative policies, while Lewis W. Douglas, who came to the presidency in 1940, was not particularly concerned with growth except as it was necessary to add younger lives and better risks to the body of policyholders and as it fostered an agency force of such

[28] See New York Laws, chapter 33 of 1909. Later amended by chapter 697 of 1910, chapter 369 of 1911, chapter 304 of 1913, chapter 360 of 1916, chapter 511 of 1917, etc.

[29] These changes were made much to the amazement and surprise of Theodore Roosevelt when Charles Evans Hughes was governor of New York, see *Chicago Daily Tribune*, March 4, 1919.

[30] Resolution of Oct. 25, 1910. The limit on new business was $170,000,000. This restriction was not removed until June 27, 1917, when new business was easy to get. See *Minutes of the Board of Trustees*, Nov. 29, 1910, and June 27, 1917. After this latter date the Company had at various times to get permission from the Superintendent of Insurance, as provided for in the law, to exceed the legal limit. Legal limits on new business have never been very effective.

excellent quality that it would effect an initial selection of risks—goals which would ultimately reduce the cost of insurance. He held that security and cost were the most critical criteria by which life insurance operations should be measured.

In spite of the fact that The Mutual's management since 1907 has not accentuated the virtues of size, that the Armstrong Investigation had deleterious effects on the sale of life insurance, that for ten years a policy of restriction was followed, and that industrial and group insurance were never sold, The Mutual Life has had a remarkable growth. During World War I, the Company's new business nearly trebled, and from 1914 to 1929, it nearly quadrupled, while its insurance in force tripled from 1907 to 1930. During the depression of the thirties, new business fell off, but insurance in force, after declining from 1930 to 1933, remained fairly steady in the next few years. It started upward in 1943.

THE AMERICAN ECONOMY AND LIFE INSURANCE, 1907–1943

The major changes which have taken place in life insurance in the last thirty-five years—great overall growth, marked expansion of insurance among low- and middle-income groups, and the development of contracts to meet specific needs—have resulted mainly from conditions created by the evolution of the American economy. Life insurance, like all other great social institutions, has tended, on the one hand, to adapt itself to its environment and, on the other, to effect alterations in that environment. But as the whole is larger than any of its parts, so a given institution is, in the long run, more profoundly influenced by its environment than is the total environment by a single institution.

One of the most important features of the environment in which American life insurance has operated since 1907 has been the growth of economic activity. Although no virginal "trans-Mississippian" territories remained to be developed and foreign business had to be forgone by many New York companies because of statutory limitations on new insurance placed in force and hostile foreign legislation,[31] the economy of the United States expanded so greatly that life insurance had fertile soil

---

[31] Canada is, of course, excepted.

FOREIGN BUSINESS OF UNITED STATES COMPANIES

(Insurance in force, in thousands of dollars)

Year	Amount	Percent of Total	Year	Amount	Percent of Total
1900	$781,041	9.21	1920	$663,689	1.57
1905	1,142,063	8.27	1925	150,397	0.22
1910	1,026,431	6.26	1930	114,557	0.11
1915	982,204	4.31	1935	91,213	0.09

into which to push its roots. The sheer growth of American business goes far, indeed, toward explaining how life insurance was able to reach such remarkable heights within the period under survey.

Production, basic to all economic expansion, was greatly augmented, even though the rate of increase became less rapid and more irregular than it had been in the nineteenth century. Reference to Chart I, page 7, gives ample testimony to this fact. The volume of agricultural production grew from an index of 83 in 1921 to 110 in 1940,[32] while that of industrial production went up from an index of 158 in 1909 to 373 in 1939.[33] Certain "new" industries, such as the telephone, the automobile, the radio, the airplane, plastics, and chemicals, and some "new" crops, such as soy beans and alfalfa, grew at an enormous rate, because they were merely being fitted into an economy which was already highly developed.

Increased production meant that goods were available to sustain a larger population; and the population did increase as is shown in Table 36.

TABLE 36

POPULATION OF THE UNITED STATES [a]

Year	Number	Percentage Increase over Preceding Census
1910	91,972,266	21.0
1920	105,710,620	14.9
1930	122,775,046	16.1
1940	131,669,275	7.2

[a] *Census Reports,* Department of Commerce, Bureau of the Census.

That the rate of increase of the population was not greater is attributable to many factors of which the desire for a higher standard of living rather than more children and a falling off in immigration were of primary importance.[34] The standard of living, as measured in dollars expended annually per capita for consumption, rose from $293 in 1909 to $571 in 1940.[35] This improvement was made possible by new mechanical techniques, an increased division of labor in manufacturing establishments, and the use of more mechanical power per capita—the amount of in-

---

[32] *Statistical Abstract of the United States* (1942), p. 742.

[33] *Ibid.,* p. 886.

[34] The birth rate per thousand of population was 25.0 in 1915 and 18.9 in 1941. The average family had 4.7 persons in 1900, 3.8 in 1940. Immigration was 1,285,349—an all-time high —in the 1907 fiscal year and was 51,776 in the 1941 fiscal year. The total number admitted in the period 1905–1909 was 4,947,239; in the period 1935–1939, 272,422. *Statistical Abstract of the United States* (1942), pp. 44, 105, 122.

[35] The 1909 figure is from National Industrial Conference Board. The 1940 figure is derived by Mutual Life Research Division from Department of Commerce data.

stalled horsepower in the country rising from 42,000,000 in 1899 to 1,230,816,000 in 1935.[36]

The increase in the population meant a larger potential market for life insurance, while the higher standard of living resulted in attempts

CHART XIII

PROPORTION OF POPULATION IN EACH AGE DISTRIBUTION OF TOTAL POPULATION, 1850–1980; ESTIMATED AFTER 1930

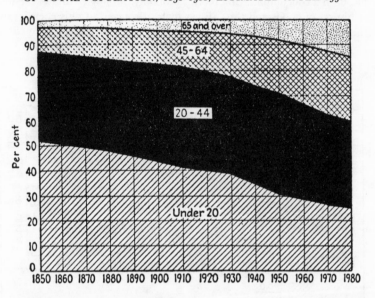

to provide the amenities of life after working days were over—attempts that created an enlarged demand for combination life insurance, endowment, and annuity policies. Furthermore, the average length of life of white males in this country was raised by improved medicine, public health, and living conditions from 48.23 in 1900–1902 to 63.65 in 1942 and for white females from 51.08 to 68.61 between the same dates.[37] The greatest advances were attained in the younger age group rather than in the older, which meant that although the population lived in general to a more advanced age, the chances of living beyond three score years and ten were not much enhanced.

[36] Wright, *Economic History of the United States*, p. 668.

[37] *Statistical Bulletin, Metropolitan Life Insurance Company*, April, 1944, pp. 6–7. Since 1900, the expectation of life at birth of colored persons has increased 21 years.

This alteration in the age composition of the population of the United States and the difficulty older persons encounter in finding employment have tended to increase the demand for life insurance savings plans to provide for old age.

The field for life insurance has been further widened by the extension of our use of money as a measure of value and as a medium of exchange. In earlier chapters a point has been made of the fact that life insurance has been a concomitant of a money economy. Money facilitates the distribution of goods and thus allows man to concentrate his energies on the production of one product rather than to disperse them in an effort

CHART XIV

DISTRIBUTION OF THE LABOR FORCE, 1870–1938

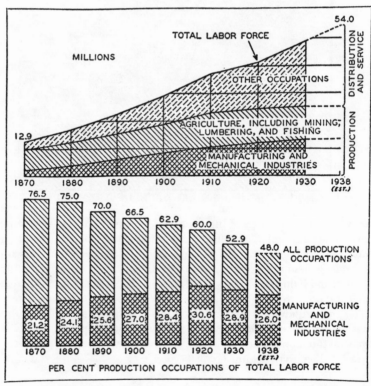

Source: National Industrial Conference Board, *Studies in Enterprise and Social Progress,* p. 48.

to produce everything he needs. The "one" product can be exchanged for cash or credit, which in turn can be used for the purchase of consumers' goods. Economic interdependence results from this process and so, too, does the concentration of the means of production in the hands of fewer individuals. When a person can no longer find employment for his labor or for his capital, he has to live from savings. Under these circumstances life insurance is a boon, for it not only furnishes protection from the economic consequences of early death but also makes possible the accumulation of a reserve.

During the last thirty-five years the use of money has been greatly extended. In agriculture, farmers have to a large extent produced money crops rather than diversified products to meet their own needs. In industry, the trend has been similarly toward specialization and the division of labor, with little or no thought that the immediate workers will consume all that they turn out. Commerce has grown by leaps and bounds, as is evidenced by the ever larger number of persons engaged in trade, which means that economic interdependence is being augmented.

Finally, the market for life insurance has been enlarged by the continued urbanization of our population, for, as has been pointed out previously, the inhabitants of urban areas have need of more life insurance proportionately than persons residing in rural areas. In 1920 the number of people employed in manufacturing exceeded for the first time the number engaged in agriculture and the value added to goods by manufacturing, which had passed the value of agricultural products in 1899, greatly increased in excess. This industrialization made urbanization on a large scale possible, and by 1940 56.5 percent of the population was living in places of 2,500 or larger and 12.1 in cities of 1,000,000 or more.[38]

LIFE INSURANCE AND THE BUSINESS CYCLE, 1907–1943

Although urbanization, the extension of our money economy, a higher standard of living, the lengthening of the average expectation of life, and the growth of population enlarged the market for life insurance in the period 1907–1943 and made possible an increase in the amount of insurance in force, the life insurance business did not enjoy a steady, unbroken expansion. Life insurance seems to have become more susceptible than it was formerly to fluctuations in economic activity—to

[38] *Statistical Abstract of the United States* (1941), p. 7, and *Sixteenth Census of the United States* (1940).

expand with greater speed in periods of prosperity and to contract to a greater extent in periods of depression. This fact may be explained chiefly on the grounds that (1) life insurance per capita is larger than it was, (2) that the savings factor in life insurance has been stressed, with the result that insurance companies are more liable to the withdrawal of funds than they were, (3) that increased surrender values have encouraged this trend, and (4) that the swings of the business cycle in recent times have been exceptionally violent.

During the early part of the twentieth century the downward sweeps of the business cycle were not so pronounced as they were to become after World War I. From 1897 to 1920 the United States enjoyed a long-term, economic prosperity which was only paralleled in our history by the good times after 1792 and those after 1847. As in these earlier periods, so, too, after 1896, the trend of wholesale prices was upward. There was an increase in the world supply of gold, particularly from the South African fields, and an expansion of credit. Farmers were more prosperous than they had ever been before, because of a rise in agricultural prices which exceeded the rise of the general price level. Industry expanded rapidly, finding new outlets for its goods in foreign markets, commerce profited from an increased exchange of goods, and railroads prospered from the larger volume of traffic.

Depressions have always been less severe and of shorter duration during upward secular trends in prices and business activity than they have in long-term downward trends—and the depressions between 1900 and 1920 were no exception to the rule. The recession of 1903, the "panic" of 1907, the war crisis of 1914, and the contraction in 1919 immediately following the cessation of hostilities were all of minor depth and scope. The depression of 1907, which reached its trough in June, 1908, was aggravated unnecessarily by the lack of a reserve of lending power in the New York money market, but this insufficiency was remedied by the temporary Aldrich-Vreeland Act of 1908 [39] and the Federal Reserve Act of 1913. The "outbreak of war crisis" in 1914 was likewise made worse by special factors—the drain on American gold because of large imports of foreign goods early in 1914, an unusual amount of short-term foreign loans in this country, the dumping of foreign-owned American securities onto the market, and the temporary reduction in the export trade. But these difficulties were soon overcome, and war orders ushered in an extraordinary boom. Similarly, the minor setback to business in 1919,

---

[39] The Aldrich-Vreeland Act provided for the authorization of an issue of emergency national bank note currency to meet demands for money in times of stringency.

which was influenced by problems of demobilization, gave way shortly
to prosperity as the demand for civilian products increased and European nations placed orders in the United States for goods with which
to get through the winter.

Life insurance was buoyed up by these relatively good times. During
this period total ordinary insurance slipped backward only once, and
that was in 1906, when the effects of the Armstrong Investigation were
most severely felt. The amount of new ordinary insurance written was,
however, more directly influenced by business conditions than insurance
in force. A decided falling off in new insurance was registered in 1906;
the 1905 figure was not topped until 1911; a reduction took place in
1914; but in 1919 there was no setback. The Mutual Life's new insurance series shows a strong reaction to the Armstrong Investigation, but
not to the panic of 1907, a slight decline in 1914, and a large increase in
1919. Surrenders and lapses were the most sensitive of all aspects of the
life insurance business. They increased greatly from 1905 to 1906, were
high again in 1914, but were not much affected by the recession of 1919.
In The Mutual Life surrenders reached peaks in 1908 and 1915, and
started up in 1919, while lapses attained turning points in 1906, 1913,
and 1918.

In May, 1919, revival from this first post-war recession began, the
price index soaring from 198 to an all-time peak of 244 in May, 1920,
and bank loans and discounts rising 23 percent from October, 1919, to
June, 1920. In the spring of this latter year contraction was visible, as
European nations, having resumed production, reduced their purchases
in America and Americans went on a buyers' strike because of high
prices. Prices fell precipitously from the peak to 136 in June, 1921, agricultural prices sank even more rapidly and much lower, and bankruptcies became more numerous than in any previous comparable length
of time.

This second post-war depression was not an auspicious inauguration
for the "torrid twenties." Nevertheless, recovery began in the fall of
1921, industrial production increased, commercial activity was great,
agricultural output held up remarkably well, and strange to relate, because of its rarity in the upward swing of the cycle, price levels remained
almost stable.[40] In view of these conditions some observers envisaged a
"new era" in economic history—an era of prolonged prosperity, in which
the business cycle would disappear. More perspicacious economists
pointed out, however, that all was not well in the body economic. World

[40] Prices rose slightly from 1922 to 1926 and declined a little from that date to 1929.

War I had created many maladjustments, of which the most threatening were the contraction of enormous public and private debts while prices were high and then the creation of conditions—the destruction of production equipment, the loss of markets, and after 1920 low price levels—which made repayment of debts without monetary depreciation almost impossible. Some industrial lines showed definite weakness because of overproduction, especially tin, rubber, copper, and coal. Railroads and public utilities were caught in rising costs and the rigidity of rates. Immense foreign loans tended to keep interest rates high. And worst of all, heavily indebted agriculture was faced with abnormally low prices.[41] Finally, a speculative craze hit the security exchanges. As money began to find investment in stocks, the prices of shares rose. Before long money was being borrowed at 10 per cent to buy stocks, which if dividends on the basis of earnings were paid, would yield only 2 percent on the purchase price. From 1926 to September, 1929, the index of 421 common stocks in New York rose from 100 to 225, and in the twenty months ending in September, 1929, the value of stocks on the New York Exchange increased by more than $51,000,000,000. In the early fall of 1929 stock prices had become sticky; speculators began to sell; between September 3 and November 13 share values on the New York Exchange fell by $30,000,000,000, and by June, 1932, stock prices had reached an index of 34 (1926 = 100).

The depression which followed this stock market crash was deep, and the bottom of it was not reached until March, 1933.[42] Prices fell from 95.3 in 1929 (1926 = 100) to 64.8 in 1932, industrial production declined from an index of 311 in 1929 to 192 in 1933, bankruptcies increased by one-third during the same time so far as liabilities were concerned, and unemployment rose to unprecedented heights. By the time business was rounding the corner, the Roosevelt Administration launched its New Deal program for (1) a more equitable and socially desirable distribution of wealth and income, (2) the maintenance of high wage levels and shorter working hours for labor, (3) higher farm prices, and (4) priming the economic pump by public works and other spending projects. Desirable as these and other measures may have been, they tended to keep costs of production high, while prices remained low, thus discouraging capital from seeking employment. At the beginning of 1934 the general

---

[41] From 1914 to 1918, 33,000,000 additional acres in the United States, Australia, Argentina, Canada, and India were put down to wheat. These countries had 50 percent of the world's exports of wheat in 1913; 94 percent in 1928. The corresponding percentage of the Danubian countries fell from 40 to 5 during the same period.

[42] The turning points in the business cycle used here are those prepared by the National Bureau of Economic Research.

CHART XV
SURRENDERS AND LAPSES, 1907–1943

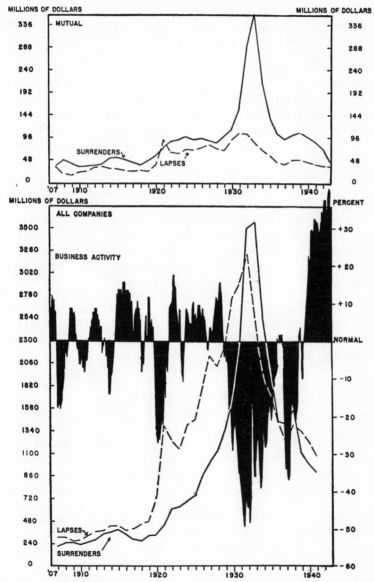

Source: New York Insurance Department, *Reports,* (Albany, 1908–1942); The Cleveland Trust Company, *American Business Activity since 1790* (Cleveland, 1944).

price level was 25 percent lower than that of 1929 and agricultural goods were 45 percent below the 1929 mark. In order to raise prices, the dollar was devalued in terms of gold, and, although temporarily and to an unexpectedly small extent, prices did rise, the chief effect of devaluation was to stimulate the mining and importation of gold and the keeping of interest rates down. These rates became so low and the government itself became such an important lender of money that institutional investors, like life insurance companies, were sorely hit.

From April, 1933, there was very slow and moderate recovery to a peak in April, 1937. At the latter date, wholesale prices were only 8 percent below the 1929 level; the realized national income was 50 percent more than it had been in 1933; industrial production was at an index of 303 as compared with 311 for 1929, but unemployment was still rife. The last half of 1937 brought a sharp reaction in which the number of unemployed doubled, prices slumped by 10 percent, agricultural prices by 25 percent, and industrial production returned to the 1934 level. Recovery from this recession was extremely slow, prices remained low and unemployment remained high. With the outbreak of war in Europe in September, 1939, and more especially with the entry of the United States into the conflict in December, 1941, business jumped into the revival and then into the boom phases of the cycle. All curves portraying prosperity went upward, but they contained in them the threat of inflation, the creation of new maladjustments, of which the Federal debt will probably be the most serious, and indications that the fall following the boom may be a hard one.

The reaction of ordinary life insurance to these up and downs of business has followed what has become and promises to remain a fairly definite pattern. In the rather mild depression of 1920–1921 the insurance in force of all companies did not decline, nor did the outstanding insurance of The Mutual Life fall off, but in 1932 the story was different. The ordinary insurance of all companies did not pass the 1931 figure until 1940. New ordinary business of all companies, on the other hand, started downward in 1930 and has not regained the ground lost—a condition which The Mutual Life has shared. In 1940 and 1941 some increase was registered, but the gains did not hold in 1942. Surrenders for all companies more than doubled from 1930 to 1932, while other voluntary terminations grew considerably—and again The Mutual Life contributed its part to these increases. The more life insurance is considered as a means of savings, the greater will be such runs in poor times.

XIV. Recent Trends in Policy Contracts

IN ITS EFFORTS to curb cut-throat competition among life insurance companies and to do away with those forms of life insurance contracts, which were deemed to be misleading or disadvantageous to the public, the Armstrong Committee proposed and secured the enactment of a law which required companies in New York State to issue only prescribed, standard policies. The cue for this action had been given by experience in the field of fire insurance, where the system had worked well; and the drastic step was taken when a weeding out of undesirable policies from the many in existence seemed impracticable. Thus, on January 1, 1907, when the new law went into effect, The Mutual Life could write business only on the same forms as other New York companies, and these contracts were limited to life, single premium life, endowment, single premium endowment, limited payment life, joint life, term, and five types of annuities.

In some respects the standard forms marked a step forward, but in others they were less progressive than the contracts previously issued by The Mutual Life. Thus, the new forms omitted guaranteed cash surrender values, although they contained loan values, and they offered such a small choice of policies that the drafting of an insurance plan to meet the particular needs of an individual was made more difficult, although this problem was partially solved by the introduction of three optional modes of settlement. These arrangements for paying death claims, which had been granted in part prior to 1907, provided that (1) the proceeds from insurance might be left with the insurer at 3 percent interest until the death of the beneficiary; (2) such proceeds might be paid out in equal annual installments over a prescribed number of years with any remainder at the death of the beneficiary going to his estate; (3) they might be paid to the beneficiary as a life annuity with a minimum of twenty annual payments guaranteed. Other provisions in the 1907 policies were that dividends be paid annually, that the insured could reserve the right to change the beneficiary, that the automatic settlement on lapsed policies was extended term insurance rather than paid-up insurance, and that in event of lapse the policy could be reinstated within three years, upon evidence of insurability and the payment of defaulted premiums with interest.[1]

From the beginning the standard forms were subjected to severe criticism. The companies felt that stereotyped contracts needlessly curbed competition and mitigated against the furnishing of adequate protection. Furthermore, to have standard forms prescribed by all states meant that different kinds of contracts would have to be provided for each jurisdiction. The Superintendent of Insurance for the State of New York endeavored to overcome some of these difficulties by approving other contracts than those first issued in 1907. Thus, The Mutual Life was permitted to write a joint life limited payment policy, yearly renewable term insurance, an educational fund form, and a continuous installment life contract,[2] and it was allowed to guarantee cash surrender values. In order to meet competition in other states, however, The Mutual Life adopted policy forms which were more liberal than those forced upon it in New York. New Yorkers did not like this turn of events, and they joined their voices with those of the companies and of the Committee of Fifteen [3]—the latter represented insurance officials of various states—in a chorus against standard forms. In the face of this opposition New York State decided to abandon its position in the matter as of January 1, 1910.

With the dropping of standard forms, however, the State of New York did not intend to let conditions revert to what they had been prior to 1905. It decided that sufficient control could be exerted by requiring the companies to secure state approval of all contracts delivered in New York and by insisting upon the insertion in policies of certain standard provisions. These provisions, as amended from time to time, were in 1942 the following: [4]

a) that the insured is entitled to a period of grace of thirty days in which to pay premiums, but if a claim arises during this grace period the policy

[1] In case of misstatement of age, the amount payable was defined as the amount the premium paid would have purchased at the correct age.

[2] The joint limited payment life was introduced in 1907, the other three contracts, in 1908. The Educational Fund was a yearly renewable term policy which each year decreased in amount so that the proceeds at death would be just sufficient to provide for annual installments of the amount selected in the application until the beneficiary attained a certain age. Information on these and other contracts of the period 1907–1942 has been obtained from a file of policies maintained by the actuary of The Mutual Life.

[3] The Committee of Fifteen grew out of a conference, held in Chicago in February, 1906, by state governors, attorneys-general, and insurance commissioners. Its recommendations provided a guide for subsequent legislation.

[4] Insurance Law, State of New York, section 155. The dates of various changes are available in McKinney's *Consolidated Laws of New York Insurance Law* (Brooklyn, Edward Thompson Co.).

shall be considered in force and any sums due on it may be deducted from the amount payable in the settlement;

b) that the policy shall be incontestable after it has been in force from date of issue for a period of two years during the lifetime of the insured [5] except for non-payment of premiums, for violation of the conditions relating to military and naval service, and at the option of the insurer for disability benefits and additional death benefits resulting from accident;

c) that the policy or the policy and the application shall constitute the entire contract;

d) that if the age of the insured has been misstated, any amount payable under the policy shall be such as the premium would have purchased at the correct age; [6]

e) that dividends be paid annually;

f) that the options available in the event of default after premiums have been paid for three years shall be indicated, together with a table of loan, surrender, and other values. The surrender charge is limited to two and one-half percent of the face amount of the policy.

g) that policy loans may be obtained up to the cash surrender value at the rate of 5 percent;

h) that the reserve basis used in determining non-forfeiture benefits or annuity payments be specified;

i) that the policy may be reinstated upon evidence of insurability within three years of the time of default unless the cash surrender value has been exhausted by payment or unless the period of extended insurance has expired.

j) that no policy of life insurance shall be delivered or issued for delivery which excludes liability for death except under the following provisions:

1) inside the United States and Canada in the event of death occurring as a result of service in the military, naval, or air forces of any country at war, declared or undeclared, or in any ambulance, medical hospital or civilian non-combatant unit serving with such forces, either while serving with, or within six months after termination of service, in such forces or units; or outside the United States or Canada while in such forces or units;

2) in the event of death occurring within five years from the date of issue of the policy, as a result of war, declared or undeclared, when the cause of death occurs while the insured is outside the United States or Canada and the insured dies outside such areas or within six months after returning thereto;

3) in the event of death occurring as a result of suicide within two years from the date of issue of the policy;

---

[5] The phrase "during the lifetime of the insured" was inserted after the case of *Monahan vs. Metropolitan Life Insurance Co.* (1918) 283, Illinois 136, 140. The court ruled that in the absence of a "during the lifetime of the insured" phrase, the policy was not contestable even in the case of fraud, if the insured died prior to the expiration of the contestable period.

[6] Insurers are forbidden to ante-date policies more than six months in order to give the insured lower premium rates, Insurance Law, State of New York, section 156.

4) in the event of death occurring as a result of aviation under conditions specified in the policy;

5) in the event of death occurring within two years of the date of issue of the policy as a result of a specified hazardous occupation or while the insured is resident in a specified foreign country;

6) in any of the above cases, the Company shall pay upon the death of the insured an amount not less than the reserve on the face amount of the policy, except in the case of death occurring in military service outside the United States and Canada, the Company shall pay the gross premiums charged, less dividends paid.

POLICIES WITH A LARGE SAVINGS OR INVESTMENT ELEMENT

The substitution of standard provisions and state approval of contracts for standard forms allowed life insurance companies to increase the number of types of life insurance contracts which they offered to the public. Although the bulk of business has been in ordinary life, limited payment life, endowment, term, and annuity contracts, various combinations of these forms and the extension of some of the principles which they embody have been important in the last thirty-five years.

When the standard provisions replaced standard forms (January 1, 1910), The Mutual Life simply introduced into New York State those policy forms which it was using in other states, for they contained the required terms. Shortly thereafter, however, the Company began to extend its line with the idea of meeting more of the specific insurance needs of a larger number of people.

One class of new policies had as its aim the accentuation of the savings or investment element in life insurance—an element which is large in limited payment, endowment, and annuity contracts. Arrangements of many kinds may be made on these basic plans, but a few of them as made available by The Mutual Life deserve special mention. Since 1907 the Company has allowed endowments to be paid as annuities, as provided for in the optional modes of settlement, which makes possible the securing of a steady income in later years when the need for life insurance has presumably diminished.[7] From 1924 to 1930 The Mutual Life issued a few retirement endowment and income contracts which paid a monthly income beginning with the end of the endowment period and in addition the face amount of the policy at this time or at prior death. In 1935 the Company adopted the endowment annuity plan whereby the insured would receive after a given age (55, 60, 65) monthly payments for life,

[7] In 1923 the Company introduced a single premium endowment monthly life income policy.

with ten years payments certain and whereby, in case of his death prior to the maturity date, his beneficiary would get the face amount of the policy. Efforts were increasingly made to provide for endowments maturing at specified ages to coincide with the wishes of applicants—a part of a general tendency toward "tailor made" contracts. Also, a trial was given between 1923 and 1928 to the practice of writing insurance through savings banks with the end in view of guaranteeing a minimum savings plan. The insured dealt only with the bank, and the Company only with the banks, but this scheme was abandoned because of the confusion to which it led.[8]

Contracts which are of the strictly investment type are annuities. In 1907 The Mutual Life had among its offerings a single premium life annuity, a joint and survivor annuity payable until the death of the last survivor, a deferred annuity which provided for annuity payments beginning after the lapse of a certain number of years, and a survivorship annuity with payments to the beneficiary beginning with the death of the insured. In subsequent years this list was considerably enlarged. In 1908 the Company began to write deferred survivorship annuities with payments beginning after a given number of years following the death of the insured; in 1911 it added a cash option deferred annuity; in 1913, an annuity certain followed by a deferred annuity, which provided for payments certain for the number of years selected in the application and, if the annuitant lived beyond this period, for an annuity until death; [9] in 1931 a retirement income plan [10] and a temporary annuity which are

[8] This scheme seems to have been devised by Edward A. Woods of The Equitable in 1921. He made an arrangement with the Peoples Savings and Trust Company of Pittsburgh whereby a depositor in the bank agreed to deposit a given amount every month for a stipulated number of years. The bank guaranteed to pay the depositor a given sum in case of death before completing the payments. The bank, in turn, covered its risk by paying premiums on a policy with The Equitable. This plan of "insured savings" has been strongly opposed from certain quarters. See *Eastern Underwriter*, Jan. 14, Nov. 18, and Dec. 16, 1921, and Oct. 16, 1925. The Mutual had an arrangement of this kind with the Harris Trust Co. of Chicago.

[9] From 1919 to 1929 the Company wrote a single premium life and annuity plan. From time to time the provisions of the various contracts were altered. This was true of June, 1917, the latter part of 1923, and the early months of 1924, 1932, 1935, and 1940. Between 1928 to 1931 the Company wrote an investment annuity plan. It provided for annuity payments during the life of the annuitant and the payment of a sum at his death. It was little more than an annuity, plus a single deposit at a guaranteed minimum rate of interest.

[10] This contract provided for a monthly life income with five years' payments certain to the annuitant if he were living on the maturity date and for payment to the beneficiary of the cash value of the contract if the annuitant died before the maturity date, or of the remaining payments certain if the annuitant died within the five years after the maturity date. This plan was in a way a substitute for the retirement endowment and income contract which was dropped in 1930 and for the cash option deferred annuity which was discontinued in 1931.

well described by their names; and in 1932, a refund annuity [11] which aimed to prevent loss on an annuity contract in case of early death by paying to the annuitant's beneficiary the excess of the single premium

CHART XVI

GROWTH OF THE ANNUITY BUSINESS IN THE MUTUAL
LIFE, 1907–1943

*Premiums Received for Annuities as Percentage of
Total Life Insurance and Annuity Premiums*

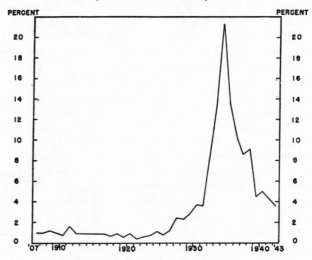

over the annuity payments made—a contract which was replaced in 1939 by a life annuity with payments guaranteed for ten years.[12]

The amount of annuity business was not large in proportion to that on other forms of contracts until about 1928. With the coming of the deep depression of the early thirties and low interest rates, many persons felt that life insurance and annuities afforded excellent investment opportunities.

They realized that premiums were computed on the supposition that money would earn 3 percent or more,[13] that the interest rates guaranteed

11 The refund annuity was similar to a life annuity except (1) that payments were to be continued until the total payments made by the Company equaled the single premium paid, whether or not the annuitant was living, (2) that after two years and before all the guaranteed payments had been made, the contract could be surrendered for the discounted value of the remainder of such payments and (3) that a beneficiary was named in the contract.

12 Under this contract surrenders were allowed only after the death of the annuitant and before all the ten-year payments certain had become payable.

13 From 1909 to 1924 annuity premiums were based on the British Offices Experience

under optional modes of settlement were high, and that the mortality rate among annuitants was low and hence favorable to them. Many persons even borrowed from banks at 2 percent in order to buy life insurance and annuities. The business done in single premium insurance and in annuities grew by leaps and bounds, reaching a peak in 1935.

As interest rates fell, the tendency to invest in single premium insurance policies and annuities naturally increased as long as the premium rates were not increased. This meant that the companies were getting large sums for investment at current rates lower than the rate being earned on the existing assets. In addition, the mortality among annuitants was increasingly lower than had been assumed. The result was that rates for all types of single premium contracts were increased. Other steps were taken to curtail this "watering down" of the interest yield through the dumping on the companies of large sums primarily for investment purposes. Thus, agents' commissions on annuities and single premium policies were reduced in 1930; amounts of insurance and annuities to be written on single premium basis were limited in 1934

TABLE 37

SINGLE PREMIUM EXPERIENCE: THE MUTUAL LIFE, 1930–1943 [a]

(In thousands of dollars received)

Year	Total New Premiums Life Insurance & Annuities	Single Premiums Life Insurance & Annuities	Percentage
1930	19,971	5,011	25.1
1931	19,746	8,488	43.0
1932	18,364	7,581	41.3
1933	22,761	11,095	48.7
1934	36,458	22,050	60.5
1935	60,029	41,792	69.6
1936	31,727	19,174	60.4
1937	26,970	17,780	65.9
1938	22,079	13,400	60.7
1939	18,830	12,091	64.2
1940	14,015	8,184	58.4
1941	10,858	5,346	49.2
1942	7,101	1,866	26.3
1943	7,401	1,789	24.2

[a] Excludes premiums for disability benefits, double indemnity, and dividends applied to purchase dividend additions.

Select Tables of Mortality for males and females and 3 percent interest, the McClintock Annuity Table being discarded. In 1924 the American Annuitants Select Table, male and female, and 4 percent was adopted. In 1933 the interest rate used was reduced to 3¾ percent, males were set back one year and females five years—measures which, of course, raised the rates. The interest factor was lowered to 3½ percent in January, 1935, and to 3 percent in November, 1935. In July, 1938, the 1937 Standard Annuity Table, with males set back 1 year and females 6 years, and 3 percent interest was adopted; in December, 1939, the interest rate assumed was dropped to 2½ percent, and in December, 1941, life annuities were set back 2 years for males and 7 years for females, while the interest rate was 2 percent. Rates on single premium life insurance were raised in 1935, 1939, and 1941.

and again in 1941; and in 1942 the writing of single premium insurance and some annuities were restricted to The Mutual's full-time agents.

LOW COST INSURANCE AND SPECIAL PLANS

Contracts which provide for a large element of savings are suitable for those who can afford them, who look forward to retirement, or who desire to make special provision for dependents, but they do not meet by any means the needs of all. In fact, during the depression years there was a growing demand for insurance requiring low premium payments, and, paradoxical as it may seem in the light of the discussion in the previous section, for insurance without any "savings" element, i. e., term insurance.

The type of insurance which superficially appears to have the lowest cost is short period term, for it provides protection against the "contingency" of death rather than, like ordinary life, the certainty of death —a fact that may make its reputed cheapness illusory. The usual form of a term policy provides insurance for a definite period—five, ten, fifteen, or twenty years—and contains the privilege of exchanging the contract for an ordinary life, limited payment life, or endowment policy, either as of the attained age or as of the original date, during all except the last few years of the term period. This kind of term policy was issued by The Mutual Life from 1907 to 1927 and again from 1938 onward, and has had a certain popularity.[14] A different type of term policy made available by the Company after 1923 was automatic convertible term, which provided for an automatic change at the end of the term period to a permanent insurance plan selected in advance.[15] The Company also wrote yearly renewable term contracts, running to age 65 or for a specified period of years with an annually increasing premium and the privilege of changing under certain restrictions to permanent insurance.[16] Finally, The Mutual Life adopted in 1942 a "term to age 65" policy at a level premium rate.

[14] Exchange was not granted on 5 year term. As originally written, 80 percent of the reserve at the time of exchange was applied toward payments of the premiums on the new policy; the age of the insured on the new policy was his attained age at that time; and the policies which he could select were those written at the time of change. In the case of exchange for policies as of original date, one of the important restrictions was an age limit of 55 years.

[15] At first the length of term insurance was one year, later it was any number of years up to ten; and then one, two or three years. Under convertible term, the policyholder was not in danger of being unable to get a policy with the provisions which he wanted because the insurer had discontinued it. He selected his permanent plan when he took out his convertible term policy.

[16] These policies were written from 1908 to 1938. They were replaced by the very similar "term with increasing premiums" in 1938, but this policy is issued only in one State.

TABLE 38

ANALYSIS OF THE MUTUAL LIFE NEW BUSINESS PAID FOR

(By plan of insurance)

Plan	YEAR 1943				YEAR 1942			
	Number of Policies	Percentage of Total Number	Amount of Insurance	Percentage of Total Amount	Number of Policies	Percentage of Total Number	Amount of Insurance	Percentage of Total Amount
Ordinary life	1,325	2.36	$5,002,471	2.93	1,528	2.57	$6,795,002	4.35
Life to 85	11,230	20.00	33,766,923	19.80	15,288	25.74	38,166,611	24.42
Preferred risk	4,669	8.31	35,856,494	21.02	4,609	7.76	32,795,834	20.99
Limited payment life								
Less than 20 payments	396	.70	1,820,698	1.07	387	.65	1,136,158	.73
Twenty payments	10,800	19.23	20,904,757	12.25	10,821	18.22	18,645,469	11.93
More than 20 payments	3,857	6.87	8,519,685	5.00	4,779	8.05	8,819,670	5.64
Family income	1,707	3.04	8,369,787	4.91	1,296	2.18	6,028,997	3.86
Double protection	129	.23	391,732	.23	329	.55	978,795	.63
Juvenile	6,606	11.76	8,240,112	4.83	6,666	11.22	7,918,255	5.07
Total life plans	40,719	72.50	122,866,059	72.04	45,703	76.94	121,284,791	77.62
Endowments								
Less than 20 years	1,630	2.91	5,185,092	3.04	847	1.43	1,935,885	1.24
Twenty years	3,341	5.95	6,773,277	3.97	2,612	4.40	4,347,520	2.78
More than 20 years	5,897	10.50	14,417,205	8.46	5,508	9.27	10,378,185	6.64
Endowment annuity	1,174	2.09	5,862,756	3.44	886	1.49	3,626,964	2.32
Juvenile endowment	1,428	2.54	1,988,366	1.17	511	.86	668,946	.43
Total endowments	13,470	23.99	34,226,696	20.08	10,364	17.45	20,957,500	13.41
Five to 20 years term	1,152	2.05	6,972,796	4.09	1,958	3.30	9,260,103	5.93
Term to 65	97	.17	507,310	.30	155	.26	774,557	.50
1 to 4 years term	298	.53	2,129,858	1.25	808	1.36	2,458,508	1.57
Term increasing premiums	4	.01	20,000	.01	21	.03	84,500	.05
Family income rider a	...	...	2,158,592	1.26	...	...	...	...
Total term	1,551	2.76	11,788,556	6.91	2,942	4.95	12,577,668	8.05
Life single	72	.13	251,750	.15	67	.11	281,563	.18
Endowment single	331	.59	1,336,373	.78	260	.44	864,680	.55
Joint life	17	.03	74,080	.04	26	.05	34,000	.02
Miscellaneous	...	...	...	...	37	.06	257,170	.17
Grand total	56,160	100.00	170,544,114	100.00	59,399	100.00	156,257,372	100.00
Automatic term conversion	1,496	2.66	4,953,839	2.90	1,695	2.85	5,924,647	3.79
Special term	1,222	2.18	3,348,411	1.96	2,174	3.66	4,337,321	2.78
Retirement inc. (annual income)	475	...	217,193	...	536	...	503,662	...

a Added to 519 policies.

Although the advantages of term insurance have been emphasized by so-called insurance "counsellors," it has certain important drawbacks. For example, renewable term insurance (under which the insurance can be renewed for successive periods up to a specified age) presents some practical difficulties to the company while the increasing premiums are an obvious objection from the insured's point of view. The best and most practicable plan where insurance is required for the whole of life is either ordinary life or limited payment life. There is, however, a considerable demand and a legitimate need for term insurance covering relatively short periods, and, especially in recent years, The Mutual has increased the variety of its term insurance contracts. The conversion privilege renders such contracts suitable for many who, for the time being, are unable to pay the higher premiums for insurance on a permanent plan.

In addition to extending its line of term insurance, The Mutual Life has endeavored to lower the cost of insurance by issuing preferred risk policies. By placing in one class applicants who meet high physical, moral, financial, and family health record standards, it is possible to furnish insurance at lower cost. This step was taken in 1941, when the Preferred Risk Modified Life policy was first issued. In addition to higher standards of selection, this policy is not issued for amounts less than $5,000, a rule which further reduces the cost because of the lower expense per $1,000.[17]

Another low-cost policy is the survivorship annuity, which has been available throughout most of the period under survey. Closely related to the survivorship annuity is the continuous installment policy, re-named "life income" in 1919 in the hope that this term would be more descriptive.[18] Being a combination of ordinary life and deferred survivorship annuity, it guaranteed a given number of payments ("payments certain") after the death of the insured and continued payments during the remaining lifetime of the original beneficiary. This contract was pushed hard for some years, but as time went on it was criticized because it required level premiums and provided for a decreasing amount of insurance. It was dropped by the Company in 1939[19] on the

---

[17] This policy is not to be confused with another contract which was issued in 1917 as a modified endowment, was called a modified life after 1919, and was discontinued in 1928 as a separate policy, although its main feature could be obtained on the ordinary life or limited payment life plan. This plan was devised for applicants who had an impairment which made them ineligible for insurance for life, but which would not lead to excess mortality for some years.

[18] The single premium continuous installment income was made available in 1913.

[19] The policy has no face amount. The sum payable is the annuity to the beneficiary, and

grounds that the type of service which it rendered could be better obtained by other contracts.

More popular methods of providing insurance payable in the form of income to the beneficiary than the "continuous installment" policy have been devised in recent years through the introduction first of the "Family Protection Policy" and later of the "Family Income Policy." Both these policies are combinations of term and whole life arranged to produce an income in the event of the early death of the insured. The Family Protection Policy, which was written by The Mutual Life from 1934 to 1942,[20] provided that if the insured died within a selected period (10, 15, or 20 years), an income would be paid during a specified number of years, and the face amount of the contract would be paid at the end of this time. The family income plan, which was first issued by the Company in 1940, was essentially like the latter, except that installments to be paid, if death of the insured occurred during the selected period, would be only for the remainder of the period rather than for a fixed number of years—a provision that thus made for a decreasing amount of insurance. Closely related to these contracts is the double protection plan, which the Company added to its offerings in 1942. It is a combination of term insurance to age 65 and life insurance paid-up at age 85. If the optional settlement for installments for a prescribed number of years to the beneficiary is exercised, the double protection policy is very similar to the family protection policy.

The Mutual Life has also introduced other plans to meet the special needs of applicants. Although the age at which persons could take out insurance was lowered from fifteen to ten in 1924, there was a demand for juvenile policies covering ages from birth to nine, and the Company began to write them in small amounts in 1938.[21] A "pay roll deduction plan," renamed the "salary savings plan" in 1942, was begun in 1925 for groups where premiums were to be forwarded to the Company by a common remitter [22]—an arrangement designed especially to facili-

---

accordingly it decreases as the beneficiary becomes older. A point may be reached at which premiums exceed the possible benefits. See Maclean, *Life Insurance*, pp. 66 ff.

[20] In 1934 the family protection plan was provided by a rider on an ordinary life policy. In 1937 a separate form was used. The policy was dropped in 1942, because similar types seemed more desirable.

[21] They were somewhat altered in 1939. A supplemental premium protection contract is available to safeguard the juvenile policy in case the applicant dies. This "insuring insurance" is accomplished by a contract which provides that in the event of the death of the applicant while the policy is in force the Company will waive premium payments becoming due before the anniversary of the policy on which the insured attains the age of 21.

[22] This plan was not group insurance, for there was no master policy and no given proportion of a group had to be insured. Individual contracts were made with the members of a group. They were appreciably the same as the regular policies, save premiums might be paid monthly and insurance might, after 1940, be taken without medical examination.

tate collection of premiums from employees of a common employer. Nonmedical insurance was offered in 1939 to inhabitants of small towns and cities who were not engaged in hazardous occupations.[23] Monthly premium payments were permitted in 1941 on both new and existing policies.[24] Ordinary life policies were replaced in 1941 by life paid-up policies at age 85. Finally, substandard insurance was added to the Company's long list of offerings in 1942.

DISABILITY AND ACCIDENT BENEFITS

In their efforts to meet the special needs of the public, life insurance companies provided in the period now under survey, as additions to their contracts, certain extra benefits in case of total and permanent disability or in case of death resulting from accident. The first insurance of this kind appeared in Germany in 1876 and was issued by American fraternal orders in the next year. In 1894 Arthur Hunter, an American actuary, prepared premiums for a policy which would waive the payment of premiums in case of disability and the Fidelity Mutual and the Phoenix Mutual placed disability clauses in their contracts in 1896.[25] The Travelers in 1904, the Reliance in 1905, the Minnesota Mutual in 1906, and the New York Life in 1910 began to issue policies which provided for the waiving of premiums in case of total and permanent disability. Then several companies began to experiment with an annual income of 10 per cent of the face amount of the policy to be paid to the insured in case of total and permanent disability, such payments to be deducted from the face amount of the insurance at death. By 1910 five companies were offering disability income contracts, and many more, waiver of premium contracts.

The Mutual Life took its first step toward including provision for disability benefits in life insurance policies in 1913. On January first of that year contracts were issued with a provision for the waiving of premiums in case of total and permanent disability, prior to the insured's sixtieth birthday. If the payment of premiums was then waived, cash, loan, and nonforfeiture values remained the same as though pre-

---

[23] Nonmedical insurance is provided by The Mutual Life to those persons who reside in places where a medical examination would be difficult to obtain. Inasmuch as it is open to abuse and fraud, it is carefully restricted. Limits in amount are $1,000 minimum—$2,500 maximum for married women and $5,000 for males. Age limits for applicants are ten to forty-five years.

[24] Quarterly premium rates are higher than semi-annual or annual, because of added expense. Monthly rates are approximately one-third of quarterly rates.

[25] *Disability Benefits in Life Insurance Policies* (New York, Actuarial Society of America, 1932), p. 2; Stalson, *Marketing Life Insurance*, pp. 640–641; and Elston, *op. cit.*, pp. 45–46.

miums were regularly paid in cash.[26] In 1917 The Mutual Life introduced its first contract for the payment of an income in addition to waiving premiums in the event of total and permanent disability—the amount to be paid each year being 10 percent of the face amount of the policy.[27] Payment of this income was additional to and did not reduce the amount payable at death. In 1920 the income benefit was increased from $100 annually to $10 monthly for each $1,000 of insurance. Then, in August, 1922, the Company offered an arrangement for "increasing disability benefits," that is, for monthly income payments which would increase from one per cent of the face amount of the policy to one and one-half percent, if total disability lasted more than five years, and to two percent, if total disability lasted more than another five years.[28] And at the same time it was provided that total disability would be presumed to be "permanent" if it lasted for ninety days, although the Company had the right, as always, to a periodic check on the insured to determine whether or not he had recovered.[29]

In the course of time disability benefits were to prove unsatisfactory. The rate of disability proved to be much higher than expected, and the cost of the benefits was greatly in excess of the anticipated cost. This was due to a variety of causes including too liberal administration, too liberal terms of the contract, adverse attitude of the courts in contested cases, fraud and malingering, and, in general, lack of experience in this type of insurance. Most contracts stipulated that the insured was deemed to be totally and permanently disabled when he had become "wholly and permanently disabled so that he is and will be permanently, continuously and wholly prevented thereby from performing any work or engaging in any occupation for compensation or profit." [30] Both the companies and the courts were inclined to interpret "any occupation" in

[26] In April, 1914, the waiver of premium benefit was changed to provide for automatic termination of the provision upon the insured's entering the military or naval service of any country at war or engaging in any civilian capacity in connection with actual warfare. This change was made because of the Mexican border clash.

[27] On continuous installment policies the income payment was the same as the normal income after death. It was first offered by the Fidelity Mutual in 1904. See Amrhein, *Liberalization of the Life Insurance Contract*, p. 292.

[28] The leaders in this step were The Mutual Life and the New York Life, Elston, *op. cit.*, p. 46.

[29] In February, 1926, disability benefits were further liberalized by adding the provisions (1) that income payments should be due as of the date proof was received, if received within the first month, or at the end of the first month, if received later, and (2) that in the case of lapsed policies, if no premium was in default more than six months and if the insured became totally disabled on or before the due date of the premium first in default and if proof was furnished that such disability had existed continuously, the policy would be reinstated and benefits would be paid.

[30] *Flitcraft Manual* (1929), p. 429.

a liberal manner, and a few courts do go so far as to declare that any occupation means own or former occupation.[31]

In July, 1930, standard provisions drafted by the National Convention of Insurance Commissioners for disability benefits were adopted by The Mutual Life—provisions which among other things did away with increasing income benefits, required four months of total disability before permanent disability was presumed to exist, and continued to exclude disability begun after sixty years of age.[32] Even with these changes and with higher rates, experience with disability benefits continued to be adverse. Frauds could not be completely eliminated in spite of the vigilance of a special bureau of disability claims,[33] and the number of claims continued to exceed those originally expected. At last, The Mutual Life decided that disability income benefits could no longer be safely issued and withdrew them from its list of offerings on January 1, 1932—an action that was taken at about the same time by many other companies.[34] Then, with losses on disability contracts remaining high, the question arose as to a reduction of dividends on those policies following the well-established theory that dividends should be in direct ratio to the contribution made to the surplus.[35]

Although disability income contracts did not prove to be practicable as written, The Mutual Life continued to offer the waiver of premium provisions in its policies. Beginning in 1918 The Mutual also included in all standard policy forms, if requested, a provision for payment of double the face amount in event of death by accidental means. This was known as "double indemnity" or "additional accidental death benefit." At first two forms of double indemnity were available: (1) "Travel D.I.," which covered only accidental deaths while traveling in a "common carrier" (such as a train, bus, etc.),[36] and (2) "General D.I.," which

---

[31] Patterson, *Cases and Other Materials on the Law of Insurance*, pp. 207–209.

[32] At the same time, the Company changed its provisions for double indemnity, the chief change being automatic termination at age of seventy. In 1932 termination was changed to age sixty-five.

[33] Set up in the Company at the end of 1924. *Minutes of the Board of Trustees*, Dec. 31, 1924.

[34] *Minutes of the Board of Trustees*, Sept. 30, 1931. One company continues to issue a disability income benefit policy with the benefit based on loss of earned income resulting from disability. Others have greatly reduced the benefits.

[35] This practice has been supported by the courts. Among other decisions, see *Rhine vs. New York Life* (1936) 273, New York, and *Rubin vs. Metropolitan Life Insurance Co.* (1938) 278, New York 625.

[36] This benefit, which was provided for on payment of an additional premium, was available only in connection with ordinary life, limited payment life, and endowment policies which also provided for disability benefits. The double indemnity provision was abrogated if the disability benefit provision terminated before the insured reached age 60. This travel double indemnity was discontinued July, 1920, because of the slight demand for it after the introduction of a general double indemnity provision.

covered any accidental deaths other than those specifically excluded.[37] Later, Travel D.I. was dropped, since there was very little demand for it. Experience showed that certain exclusions were necessary in order to avoid the additional liability in cases where death was not really due to an accident or where the circumstances of the death might lead to a suspicion of suicide. Such exclusions included "accidental" deaths resulting from disease, from self-inflicted injuries, from the taking of poison, or from the inhaling of gas.

As in the case of disability benefits, experience indicated that modifications in the original forms of contract and in the terms of insurance were necessary if loss was to be avoided. Thus, the fact that the accident

TABLE 39

ACCIDENT EXPERIENCE AMONG THE MUTUAL LIFE
POLICYHOLDERS [a]

| | DEATH RATE PER 100,000 | | | DEATH RATE PER 100,000 | |
Year	All Accidents	Auto Accidents	Year	All Accidents	Auto Accidents
1913	74	9	1928	77	23
1914	72	9	1929	80	31
1915	84	13	1930	81	30
1916	87	13	1931	79	31
1917	92	11	1932	71	28
1918	104	11	1933	69	30
1919	120	13	1934	70	30
1920	74	12	1935	72	34
1921	75	17	1936	64	28
1922	71	16	1937	70	32
1923	64	16	1938	63	27
1924	74	20	1939	59	27
1925	69	20	1940	65	29
1926	71	23	1941	66	33
1927	71	22	1942	50	17
			1943	46	15

[a] "Death Rates per 100,000 from All Accidents and Automobile Accidents in Calendar Years 1913 to 1943."

death rate increases with age was not, at first, fully appreciated. In the original contracts the extra premiums were the same at all ages, and coverage continued for the whole of life. Later, premium rates were graded on an increasing scale with age, first to age 70, then to age 65, and coverage was limited.

While there is no logical basis for a double indemnity benefit, the low cost in relation to the high additional benefit makes it exceedingly at-

[37] The provision terminated if within two years the insured engaged in military or naval service outside the continental limits of the United States and Canada or if within two years or such shorter period as World War I continued, the insured traveled or resided outside these limits.

tractive, and a large proportion of the insurance written since 1918 has contained provision for this additional benefit. The chief disadvantage from the Company's point of view is the relatively large number of improper claims, many of which lead to expensive law suits. Undoubtedly many claims have to be paid for which the Company is not really liable, and, as indicated above, it has been necessary to introduce many limitations into the contract in order to avoid such improper payments. On the whole, however, double indemnity has been a substantial benefit to policyholders and has not been unprofitable to the Company. It has become a well-established feature in modern life insurance policies.

OTHER CHANGES IN LIFE CONTRACTS

In addition to offering a large number of policies designed to meet special needs, The Mutual Life changed the terms of its contracts from time to time to accomplish five main tasks—(1) to give policies more flexibility of settlement, (2) to aid those who were in temporary financial difficulty, (3) to conform to state laws, (4) to aid its policyholders in maintaining or increasing their insurance with the Company, and (5) to eliminate or reduce its liability in connection with such special risks as aviation activities or participation in war. Such restrictions were necessary to prevent selection against the Company by persons subject to these special hazards.

One of the most notable steps forward in this period was the development of liberalization of contractual provisions regarding the modes of settlement of insurance benefits. Attention has already been called to the first three optional modes of settlement in the standard policies of 1907 —(1) the option to leave the proceeds of insurance with the Company at interest, (2) the option to receive equal installments, including both principal and interest, for a fixed number of years,[38] and (3) the option to receive equal installments for twenty years certain and thereafter for the remaining lifetime of the beneficiary, the amount of the installments depending on the age of the beneficiary. In 1925 other fixed periods were provided under option 3, and a new—the fourth—optional mode of settlement was added to the list to provide payment of an income of selected amount until the principal and interest were exhausted.[39] Finally, in 1934 the fifth optional mode was made available—a method of

[38] This arrangement was liberalized in January, 1911. Monthly, quarterly, and semiannual installments were then permitted, under both option two and option three.

[39] Another change at this time provided that no guaranteed payment or installment should be for less than $10, but the previous restriction that the proceeds be at least $1,000 was removed.

settlement which allowed the proceeds of a policy to be used for the purchase of a life annuity to the beneficiary at a rate slightly more favorable than the rates in use at the date of the settlement for ordinary cash purchases.[40]

Other liberalities and changes favorable to policyholders were made during this period. The right was given to policyholders to apply, within a specified period after taking insurance, for additional amounts without medical examination.[41] In 1941 it allowed the monthly payment of premiums. The period of "incontestability" was, for a time, reduced to one year instead of two,[42] but this was later modified to provide that the policy would be incontestable after it had been in force, during the lifetime of the insured, for two years.[43] This was necessary to prevent improper claims when death occurred during the contestable period, but the claim was withheld until the period had expired.

On the other hand, on the outbreak of World War II it became necessary to include in all new policies a "War and Aviation" clause eliminating the special risks of active participation in war. Similar action was taken by other companies. Policies previously issued contain in general no such restrictions. In general the "War and Aviation" clause provides that in event of death while in service outside the "home areas" or in event of death resulting from actual warfare inside these areas or in event of death as a result of aviation, other than while traveling as a passenger on a regularly scheduled flight, the company's liability is limited to the return of the premiums paid with interest.

Another phase of the life insurance contract which underwent change between 1907 and 1943 pertained to the cash value of policies—values which form the basis for determining the amount of policy loans and nonforfeiture or surrender values. The first terms adopted after the Armstrong Investigation for surrenders stipulated that a surrender value would be granted after premiums had been paid for three full years, that prior to the payment of ten annual premiums the surrender value should be no less than 80 percent of the reserve, and that thereafter it should be the full reserve. In the 1908 forms, used by The Mutual Life

---

[40] In 1940 the optional modes of settlement were made available for election within one month after the maturity of the policy, besides being available when the policy was in force or became payable. Also, in 1940 the fifth mode of settlement, which had previously been available on request as a rider, was attached to all new issues for which it was suitable.

[41] The period in which this might be done was increased from 60 days to 3 years in 1926, although there were limits on additional insurance taken in this way.

[42] That is, unless the insured died in the first year after he had taken out his policy. In that event the contestable period remained two years.

[43] Maclean, *op. cit.*, pp. 208–209.

CHART XVII

CHARACTERISTICS OF THE MUTUAL LIFE'S INSURANCE IN FORCE

(By amount of insurance)

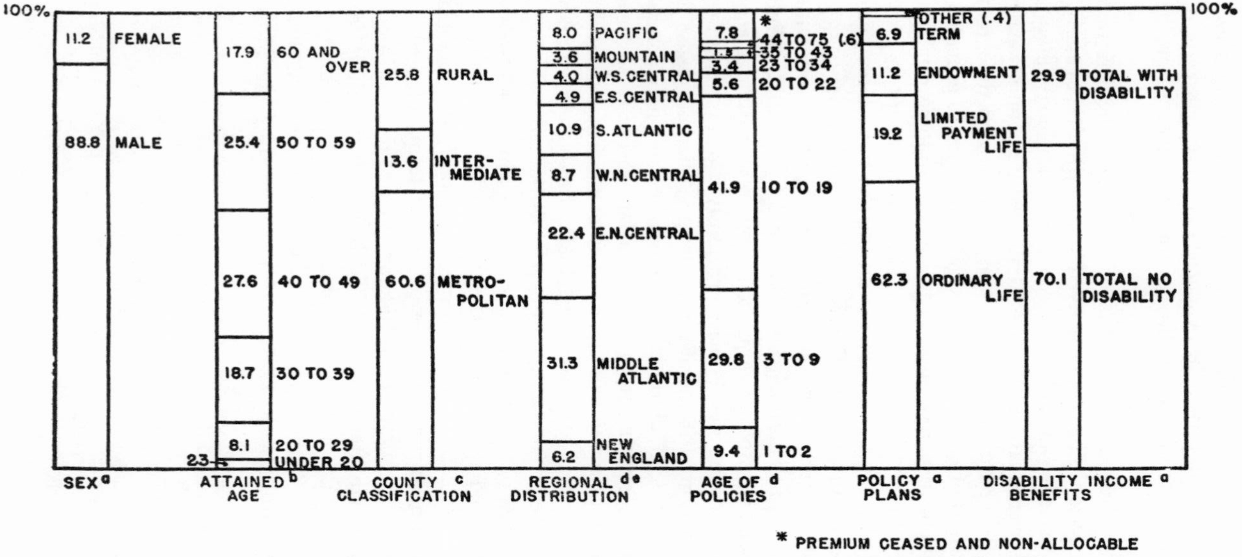

100%						100%
11.2 FEMALE	17.9 60 AND OVER	25.8 RURAL	8.0 PACIFIC / 3.6 MOUNTAIN / 4.0 W.S.CENTRAL / 4.9 E.S.CENTRAL	7.8 * / 44 TO 75 (.6) / 35 TO 43 1.8 / 23 TO 34 3.4 / 20 TO 22 5.6	OTHER (.4) / 6.9 TERM / ENDOWMENT 29.9	TOTAL WITH DISABILITY 29.9
	25.4 50 TO 59	13.6 INTER-MEDIATE	10.9 S.ATLANTIC		11.2 ENDOWMENT	
88.8 MALE			8.7 W.N.CENTRAL	41.9 10 TO 19	19.2 LIMITED PAYMENT LIFE	
	27.6 40 TO 49	60.6 METRO-POLITAN	22.4 E.N.CENTRAL			
	18.7 30 TO 39		31.3 MIDDLE ATLANTIC	29.8 3 TO 9	62.3 ORDINARY LIFE	TOTAL NO DISABILITY 70.1
	8.1 20 TO 29 / 2.3–5 UNDER 20		6.2 NEW ENGLAND	9.4 1 TO 2		
SEX ᵃ	ATTAINED ᵇ AGE	COUNTY ᶜ CLASSIFICATION	REGIONAL ᵈᵉ DISTRIBUTION	AGE OF ᵈ POLICIES	POLICY ᵃ PLANS	DISABILITY INCOME ᵃ BENEFITS

* PREMIUM CEASED AND NON-ALLOCABLE

ᵃ Sample of insurance in force December 31, 1940, issued 1919–1938.   ᵇ Insurance in force July 1, 1940.

ᶜ Based on 1939 and 1940 full year paid for issues. The classification by county follows the 1930 census. Metropolitan counties contain or are adjacent to counties containing one or more central cities of 50,000 or greater and have a population density of 150 or more per square mile. Rural counties are those in which 50% or more of the population live in communities of 2,500 or less. All other counties are classified as intermediate.

ᵈ Insurance in force December 31, 1940.   ᵉ Geographical divisions established by the Bureau of the Census.

for states other than New York and introduced into New York in 1910, surrender values were stipulated in dollars and cents and were more generous than the minimum required by law. In 1913 the legal surrender charge was fixed at not more than 1½ percent of the face amount of the policy during the first ten years of full premium payments and less thereafter, but, as earlier, the charge actually levied decreased steadily as more premiums were paid.[44] The right to obtain loans on policies, made mandatory in the State of New York in 1907, has been granted by The Mutual Life for amounts up to the cash value of a policy,[45] the interest charge having been on new policies 5 percent in 1913, 6 percent from 1913 to 1939, and 5 percent since 1939. The liquidity which was thus given life insurance policies elicited expressions of fear of runs on life insurance institutions, and these fears were realized in the depression which followed 1929.[46] At the time of the "banking holiday" (1933) state insurance departments declared a partial moratorium on surrenders and policy loans, although no important insurance company asked that such a step be taken. Nevertheless, this episode gave companies an opportunity to revise their practices as regards loans and surrenders—a revision which consisted in augmenting surrender charges and in delaying the granting of policy loans. Thus, on January 1, 1935, The Mutual Life announced that the surrender charge on new contracts would be not more than 2½ percent of the face amount of the policy or 20 percent of the reserve, whichever was greater, that some deduction would be made until the twentieth year, instead of the tenth year, and that the payment of cash surrender values or the granting of policy loans might be deferred not more than six months after request had been made.[47]

Policy loans, which all too frequently lead to surrenders, and surrenders themselves are discouraged by life insurance companies. Every effort is made to keep the insurance on their books in force. Contract provisions as to reinstatement of lapsed policies are liberal. In 1917 The Mutual Life abolished the interest charge during the period of grace,[48] temporarily extended in March, 1933, the grace period, and beginning in 1940, provided on request for automatic premium loans, that is, the

[44] The surrender charge aims to cover the cost to the Company of having a policy stopped. See *The Mutual Life Insurance Company vs. Nelson*, 183 S. 636. Also see testimony of W. A. Hutcheson, Temporary National Economic Committee, Part 10, p. 4626.

[45] Loans were granted before premiums for three years had been paid, if the remaining cash value of a policy was sufficient to pay premiums to the end of three years.

[46] See pp. 305–308, 379–380.

[47] In January, 1926, the Company decided to grant loans up to $600 through the agencies. In 1927 this maximum was changed to $1,000. About 90 percent of the loans were thus handled in this way.

[48] *Minutes of the Insurance and Agency Committee*, Nov. 16, 1917.

automatic granting of a policy loan to meet premiums not paid in cash. As a general conservation measure the company established in 1906 a Policyholders' Service Bureau, which follows up lapsed policies and gives advice and assistance to policyholders in regard to maintaining their insurance.[49]

The major change which The Mutual has made since 1906 in computing premiums and reserves was to lower the rate of interest assumed for life insurance premiums from 3½ to 3 percent in 1907. The American Experience Table of Mortality has been continuously employed by the Company since 1868. A few other companies have in recent times adopted more modern tables and lower rates of interest. The Mutual Life has never taken advantage of the modified reserve systems permitted by law—the select and ultimate method made permissible in New York State by the Armstrong legislation or the modified preliminary term system (Illinois Standard) introduced in 1923—but has always employed the full net level premium reserve basis in determining its reserve liability. Premiums have been loaded for expenses by one-sixth of the net premium for ordinary life plus one-sixth of the net premium for the plan.[50] In the apportionment of dividends there has been some refinement of procedure, but no basic changes, although in 1917 the Company placed a clause in new policies which stipulated that dividends would not be paid for the first policy year unless any premium then due was paid.[51]

The actuarial work of The Mutual Life during the period which has been described in the preceding pages has been in the hands of persons who have stood at the top of their profession. From 1888 to 1911 the Company's actuary was Emory McClintock, one of the greatest of American actuaries and the first American to be made a Fellow of the Institute of Actuaries of Great Britain (1874). From 1911 to 1940 The Mutual's

[49] Originally called Restoration Bureau. Its name was changed in 1928. At this later date service representatives in the field were appointed for personal contact with policyholders. In addition to conservation programs, the Policyholders' Service Bureau tries to straighten out problems arising between policyholders and the Company.

[50] For endowments after 1909 the loading was ⅙ of the net premiums for ordinary life plus ¹⁄₁₂ of life limited net premium plus ¹⁄₁₂ of the endowment net premium.

[51] The law of 1934 on this point, section 83, New York Insurance Law, reads "every such corporation shall apportion the remaining surplus equitably to all other policies entitled to share therein and such apportionment in the case of any policy shall not after the first policy year be made contingent upon the whole or any part of the premiums for the subsequent policy year." In 1939 New York State enacted a law to the effect that no dividend should be paid on the first policy year unless "upon reasonable assumptions as to expenses, mortality, policy and contract claims, investment income and lapses it was actually earned in such year." Chapter 882 of the Laws of New York State, 1939. This law made little difference in practice since the Insurance Department agreed that first-year expense could be amortized in determining whether a first-year dividend had been "earned."

actuary was William A. Hutcheson, an authority on life insurance history and an interested student of the Company's past. He was followed briefly in 1941 by Wendell M. Strong, who possessed a remarkable combination of legal and actuarial training and knowledge. Strong, who retired because of poor health, was succeeded by Joseph B. Maclean, the author of the most widely used textbook in America on the subject of life insurance. Actuaries who have been in the service of The Mutual Life have played an outstanding role in the actuarial profession, and more presidents of the Actuarial Society of America have been chosen from The Mutual Life than from any other single company. Sheppard Homans was instrumental in founding the Society and was its first president, while David Parks Fackler, John S. Thompson, Emory McClintock, William A. Hutcheson, Wendell M. Strong, and Joseph B. Maclean have all been honored by election to its chief executive post. Furthermore, many members of the Company's Actuarial Department have been active in the Society's work—in its actuarial courses, its examinations for membership, and in its publications. They have contributed much to the maintenance of high standards in the profession.[52]

[52] The Company's actuaries have played a less prominent role in the American Institute of Actuaries, founded in 1909, for this body, whose purposes are similar to those of the Actuarial Society, draws largely upon members of the profession located in the West.

XV. Toward Informed Selling and Scientific Selection of Risks

THE GROWING AND INSISTENT DEMAND of persons in all walks of life and in all conditions of health and fortune for some kind of protection against the financial hazards of death has led not only to the variety of policy forms discussed in the last chapter but also to a more scientific selection of risks and to "informed selling." The last thirty-five years have witnessed a more accurate appraisal of the expectation of life than was ever before possible, the grouping of applicants for insurance into classes according to the risk involved, and the establishment of special premium rates for each classification. Furthermore, within this time span there has been a development in the marketing of life insurance so that selling is no longer a "hit-or-miss" affair, but a business profession of a highly technical nature. These changes in selection and marketing were given an initial impetus by the Armstrong Investigation and the events which immediately followed it. The condemnation of some of the old selling practices, limitations on the cost of getting new business, and a temporary falling off in production caused some of the old-type agents to retire and the others to tap new markets. In this scramble for sales, great strides were made toward selling insurance for business purposes, for the preservation of estates, for the creation of trusts, for the payment of taxes, and for providing an income—types of insurance which called for astute "programming." To provide men who were qualified to write insurance to meet the new requirements of the market, insurance companies and educational institutions began to introduce courses in life insurance salesmanship. Soon company agencies were being manned by a new class of men and women; states were requiring (New York in 1940) written examinations of those who wanted licenses to sell insurance, and high technical standards were set for those who aspired to become "chartered life underwriters."

The marketing force of The Mutual Life experienced this general evolution and profited from it. On the morrow of the Armstrong Investigation, however, the future of the agency department did not look bright, for disruption was to precede improvement. In the first place, the few remaining general agencies were transformed during 1905 and 1906 into managerial agencies, a process which eliminated some of the large organizations, like that of Colonel Raymond, and which, because of the establishment of more than fourteen new agencies, was expensive.[1] Several of the managers both at home and abroad were dismissed or transferred to new posts, and managers' salaries were fixed at reduced amounts, although they could be augmented by commissions on personal sales of insurance. New contracts had to be negotiated with all the agents along lines so rigidly restricted by law[2] that The Equitable, the New York Life, and The Mutual Life decided by agreement upon uniform commission schedules beginning in 1907. These rates, which marked a great reduction in those formerly paid, were graduated according to type of policy. They consisted, in most instances, of a percentage of the first year's premium, and of a small percentage of renewals for nine years.[3] Lower commissions,[4] the abolition of unsecured "advances" to agents,[5] the doing away with salaries to subagents,[6] and a drastic falling off in new business because of public feeling against life insurance companies led many of The Mutual's salesmen to become discouraged and to resign. One-half of the "real insurance men," according to the Manager of the Agency Department, George T. Dexter, severed their connections with the Company at the beginning of 1907.[7] Such an exodus of agents only added to the management's difficulty in restoring the usual flow of new business.

In the ensuing years the whipping of the agency force into an efficient organization was one of the chief problems of the Company's administration. President Peabody, who was more interested in the real estate investments of the Company than in marketing insurance and, as we have seen, believed in limiting the size of The Mutual Life, adopted a policy almost of *laissez faire* toward the agencies. Nevertheless, in 1910 the system of compensating agency managers was altered so that in addi-

---

[1] *Insurance and Agency Committee*, March 5, 1906. After the creation of more than one agency in New York, the Company established a Metropolitan Clearing House to attend to the collection of premiums on policies in the New York area and to the general servicing of these policies. In other districts the agencies handled such matters, although clearing houses were later set up in Philadelphia and Chicago.

[2] For details of these restrictions see above, p. 226.

[3] *Insurance and Agency Committee*, June 12, 1906, and June 28, 1906. Also circular letters to managers following these decisions.

[4] The ratio of commissions to premiums on new business dropped from 71.49 percent in 1905 to 45.20 percent in 1907.

[5] "Reports of Official Examinations," *Annual Report of the Superintendent of Insurance of the State of New York* (Albany, 1910), Miscellaneous, p. 735.

[6] *Insurance and Agencies Committee*, Jan. 5, 1906.   [7] *Ibid.*, Dec. 19, 1907.

tion to a base salary and commissions on personal sales the managers received a special reward for the production of their agency,[8] and extra sums were granted them for aiding agents who were just getting started, for agency advertising, and for such other agency expense as training salesmen.[9] In 1914 a new plan for remunerating managers was adopted [10] whereby the agencies were divided into three classes according to the population and the costs of living within the agency territory.[11] Each class had its own salary scale, plus sums arrived at by a special formula. This system operated so successfully that in its essential features it has remained in use to the present time. The only changes of importance in it have been alterations in the rates to meet fluctuating living costs and business conditions [12] and a monetary encouragement to keep insurance in force as well as to place it on the books.[13]

The duties performed by the managers of agencies of the "branch offices," as they are sometimes called, have tended to increase throughout the years. To the fundamental task of organizing an agency force in a district, of making contracts with agents, of forwarding applications for insurance and premiums to the home office, of distributing new policies to insureds, and of getting new business written, managers have been given one job after another. They have to train agents, to assume (since 1926) many of the details pertaining to policy loans, to pay (since 1929) certain death claims, and gradually to share more of the responsibility for maintaining insurance in force—for the conservation work of the Company.[14] Thus the managers are salesmen, sales directors, and educators. They are key men in the marketing organization of the Company.[15]

[8] *Ibid.*, Nov. 24, 1909.

[9] *Report on the Examination of the Mutual Life by the Superintendent of Insurance for the State of New York for the Three Years Ending Dec. 31, 1911* (Albany, 1913), p. 8.

[10] *Minutes of the Insurance and Agencies Committee*, April 17, 1914.

[11] Twenty-five agencies were placed in the first class; 25 in the second, and the remainder in the third. In 1941 37 were in the first, 24 in the second, and 16 in the third.

[12] Beginning July 1, 1917, the base salaries were increased because costs of living were rising. When large amounts of new business were being written (1928, 1929, and 1930), remuneration from one part of the formula was lowered. When new business was difficult to get, the rate was again raised (1936).

[13] Circular letter to managers, December 2, 1918, indicated a step in this direction. The most recent plan is called Compensation for Agency Efficiency and Conservation Persistency.

[14] The number of service representatives of the Policyholders' Service Bureau has recently (1942) been reduced because of a shift of the work of conservation to the agencies. Mention should be made here of the fact that for about two years prior to 1906 policies were issued from Chicago in order to speed up the issuing of insurance in the Middle West. This system was soon abandoned because of the added expense.

[15] *Report of an Examination of The Mutual Life Insurance Co. of New York by the New York State Insurance Department for the Years 1936, 1937, 1938* (Albany, 1940), p. 25.

ORGANIZING FOR SALES: THE AGENTS

The managers need, of course, a corps of responsible, energetic, and intelligent agents for the actual selling of life insurance. To secure them simply by raising commission rates has not been possible because of the rigid limitations established by law. The task, therefore, has had to be accomplished by making a careful selection of prospective agents, by giving them adequate training, and by allocating to them markets sufficient to permit the making of a living. How difficult this problem has been can be gleaned from the fact that of the 10,680 agents under contract to six life insurance companies (The Mutual Life was not one of them) in 1930, a third of them produced no business at all for their companies, another third sold no more than $25,000 apiece, and only 10 percent produced more than $100,000.[16] It is obvious from these figures that many agents hold contracts only on the off-chance that they might make a sale, that many more devote only a small proportion of their time and energies to the work, and that still others are not successful salesmen.[17] Consequently, the turnover among the members of life insurance companies' sales forces has been very large, having been estimated at from one-fourth to one-third of the total number per year.[18]

Life insurance companies have in the last few years endeavored to remedy this situation by increasing the number of full-time agents and by decreasing the number who operate on a part-time basis. The Mutual Life took steps in this direction in 1930 and again in 1942 by establishing particularly favorable conditions for and reserving to its full-time field representatives the writing of some classes of risks.[19] But the Company's greatest contribution to the cause was the institution in 1943 of its Lifetime Compensation Plan—a plan that has been heralded as the greatest advance made in compensating agents since the Armstrong Investigation of 1905.

Under the former system of commissions, agents were paid almost exclusively for sales, which in the earlier history of insurance was entirely satisfactory. But as companies have grown older, as life insurance has been employed for an ever greater variety of financial exigencies, and as individual agents have built up large clienteles, the work of servicing existing policies has become enormous. Furthermore, commissions

[16] Stalson, *Marketing Life Insurance*, p. 626.   [17] *Ibid.*, p. 627.
[18] J. V. E. Westfall, *Relation of the Agent to Some Executive Problems* (New York, Association of Life Insurance Presidents, 1920). See also the investigation of the Life Insurance Sales Research Bureau of 1943.
[19] See *Points*, Feb. 2, 1942.

based largely on new sales resulted in great fluctuations in agent's incomes; they offered no incentive to the agent to remain with his company and differed but slightly whether the insurance remained on the books or was shortly surrendered.

To correct these various faults in the existing method of payment and to reduce the cost resulting from the turnover of agents, The Mutual Life devised its new method of compensating agents. The basic aims of the arrangement are to level out remuneration over longer periods, to reward agents for quality and persistency of and for service on policies, and to provide a retirement income for salesmen. Furthermore, an incentive to remain with the Company is given because certain of the rewards are canceled if an agent severs his connections with the Company without good cause. Finally, the new plan results in no increase of selling costs; and it meets fully the requirements of the New York insurance law, which was amended, April 23, 1943, especially to permit the changes here set forth.

Selection of the right kind of persons for selling life insurance is an especially knotty problem, for the attributes which make for successful selling are extremely difficult to evaluate. A definite attempt has been made, however, both by The Mutual's agency managers and the home office to enlist a high class of men and women in the field forces. This has been done largely by urging members of the Company's organization to recommend promising persons to the managers and agency department, by personnel recruiting among college graduates, and by advertising the practical advantages of life underwriting.[20]

Training life insurance agents is, on the other hand, a tangible thing and has come to be provided on a large scale by insurance companies and by educational institutions. The earliest form of agency training consisted largely in the sending of company representatives into the field to lecture to agents on the subject of insurance and in attaching the trainee to a successful salesman or agency supervisor in the hope that all the techniques of the trade would be readily acquired. At the beginning of the twentieth century, however, The Equitable and the Travelers experimented with home office training courses; instructors in insurance began to be appointed in universities,[21] and schools of sales-

---

[20] The Mutual Life has issued several interesting pamphlets for this purpose—*Life Insurance in Action; Making a Living as a Life Insurance Representative;* etc.

[21] For a detailed account of these developments see Stalson, *op. cit.*, pp. 576 ff. According to him the first university course in insurance was given at Harvard University in 1897. The best known of the teachers of life insurance is Solomon S. Huebner of the Wharton School at the University of Pennsylvania.

manship began to put in an appearance.[22] The most famous of the latter institutions were the Carnegie School, founded in 1919 and transferred to the University of Pittsburgh in 1923, and the New York University School, founded in 1920. This "school training" plan, which envisaged the giving of courses for about three months, failed to prosper and has largely disappeared. University instruction in insurance has, on the other hand, been successful, especially at the Wharton School, University of Pennsylvania, and had developed by 1932 to a point where teachers of insurance were numerous enough to form the American Association of University Teachers of Insurance.

The most important steps in the training of agents were taken, however, by the life insurance industry itself. The National Association of Life Underwriters, which was established in 1890 for the purpose of elevating the position of the agent, advanced from 1907 onward the idea of raising life insurance selling to the level of a profession.[23] In 1912 it started a campaign to educate the public, especially the colleges, in life insurance salesmanship. It sponsored the famous textbook on life insurance by Solomon S. Huebner (1915), it furthered the idea for sales congresses in which the problems of selling were discussed (one of the earliest of such gatherings was presided over by Alexander E. Patterson, now executive vice president of The Mutual Life), and it launched the American College of Life Underwriters (1927) and the Chartered Life Underwriter movement. This last-named project aims to raise by rigid examinations the profession of the life insurance agent to a status comparable to that of the certified public accountant. The American College of Life Underwriters sets standards for a course of study in preparation for the Chartered Life Underwriter tests. Lastly, the industry gave birth to the Life Insurance Sales Research Bureau (1920), which investigates all kinds of sales problems, and to the Institute of Life Insurance (1938), which devotes its attention to institutional questions.

For their part, the life companies contributed much toward the movement for training agents and for informed selling. The trail blazers in this matter were undoubtedly the Phoenix Mutual and The Equitable Society, especially the latter's Edward A. Woods, director of an agency from 1890 to 1927. The Mutual Life early recognized, however, that life insurance selling could be taught and that its agents should be capable of working out the best possible schemes of coverage for their clients.

[22] The first of these was the Cerf School of Salesmanship, organized by the New York general agent of The Mutual Benefit.
[23] *Eastern Underwriter*, Aug. 22, 1907.

Accordingly, the Company employed Jacob A. Jackson, chief of its Literary (publicity) Bureau, to deliver, beginning in 1905, a series of lectures on the subject of life insurance to college students and to The Mutual's agents and to publish the remarkably lucid *Educational Leaflets* (New York, 1903). In some of the Company's agencies, especially in that of Ives and Myrick of New York, classes were given after 1909 to prospective insurance salesmen in an effort to teach them not only what to sell but also how to sell it. To Charles E. Ives should go much of the credit for setting the example in The Mutual Life of training agents and also for furthering the ideas of "programming"—of integrating a person's life insurance with his financial and family needs. This latter idea had been propounded in the early sales literature of the Company, it was used by C. M. Lovelace, head of the Carnegie School,[24] and it was also advocated by Ives in a pamphlet, *The Amount to Carry—Measuring the Prospect,* first published in 1912.

Another important step forward in The Mutual's program for training agents was taken in 1932, when the Life Insurance Sales Research Bureau prepared the Company's first formal training course for agents. In 1934 the Company published the first edition of its very remarkable *Text Book*—a book which has recently been revised. In 1940 The Mutual Life joined the Cooperative Fund for Underwriter Training, which has as its aim the defraying of part of the expenses for the Chartered Life Underwriter examinations. Finally, agents have been provided by the home office with various kinds of literature and equipment to facilitate their work—rate books, different types of "programming" forms, and *The Estate Coordinator,* which is a book, given to clients, with a complete record of their life insurance holdings.[25]

In addition to the training and the programming aids which The Mutual Life has given its salesmen, the Company has attempted in a great variety of ways to encourage and assist its field representatives. One of its most successful methods of doing so has been to hold national educational meetings—The National Field Club Conferences—for those agents who have produced a given amount of new business in any one year. These meetings, attended by Mutual's more successful representatives, have provided an excellent opportunity for an exchange

---

[24] Stalson, *op. cit.,* p. 640.

[25] To these aids for agents might be added the publications of the general insurance press. The Spectator Company publishes an extremely useful *Yearbook,* containing statistical and other information about all companies; Alfred M. Best & Co. publishes the *Life Report,* which is a manual giving information about all companies useful to salesmen; The National Underwriter Company publishes the *Diamond Life Bulletin,* and the Flitcraft Company brings out the *Life Insurance Manual.*

What's your Social Security I.Q.

60,000,000 Americans own Social Security cards . . . have money recorded in their accounts on the government's books. Yet many lack a clear understanding of how Social Security works. Here are five simple questions about Social Security. If you can answer *all* correctly, your knowledge of this important subject is probably "above average".

> 1. Who pays the cost of Social Security?
>
> 2. Would a private income of $100 a month prevent you from accepting a Social Security check at 65?
>
> 3. Do children ever receive benefits on the death of their father?
>
> 4. Can a married couple over 65 live comfortably on Social Security alone?
>
> 5. Does Social Security make ownership of Life Insurance less or more desirable . . . and why?
>
> *Correct Answers below*

Wouldn't you like to learn how Life Insurance and Social Security can work together for your family welfare? The Mutual Life representative in your community knows the Social Security rules. Let him show you what Social Security will do for you . . . how much other income may be needed if your family—or yourself at 65—are to accept Social Security and still live in reasonable comfort.

FREE *Social Security* HELPS

1. This special FILE lists the 7 types of official records required to collect Social Security benefits and also provides a place for their safe keeping. 2. This handy FOLDER gives help in estimating your future benefits from Social Security and your life insurance policies. To have both, just mail this coupon today.

NAME_____ AGE_____

ADDRESS_____

OCCUPATION_____

100th Anniversary Year
THE MUTUAL LIFE
INSURANCE COMPANY of NEW YORK
"First in America"   Lewis W. Douglas, *President*

34 NASSAU STREET   NEW YORK CITY

CORRECT ANSWERS: 1. Employers and employees contribute equally through a special Federal tax. **2.** Possession of income, such as from investments or life insurance, does *not* affect Social Security payments. But, as a rule, no one regularly engaged in commercial employment can receive a Social Security check. **3.** Yes, until age 16 (18 if in school.) The widow also receives benefits so long as such children are in her care. **4.** Social Security checks for an over-65 couple will not usually exceed $40 to $60 a month. To live comfortably, most couples require more. **5.** More desirable. Without extra income, such as life insurance provides, you or your widow may not be in a position to accept Social Security when due.

REPRODUCTION OF ADVERTISEMENT APPEARING IN THE
SATURDAY EVENING POST, NOVEMBER 27, 1943

of ideas between the home office and the field forces, for the discussion of sales problems, and for inspirational activity.[26] In April, 1936, the Company adopted a system for guaranteeing payments for a maximum of thirteen weeks to new agents in the hope that such guarantees would attract career underwriters to the field forces.[27]

THE HOME OFFICE; ADVERTISING; GEOGRAPHICAL LIMITATION OF THE MARKET

With the growth of the managerial agencies, agency training, programming, and a multitude of other sales activities, the Agency Department in the home office was greatly enlarged. From a staff of forty in 1906,[28] this department has grown until at present it employs sixty-six persons, organized into sections to deal with various aspects of the work. The department is administered by a corps of officers who stand high in the councils of the Company, have had extensive experience in the field, and are intimately acquainted with all kinds of questions concerning actual selling. It is represented in the Association of Life Agency Officers, which was founded in 1917 to study the problems of managing an agency department.

From agency work have gone most of the undesirable practices which appeared in life underwriting prior to 1905. Rebating and twisting, that is, getting a policyholder to change his insurance either from one company to another or from one policy to another within a company so that new commissions will be paid, have been prohibited by law, and raiding sales forces has been practically nonexistent because of intercompany coöperation in preventing it. Life insurance advertising has also been greatly altered, for, aside from a few public statements after the Armstrong Investigation to allay the fears which had been aroused, it has been largely of an institutional nature. Gone entirely are the bitter

---

26 Prizes for the largest amounts of new business were awarded in 1906. They were abolished in 1907. In 1913 the Field Club was first established. At that time there were three clubs—one Eastern, one Southern, and one Western—and three separate conventions were held. In 1914 the National Field Club was founded. In 1919 the original regional conventions were abolished, but the Clubs were continued as membership organizations until 1923. The only years since 1913 in which a Field Club convention has not been held were in 1918, when the money required for such a meeting was used to purchase an ambulance for overseas troops, and in 1942, when the meeting was canceled to reduce travel on overburdened railway lines.

27 The maximum amount to be guaranteed is $50 a week. The period of thirteen weeks may be extended under some circumstances. Repayment to the Company of these guarantees is provided for all first year commissions on insurance placed during the guaranteed period and on part of such commissions thereafter. Less than half of such guarantees were repaid up to the end of March, 1939.

28 This number excluded those in the Foreign Agency Department.

recriminations which marked insurance publicity in the third quarter of the last century, and in their place have appeared descriptions of or appeals for life insurance in general.[29] The Company's house publications—*Points, Our Best Assets*, and beginning in 1942 *The Mutual Circle*—have all been of a dignified character. The annual reports of the Company to policyholders have also been improved, especially since 1939, in that the condition of the Company has been explained with great frankness, technical material has been put into understandable terms, and graphs have been used to illustrate essential problems.

In addition to advertising, certain events have made the need for insurance strongly felt. In World War I and World War II governmental provisions for insuring members of the armed forces and the increased risk to life seem to have popularized the idea of life insurance with the masses. It may be, too, that the Social Security Act is having a similar effect, for the protection which it renders brings the concept of insurance to the attention of a large number of people and by implication indicates the need for additional coverage with private institutions. Be that as it may, the fact remains that the market for life insurance has been deepened in the last twenty-five years.

The territorial extent of the market, in so far as The Mutual Life and most other American companies are concerned, has, on the other hand, tended to shrink since 1905. The Mutual withdrew from Texas in 1907 because of the Robertson Law, which required the investment of certain funds and the deposit of a percentage of the reserves on policies held by Texans in Texas securities.[30] Before the end of World War I The Mutual had ceased writing new business in all foreign countries except Canada, but it withdrew from there in 1932, from Hawaii in the same year, and from Alaska in 1934.[31] Either hostile legislation, investment requirements, war conditions, or lack of new business has been responsible for these steps. From this restriction of the area in which the Company writes new insurance a more intensive cultivation of the districts worked has resulted. Concentration of effort has tended to reduce selling costs and to provide better supervision of the field forces.

[29] The Mutual's advertising immediately after the Armstrong Investigation was handled by N. W. Ayer and Sons. See *Minutes of the Insurance and Agency Committee*, Jan. 16, 1908. For a history of this advertising Company consult Ralph M. Hower, *The History of an Advertising Agency: N. W. Ayer and Sons at Work, 1869–1939*, Cambridge. For an example of recent Mutual Life Advertisements, see *Saturday Evening Post*, November 27, 1943.

[30] *Minutes of the Insurance and Agency Committee*, June 26, 1907.

[31] Dates of withdrawal of the Company from writing new business in the following jurisdictions: Alaska, January 1, 1934; Cuba, December 31, 1917; Hawaii, April 15, 1932; Philippine Islands, never licensed; Texas, July 11, 1907; Canal Zone, never licensed; Canada, August 1, 1932; Mexico, October 15, 1911.

Today insurance is sold in every state in the Union, with the exception of Texas, and in amounts that are roughly in proportion to state population and wealth.

The new trends in life insurance have had an important bearing upon the selection of risks. In the case of industrial insurance, the tendency has been to minimize the role of selection and to issue policies to nearly all applicants. In the case of some of the smaller companies, on the other hand, great care in selecting risks has been exercised not only by demanding that high medical requirements be met but also by limiting insurance to those who live in a given locality or who practice a certain profession. But in the case of companies like The Mutual Life, which do a large ordinary business, evolution has been in the direction of offering insurance to more and more people, of endeavoring to maintain definite standards of insurability, of classifying those who make application for insurance into three main groups—preferred, standard, and substandard—and of scaling the premiums for each group according to the risks involved.[32]

Long before 1907 The Mutual Life had liberalized its selection on Southern risks, on travel, and on a number of other special classes because of increased knowledge and actual improvement in experience. This policy rested on a belief that either the dangers which had led to the charging of extra premiums for certain risks had been greatly reduced or safe cases could be picked out of admittedly poor classes of risks by use of a superior technique developed by the Company. To a large extent the former conviction was well founded, for obviously

[32] These trends were clearly set forth in the *Annual Report of The Mutual Life's Inspector of Risks* in 1920:

"In their underwriting policy, life insurance companies seem to be divided in two classes:

"1st—Those that limit their field to sections, localities and classes which produce the best risks; barring from solicitation whole areas of the country and entire industries. . . .

"2nd—Those whose policy is to open wide the insurance field, apparently caring little for the effect on mortality and consequently on dividends.

"It would seem that The Mutual Life is in position to establish a third class; one which opens wide the field and; by skilled individual selection, procures a good mortality at the same time. That we are well on our way toward this goal is apparent from the fact that we write freely at present in all parts of the United States; only a very few industries and these the most extremely hazardous are closed to solicitation, and this on terms as liberal as any of our competitors. . . .

"Whether in its final [test] this policy could be made to result in the best mortality [rates] achieved by any company, and at the same time the most liberal underwriting opportunity offered by any, only time can tell. But there is no doubt that we have gone far enough on our way to show that there is an opportunity for, at the very least, a close approach to such a result."

steamboat and railroad travel had become relatively safe, and mortality rates among Southerners had greatly improved.[33] Much also could be said in favor of the latter contention, for The Mutual Life employed the "individual" method of selection, which meant that a decision on every application for insurance was reached, not by following a set of hard and fast rules, but by the total impression made on the examiner by the data before him.

The successful operation of this system of selection involved keeping abreast of all the changes affecting mortality. This the Company attempted to do and continued a long-established tradition of research among its examiners. Of the many problems which these men studied, that of occupational selection was one of the most important. For years attention had been given to this question, and those engaged in certain occupations were arbitrarily excluded from insurance or were "rated up," that is, were charged extra premiums. In 1907 The Mutual's Inspector of Applications, an officer who was later called Inspector of Risks and finally Supervisor of Risks decided that The Mutual's information on occupational risks had become antiquated and undertook the task of reclassifying it. A careful study was made of occupational mortality, and as a result a number of previously ineligible occupations were admitted to insurance.[34] Subsequently industrial plants were periodically inspected; the Company's experience with various occupational groups was reviewed annually; and underwriting rules were accordingly altered from time to time. Not all the changes effected were in the direction of greater liberality, but the net result was a widening of the acceptable field through increased knowledge of the risks and the charging of extras only where such rates were necessary.[35]

The work of The Mutual Life in occupational selection was considered so valuable that when the Joint Committee on Mortality of the Association of Life Insurance Medical Directors and of the Actuarial Society of America recommended a revision of the "occupational code," The Mutual was chosen as one of six companies to do the work. The result of this revision was the publication in 1926 of a code with more

---

[33] There was a steady improvement in the Company's experience on Southern business. In 1915 a definite mortality saving on Southern risks was registered. *Annual Report of The Mutual Life's Inspector of Risks,* 1916. Further improvement was still desired, however, and was noted with satisfaction in each of the next eight years. After that date Southern business presented no particular difficulties, although especial care in selecting Southern risks continued to be exercised.

[34] *Annual Report of the Inspector of Applications,* 1907.

[35] In the ten years preceding World War I several of the Company's underwriters studied chemistry at Columbia University in order to deal more intelligently with the question of industrial hazards. *Annual Report of the Inspector of Risks,* 1916.

than one thousand classifications and about two thousand six hundred occupational titles—a body of information that has remained in use, with minor amendments, to the present time. This investigation seemed so worth while that representatives of the coöperating companies continued to meet to discuss occupational risks throughout 1926. Subsequently the Home Office Life Underwriters Association appointed a Standing Occupational Committee to formalize their findings. This Committee, composed of one member from each of ten companies and including a representative from The Mutual Life,[36] has regularly published its findings in the *Proceedings* of the Association—a collection of data which is the most extensive and authoritative on the subject of occupational underwriting in existence today.

The Mutual Life's medical department also carried on important research pertaining to medical selection. In 1907 Dr. Brandreth Symonds published two important papers—"The Influence of Family History on Medical Selection" and "The Influence of Build on Medical Selection"—which for long influenced the acceptance of applications both in The Mutual Life and in other companies. Also, in 1907 The Mutual began to measure blood pressures by use of the sphygmomanometer, in 1913 it demanded that blood pressure readings be taken for all applicants in agency cities, and in 1925 it made such readings a routine part of all examinations. These steps may be considered to comprise one of the major developments in the recent history of medical selection, for the general use of information on blood pressure has made possible the refusal of countless undesirable risks which would otherwise have been accepted. Experience has shown, moreover, the need for stricter standards on blood pressures and also for more rigid rules governing the closely allied question of overweight.

Advances in medical knowledge and statistical studies of experience with various types of impairment made selection ever more precise. For example, in 1923 an investigation demonstrated the feasibility of reducing from ten to five years the period of postponement required for risks with a history of gastric ulcer. In 1924 the development of a method of quantitative analysis of urinary albumin permitted liberalization of selection on this condition. And in the same year a long step forward was taken in establishing methods of correct diagnosis and scientific selection of goiter cases. A simplification of the method of taking basal metabolism readings in 1925 aided in handling cases in which this in-

[36] Morris Pitler of The Mutual Life was the second chairman of this committee.

formation was important, and in 1928 standards were established for the more accurate diagnosis of diabetes by means of the blood sugar tolerance test. The Company was able in 1925 by a more extensive use of chest X rays to cut the postponement period for applicants with a history of pulmonary tuberculosis from ten to five years. By requiring in 1935 X rays from all applicants with a history suggesting tuberculosis it was able to reduce postponement from five to three years and the minimum age limit for such applicants from thirty-five to thirty.

In the case of major surgical operations, many of which were once thought to make a patient uninsurable at standard rates for periods of from five to ten years, statistical studies made possible gradual reductions in these postponement periods until in the middle nineteen-thirties many cases were accepted after one to five years. The technique of visualizing the gallbladder and the kidneys, perfected about 1930, made possible the selection of applicants who had had trouble with these organs with much greater accuracy than in the days when clinical history alone had to be relied on. The development of the modern type of electrocardiograph has also been of great importance in medical selection, for it has made possible a better diagnosis of questionable heart conditions.[37] The discovery of vitamins and the subsequent research into their nature and effects have permitted the acceptance of many risks which were formerly rejected. Thus, such conditions as beriberi, pellagra, multiple neuritis of unexplained origin, and night blindness are now known to be caused by a vitamin deficiency and are considered acceptable for insurance after about a year of satisfactory treatment.

Medical statistics have also played an important role in determining selection policies, for actual experience is one of the chief factors on which to rely. Consequently, The Mutual Life has adopted the latest methods of assembling and analyzing data on medical impairments. In 1932 The Mutual Life prepared a new General Code of Impairments, designed for use in the punched card system. This material permits the Company to conduct more detailed, accurate, and scientific medical impairment studies than ever before. A special Research Section in the Supervisor of Risks Department collects information on selection outside The Mutual's own experience,[38] and the Statistical Department prepares an analysis, on the following subjects from Company data:

[37] In 1936 The Mutual Life established its own X ray and electrocardiographic laboratory in the home office.

[38] Thus, health and sanitary conditions in foreign countries are kept under scrutiny in order to facilitate underwriting risks on travel or residence outside the United States.

Annual Statistical Report on Mortality, Double Indemnity and Disability
Mortality Experience by Agency at Issue
Mortality Experience by Size of Policy
Mortality Experience of Corporation and Creditor Insurance
Report of Rejected Cases for Moral Hazard
Mortality Experience of Foreign Born Classes
Mortality Experience by Residence at Issue
Mortality Experience by Habits as to Alcohol
Mortality Experience of Large Risks—$50,000 and over
Report of Lapse Rates
Mortality Experience by Medical Impairments
Mortality Experience of Additional Insurance without Further Medical
    Examination
Report of Effects of Occupation on Mortality
Mortality under Reinstated Policies
Mortality Experience on Term Policies

SPECIAL RISKS

In addition to occupational and medical hazards, there are several classes
of special risks which have presented exceptionally knotty problems to
underwriters. One of these classes was made up of women who, according to an ancient life insurance tradition, exercised "an initial self-
selection against the Company." [39] The Mutual's experience came to
show that this old belief was entirely untrue or at least greatly exaggerated. Consequently, by 1921 most of the selection restrictions on
women were removed, and the two sexes began to be underwritten on
nearly the same basis. [40] Another special class was composed of those who
used alcohol to excess. As we have seen in earlier chapters, an immoder-
ate use of intoxicants had long been considered an unfavorable feature
from a life insurance standpoint, even though in the early nineteenth
century a British company had charged an extra premium for a person
who was a total abstainer. But in 1915 a study of The Mutual's experience seemed to indicate that another old prejudice was not entirely warranted. Consequently, in 1915 a somewhat more liberal attitude was
taken toward this class of risk, although during prohibition a partial
return to strict selection had to be made. [41]

Large amounts of insurance on one life also constitute a special class
of risk. The Mutual Life took pride in being considered a large risk

---

39 *Annual Report of Inspector of Risks*, 1915.
40 *Ibid.*, 1921. It should be added that in 1917 self-supporting spinsters were accepted for
waiver of premium and disability benefit.
41 *Ibid.*, 1917.

company and cultivated the issuing of policies for large sums. In 1927 it raised the limit for its own retention on a single life to $350,000 and in 1929 to $500,000. Similarly, the limit for waiver of premium was successively increased from $50,000 to $250,000, and that for double indemnity from $25,000 to $50,000. These high limits, combined with liberal practices as regards blood pressure and overweight, resulted in insuring a number of questionable cases for large amounts. When this became apparent, a reduction in the limits was made (1942), $250,000 being set as a top for insurance, $100,000 for waiver of premium, and $25,000 for double indemnity.[42]

The development of aviation created still another case apart. In the early and experimental stages of this industry the hazard of flying could not be covered. Standard premiums did not provide for this new risk, and experience on which to base extra charges was entirely lacking. The problem was merely how to avoid the risk, and since a clause restricting coverage had to be limited by law to the contestable period, applicants who engaged in aviation had to be rejected.[43] Up until 1928 this rule applied to all pilots and to all persons who flew as passengers. In that year The Mutual Life first issued coverage to applicants at standard rates if they flew as passengers in planes operated by licensed pilots and if the number of their flights did not exceed four per year.[44] With the increasing safety of aviation, the Company gradually liberalized these restrictions. The rate of progress can be measured by the facts that in 1934 the limit for standard insurance had been raised to twenty flights and the rate for additional flights reduced to ten cents and that by 1940 the same figures had become fifty flights and approximately three cents. In 1940 all restrictions on scheduled passenger flying (with the sole exception of lower double indemnity limits for excessive flying or flying more than 750

[42] Prior to 1937 insurance on one life in excess of $350,000 was reinsured in other companies. In 1937 reinsurance was discontinued, and in 1940 the maximum amount taken was lowered to $350,000. In 1941 the limit on waiver of premium was reduced to $125,000.

[43] In 1918 a clause was adopted to exclude liability for death resulting from aviation during the contestable period. Its use was limited, however, both because need for it was not then very great and because its nature made it of little value anyway. In 1923 it was replaced by a clause under which the policy was canceled if a flight was made during the contestable period. Neither of these clauses was intended for general use, of course, being endorsed on a policy only to cover the hazard of resumption of flying by an applicant who had flown in the past and then discontinued the practice. It was possible, however, to use a permanent restriction of coverage in the Double Indemnity clause, so this provision excluded liability for death as a result of "participation in aeronautics."

[44] If more than four flights per year were made, the extra premium charged was $.50 per $1,000 of insurance per flight, assessed in units of $2.50. Licensed pilots who were not pilots by profession, were accepted for a short time with an extra annual premium of $1 per $1,000 of insurance per flight, assessed in units of $5 with a $10 minimum.

miles over water) were completely removed. Although the hazards of regular air transport have not been entirely eliminated, they have been sufficiently reduced so that no extra premium is needed.[45]

TABLE 40

SCHEDULED FLYING STATISTICS

U.S. Companies—Domestic and Foreign Service [a]

Year	Passengers Carried	Passenger Fatalities	Passenger Fatalities per 1,000 Passengers Carried
1927	8,679	1	.120
1928	49,713	15	.300
1929	173,405	18	.100
1930	417,505	25	.060
1931	531,662	26	.049
1932	547,560	25	.046
1933	576,612	12	.021
1934	572,265	21	.037
1935	874,116	15	.017
1936	1,166,043	46	.039
1937	1,289,735	51	.040
1938	1,536,111	32	.021
1939	2,094,909	19	.009

[a] *Transactions of the Actuarial Society of America*, XXXIII (1927–1929), 490; XLI (1930–1939), 244.

Unique problems of selection have also come into being in connection with the writing of special benefits such as double indemnity and disability. Double indemnity presented a particularly involved situation, because the premium for this coverage was so small that any great deviation from normal was sufficient to rule out an applicant. The major field to which attention had to be given was that of industry, for many occupations which experience a satisfactory overall mortality are subject to an accident rate twice that of normal. Consequently, a complete revision of The Mutual's occupational rating schedule was necessary to indicate eligibility or ineligibility for double indemnity.

In the case of income disability benefits, especially those providing

---

[45] Coincident with the increased safety of air travel on scheduled airlines was the improvement in all other forms of aviation. A great advance in the handling of these cases was made in 1930, when the New York Court of Appeals in *Metropolitan Life Ins. Co. vs. Conway* ruled that the aviation risk could be excluded permanently from life policies rather than only during the contestable period. This decision made it possible to offer limited coverage to pilots and private plane passengers who had previously been rejected for insurance, and The Mutual adopted clauses of that type. In 1940 the Company decided, however, that airline crews could safely be offered unrestricted coverage for an extra premium. The practice adopted provided annual extras of $20 per $1,000 for pilots and co-pilots and $15 per $1,000 for stewards and hostesses. A year later the extra for pilots and co-pilots was reduced to $15. Further progress in the underwriting of aviation cases was interrupted when the United States entered World War II. The universal use of a war clause excluding aviation risks stopped for the time being further changes in the selecting of aviation risks.

for an increasing amount of income and those containing the ninety-day clause (1922), extreme caution in selecting risks had to be used. Experience in handling waiver of premium contracts did not prove to be a sufficient guide for disability policies, and the problems involved in the two cases turned out to be entirely different. The terms of the disability policies were altered so frequently that the Company could not measure the probable future experience. Court decisions and the depression of the thirties provided incentives for those with disability contracts to take advantage of the Company by becoming "disabled." Consequently, losses on disability began to pile up, and a decision was finally taken to cease issuing policies of this kind.

Juvenile insurance, first written by The Mutual Life in 1938, also presented entirely new considerations in selecting risks, for the standards employed for adults had to be revised in underwriting children from six months to ten years of age. Nonmedical insurance, offered by the Company in 1939 in amounts of not less than $1,000 and for not more than $2,000 to residents of rural areas, threw an especial responsibility of selection upon the agent and the inspection service. Nonmedical insurance on the monthly premium, salary deduction plan [46] required a careful inspection of the group applying for the insurance and especial attention to industrial health hazards. Finally, the preferred risk modified life policy necessitated the establishment of standards above those demanded for ordinary life, and substandard insurance, the fixing of minimum requirements.

Of all special problems of selection those created by modern war are perhaps the most perplexing, because mortality rates may fluctuate widely with the intensity, duration, and frequency of conflicts. In the Civil and Spanish American Wars they were dealt with by extra premiums and by refunding any charges in excess of what was needed to cover exceptionally high mortality. During World War I a not-dissimilar procedure was followed, although the circumstances were profoundly different. In the earlier periods, policies contained clauses restricting coverage for service in armed forces during wartime. By 1914, however, the contracts issued by most companies did not have war exclusion clauses, yet the added risk of warfare had to be eliminated or covered by extra premiums in new policies to prevent unfavorable selection. Accordingly, at first The Mutual Life introduced clauses into its new contracts which excluded war risks, although provision was made for the return of premiums in the event of death caused while in service.

[46] Made available in 1940.

As more mortality experience was gained, however, the Company began to grant war coverage upon the payment of extra premiums.[47] When the United States entered the conflict, it was decided to charge 10 percent of the face amount of the policy for persons in the armed forces and from 2.5 to 5 percent for civilians traveling to Europe or serving in the Red Cross, Y.M.C.A., or Knights of Columbus. After the cessation of hostilities the actual mortality incidental to the War was calculated, and as the extra premiums collected had been more than sufficient to cover losses, the excess was refunded to policyholders or to their beneficiaries. Of the amounts collected under the 10 percent extra, 30.5 percent was refunded, and of the sums paid for service in civilian auxiliary forces, 100 percent was returned.[48]

Soon after World War I war clauses were again dropped from The Mutual's contracts, so when World War II began, the underwriting of war risks was in a situation similar to that of 1917. Mortality experience in the earlier conflict had provided, it was thought, a very limited guide for future policy, for no one knew whether or not the new war would be bloody, would last a long time, would become widespread, or would lead to epidemics. Without some fairly accurate estimate of what wartime mortality would be, the fixing of suitable extra premiums was almost impossible. And to make matters worse, state laws varied considerably as to war exclusion clauses and as to the conditions for eliminating risks or charging extras. Consequently, American life companies failed to reach any uniformity of position in the early part of World War II, and confusion reigned in the practices adopted. In the autumn of 1939 The Mutual Life adopted clauses to exclude war risks on such new policies as seemed to require them, and in the next two years they altered these provisions to meet special circumstances. This effort to distinguish among the risks likely to be particularly exposed to the hazards of war was continued so far as the reinstatement of lapsed policies was concerned after America's entry into the conflict, insertion of the war clause being determined by sex, age, occupation, and marital status. New policies, however, contained a war clause, although it provided for

[47] Because little new insurance was being written in Europe and most of the policies in force there had large reserves, no great losses were envisaged from war casualties of Europeans. *Minutes of the Board of Trustees*, Sept. 30, 1914. During the trouble with Mexico in 1916 insurance on the lives of officers in the armed forces was refused. It was accepted, however, in 1917.

[48] The partial refund of the military service extras resulted from the fact that the policyholders were exposed for an average duration of less than a full year. On an annual basis the extras charged were just about adequate to cover losses.

the return of premiums or the reserve in case of death from war.[49] The Company, along with other New York State institutions, followed the state's standard provision, adopted in the spring of 1942, which excluded liability from death occurring as *a result of* military, naval, or air service inside the United States or Canada or from death resulting from any cause while the insured was serving with the armed forces outside the United States or Canada.

METHODS OF SELECTION; RESULTS OBTAINED

With the increasing complexity of selecting risks and with the growth of the Company, there was a marked expansion in the number of persons engaged in selection. On the other hand, little change was made in the fundamental organization of this phase of the business, for before 1907 all the bureaus having to do with selection were brought together under one officer, and they have remained thus grouped to the present time.[50] Methods of handling certain aspects of risk selection have, however, been altered from time to time. One of the most important developments has been the growth of lay underwriting, that is, the approving of applications for insurance by persons without medical training. Prior to 1917 every case had to be passed upon by members of the medical department, but after that date medical examiners received only those cases on which the lay underwriters believed professional advice was necessary.[51] Another change, effected in 1942, was the disbanding of the National Commercial Agency and the placing of the work of inspecting moral hazards in the hands of two agencies not connected with the Company.[52] Finally, The Mutual Life's long-established practice of individual selection was abandoned in favor of the numerical system [53]—a change which was discussed by the officers at a meeting in Ponta Vedra (1941). The new method requires the underwriter to give a numerical score for the principal factors in the application and to decline or rate up cases which have a total number of points above predetermined

[49] *Circular letter to Managers*, Dec. 9, 1941.

[50] This was one of the earliest examples of a combination of "line" and "functional" organization within the Company. The Managers of Selection have been Dr. Grenville M. White (1906–1928), Dr. P. Maxwell Foshay (1928–1939), Dr. Eugene F. Russell (1939–1941), and Leigh Cruess (1941–   ).

[51] This system has required a great saving of time, effort, and expense and has operated satisfactorily. At the present, final decisions are made by lay underwriters on well over half of all applications received.

[52] These are the Retail Credit Company of Atlanta, Georgia and the Hooper Holmes Bureau of New York City. The change was made in order to get better service at lower costs.

[53] Introduced by the New York Life in 1904.

TABLE 41

NUMBER OF DEATHS AND DEATH RATES

(Per 100,000

Cause of Death	1912		1915		1920		1925	
	No.	Rate	No.	Rate	No.	Rate	No.	Rate
Typhoid and paratyphoid fever	107	21	110	21	58	9	61	8
Influenza	70	14	69	13	653	99	173	22
Acute peri-endo and myocarditis	36	7	133	25	85	13	65	8
Pneumonia all forms	473	95	531	99	637	97	383	48
Tuberculosis all forms	520	104	438	82	404	62	361	45
Cancer and other malignant tumors	466	93	500	94	678	103	744	94
Diabetes	143	29	143	27	211	32	167	21
Cerebral hemorrhage, etc.	710	142	721	135	803	122	715	90
Angina pectoris and coronary disease	197	40	231	43	310	47	314	40
Chronic heart disease	634	127	616	115	818	125	1,261	159
Arteriosclerosis	240	48	269	50	267	41	235	30
Nephritis (acute and chronic)	579	116	619	116	583	89	692	87
Diseases of stomach and duodenum	100	20	94	18	92	14	85	11
Appendicitis	76	15	103	19	104	16	143	18
Disease of liver and gall bladder	172	34	164	31	167	25	152	19
Diseases of bladder and prostate	71	14	109	20	119	18	96	12
Diseases of pregnancy and puerperium	21	4	15	3	19	3	20	3
Suicide	139	28	170	32	148	23	162	20
Homicide	37	7	23	4	39	6	48	6
Automobile accidents	43	9	67	13	76	12	162	20
All other accidents	306	61	336	67	372	57	342	43
War claims (not included in above)	...	...	..	...	...	...	...	...
Total deaths from all causes	6,341		6,625		7,763		7,329	

minima. It is argued that this detailed analysis prevents the examiner from being either too lenient or too severe and from making egregious errors.[54]

Methods of underwriting have also profited much from underwriters' professional organizations. The Association of Life Insurance Medical Directors has provided a clearing house for problems dealing with medical selection and has made possible an exchange of information about applicants. The Home Office Life Underwriters Association, founded in

[54] Oscar H. Rogers and Arthur Hunter, "The Numerical Method of Determining the Value of Risks for Insurance," *Transactions of the Actuarial Society of America*, XX, Part 2, 273 ff.

FROM PRINCIPAL CAUSES: THE MUTUAL LIFE

men and women)

1930		1935		1940		1941		1942		1943	
No.	Rate	No.	Rate	No.	Rate	No.	Rate	No.	Rate	No.	Rate
34	3	8	1	4	0	3	0	2	0	6	1
123	12	27	3	88	10	94	10	56	6	39	4
55	5	43	5	58	6	48	5	...	...	...	...
453	45	554	62	323	35	271	30	248	27	277	30
345	34	292	33	207	23	185	20	170	19	177	19
971	96	1,095	122	1,230	135	1,230	135	1,276	140	1,219	133
221	22	217	24	283	31	236	26	233	26	191	21
774	77	499	56	924	101	784	86	352	93	867	95
634	63	1,227	137	1,931	212	1,991	218	2,033	223	2,088	228
1,497	143	1,383	155	1,528	167	1,337	146	1,245	136	1,221	133
404	40	524	59	179	20	182	20	174	19	223	24
709	70	573	64	752	82	649	71	603	66	557	61
144	14	95	11	133	15	113	12	99	11	93	10
207	20	159	18	123	13	77	8	67	7	43	5
154	15	160	18	176	19	154	17	126	14	138	15
134	13	147	16	129	14	106	12	131	14	111	12
39	4	23	3	22	2	25	3	19	2	15	2
348	34	265	30	306	34	205	22	210	23	121	13
46	5	26	3	20	2	14	2	20	2	18	2
308	30	301	34	262	29	300	33	159	17	136	15
469	46	316	35	307	34	293	32	273	30	264	29
...	...	...	...	...	...	...	...	154	17	449	49
8,983		9,258		9,981		9,206		9,098		9,204	

1931 and presided over during its first year by Austin D. Reiley, Supervisor of Risks of The Mutual Life, has raised the quality of selections relating to other than medical factors.

The best imaginable methods of selecting risks, however, cannot determine which individuals who measure up to certain standards are going to be the first victims of accidents, of certain communicable diseases, and of death. The influenza epidemic of 1918–1919, which caused the death of 2,788 Mutual Life policyholders, is a case in point. Selection had practically no effect on eliminating those who were to succumb to this disease. In fact, Mutual Life's experience seemed to indicate that mortality from influenza was greatest among the younger policyholders and was just as great among the newly insured as among holders of policies who had been insured for some years.[55] Fortunately, medical science has removed the scourge of many diseases. Sulfa derivatives have diminished the danger of death from pneumonia, improved diagnosis

TABLE 42

RATIO OF ACTUAL TO EXPECTED MORTALITY AND AVERAGE AGE OF POLICYHOLDERS IN THE MUTUAL LIFE

According to the American Experience Table 1907–1943

Year	Ratio of Actual to Expected Mortality	Average Age of Policyholders	Year	Ratio of Actual to Expected Mortality	Average Age of Policyholders	Year	Ratio of Actual to Expected Mortality	Average Age of Policyholders
1907	84.81	...	1920	66.74	...	1933	69.17	45.3
1908	77.59	...	1921	56.45	...	1934	68.64	45.8
1909	78.52	...	1922	59.83	...	1935	65.84	46.0
1910	78.47	...	1923	63.42	...	1936	66.11	46.3
1911	76.99	...	1924	56.27	43.2	1937	64.35	46.5
1912	72.82	...	1925	52.83	...	1938	61.39	46.6
1913	75.28	...	1926	51.42	...	1939	62.69	46.8
1914	75.04	...	1927	54.46	...	1940	61.86	46.9
1915	73.53	...	1928	54.88	...	1941	60.63	47.1
1916	75.75	...	1929	59.95	...	1942	56.59	47.2
1917	71.66	...	1930	63.04	44.0	1943	60.36	...
1918	95.74	...	1931	65.32	44.3			
1919	63.05	...	1932	65.61	44.8			

and treatment of tuberculosis have improved the mortality rate from this disease, vaccinations have reduced deaths from diphtheria and smallpox, better care of obstetric cases has lowered the number of deaths due to childbirth, and modern sanitation has reduced the prevalence of typhoid. The mortality rates of life insurance companies reflect the general improvement in public health and the progress of medical science.[56] The Mutual Life has shared in this trend.

[55] In 1919 68.3 percent of the total influenza deaths in The Mutual Life were below 40 years of age. *Mortality Report for 1919*, p. 5.

[56] See Louis I. Dublin and Alfred J. Lotka, *Twenty Five Years of Health Progress* (New York, San Francisco, 1937); testimony of Louis I. Dublin before the T.N.E.C. Committee, *T.N.E.C.*, Part 12, p. 985; and the *Information Bulletin*, published by The Mutual's Supervisor of Risks. The Mutual Life has been unable to engage in the welfare work undertaken by some of the industrial companies. Such enterprises are largely effective among the working classes.

XVI. Investing for Security

O F ALL THE PROBLEMS which face American life insurance companies today, none is more important than that of investments. Policy contracts may be altered, agents may sell more insurance, and new methods of selecting risks may be devised without fundamentally affecting the insurance business; but if the assets of life companies are not zealously protected, the advantages provided by insurance become *ipso facto* endangered. In these changing times, when wars, depressions, and an almost revolutionary attitude toward money have profoundly modified our economic system, the investing of life insurance funds has taken on a new aspect. Every energy has to be exerted, first, to make assets secure and, secondly, to earn enough interest on them to cover the rate assumed in computing premiums.

In an effort to increase the safety of life insurance investments, New York State established after the Armstrong Investigation rigid restrictions upon the placement of funds. According to the terms of the law which was enacted in 1906, life companies were no longer to own common stocks, bonds secured by stocks, or real estate that was not actually necessary for the conduct of business, nor were the companies in the future to underwrite new issues.[1] This legislation, which was followed in a general way by most other states, meant that life insurance investments were and have remained limited largely to mortgage loans, policy loans, and high grade corporate, municipal, state, and government bonds. The only important exceptions have been that in 1928 life companies were allowed to invest 2 percent of their assets in certain preferred or guaranteed stocks,[2] that since the early part of the "great depression" of the thirties life insurance commissioners have been lenient in permitting the management of foreclosed real estate, that permission has been granted to engage in low-cost housing projects, and that in 1939 the

---

[1] Common stocks, collateral trust bonds, and real estate had to be disposed of within five years. The fact should be mentioned here that no mortgage loan in New York State may be in excess of two-thirds of the value of the property. See above, Chapter XII, and also *T.N.E.C.*, Monograph 28, p. 372.

[2] *Laws of the State of New York* (Albany, 1928), Chapter 539.

tests for permissible securities were made more practical.[3] In so far as life companies have thus been prevented from engaging in speculative enterprises and have had their entrepreneurial activity restricted to the field of life insurance, the legislation has probably been sound. Yet the salutary effect of such laws is limited, for the most serious investment problems of life insurance companies arise from the condition of the money market and from the state of business activity.

In an economy which is expanding rapidly or which is experiencing a diminution of the purchasing power of its monetary unit, the demand for capital is usually much greater than in an economy which is growing very slowly or which is witnessing an augmentation of the purchasing power of its money. Over the whole period now under survey, that is, from 1907 to 1943, the productive capacity of the United States grew considerably, and prices rose to some extent. Consequently, there was an over-all increased demand for capital, but this demand fluctuated widely, as can be seen from statistics on private long-term—mortgage and bonded—debt. Thus, in 1938 the total of such indebtedness was about thrice what it had been in 1907. The rise was steady from 1907 to 1914, rapid from 1914 to 1920, retarded somewhat in the depression of 1920–1921, when prices collapsed and inventory losses had to be taken, was accelerated again from 1921 to 1930, and then was transformed into a decline, the shrinkage having been 18 per cent from 1930 to 1937.[4]

A detailed analysis of long-term debt statistics shows at once that the capital demand of various branches of the economy was by no means the same. The amount of money in non-farm mortgages grew at an annual average of 6.2 percent between 1900 and 1919 and of 12.23 percent from 1920 to 1928, but the total subsequently declined by 26 percent from 1930 to 1937—the greatest contraction of any of the classifications to be considered. Farm mortgages followed the general trend upwards to World War I, soared with the high agricultural price levels of 1914–1919, were reduced at an annual rate of 1.6 percent from 1924 to 1930, and collapsed by 23 percent during the years 1930–1937. In the case of railroad debt, the rise was rapid to 1912, was slow from 1912 to 1930, and was changed into a decline from 1930 to 1938 of almost 7 percent. For manufacturing, mining, quarrying, services, and trade the increase in long-term debt was steady to 1930, but the decrease amounted to 12 percent in the next eight years. Only for public utilities was there no decrement in total capital debt, yet even in this category the rate of annual increase, which was 7.11 percent in 1930, fell to only 2 percent in 1938.

[3] *Insurance Law of the State of New York*, section 84. It should be noted here that following the T.N.E.C. investigation the Association of Life Insurance Commissioners has each year made the requirements for valuing assets more stringent.

[4] *Studies in Enterprise and Social Progress* (New York, 1939), p. 68.

CHART XVIII

PUBLIC AND PRIVATE LONG-TERM DEBT, 1907–1942

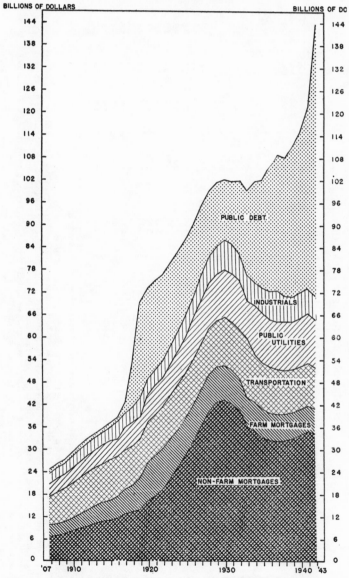

BILLIONS OF DOLLARS

BILLIONS OF DO

PUBLIC DEBT

INDUSTRIALS

PUBLIC UTILITIES

TRANSPORTATION

FARM MORTGAGES

NON-FARM MORTGAGES

TABLE 43

STOCK AND BOND YIELDS—PER CENT, 1922–1943 [a]

			BONDS						STOCKS			
	U.S. TREASURY (TREASURY DEPT.) [b]	MUNICIPAL (BOND BUYER) (20)	CORPORATE (MOODY'S INVESTORS' SERVICE)				MUNICIPAL (STANDARD & POOR'S CORP.) (15)	PREFERRED [c] (STANDARD & POOR'S CORP.) (15)	COMMON (MOODY'S INVESTORS' SERVICE) [d]			
YEAR			Total	Industrial	Railroad	Public Utility			Total [e] (200)	Industrial (125)	Railroad (25)	Public Utility (25)
1922	4.30	4.21	5.95	6.04	5.89	5.93	4.23	6.14	….	….	….	….
1923	4.36	4.27	6.04	6.04	6.24	5.83	4.25	6.12	….	….	….	….
1924	4.06	4.21	5.80	5.90	5.90	5.61	4.20	6.08	….	….	….	….
1925	3.86	4.13	5.47	5.61	5.51	5.29	4.09	5.90	….	….	….	….
1926	3.68	4.14	5.21	5.37	5.13	5.11	4.08	5.78	….	….	….	….
1927	3.34	3.99	4.97	5.10	4.83	4.96	3.98	5.51	….	….	….	….
1928	3.33	4.05	4.94	5.10	4.85	4.87	4.05	5.12	….	….	….	….
1929	3.60	4.31	5.21	5.31	5.18	5.14	4.27	5.12	3.5 [f]	4.0 [f]	4.4 [f]	2.6 [f]
1930	3.29	4.12	5.09	5.25	4.96	5.05	4.07	4.95	4.6	4.9	5.6	3.7
1931	3.34	4.07	5.81	6.08	6.09	5.27	4.01	5.04	6.2	6.4	7.8	5.4
1932	3.68	4.77	6.87	6.71	7.61	6.80	4.65	6.13	7.4	7.3	6.3	8.0
1933	3.31	5.14	5.89	5.34	6.09	6.25	4.71	5.75	4.4	3.7	2.7	6.9
1934	3.12	4.22	4.96	4.52	4.96	5.40	4.03	5.29	4.1	3.4	3.0	6.9
1935	2.79	3.38	4.46	4.02	4.95	4.43	3.41	4.63	4.1	3.5	4.0	6.3
1936	2.65	2.93	3.87	3.50	4.24	3.88	3.07	4.33	3.5	3.4	2.7	4.5
1937	2.68	3.03	3.94	3.55	4.34	3.93	3.10	4.45	4.8	4.8	4.3	5.5
1938	2.56	2.99	4.19	3.50	5.21	3.87	2.91	4.34	4.4	3.9	5.3	6.4
1939	2.36	2.82	3.77	3.30	4.53	3.48	2.76	4.17	4.2	3.9	3.7	5.5
1940	2.21	2.52	3.55	3.10	4.30	3.25	2.50	4.14	5.3	5.3	5.4	5.7
1941	1.95	2.15	3.34	2.95	3.95	3.11	2.10	4.08	6.2	6.3	6.5	6.6
1942	2.02	2.25	3.34	2.96	3.96	3.11	2.36	4.31	6.6	6.4	7.7	7.9
1943	1.91	1.90	3.16	2.85	3.64	2.99	2.06	4.06	4.8	4.5	6.9	5.8

Note: Figures in parentheses indicate number of issues; data not available in cases of omission.

[a] *Statistical Abstract of the United States* (1942), p. 349; *Survey of Current Business*.

[b] Prior to 1926 average yields of all outstanding Treasury Bonds due or callable after 8 years, together with certain Liberty Loan issues; beginning 1926, average yields are based on all outstanding partially tax-exempt Treasury Bonds not due or callable for 12 years or more.

[c] High grade noncallable, including public utility and industrial.

[d] Average of monthly figures computed by dividing the aggregate annual dividends being paid as of the end of each month by the market value of all outstanding shares of the companies as of the same date.

[e] Includes 15 banks and 10 insurance stocks.

[f] Average of figures for June to December.

Thus, it would seem that from 1907 to 1914 investment opportunities were numerous, although not dramatic, especially in non-farm mortgages and in railroads. During World War I private capital demand was large for farm mortgages. From 1921 to 1930 demand was again exceptional, with non-farm mortgages, public utilities, and industrials leading the way. Until 1939, at least until after the outbreak of World War II, real difficulty was experienced in finding satisfactory outlets for the investment of accumulated funds, utilities offering the greatest opportunities.

As we shall see shortly, the demand for capital profoundly influenced the investment policies of life insurance companies, but before passing to that subject let us consider more in detail the situation during the depressed years of the thirties. New capital issues fell off more rapidly than the total debt, and refunding operations, which resulted invariably in lower interest rates, increased considerably.[5] Dealings in bonds on the exchanges dwindled to a point which indicated the lack of market for long-term funded securities. The quality of investments also declined temporarily, although the Securities and Exchange Commission, created as a result of legislation in 1933, and the Public Utilities Holding Act of 1935 have tended to curb the flotation of unsound issues.[6] Finally, bond yields were diminished markedly with the fall in interest rates, the yield on United States governments having declined from 4.36 in 1923 to 1.91 in 1943 and that on corporate bonds from 6.04 in 1923 to 3.16 in 1943.

The dearth of investment opportunities was alleviated somewhat in the thirties by an enormous expansion of governmental borrowing. Yet government bonds had low yields, and they provided capital which was in part used to finance undertakings in competition with institutional investors. The Federal Land Banks, created in 1917, and the Federal Farm Mortgage Corporation of 1933 cut into the farm mortgage market, the Reconstruction Finance Corporation, established in 1932, assisted in financing commerce and industry, the R.F.C. Mortgage Corporation, set up in 1935, and the Home Owner's Loan Corporation (1933), took a share of non-farm mortgages, and a host of other agencies assumed a large part of the nation's investment demand.[7] The aggregate "loans" of

---

[5] See Table 58, Appendix. [6] *T.N.E.C.*, Monograph 28, p. 374.

[7] Reconstruction Finance Corporation; Electric Home and Farm Authority; Export-Import Bank of Washington; R.F.C. Mortgage Company; Federal National Mortgage Association; Disaster Loan Corporation; Federal Deposit Insurance Corporation; Home Owner's Loan Corporation; Federal Savings and Loan Insurance Corporation; Federal Housing Administration; Federal Land Banks; Federal Intermediate Credit Agricultural Marketing Act Revolving Fund; Regional Agricultural Credit Corporation; Production Credit Corporations;

all governmental corporations and credit agencies were reported by the Treasury Department to have amounted in 1934 to $3,223,000,000, in 1936 to $8,312,000,000, and in 1943 to $7,686,000,000. These were large sums in view of the shrinkage in the investment market.

INVESTMENT PORTFOLIOS OF LIFE INSURANCE COMPANIES

Immediately after the Armstrong Investigation the main investment concern of life insurance companies in those states which had enacted legislation restricting the classes of securities permissible for insurance funds was to comply with the new requirements. Accordingly, life companies began to throw their disqualified holdings upon the market. They sold that real estate, both at home and abroad, which was not needed for the conduct of their business, they dumped their stocks and collateral trust bonds upon the market, and they withdrew their deposits from partially owned banks and trust companies. The chief effect of this action appears to have been the weakening of the market for equity securities—life insurance companies reduced their holdings of common stocks by 36 per cent between 1906 and 1911—and to have threatened the very existence of some banking institutions. It seems clear that compliance with the new laws contributed directly to the panic of 1907, for that crisis took the form of lowered stock exchange prices, runs on trust companies, and ultimately to a severe stringency of money. For a time the situation was so serious that some companies appealed to state insurance commissions for delays in meeting the new legal requirements in order to avoid loss. But the panic was short-lived, losses were not so great as was feared in the depression year, and by 1911 portfolios had been altered to conform with law.

With the transformations occasioned by the Armstrong Investigation out of the way, more attention could be given to the general character of the portfolios. In the years from 1906 to 1914, when farm prices were high, when urbanization was going on at a rapid pace, and when railroads were expanding, life insurance companies had a tendency to favor the financing of these branches of our economy. Thus companies' holdings of farm mortgages increased from $262,000,000 in 1906 to $789,000,000 in 1916, of urban mortgages from $547,000,000

Emergency Crop and Feed Loan Offices; Banks for Cooperatives; Commodity Credit Corporation; Federal Farm Mortgage Corporation; Tennessee Valley Associated Cooperatives, Inc.; Farm Security Administration; Rural Electrification Administration; Public Works Administration; United States Housing Authority; Inland Waterways Corporation; United States Maritime Commission; Tennessee Valley Authority; Puerto Rico Reconstruction Administration.

CHART XIX

DISTRIBUTION OF ADMITTED ASSETS OF ALL COMPANIES, 1906–1942

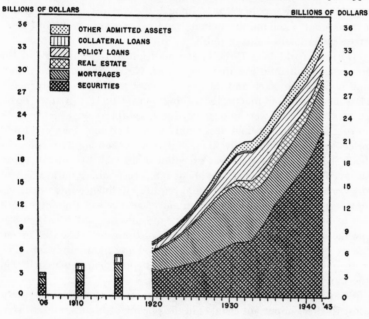

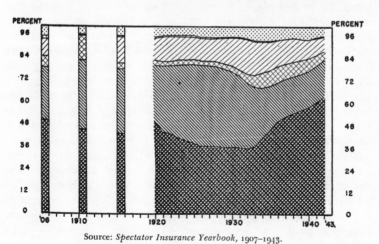

Source: *Spectator Insurance Yearbook*, 1907–1943.

to $983,000,000, and of railroad bonds from $1,000,000,000 to $1,670,000,000. The only other class of securities that increased appreciably as a *percentage* of the total of life insurance investments during these years was policy loans, although the *amount* of moneys placed in state, county and municipal bonds, in foreign governments, in United States governments, and in public utilities grew to some extent.

During World War I, the largest addition to the portfolios of life insurance companies was in governments. Nearly $800,000,000 of federal bonds were taken and the percentage of total investments in this class increased from practically nothing in 1911 to 11.5 in 1920. Loans on farm mortgages were also greatly increased (percentagewise from 12 in 1911 to 16.3 in 1920 and in amount by $645,000,000), for agricultural prices were extraordinarily high, and the demand for farm produce both at home and abroad was exceptional. In fact, by 1919 the gross income from farm products was about 150 percent above the average for the years 1910–1914, and the capital required to finance this augmentation was enormous. Loans on urban mortgages grew in amount, even if not in percentage, because of the wave of building, particularly in war production or distribution areas. None of the other classes of investments, not even industrial bonds, registered any significant gains. The great bulk of new life insurance capital was going definitely to help win the war.

With the coming of the twenties, a new set of economic conditions arose to effect important changes in the placing of life insurance investments. In the first place, Federal borrowing ceased, and, with the high market prices for government bonds, the life companies began to sell their holdings. In the second place, the collapse of farm prices in 1920 and the maintenance of relatively high prices for industrial products, led certain life insurance companies to be more reticent in making loans on farm mortgages. Although investments in these securities grew in amount from $1,127,903,000 in 1920 to $1,977,418,000 in 1927, the percentage of the total portfolios thus placed dropped from 16.3 in 1920 to 10.9 in 1930. And, thirdly, foreign governments were sold off in view of the precarious condition of public finance in most European countries and the withdrawal of the companies from overseas business. Consequently, insurance funds had to seek other channels of investment and flowed mostly into urban mortgages, railroads, public utilities, and policy loans. Urban mortgages almost quintupled in amount from 1920 to 1930, the railroad investment was increased by over a billion dollars, moneys in public utilities more than quintupled, and those in policy

CHART XX

DISTRIBUTION OF ADMITTED ASSETS OF THE MUTUAL LIFE, 1906–1943

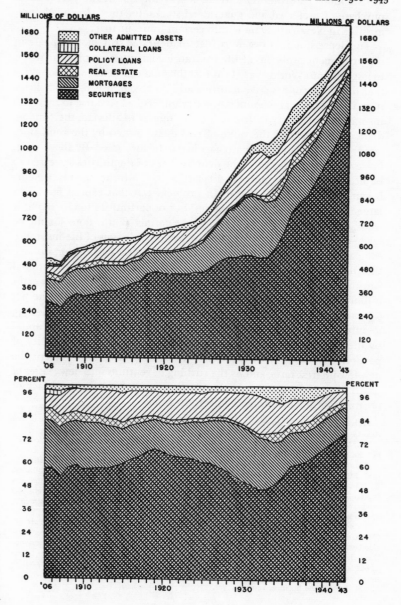

loans doubled. Furthermore, there was at the end of the period some purchase of preferred and guaranteed stocks, for they were made permissible in New York State within certain limits in 1928.

The depression that began in 1929 inaugurated still another phase in the investment problems of life insurance companies—a phase that was to last well into World War II. At first the financial shocks were so severe that little of a constructive nature could be accomplished. Policy loans increased by leaps and bounds as policyholders had recourse to their life insurance for security with which to get money to alleviate their immediate difficulties, and the value of real estate owned by the companies was greatly augmented as mortgages had to be foreclosed. By about 1934, however, this first aspect of the depressed era of the thirties appeared to be nearing its close, and new difficulties in life insurance investments began to be apparent. The main problem was that capital flowed in large amounts to the life companies, but opportunities for investing it were greatly restricted. Concerning the former point, note should be taken of the fact that from 1934 to 1940 admitted assets of life insurance companies increased annually by about one and a half billion dollars, that in 1940 their total assets came to be 10 percent of our national wealth,[8] and that the twenty-six largest companies had twenty-eight billions of dollars to invest or reinvest from 1929 to 1938.[9] Yet the net capital formation in the country amounted during the years 1919–1935 to only 5.3 billions per year.[10] The effects of the accumulation of capital by life companies were made still more serious by the inflexibility of portfolios resulting from sheer size, by an unwillingness to accept the new low-interest rates, and by the curbing of ventures into new classes of securities on account of tradition, laws, a desire for safety, and lack of organization for investments in certain fields.[11]

[8] Elbert S. Brigham, "Investing for Security of Home and Nation," *Proceedings of the Association of Life Insurance Presidents* (New York, 1941), XXXV, p. 104.

[9] *T.N.E.C.*, Part 10A, R.92, 94, and 125. From 1934 to 1938 life companies purchased 32.8 percent of all new corporate bond and notes issues.

[10] Simon Kuznetz, in his *National Income and Capital Formation, 1919–1935*, estimates that annual average gross capital formation during the period studied was $14 billions. Of this, $8.7 billions offset capital consumption and $5.3 billions represent the annual net capital formation. Forty-three percent of the $5.3 billions went into business, 39 percent was used by public agencies largely for construction, 8 percent went for foreign investments, and most of the remainder was used for residential construction.

[11] The testimony of John W. Stedman of the Prudential before the T.N.E.C., Part 28. "Mr. Gesell. That, if I may pause on it, is a very interesting point. You want a 10-year certified balance sheet, or perhaps longer, in order to get a test of the company's experience through a business cycle or over a representative number of years. That would seem to me to bar from the reservoir of capital which you have, many, many business ventures, especially new business ventures, would it not?
Mr. Stedman. New business ventures, yes.

Great as would have been the task in normal times of investing the large amounts of capital which came to the life insurance companies after 1934, it was doubly difficult because of the lack of demand for new money. In the first place a further reduction in agricultural prices and competition from Federal farm lending agencies, especially the Federal Farm Mortgage Corporation, nearly ruined the market for loans on farm mortgages. In 1928 life insurance companies held 22.3 per cent of all farm mortgages in the country and had 13.3 per cent of their portfolios in such securities, but by 1939 they owned only 12.6 percent of the total amount of farm mortgages, and in 1942 only 2.5 percent. Meanwhile certain companies had foreclosed on so much farm property [12] that they had become the largest farm landholders in the nation and received the biggest farm relief benefits paid by the Federal Government. The managerial problems thus created were enormous, for the companies had to deal mostly with tenant farmers who did not stay long on one piece of ground, who had to be instructed in farm economics, and who in general tended to "mine" the land.[13]

The Vice Chairman. Right on that point, will you develop whether or not an indisposition to purchase the securities of a new business venture is controlling?

Mr. Stedman. It would not be, in our judgment, suitable for the funds of life insurance; in other words, it is not a trustee's investment.

The Vice Chairman. Would no other consideration balance against the absence of a 10-year record?

Mr. Stedman. I think when we look back over the past 10 years I have to say no.

The Vice Chairman. I think that is one of the most interesting facts that has been brought out in this whole hearing.

Mr. Gesell. Perhaps I can develop it a little bit further, Judge. Let me ask you this: We hear a great deal these days about loans to small businessmen. Have you tried to make loans to small businessmen?

Mr. Stedman. Yes; we have.

Mr. Gesell. Can you tell us what you have done in that regard and what success you have had?

Mr. Stedman. I spoke of our having stationed in Chicago nearly a year and a half ago a man whose function it was to find, if possible, small industrial loans. We didn't want to go much below one hundred thousand, possibly fifty, and considered small industrial loans to be limited by the figure of a million dollars. Our hope was that we might make the loan as a mortgage loan, secured by a first mortgage, and write the necessary covenants on the paper. The expense of a small issue providing for a corporate trustee could not be borne. It would not be economical. The rate would be too high for the borrower. In a word we have had practically no success."

[12] As a result of foreclosures, twenty-six companies held at the end of 1938 $529,392,000 of farm real estate and had an additional $81,755,000 under contract of sale. The Department of Agriculture announced July 7, 1941, that the largest benefit payment under the crop control programs of 1939 went to the Prudential—a payment of $133,191. The second largest of $96,332 was made to the Metropolitan. Eleven other insurance companies received sums in excess of $35,000. Yields on various parts of the portfolio are unavailable. If obtained, they would have to consider losses and the amounts salvaged by foreclosure on other settlements.

[13] *T.N.E.C.*, Monograph 28, pp. 349–350.

"Other mortgages," which were largely in urban property, also caused trouble. In 1928 29.2 percent of the portfolios of life companies were in holdings of this category, but by 1942 the percentage had fallen to 16.1. Here the shrinkage in the total sums was not so great as in farm mortgages, presumably because foreclosures were proportionately not so extensive, urbanization was continuing, and competition from governmental agencies was less keen.[14] Since 1936 there has been an increase in the amounts thus placed, which indicates that even with the small number of such mortgages coming into the market, life insurance companies believe them to be good risks. In 1938 twenty-six companies realized 4.69 percent on mean gross admitted assets in urban mortgages, but they earned only 1.37 percent on foreclosed urban real estate.[15]

Investments in railroads did not provide much of an outlet for life insurance funds after 1930. From that date to 1942 the total amount thus placed had grown very little, and the percentage of the portfolios invested in railroads had decreased steadily from 1906. This was owing primarily to the lack of expansion in rails and to poor earnings. Railroads were caught in the predicament of having their rates fixed, while their costs were dependent upon market conditions, and they were faced with the stern competition of motor vehicle transportation. In 1938 only 1.23 percent, or $165,000,000, of the twenty-six leading companies admitted assets were in default, yet $141,000,000 of this amount was accounted for by railroad bonds.[16] Moreover, the percentage decline should be attributed, in part, to the fact that a large proportion of life insurance assets was placed in railroads prior to the period under consideration and that during the thirties the demand for capital was greater in other branches of the economy.

Recently the most important private channel for life insurance investments has been public utilities, because of the expansion of the telephone and electrical industries. The total amount in utilities increased from roughly $1,500,000,000 in 1929 to $5,043,000,000 in 1942—the greatest gain of any part of the portfolios in private enterprise. On a percentage basis, holdings of such investments went up from 9.1 percent of the total in 1929 to 15.8 percent in 1942. The next largest private field for life insurance funds has been in industrial bonds and stocks. Industry took nearly $1,500,000,000 of capital from life companies from

---

[14] Twenty-six companies studied by the T.N.E.C. forclosed urban mortgages amounting to $1,229,849,000 between 1932 and 1938. *T.N.E.C.*, Part 10A, p. 199.

[15] *T.N.E.C.*, Part 10A, R.227. This was on book value which was undoubtedly above market. See also Monograph 28, p. 350.

[16] *T.N.E.C.*, Monograph 28, pp. 360–361.

1929 to 1942, but opportunities here were not extensive, because of slow growth and a tendency to finance expansion out of earnings.

By far the greatest outlets for life insurance funds after the beginning of the thirties was in public bonds. States, counties, and municipalities borrowed about a billion dollars from life insurance companies between 1929 and 1942, and the Federal Government received more than eight billion dollars from the same source during the same period. The demand of the Government for "new deal" financing, especially after 1933 and then for war purposes after 1941 was by far the largest open to life insurance companies in this period, when the private investment market was relatively inactive. Yields were low, but the security was considered good, and little hesitancy was shown in going heavily into this field. What the ultimate consequences will be of large loans to the Government, which in turn lends part of the capital to private enterprise, only time can tell. This process is, however, making the Government a kind of middleman and is furthering a development toward what has been called national capitalism.

Among the other changes in life companies' portfolios has been, first, the almost complete liquidation of foreign government bonds, other than Canadian, because of their poor record. Secondly, there has been a reduction in policy loans since 1933, which may be attributed partly to the ability of banks to lend on the security of life insurance policies at lower rates of interest than the insurance companies and partly to better times. Thirdly, collateral loans have become relatively unimportant, holdings of stocks have increased since 1929, and "cash" has grown because of the lack of investment demand, because of a desire for higher liquidity, and because of the practice of retaining cash until an opportunity for making a large loan arises.[17]

The management of large portfolios, like those of the great life insurance companies, presents special problems which the small investor rarely experiences. The liquidation of large blocks of securities is only possible in a rising market, which has to be anticipated by a year or more, for otherwise the price would be forced down. This situation acts as a stabilizing factor in the bond market, it tends to lead insurance investors to operate on long term trends, and it makes the alteration of a portfolio an extremely burdensome and slow task. Size of the portfolios also renders the making of small loans extremely difficult, because few requests for small amounts come to the great institutional investors, the borrowers are widely dispersed and are hard to check, the risk is usually

17 *Ibid.*, pp. 355 ff.

greater on them than on large borrowers, and as a rule the best opportunities come first to the attention of local banks, which take their pick.

In addition to these problems, mention should be made of the fact
that, like most investment institutions, life companies shy away from
those types of investment which involve or are likely to lead to the actual
management of businesses. Life insurance is the main concern of life
insurance companies, and they do best in performing this primary function. Yet a slight evidence of a return to some entrepreneurial activity
may be discerned in low-cost housing projects and in the holding of real
estate obtained by foreclosure. Finally, life insurance companies have
been somewhat hampered by the stringent legal restrictions on their investments. The advisability of allowing, where such permission has not
already been granted, the investment of insurance funds in common
stocks has been warmly debated in recent years, but no great body of
opinion in favor of such action has been formed within insurance
circles.[18]

In general, life insurance companies prefer to place their moneys in
bonds, which can be bought directly from the issuers and for which
there is a real market. Yet the companies have been prevented since the
Armstrong Investigation from forming syndicates, and they may not
perform the services of investment brokers. Consequently, they buy
most securities from bankers or over the counter, although most industrial bonds are obtained directly, and similarly most mortgage loans are
obtained through middlemen—the mortgage brokers. According to findings of the T.N.E.C., the twenty-six largest life companies purchased
38.34 percent of their new acquisitions of corporate bonds from bankers,
32.47 percent in the open market, 27.96 percent privately from issuers,
and only 1.23 percent at public bidding. There is a possibility that a
little larger proportion of new purchases will be made as a result of
direct, public bidding. The Interstate Commerce Commission requires
public, competitive offers for railroad equipment trusts, the Securities
and Exchange Commission insists on a similar procedure for registered
public utility holding companies, and certain corporations have shown a
disposition to follow this procedure.[19] Yet life insurance companies do

18 See statement by Lewis W. Douglas, president of The Mutual Life Insurance Company
of New York, at hearings before the Joint Committee of the New York State Legislature on
Permitting Life Insurance Companies to Make Investments in Common Stocks, New York,
Oct. 21, 1941. See also, *T.N.E.C.*, Monograph 28-A.

19 The I.C.C. rule became effective June 23, 1926; the S.E.C. rule, May 7, 1941. A good
illustration of a private corporation's placing a new issue by competitive bidding is the case
of the A.T. & T. which offered a large block of debentures in 1941. This block was taken by
The Mutual Life and other large insurance companies. See New York *Times*, Sept. 27–
Oct. 2, 1941.

not want unduly to encourage this trend, for they recognize the great importance of the investment bankers in the placement of capital.

In making their investments, life insurance companies have to pay particular attention to long-range yields in order to make the rates of interest assumed in computing premiums. The yields which have been obtained by them rose during World War I, fell slightly in 1922, reached a peak in 1924, and declined steadily to 1942. World War II may reverse the recent trend, but the problem is pregnant with so many possibilities that long-range forecasting at this time is particularly precarious.

THE MUTUAL LIFE'S INVESTMENTS

The Mutual Life's experience with investments has not been dissimilar to that of the group of companies thus far treated. Although The Mutual's portfolio has differed in some respects from those of other life insurance institutions, The Mutual has encountered the same problems of interest rates and in recent years the same restricted investment market as other life insurance institutions.

Chart XX makes clear, in the first place, the great growth of The Mutual Life's assets since 1907. This increase is accounted for, in part, by the fact that the level premium reserve system leads to greater assets for some twenty or thirty years after the amount of insurance in force becomes stationary.[20] In the second place, the chart shows that the percentage and amount of real estate owned declined after 1907 (this was largely because of the sale of Company office buildings, both at home and abroad),[21] but that it rose sharply after 1933, when foreclosures became numerous. In the third place, the chart indicates that mortgage loans remained high in proportion to other parts of the portfolio until World War I, when they fell off because of large purchases of Liberty Bonds. In the fourth place, collateral loans practically disappeared because of legislation against them, but policy loans greatly increased, especially during the depression following 1929. In the fifth place, common stocks have been sold off—and, of course, this included the excellent bank stocks held in 1905—to meet the requirements of the New York State

20 John M. Laird, in his presidential address before the Actuarial Society of America, "Trends in Life Insurance and Thrift in the United States," *Transactions of the Actuarial Society of America,* XLII (1941), 258, states, "If the amount [of insurance] in force should remain at about the present figure, the reserves and assets might easily rise for twenty or thirty years but would eventually reach a fairly constant level."

21 For example, the *Minutes of the Board of Trustees* refer to the decision to sell The Mutual's buildings in Little Rock, Arkansas, May 26, 1909; in Capetown, South Africa, May 31, 1917; in London, December, 1913; in Philadelphia, January 28, 1920; in Mexico City, February 28, 1923; etc.

insurance laws. In the sixth place, cash on hand rose phenomenally during the thirties, when outlets for capital were limited, and other admitted assets—net interest and rents due and accrued, as well as net deferred and uncollected premiums—also increased.

Chart XX indicates that bonds have comprised more than one-half of The Mutual's investments since 1910 and were in 1943 75.9 percent of the total portfolio. United States governments were bought during World War I, sold off in the twenties and early thirties, and purchased again in large amounts in the later thirties, especially after the beginning of World War II. The fact that 44.4 percent of The Mutual's total admitted assets is in government securities is significant of the extent of public financing. State, county, and municipal bond holdings have also increased in recent years, but the obligations of foreign countries have been largely liquidated. The bonds of railroads were purchased in large amounts up to World War I, but have declined in total volume since 1927. Public utilities and industrials, on the other hand, have attained a more important position in recent years.

While the composition of The Mutual's portfolio has in general been similar to that of the forty-nine companies studied previously, it has differed from them in two important respects. The Mutual Life has made no loans on farm mortgages since before 1900 and as a result has obtained only urban properties under foreclosure proceedings.[22] Furthermore, in 1943, 70 percent of the Company's mortgage loans were on New York City real estate and 89 percent of the real estate acquired in the satisfaction of debt was located in New York. Finally, The Mutual Life was proportionately heavier in railroads than the average for the forty-nine companies and began to get out of them a little later. It also has had a larger proportion of its assets in United States bonds than the average and during the thirties had a greater percentage of its portfolio in policy loans, although that percentage is now below the general mean.

Like other life insurance companies, The Mutual Life has been confronted in recent years with a reduction in earnings on its invested assets. In Table 44, below, a general increase in the gross earnings on mean admitted assets from 1907 to 1923 will be noted, while from the latter date to 1943 an almost steady decline will be perceived. The table also shows the establishment of large contingency reserves, beginning in 1940 to cover possible losses and in the last few years an increase in "invest-

22 One mortgage loan of $6,000 might be classified as a farm mortgage or a mortgage on residential property. T.N.E.C., Part 10A, p. 195.

ment expenses"—an item which includes increased real estate expenses and overhead and is reflected in the difference between the gross and the net interest rates on mean admitted assets.[23]

TABLE 44

THE MUTUAL LIFE, 1907–1943

YEAR	INTEREST RATE (IN PERCENTAGE) ON MEAN ADMITTED ASSETS Gross	Net	SURPLUS RESERVES	RESERVES FOR INVESTMENT REVALUATION AND CONTINGENCIES a
1907	4.78	4.53	...	0
1908	4.81	4.57	$16,169,863.67	0
1909	4.67	4.45	17,519,350.35	0
1910	4.69	4.48	10,340,065.19	0
1911	4.67	4.48	11,310,620.38	0
1912	4.69	4.49	12,546,662.02	0
1913	4.71	4.51	10,967,506.22	0
1914	4.69	4.50	12,647,615.19	0
1915	4.76	4.57	14,625,579.16	0
1916	4.82	4.62	16,262,739.77	0
1917	4.86	4.65	17,609,997.08	0
1918	4.75	4.44	15,731,075.52	0
1919	4.62	4.32	19,551,214.93	0
1920	4.77	4.48	23,058,543.13	0
1921	5.10	4.80	28,051,586.81	0
1922	5.10	4.73	37,332,151.55	0
1923	5.19	4.77	42,714,342.37	0
1924	5.10	4.69	50,545,644.48	0
1925	5.02	4.57	53,280,203.31	0
1926	4.99	4.57	56,767,592.82	0
1927	4.88	4.53	59,843,166.81	0
1928	4.94	4.65	64,106,973.68	0
1929	4.97	4.66	62,849,592.76	0
1930	4.97	4.67	61,368,203.89	0
1931	5.03	4.72	63,030,589.89	0
1932	4.92	4.56	58,773,456.97	$9,275,166.43
1933	4.68	4.25	59,144,436.12	7,815,341.51
1934	4.32	3.85	59,605,704.55	519,535.18
1935	4.08	3.60	55,769,831.46	442,152.64
1936	3.94	3.50	61,520,866.43	0
1937	3.79	3.36	44,270,996.86	0
1938	3.73	3.27	49,548,010.59	0
1939	3.60	3.13	51,423,482.10	0
1940	3.52	3.04	27,717,636.40	29,950,000.00
1941	3.52	3.04	31,434,022.45	45,064,075.18
1942	3.30	2.79	35,538,349.82	46,465,599.72
1943	3.14	2.71	43,177,259.17	54,146,983.83

a Does not include reserves for revaluation of life insurance and annuities.
Source: Annual Statement—The Mutual Life.

[23] The method of computing investment expenses is extremely complicated. It includes not only what are clearly investment expenses—taxes on real estate, brokers' fees, cost of running the financial, real estate and policy loan departments, etc.—but also a substantial item for the general overhead of the Company. The system employed was altered in 1926, and the one used in 1941 allocated .137 percent of mean ledger assets to investment expenses. The limit by law would have been .25 percent.

THE MUTUAL LIFE'S INVESTMENT POLICIES AND PROBLEMS

The character of The Mutual Life's portfolio has been determined by certain basic principles. From 1906 to 1927 concentration in mortgage loans in New York City real estate and on railroad securities resulted largely from opinions held by President Peabody. He had great faith in both these types of securities, and, in fact, during the years of his administration experience with them was satisfactory. To have predicted the difficulties which these investments were ultimately to encounter would have required almost clairvoyant powers. Certainly, the low agricultural prices in the twenties made urban mortgages appear to be better investments than farm mortgages, and at that time no one could foresee the Government's farm relief program of the thirties, which was to rescue, in part, investments on farm lands. Moreover, the reduced earning power of the railroads because of governmental rate fixing and of competition with the automobile and truck did not become apparent until the late twenties. And, finally, the great depression of the thirties was not forecast by many persons, not even by the most sagacious students of the business cycle. Consequently, hindsight should not be employed for too disparaging judgments of Mr. Peabody's investment policies—policies, which it must be remembered, were not basically different from those of other leading life insurance executives.

The coming of the business depression in 1929, which coincided closely with the beginning of Mr. Houston's presidency and with the appointment of Dwight S. Beebe as financial manager (1928), presented The Mutual Life with new investment problems. The fall in the market values of corporate securities meant that the bond portfolio had to be reëxamined and reworked. Consequently, more attention began to be devoted to investment analysis and research in an effort to discern long-term trends upon which to act, and new methods of handling securities in the home office were introduced in order to facilitate and expedite investment operations. Rails began to be sold, as we have seen, and in their place were purchased especially governments, public utilities, and industrials. This process was greatly accelerated after Mr. Douglas became president, the total of security transactions—purchases, sales, and redemptions—in 1941 having exceeded the vast sum of $700,000,000,[24] or nearly one-half the total admitted assets of the Company. In this change of the portfolio, The Mutual Life has been a large purchaser of government bonds partly because of their safety, partly because of their

[24] See *Annual Report* (1941), p. 27.

availability, and since December 7, 1941, because of their role in financing the war.

The effect of the depression upon The Mutual's mortgage loan and real estate holdings was no less profound than on its bonds. Business conditions necessitated an investigation of all such loans and property and the adopting of measures to protect investments in every way possible. Here, again, more emphasis was placed upon research, especially after the appointment of Henry Verdelin as vice president and manager of the Real Estate Department in 1940, in order to determine neighborhood trends, obsolescence, and the earning power of property. Much of the foreclosed real estate, in an amount aggregating $15,835,000,[25] having been disposed of in 1941, the other pieces of property were put, so far as possible, upon an earning basis. This latter step required the investment of some additional funds, for the reconstruction of a building, like the Airlines Building, necessitated the employment of new moneys. Furthermore, a definite policy of securing geographical diversification of mortgage loans was adopted, and much was achieved to this end. As far back as 1928 new mortgage loaning agencies had been created in twenty-eight widely dispersed cities to make loans on "business properties in approved sections of selected towns and cities," [26] but little was accomplished along these lines until 1940. With the purchase of guaranteed Federal Housing Administration mortgages, which comprised 20 percent of the Company's mortgage portfolio at the end of 1943, The Mutual Life succeeded in reducing the percentage of mortgage loans on New York City real estate from 89 of its total mortgages in 1939 to 69.9 at the end of 1943.

The overhauling of The Mutual Life's investments has resulted in a great strengthening of the portfolio. Diversification of corporate securities has been achieved by a reduction in the amount of railroad bonds, an increase in public utilities and industrials, and by a concentration in governments. The bulk of the real estate owned is now business property. Geographical distribution of investments has been accomplished in large measure, the aim being to establish a wider territorial diversification. Finally, an added impetus has been given to the search for new investment outlets.

Another matter of fundamental concern here is the rate of interest earned. As has been stated repeatedly, the rate assumed in computing life insurance premiums is essentially a guaranteed yield and should be met by returns on investments. This point has not been impressed sufficiently

[25] See *Annual Report* (1941), p. 27.   [26] *T.N.E.C.*, Part 28, p. 15053.

upon the public, for savings on mortality have increased as yields have fallen—a fact which has tended to keep dividends proportionately greater than they possibly could have been from investment yields alone. Moreover, an interest rate is directly guaranteed on moneys which are paid to the Company for annuities or which are left with the Company under optional modes of settlement. In both cases, the rate is stipulated in the policy contract, which means that the guaranteed rate may be much higher than prevailing rates. Nor, so far as optional modes of settlement are concerned, will it presumably be less than prevailing rates, for the Company pays on them excess interest earned.[27] The burden thus placed upon the Company can be imagined from the fact that reserves on annuities, including those made under modes of settlement, amounted to $189,981,846.00 at the end of 1943 and were on an interest basis ranging from three to two percent, while moneys on deposit with the Company under optional modes of settlement totaled $142,441,949.65 in 1943, most of which was at 3 percent.[28]

This problem leads at once to a consideration of the yields on various parts of the portfolio. The highest gross rates obtained are on policy loans—loans which are not, however, encouraged because of their tendency to increase surrenders. The second highest rate has been on preferred stocks, but they form only a small part of the portfolio and are unobtainable in large amounts. Yields on mortgage loans have been in third position, while those on bonds come fourth, and those on real estate fifth. How to secure higher yields is a major problem of life insurance companies.[29]

[27] This has been the case since 1910.

[28] The rate guaranteed on policies issued from 1907 to 1939 was 3 percent; from 1939 to 1942 it was 2½ percent; Jan. 1, 1943, it was changed to 2 percent.

[29] T.N.E.C., Monograph 28, pp. 373 ff. "The consideration of common stocks as possible investment outlets does not result from any feeling that such investments will bring greater liquidity or give greater opportunities for capital gains, since these are not questions of primary importance in the handling of insurance-company portfolios. Rather, it results from the fundamental question, namely whether or not the present investment practices of the insurance companies are not sterilizing the capital markets and are not certain to bring about an eventual deterioration of the very securities upon which the companies have relied in the past. There is also merit in the proposition that if American enterprises were less burdened with corporate debt they would be more flexible and in a better position to adjust their operations in changing economic and business circumstances." British life insurance companies are allowed to invest in common stocks. See F. W. Paish and G. L. Swartz, *Insurance Funds and Their Investment* (London, 1934).

XVII. Management of The Mutual Life

IMPORTANT AS IS every branch of the life insurance business, the ultimate success of a company depends largely upon management. On the shoulders of the chief executive officer and his immediate associates rests the enormous responsibility for the felicitous functioning and proper coördinating of the specialized departments. As in all business enterprises, the executive must be able to select competent assistants to whom he can with confidence delegate authority and must have the courage to change his associates if they do not measure up to acknowledged standards. Management must formulate the basic policies to be pursued and must permeate the entire organization with an enthusiasm for the work at hand—in the case before us, for the insuring of lives as inexpensively and as safely as possible.[1]

Some idea of the arduous task of managing a life insurance company can be imagined by reflecting upon the technical aspects of the business which have been described in preceding chapters. Yet for a fuller comprehension of the role of management consideration must be given to the sheer magnitude of an enterprise like The Mutual Life. Measured by the amount of its assets, which were more than one and one-half billions of dollars at the end of 1943, this Company is one of the largest business concerns in the United States. Indeed, in 1937 there were only 749 corporations, including 331 banking and insurance institutions, in the country with assets in excess of $50,000,000. And very few business enterprises were owned by so large a number of persons as was this insurance company with its nine hundred and seventy-five thousand policy-holders.

The presidency of a large insurance company is thus one of the most important posts in America and calls for men of exceptional ability. Such men early came to the fore, and the larger companies have con-

[1] On this subject consult W. Breiby, "Supervision and Management of Life Insurance Companies," *The Spectator*, LXXXI (Oct. 5, 1933), 10; O. DeWerthern, *Behind the Scenes of Life Insurance* (New York, 1938); H. A. Hopf, *Whither Management* (St. Louis, 1931) and "Measuring Management in Life Insurance," *Proceedings of the Eleventh Annual Conference of the Life Office Management Association* (Hartford, 1934); and F. L. Rowland, "Home Office Organization," *Proceedings of the 1928 Annual Conference of the Life Office Management Association*.

tinued to find them. Especially in mutual companies, they have devoted their services to managing the funds of others. They were among the first great professional managers, as distinct from entrepreneurs who conducted businesses in which their own capital was invested. By their accomplishments they furthered a trend toward professional management which has come to be called the "managerial revolution." As we have seen, some of the early life insurance executives, in addition to performing the remarkable feats of creating a new and important industry, took a domineering and even a possessive attitude toward their companies and, in keeping with the mores of the time, used them for personal gain. Since 1906, however, all this has been changed. Although the managements of life insurance companies are still criticized for their dominant position,[2] the managers are confronted with a task to be accomplished and a body of policyholders who have neither the technical knowledge nor the time to help formulate policies. Under such circumstances presidents of life insurance companies have to assume the duties of leadership and to perform them as best they can. This situation requires the choice of men of the highest ethical standards and business morals. Fortunately, the life insurance industry has been able to select persons of this stamp with uncanny success. Since 1905 the business has established a reputation for probity that probably no other great industry or political jurisdiction of comparable size can equal.

THE MUTUAL'S PRESIDENTS SINCE 1905

The management of The Mutual Life has been exemplary in this regard. The Company's presidents, Charles A. Peabody (1905–1927), David F. Houston (1927–1939), and Lewis W. Douglas (1940–   ) have all been men of sterling character and unquestioned business ethics. Each was chosen after he had made a mark in business and public life and had clearly demonstrated his abilities and qualities. Neither of the first two was a young man at the time of his election, Peabody having been fifty-six years of age and Houston sixty-one. Curiously enough, none of the three had grown up in the life insurance business. On the other hand, each was confronted during his administration with major crises in our national life—Peabody with World War I, Houston with the great depression of the 1930's, and Lewis W. Douglas with World War II.

Charles Augustus Peabody, Jr. (1849–1931), came from a New England family. His father had early migrated to New York to practice law and to cut out for himself an important career in state and national

2 *T.N.E.C., Final Report of the Executive Secretary* (Washington, D.C., 1941), pp. 252 ff.

politics. Young Peabody was educated at Columbia College, Class of 1869, and at the Columbia School of Law, Class of 1871, and shortly after having been graduated entered under his father's tutelage upon the exercise of his profession. Gradually he became more and more interested in the handling of estates, and as a result of this specialty he acquired a wide knowledge of New York City real estate. Ultimately he was elected to the boards of several banks and other corporations, being especially influential in the Astor National Bank.

As president of The Mutual Life, Peabody was confronted with problems of the first magnitude. He took office upon the conclusion of the Armstrong Investigation and had to steer the Company through a period when life insurance was suffering from public opprobrium. His policy in meeting this situation was to conduct affairs with such scrupulous honesty and with such a reduction in expenses that public confidence was soon restored. Perhaps the events of 1905 shattered any faith which he may have had in the wisdom of greatly enlarging The Mutual Life, for he stood firm during many years, as we have seen, in a desire to keep new business within definite limits. This position brought him into conflict with The Mutual's agency managers and agents, but they had little success in trying to shake him from his convictions.[3] Furthermore, he enlarged the proportion of the Company's portfolio in mortgage loans on New York real estate and in railroad securities, for he was well acquainted with both these types of investment, and each was enjoying prosperity. Finally, he was confronted with the problem of new business during the boom in life insurance which began in the later years of World War I and continued to 1929. With people demanding more insurance protection, he "allowed" the Company to grow, but he did not take many of the obvious measures, such as writing group or industrial insurance, whereby it might have achieved great size.

David Franklin Houston (1866–1940) was born in South Carolina, was graduated from South Carolina College (1887), and received the degree of Master of Arts in political science from Harvard University in 1892. He early devoted himself to education and therein achieved success, having been in turn tutor in ancient languages at South Carolina College, superintendent of schools in Spartanburg, South Carolina, pro-

---

[3] Manager's Association, composed of the agency managers of The Mutual Life, was formed to carry pleas to President Peabody for a further consideration of Company growth. In 1918 the first president of the organization, Charles Posey of the Baltimore agency, and Julian S. Myrick, of one of the New York agencies, presented their views to Peabody. He was unimpressed by their contentions, and he remained unmoved by a similar representation made to him by some of the agents.

fessor of political science and dean of the faculty at the University of Texas, president of the Agricultural and Mechanics College of Texas, president of the University of Texas, and chancellor of Washington University, St. Louis. In 1913 Houston was appointed by President Woodrow Wilson to serve in his cabinet as Secretary of Agriculture, and in 1920, as Secretary of the Treasury. President Wilson also named him chairman of the Federal Reserve Board and the Farm Loan Board, both of which he was instrumental in creating, and to the Council of National Defense. After the close of the Wilson Administration, Houston became vice president and director of the American Telephone and Telegraph Company, president of the Bell Telephone Securities Company, a member of the board of the Prudential Life Insurance Company, a director of several corporations and banks, and a trustee of Columbia University.

As a climax to this distinguished career Houston served as president of The Mutual Life from 1927 to 1940. Hardly had he taken office and become acquainted with The Mutual Life's operations, when the "crash of 1929" occurred. To have envisaged the long duration of the depression and to have estimated correctly its effects upon life insurance would have required a person with superhuman knowledge. The Mutual Life was faced, as were all life insurance companies, with a falling interest rate, foreclosures on mortgages, declining security values, and a reduction in new business. That President Houston was able to bring The Mutual Life through these trying times as well as he did should redound to his credit. His policy was one of making changes gradually to meet exigencies as they arose, for he expected that the end of the depression would soon be reached.

Lewis Williams Douglas (1894–   ) assumed The Mutual Life's presidency on January 1, 1940, when Houston retired from that position to accept the newly created office of chairman of the Board. Mr. Douglas is descended from a family which has had a remarkable record of public service.[4] He was born in Arizona in 1894, was educated at Amherst College, and studied mining, metallurgy, and geology at the Massachusetts Institute of Technology. During World War I he served as a first lieutenant of artillery and received a decoration from the Belgian government. After the conclusion of the great conflict, he taught history and economics for a year at Amherst and then returned to his native state of Arizona to engage in mining. In 1926 he was elected to Congress, and he

---

[4] See Hugh H. Langton, *James Douglas; a Memoir* (Toronto, 1940), and *The Eastern Underwriter*, 42nd year, No. 28, July 11, 1941.

retained his seat until 1933, when he resigned to become the Director of the Bureau of the Budget. Owing to difference with the Administration over the "spending program," Mr. Douglas resigned from his position in 1934 and was made, in December, a vice president and director of the American Cyanamid Company. He accepted in 1937 an invitation to become principal and vice chancellor of McGill University in Montreal, whence he came to The Mutual Life. He is or has been a trustee of Amherst College, the Rockefeller Foundation, the General Education Board, the National Life Insurance Company' of Vermont, and a director of several important corporations and institutions.

Mr. Douglas's administration of The Mutual Life has been filled with vigorous action and important decisions. He has attempted to heal the scars caused by the depression and to diversify more widely the Company's investment portfolio. He has put new vigor into the agency force and has reorganized the process of selecting risks. He has extended the list of policies offered to the public, has raised the efficiency of the home office force, has brought much new blood into the management of the Company, and has in general strengthened the position of The Mutual Life. When America was forced into World War II, Mr. Douglas was called to serve the War Shipping Administration. In carrying on the affairs of the Company Mr. Douglas has had the capable assistance of Executive Vice President Alexander E. Patterson, who joined the organization in 1941.[5]

THE BOARD OF TRUSTEES

To mention all the officers and all the other employees who have contributed to the direction and to the day-to-day operations of The Mutual Life within the last thirty-five years would entail the listing of many hundreds of persons. Their services are not, however, to be minimized because of the anonymity which space dictates they must receive in these pages. To them belongs much of the credit for the success of The Mutual Life and to them history is grateful. Special notice should, however, be given in this place to the members of the Board of Trustees who have devoted so much of their time, thought, and energy to the

[5] Mr. Patterson entered the life insurance business with The Equitable in 1908. In 1922 he organized a new Equitable agency in New York, and in 1925 he took charge of that company's largest Chicago agency. In 1928 he joined the Penn Mutual and became general agent for that institution in Chicago and the State of Illinois. In 1937 he was elected vice president of the Penn Mutual. He was president of the National Association of Life Underwriters in 1936 and in 1939 was elected chairman of the Association of Life Agency Officers. See *Spectator*, January 15, 1942.

Company. They are the men who in the final analysis approve the general lines of policy which are to be pursued, who pass on all insurance contracts, methods of selection, agency matters, and disputable claims, and who ratify every loan which the Company makes. They constitute the controlling body of The Mutual Life and as such deserve particular recognition.

On the morrow of the Armstrong Investigation, the Board of Trustees was as profoundly altered as other phases of the business, for resignations were numerous and President Peabody was anxious to secure sympathetic supporters for the task of reorganization with which he was faced. In fact, during the three years following the Investigation thirty-two new trustees were elected to the Board. Yet continuity with the past was not entirely lost, for George F. Baker, William P. Dixon, Julien T. Davies, Augustus D. Juilliard, and Cornelius Vanderbilt retained their trusteeships for several years and played important parts in the conduct of the Company. Among the new trustees of these years were Hugo Baring, the London banker, Louis Stern, the merchant, Cyrus H. K. Curtis, of the Curtis Publishing Company, Frederick H. Eaton, president of the American Car and Foundry Company, Herman Ridder, publisher of the *Journal of Commerce,* James M. Beck, lawyer, of Philadelphia, and counsel for The Mutual Life during the Armstrong Investigation, and Henry W. Taft, lawyer, and Emory W. Clark, banker, who are still members of the Board. In subsequent years, many of the distinguished leaders of American political, professional, and business life were chosen as trustees of the Company. Of those who are no longer members of the Board, mention should be made of Woodrow Wilson, Rodman Wanamaker, the merchant, James H. Perkins, chairman of the National City Bank, Frederick A. Juilliard, merchant, Harry B. Thayer, president of the American Telephone and Telegraph Co., Myron C. Taylor, president of the United States Steel Corporation, Newton D. Baker, Secretary of War during the Wilson Administration, and Nathan L. Miller, governor of New York.

President Peabody seemed to have a penchant for lawyers and nearly one-fourth of the new trustees during his regime came from the legal profession. Of more recent date, trustees of the Company have been chosen from a wide variety of callings, as can be seen by referring to the appendix, and with a view of securing more national geographical representation. During the entire history of The Mutual Life the number of trustees classified according to the kinds of activity in which they have been engaged is as follows:

Army and		Express indus-		Medicine	2	Retailing and	
Navy	5	try	1	Mining	3	wholesaling	50
Banking	55	Hotels	2	Petroleum	3	Shipping	5
Brokerage	4	Importers	6	Public offi-		Utilities	2
Communica-		Insurance	24	cials	14	Unknown	15
tions	2	Law	44	Publishing	3		
Construction	1	Manufactur-		Railroads	10		
Education	8	ing	22	Real estate	5		

MEMBERS OF THE BOARD OF TRUSTEES, 1943

Charles E. Adams
Chairman, Air Reduction Company, Inc., New York

Joseph S. Auerbach
Partner, Davies, Auerbach, Cornell & Hardy, New York

Lewis H. Brown
President, Johns-Manville Corp., New York

Wm. Marshall Bullitt
Senior partner, Bullitt and Middleton, Louisville, Ky.

W. Randolph Burgess
Vice chairman of the Board; The National City Bank of New York, New York

W. Gibson Carey, Jr.
President, The Yale & Towne Manufacturing Co., New York

Joseph H. Choate, Jr.
Partner, Choate, Byrd, Leon, & Garretson, New York

Emory W. Clark
Banker, retired; Detroit, Michigan

S. Sloan Colt
President, Bankers Trust Company, New York

Frederick C. Crawford
President, Thompson Products Inc., Cleveland, Ohio

John W. Davis
Partner, Davis, Polk, Wardwell, Sunderland & Kiendl, New York

F. Trubee Davison
President, The American Museum of Natural History, New York

Louis W. Dawson
Vice president and general counsel, The Mutual Life Insurance Company of New York, New York

Lewis W. Douglas
President, The Mutual Life Insurance Company of New York, New York

Charles E. Dunlap
President, The Berwind-White Coal Mining Co., New York

Leon Fraser
President, The First National Bank of the City of New York, New York

Henry S. Kingman
President, The Farmers and Mechanics Savings Bank, Minneapolis, Minn.

Roswell F. Magill
Partner, Cravath, Swaine, and Moore, New York; Professor of Law, Columbia University, New York

William D. Mitchell
Partner, Mitchell, Capron, Marsh, Angula and Cooney, New York

Roland S. Morris
Partner, Duane, Morris and Heckscher, Philadelphia, Pa.

William C. Mullendore
Executive vice president, Southern California Edison Company, Ltd., Los Angeles, Calif.

William I. Myers
Dean, N.Y. State College of Agriculture, Cornell University, Ithaca, N.Y.

John K. Ottley
Chairman of the Board, First National Bank of Atlanta, Atlanta, Ga.

Alexander E. Patterson
Executive vice president of The Mutual Life Insurance Company of New York, New York

Louis H. Pink
President, Associated Hospital Service, New York

William C. Potter
Chairman of the Executive Committee, Guaranty Trust Company of New York, New York

Elihu Root, Jr.
Partner, Root, Clark, Buckner and Ballantine, New York

Franz Schneider
Vice president and chairman of the Executive Committee, Newmont Mining Corporation, New York

Gilbert H. Scribner
Senior partner, Winston & Co., Chicago, Ill.

Henry L. Shattuck
Trustee, Boston, Mass.

John Sloane
Chairman of Board, W. & J. Sloane, New York

Robert C. Stanley
Chairman and president, The International Nickel Company of Canada, Limited, New York

Robert T. Stevens
Formerly president, J. P. Stevens & Co., Inc., New York

Henry W. Taft
Partner, Cadwalader, Wickersham & Taft, New York

John C. Traphagen
President, Bank of New York, New York

Leo Wolman
Professor of economics, Columbia University, New York

Some criticism of the election of men who hold directorships in other corporations to the boards of life insurance companies has been made on the ground that interlocking relationships are thereby created.[6] This view has, however, been contested with the argument, which seems valid, that life insurance companies need the advice and direction which leaders in the business world can give and that to obtain such service prominent persons who are directors in other businesses have to be selected. Be that as it may, The Mutual's Board consists of men who receive little remuneration for the work which they do[7] and take seriously the responsibilities placed upon them. The present Board has, indeed, demonstrated a keen appreciation of the economic and social obligations of the Company and has endeavored to meet them unselfishly.

Since 1906 the law has required that the incumbent Board of Trustees prepare an "administration ticket" for each election, and from 1907 to the present there has only once been an opposition candidate.[8] In this one contested election of 1911 a single person decided to run and secured the necessary one hundred policyholders to support his candidacy. The expense involved in such a contest is large. Long lists of policyholders

[6] *T.N.E.C., Final Report of the Executive Secretary* (Washington, D.C., 1941), p. 254.

[7] The fees paid to trustees in 1941 amounted to $41,440. Article XXV of the Company's by-laws states: "No Trustee or officer of this Company shall receive any money or valuable thing for negotiating, procuring, recommending or aiding in any purchase by, or sale to this Company of any property or any loan from this Company, nor be pecuniarily interested, either as principal, co-principal, agent or beneficiary, in any such purchase, sale or loan." See also footnote 11, below.

[8] In 1911 the single opposition candidate polled 2,110 votes to an average of about 13,500 for the administration ticket. *Minutes of the Board of Trustees*, Nov. 2, 1911.

have to be made available, campaigns have to be conducted, and much time has to be spent in counting votes. In view of these facts and to save companies needless expense, the New York State law regarding elections in mutual life insurance companies was slightly altered in 1915.[9] Since that date twenty-five policyholders must petition the Superintendent of Insurance for permission to make a nomination, and the opposition ticket must be certified by one-tenth of one percent of the qualified voters, which in The Mutual Life would require about 975 signatures. This provision, which aims to prevent "nuisance" tickets or the nomination of persons who are not qualified for the duties of trusteeship, corrected an obvious abuse,[10] yet it permits action by policyholders in a company the size of The Mutual Life. The fact remains, however, that policyholders do not take much interest in the annual elections, the administration ticket usually being approved by a handful of voters.[11] In order to correct this situation—to make policyholders more fully aware that they are *members* of a great cooperative enterprise—a new system of bringing policyholders into closer contact with the management is being sought.

ADMINISTRATIVE ORGANIZATION AND EXPENSES OF THE HOME OFFICE

Since 1906 important changes have taken place in the administrative organization of The Mutual Life. As we have seen in earlier chapters, the work of the Company was divided into departments, each with an executive head who distributed responsibilities to his subordinates. This so-called "military" or "line" plan of organization was necessary to accomplish the highly specialized tasks of the insurance business, but it tended to lead to over-departmentalization—to one department's not

9 *New York Laws of 1915*, chapter 617. See the *Report of the Superintendent of Insurance* to the State Legislature for 1915 on this subject.

10 In 1913 a person attempted to run for the Board presumably to secure a position for himself. State authorities prevented this action on the ground that it would create an unnecessary expense for the Company.

11 *T.N.E.C.*, Monograph 28 (Washington, D.C., 1941), p. 16. It might be added that from 1906 to 1937 one-half the members of the Board stood for election every year. By action of the Board November 24, 1937, and pursuant to section 52 of the Insurance Law of the State of New York, the Board was divided into three classes, each class of twelve standing for election every three years. In 1939 an election for the full Board was held and the classes were determined by length of service. The Insurance Law of the State of New York, section 48, paragraph 5, which went into effect January 1, 1940, requires that a majority of the trustees of a mutual life insurance company be residents of this state or of adjoining states. According to section 56, paragraph 2, all but four trustees must be policyholders in a mutual company. At least two of the principal officers of the Company, but always less than a quorum of the board, must be members of the board of directors or trustees. Section 62 of the New York law enacted March 4, 1940, provides that a trustee vacate his seat if he fails to attend the regular meetings of the board or to perform his duties as trustee for six successive meetings, unless excused by the board.

coöperating fully with other departments. To correct this fault there has been a trend in recent years toward a type of organization known as "functional" or "staff control," whereby managerial policy flows from specialists in the form of instructions or advice to every department or phase of the business anywhere within their province of interest. This system combined with the former "line" plan is the one employed by The Mutual Life. It is one that maintains the efficiency of the earlier scheme with the integration of the latter.

On the morrow of the Armstrong Investigation little attention was given to administrative organization, for all eyes were focused upon changes to prevent a repetition of those things which had just been subjected to criticism. Consequently, most of the alterations in the Company's administrative structure were at that time designed to create stricter control of those phases of the business involving expenditure of funds. The new by-laws and code of organization adopted in 1906 [12] made provision that neither trustees nor officers might receive any valuable thing for their services in addition to prescribed fees or salaries or take action in any matter in which they had a personal financial interest, that the bureau of supplies be placed in charge of the secretary, who was required to get competitive bids for all large purchases, that all agency contracts be limited to certain rules laid down by the Agency Committee of the Board, that all proposals for expenditures in excess of a fixed amount be approved by the Board of Trustees, the president, or other designated officer before the expenditure was made,[13] and that, as required by law, all salaries in excess of $5,000 be approved by the Board of Trustees. The only important step toward functional organization was the creation within the Board of a General Committee, composed of one trustee from each standing committee, the president, and the vice president, to recommend salary changes to the Board and to set limits for investments by the finance and real estate departments.

For many years no major change in the structure of The Mutual Life was made. When Mr. Douglas became president in 1940, however, several alterations were effected. Mr. Houston was elected chairman of the Board, an office which existed for only about a year, the duties of the then-existing registrar pertaining to the issuance of policies were transferred from the Secretary's Department to a Bureau of Applications and Issue under the Manager of Selection, and the Purchasing Agent's Department was placed in the Purchasing Division of the Secretary's De-

---

[12] *Minutes of the Board of Trustees*, May 7, 1906.
[13] This arrangement made possible the abolition of the Committee on Expenditures.

partment. These changes, which had been envisaged by Mr. Houston, were followed by other measures which aimed to cut through strictly departmental lines. A vice president, subsequently made executive vice president, was appointed in 1941 to take charge of over-all insurance operations, as distinguished from investment operations, and a second vice president was chosen to assist in knitting together the work of various insurance branches of the Company. A research assistant to the president was named to study economic questions for the purpose of keeping all departments concerned with such matters informed of trends. Another research assistant to the president was appointed to deal more specifically with the Company's budget in an attempt to control expenses.[14] A third assistant to the president was given charge of relations with policyholders and the public. A supervisor of planning was also added to the Executive Department, and so too was the personnel director—an official who had formerly been a member of the Secretary's Department. Within the Board of Trustees, a Nominating Committee was established,[15] the General Committee was abolished, and a new Executive Committee was created to "exercise general supervision and control of the affairs of the Company," to "coördinate the work of the other Committees," and to "give consideration to questions of general policy." Lastly, meetings of officers of various departments began to be held for the purpose of threshing out problems which overlapped departmental lines.

The very definite attempt which has thus been made to combine the "line" with the "functional" plan of organization has stimulated a new interest within the Company in problems of home office management. The Company has, however, always been concerned with these matters. It welcomed the establishment of the Life Office Management Association in 1924—an organization composed of officers of about one hundred and fifty companies, devoted to the study of managerial problems. It has supported the Life Office Management Association Institute, which provides an educational program for and gives examinations to those interested in management; it has lent its prestige through the personal activity of its officers to courses given on life insurance management by the Insurance Society of America; [16] and it has made available to its own

---

[14] The Mutual Life's expenses had become based largely on the expenses of previous years and did not necessarily have a direct relationship to the business being transacted.

[15] From 1908 to 1940 no Nominating Committee of the Board seems to have been in existence. *Minutes of the Board of Trustees,* January 16, 1940.

[16] This society was founded in 1902. It has an excellent library on general insurance—a library which has been of great value in preparing this book.

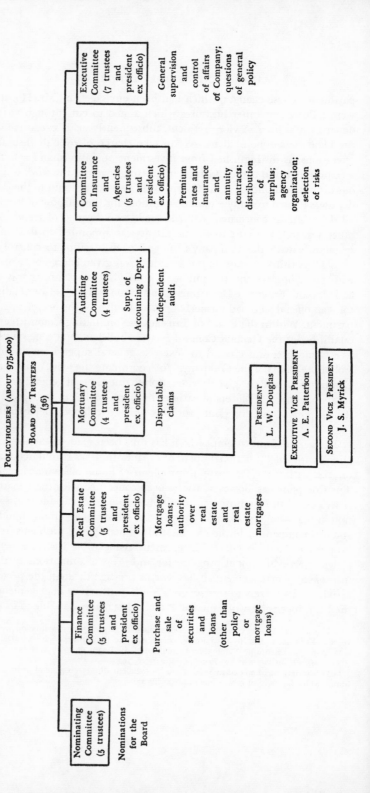

CHART XXI

THE MUTUAL LIFE INSURANCE COMPANY OF NEW YORK ORGANIZATION CHART, 1943

POLICYHOLDERS (ABOUT 975,000)

BOARD OF TRUSTEES (36)

Nominating Committee (5 trustees)

Nominations for the Board

Finance Committee (5 trustees and president ex officio)

Purchase and sale of securities and loans (other than policy or mortgage loans)

Real Estate Committee (5 trustees and president ex officio)

Mortgage loans; authority over real estate and real estate mortgages

Mortuary Committee (4 trustees and president ex officio)

Disputable claims

Auditing Committee (4 trustees)
Supt. of Accounting Dept.

Independent audit

Committee on Insurance and Agencies (5 trustees and president ex officio)

Premium rates and insurance and annuity contracts; distribution of surplus; agency organization; selection of risks

Executive Committee (7 trustees and president ex officio)

General supervision and control of affairs of Company; questions of general policy

PRESIDENT L. W. Douglas

EXECUTIVE VICE PRESIDENT A. E. Patterson

SECOND VICE PRESIDENT J. S. Myrick

EXECUTIVE DEPARTMENT

Research assistant to president, E. C. Wightman, insurance research, budget
Research assistant to president, D. B. Woodward, economic and statistical research
Assistant to president, C. B. Reeves, advertising, publicity, policyholder relations
Planning supervisor, H. Knauss, general planning, planning supervision
Personnel director, H. R. Bixler, personnel supervision
Assistant secretary, R. R. Stroud, secretary to committees and Board of Trustees

Vice president and manager of selection, L. Cruess	Vice president and manager of agencies, J. R. Hull	Vice president and financial manager, D. S. Beebe	Treasurer, S. F. Silloway	Vice president and actuary, J. B. Maclean	Secretary, W. T. Johns	Comptroller, F. W. Miller	Vice president and general counsel, L. W. Dawson	Vice president and manager of real estate, H. Verdelin
Inspection of risks; Medical Dept.; supervisor of risks; Bureau of Investigation; Bureau of Applications and Policy Issue; Statistical Bureau; investigation of claims; approval of claims	Agency organization; acquisition of new business; collection of premiums, etc., at agencies	Purchase and sale of securities; supervision of security investments	Custody of cash and securities, bank accounts and payments, policy loans	Premium rates; dividends; surrender values; reserves; collection of information tables, etc.; insurance in force; financial statements; policy forms; certification of contract payments	Correspondence and mail; files and archives; purchasing; policy registry; restaurant, telephones	Accounting; financial statements; audits; premium records; certification of all payments; superintendent of financial records of treasurer and of Manager of Real Estate Dept.; administrator of foreign business; surety bonds	Conducts all legal business; approves forms and contracts; Bureau of Disability Claims; approves disability and double indemnity claims	Loans on real estate; supervises and operates real estate and mortgage loans

home office employees since 1934 a series of lectures which prepare for the LOMA Institute examinations.

In addition to these efforts to increase the technical knowledge of its personnel, The Mutual Life has taken various steps to build morale among its employees. In 1912 it adopted a new and liberal old age retirement program and in 1926 began to grant retirement payments for total and permanent disability and allowances for illness.[17] In 1909 it encouraged the founding of The Mutual Life Association—an organization of The Mutual employees which sponsors athletic programs, social gatherings, and educational activities, pays death benefits, and provides shoppers' service. Finally, in 1942 the Company established a house organ—*The Mutual Circle*—which carries news of employees and of the institution for which they work.

The purpose of such measures and of organizational changes is to increase the efficiency of the home office and consequently to cut overhead costs to the minimum.[18] One of the characteristics of overhead costs in the life insurance business is that while the amounts of new business sold in various years may fluctuate widely, the organization to handle the maximum amount of new business cannot easily be contracted. Accordingly, efforts have to be made steadily to increase or at least to maintain at a fairly constant level new business and the amount of insurance in force. A second characteristic of life insurance expenses is that they tend to be lower in relation to premium income in the large institutions, for unit costs are reduced by large transactions.[19] The expenses of The Mutual Life in the last thirty-five years have tended to bear out these generalizations. The Company's ratio of expenses to premium income has been considerably reduced since 1905, although services to policyholders have been greatly increased. Salaries have been at a level generally below those of industrial corporations of comparable size and certainly not in excess of those of other large insurance companies. Certain items of expense have, of course, varied with altered economic conditions, the main increase having been premium taxes and taxes on and maintenance of the real estate which was acquired by foreclosure during the depression of the 1930's.

17 *Minutes of the Board of Trustees,* April 24, 1912, March 24, 1921, Aug. 25, 1926, Oct. 27, 1926, Jan. 26, 1927, Nov. 28, 1928, Feb., 26, 1930, and Dec. 23, 1939. In 1940 a retirement plan for the field forces was adopted, *ibid.*, Dec. 18, 1940.
18 See J. M. Clark, *Economics of Overhead Costs* (Chicago, 1923) and Charles K. Knight, *Advanced Life Insurance* (New York and London, 1926).
19 H. A. Hopf, *Management and the Optimum* (1935), pp. 26 ff. Care should, however, be exercised in using these findings, for they are based on net actuarial premiums. See also *Spectator Yearbook.*

RELATIONS WITH OTHER COMPANIES, GOVERNMENT, AND THE PUBLIC

Among the many changes which have taken place in American life insurance during the last thirty-five years, none is more striking than that pertaining to the relations among life insurance companies. The severe competition which was in evidence prior to 1905 and was condemned by the Armstrong Committee has almost entirely disappeared, and in its place has developed a spirit of friendliness and even of coöperation. Companies refrain entirely from attacks on one another in their advertisements, but rather devote their publicity generally to spreading knowledge about and interest in life insurance. They exchange information on various aspects of the business through trade associations and through private conferences.[20]

Such coöperative practices were criticized by the secretary of the Temporary National Economic Committee on the ground that they were intercompany or cartel arrangements.[21] During the Armstrong Investigation, on the other hand, coöperation of the recent kind would have been welcomed, for it would have mitigated the evils of competition. A close analysis of exchanges among life insurance companies shows conclusively that intercompany conferences aim to provide greater safety and more liberal policy contracts. Decisions reached do not increase the cost of insurance for the mass of the insured, because under the system of mutualization savings are distributed among or held to the account of the policyholders. Nor do they aim to eliminate the small companies from the field, but rather tend to destroy uneconomic rivalry and to eliminate unsafe practices.

The kind of coöperation which exists within the life insurance industry can be illustrated by the establishment (1941) in the State of New York of the Life Insurance Guaranty Corporation. This institution, created by law after consultation with the life insurance companies of the state, has for its purpose the creation of a fund, made up of contributions on a *pro rata* basis from all companies, which will be used to assist insurers that may get into financial difficulty. The corporation thus plans a levy upon the strong institutions to care for the weak[22]

In spite of the spirit of good feeling which exists and has existed for at least a quarter of a century among life insurance companies, competi-

---

[20] Conferences held under the auspices of Arthur Hunter, formerly actuary of the New York Life, and known as the Hunter Conferences, are a case in point. See *T.N.E.C.*, Monograph 28, pp. 153 f.
[21] *T.N.E.C.*, *Final Report of the Executive Secretary*, pp. 255 ff.
[22] Chapter 481 of the New York Laws of 1941.

tion within the industry has been very real. The cost of the same kind of insurance varies from company to company, not because of differences in premium rates, but because of differences in dividends. Thus, for a twenty-payment life policy issued at age 35 there are one hundred and sixty-three different costs among one hundred and ninety-seven companies. Furthermore, competition among life underwriting institutions takes the form of attempting to provide especially attractive contracts—contracts which begin to pay dividends in the first year, which offer especially attractive modes of settlement or conversion privileges, and which aim to give protection for specific needs. Thirdly, rivalry for insurance business may appear in the standards of selection which are set for applicants, some companies having less stringent requirements than others. Finally, companies compete with one another by providing services of various kinds to policyholders—services which have been steadily increasing in recent years. No one who has had intimate contact with the life insurance industry—above all no agent—would conclude that good feeling and collaboration have destroyed competition.

Parallel with the improvement in relations among life insurance companies there has been in the last thirty-five years a marked amelioration in the relations between companies and the state governments. The triennial state examinations of The Mutual Life have been free from any serious criticism, although they have in a thorough and competent manner probed not only into the solvency of the institution but also into its manifold practices. All matters dealing with legislation are now handled by the Life Insurance Association of America or by the American Life Convention. The former organization, founded in 1907, is one of the leading fact-finding and research institutions in the industry. It offers no support to political parties or to state politicians. It only exercises the right, which is the basis of the democratic process, of making the interests of life insurance policyholders known to legislators, insurance commissioners, and the public. The latter body, which was founded in 1906 and draws most of its strength from among the Middle Western, Western and Southern companies, performs a similar service for its members.

From the Federal Government have come the only two important investigations of life insurance in recent years, and both of these were aimed at the "concentration of economic power" rather than specifically at life insurance. The first, conducted by the Pujo Committee in 1912,[23]

23 Their report is called the *Money Trust Investigation* (1912).

took testimony on the subject of life insurance, but nothing was uncovered which led to remedial legislation or further control. The second, that by the Temporary National Economic Committee in 1940, went into life insurance both intensively and extensively. Such problems as state control, the earnings on investments, the nature of insurance companies' portfolios, the advisability of investing in common stocks, industrial insurance, and the participation of policyholders in management were treated in great detail. What the ultimate effects of the T.N.E.C. findings will be, time alone can tell. Some life insurance leaders believe that the investigation will mark as important a turning point in the industry as the Armstrong Investigation, while others are of the opinion that it will prove to have been but a passing phantom. To date it has led chiefly to a tightening up of the insurance departments of some of the Middle Western and Southern states, to a search for new outlets for investments, particularly in low-cost housing and in small loans, and to a process of soul searching in many companies in an effort to improve conditions along lines suggested by the many volumes of testimony taken by the committee.[24] Valuable as the fact-finding work of the T.N.E.C. may have been, life insurance carriers generally have indicated some resentment at the way Federal investigations are conducted. They maintain that the hearings take the form of trials, with the companies on the defensive and no adequate form of rebuttal granted them. In this particular instance, moreover, they point out that the T.N.E.C. did not limit its inquiry to the problem of concentration of insurance in a few large institutions—a concentration which incidentally was found not to have led to high rates or misuse of influence—but that the Committee extended its investigation to all phases of the insurance business.

On the question of the taxation of life insurance, leaders in the industry have also not approved of governmental policy. They argue that to tax life insurance is to discourage thrift and is no more justified than is a tax on mutual savings banks. In spite of this contention, however, most states levy both license fees for conducting life insurance operations within their borders and in addition taxes on premiums—taxes that average about 2 per cent of premiums in all states. The income from this source greatly exceeds the cost of maintaining state insurance de-

24 *T.N.E.C., Investigation of Concentration of Economic Power, Study of Legal Reserve Life Insurance Companies,* Monograph 28; *Statement on Life Insurance,* Monograph 28a; *Final Report of the Executive Secretary;* and *Hearings before the Temporary National Economic Committee,* Parts 4, 10, 10a, 12, 13, and 28. See John M. Laird, "Highlights of the Federal Investigation," *Transactions of the Actuarial Society of America,* XLI (1940), 385 ff.

partments, about 95 percent of the revenue obtained going into the general funds of the states.[25] Unjustified as such taxes may be, they have been retained and increased because of the ease of collection and the apparently slight effect which they have had upon the growth of insurance.

Federal taxation of life insurance companies is, however, quite another and probably more serious matter than state taxes. The first levies of this kind were stamp taxes employed in the Civil War and then in the Spanish American War and were not burdensome. With the enactment of the Corporation Excise Tax of 1909 and the ratification of the sixteenth amendment to the Constitution in 1913—an amendment which made an income tax constitutional—Federal taxation of life insurance companies entered a new phase. These laws immediately brought up the question of what constituted income or profits in a life insurance company.[26] After much confusion and considerable complaint, especially during World War I, when the tax rates were augmented,[27] some order was achieved by the Revenue Act of 1921. This law recognized that the "income" of life insurance companies was not comparable to that of other corporations and provided a special formula for determining how to arrive at a taxable income figure. In brief, Federal taxation has been limited since 1921 to levies on an amount obtained by subtracting certain specified deductions from investment income.[28] In view of the heavy state tax burden, justice demands that Federal taxation of life insurance companies be kept, as it has been thus far, relatively low. Yet

[25] *Bulletin*, No. 49 (Feb. 2, 1939), Insurance Department of the Chamber of Commerce of the United States. Note should also be taken of the fact that in 1934 New York City introduced a local premium tax at the rate of $\frac{1}{10}$ of 1 percent.

[26] See the attitude taken by The Mutual Life in these matters, *Annual Reports*, Nos. 69, 71, 81, 83.

[27] Up to 1921 life insurance companies paid taxes on the same basis as other corporations.

[28] It provided that the basis of taxation should be "net income." This was obtained by deducting from gross income, which included premiums, interest, and profits, the total of insurance expenses, taxes, payments on policy contracts (including dividends on premium paying policies), increase in policy reserves, depreciation, tax-exempt interest, interest on indebtedness, dividends received, and interest required to maintain the policy reserve. In 1938 the law was further changed to provide that life insurance companies be not taxed on profits derived from the sale, redemption, or payment of securities and to prevent them from deducting any losses from such transactions in determining net taxable income. Furthermore, they are exempt from the capital-stock and excess profits taxes. The net investment income subject to taxation is the gross investment income from interest, dividends, and rents—on a cash basis—less several specified deductions: (1) interest from tax-exempt securities, (2) 4 percent on the average amount for the year of all policy reserves, (3) 2 percent on funds held for deferred dividends, (4) investment expenses, (5) certain expenses and taxes on real estate held, (6) depreciation, and (7) interest paid on indebtedness. In 1942 there was a sharp reduction made in the deductions allowed on account of earnings required to maintain policy reserves. See Joseph B. Maclean, *Life Insurance*, Sixth edition (New York, 1945), *loc. cit.*

projects are being continually advanced for increasing it and have been strongly advocated since the outbreak of World War II.

In its relations with the general public The Mutual Life has been particularly fortunate. The misapprehensions aroused in 1905 were soon quieted, and confidence was restored. The Company has enjoyed

TABLE 45

ACCUMULATED RECORD OF RECEIPTS, DISBURSEMENTS, AND
LEDGER ASSETS: THE MUTUAL LIFE

	Total 100 Years
Receipts	
Insurance premiums	$4,895,549,260.96
Annuity premiums	499,923,247.20
Policy receipts	$5,395,472,508.16
Dividends deposited	18,940,576.07
Annuity installments deposited	465,845.68
Interest and rents	1,693,331,878.52
Profit and other receipts	167,888,229.10
Total receipts	$7,276,099,037.53
Disbursements	
Death benefits	$1,639,425,391.55
Matured endowments	313,350,773.16
Disability	113,680,031.45
Double indemnity	21,962,029.12
Annuities	231,583,234.18
Surrenders	1,182,890,485.05
Dividends	1,013,516,881.14
Total policy payments	$4,516,408,825.65
Dividend deposits withdrawn	12,342,602.18
Annuity installment deposits withdrawn	180,723.75
Expenses	962,961,927.91
Losses and other payments	222,916,408.81
Total disbursements	$5,714,810,488.30
Net receipts (ledger assets)	$1,561,288,549.23
Accumulated for policyholders	1,535,192,962.00
Yearly average of excess	$6,561,292.79

a reputation for its many contributions to the industry, its conservative policies, and for its long and successful history. Its large number of policyholders and business people more generally have been its loyal supporters. Its hundred-year record is one of which it can be proud and which in itself constitutes a strong argument for mutual life insurance.

A GLANCE IN RETROSPECT

As one looks back over the history of life insurance in America during the last hundred years, one cannot fail to be impressed by the record.

This industry has aimed to provide an element of financial security in our society and has in large measure succeeded in attaining its goal. Dependent as is modern man upon money with which to satisfy his daily wants and engaged as he is in economic activity which members of his family cannot always continue for the purpose of earning their own livelihood, it is not easy for him to lay aside sufficient sums to care after his death for those who look to him for support. By sharing risks with others, however, he can immediately and at small cost make provision for his dependents in the eventuality of his death, and by the thrift which insurance promotes he can begin a system of regular savings to meet his other expected future financial obligations. That life insurance has furnished an appreciable amount of security for Americans can be seen from the fact that the total amount of insurance in force with private companies approximates the annual national income and that in 1942 life insurance companies paid out to policyholders and their beneficiaries the sum of $2,443,241,867.

Yet the social value of life insurance is not limited to the services rendered the insureds—it is greatly enhanced by the fact that life insurance amasses large amounts of money which are invested largely for the purpose of providing our nation with capital goods. Real estate developments, railroad systems, public utilities, farms, many industries, and all our political jurisdictions have found in life insurance funds part of the capital which they have required. The financial magnitude of life insurance companies permits giving assistance to the largest private undertakings and is an important source of governmental borrowing. Moreover, the conservative and long-range character of life insurance investments lends stability to the investment market and makes of life insurance companies one of the safest of savings institutions. As was pointed out on an earlier page, not a single life insurance company doing business in the State of New York has failed in the last thirty-two years with ultimate loss to policyholders.

In the growth of this great institution of life insurance The Mutual Life has played a major role. It was the first life insurance company still in existence to write insurance for the general public on a mutual basis. In the period from 1843 to 1870—a period of pioneering and of dramatic accomplishment—The Mutual Life, by its success, gave great popularity to mutuality in insurance. It launched on an important scale the idea of personal solicitation of new business, because its founders realized that in the absence of working capital new insurance had to be placed on the books at once and premiums had to be received if the enterprise were to be a success. The Company drew up the first important American mortality table—the American Experience Table—it popularized the idea of annual dividends, it originated the contribution system of distributing surplus, it furthered the concept of adequate and legal reserves, and it devised practical methods of selection. The second period of the Company's history was one of great growth—a period when the principles of life insurance which had been established earlier were made operative on a large scale. These years from 1870 to 1905 were marked by strong leaders, who knew how to and who did raise life insurance to a position of first importance in the financial, economic, and social structure of our society. It was a time, furthermore, when most of the terms of the insurance contract were made more liberal, when deferred dividend policies were widely used, and when severe competition existed among the companies. The third period of life insurance history—from 1905 to 1943—has been characterized by continued growth of the institution of insurance and by a renewed effort to extend the benefits of sharing risks to the largest possible number of persons. In this effort, business ethics have been exemplary and the record for safety has been excellent. In the 1930's life insurance companies weathered one of the worst business depressions in modern history; they have lived through one world war, and they are living through another with courage and hope.

What the future holds in store for the life insurance industry it is not our task to prophesy. If, however, the achievements of the past are a gauge for measuring the social usefulness of sharing risks in years to come, it is safe to speculate that the prospects for the institution of life insurance are bright.

Appendices

Charter of The Mutual Life Insurance Company of New York

CHAPTER 246.

An Act to incorporate the Mutual Life Insurance Company of New York.

Passed April 12, 1842, by a two-thirds vote.

The People of the State of New York represented in Senate and Assembly do enact as follows

1. William H. Aspinwall, James Brown, John W. Leavitt, Elihu Townsend, James S. Wadsworth, Philip S. Van Rensselaer, Gouverneur M. Wilkins, John V. L. Pruyn, Thomas W. Olcott, Charles L. Livingston, Joseph Blunt, Jacob P. Giraud, John C. Cruger, Alfred Pell, David C. Colden, Jacob Harvey, Robert B. Minturn, Mortimer Livingston, Rufus L. Lord, Arthur Bronson, Henry Brevoort, Theodore Sedgwick, Stacy B. Collins, Robert C. Cornell, James Boorman, James Campbell, William Moore, Morris Robinson, Zebedee Cook, Jr., Jonathan Miller, Fitz Greene Halleck, John A. King, T. Romeyn Beck, Richard V. De Witt, Gideon Hawley, and James J. Ring, and all other persons who may hereafter associate with them in the manner hereinafter prescribed, shall be a body politic and corporate by the name of "The Mutual Life Insurance Company of New York."

2. In addition to the general powers and privileges of a corporation, as the same are declared by the third title of the eighteenth chapter of the first part of the Revised Statutes, the corporation hereby created shall have the power to insure their respective lives, and to make all and every insurance appertaining to or connected with life risks and to grant and purchase annuities.

The real estate which it shall be lawful for the said corporation to purchase, hold and convey, shall be

1st. Such as shall be requisite for its immediate accommodation in the convenient transaction of its business, or,

2d. Such as shall have been mortgaged to it in good faith by way of security for loans previously contracted, or for moneys due, or

3d. Such as shall have been conveyed to it in satisfaction of debts, previously contracted in the course of its dealings, or

4th. Such as shall have been purchased at sales upon judgments, decrees or mortgages obtained or made for such debts;—

The said corporation shall not purchase, hold or convey real estate in any other case or for any other purpose, and all such real estate as shall not be necessary for the accommodation of said company in the convenient transaction of its business shall be sold and disposed of within six years after the said company shall have acquired title to the same, and it shall not be lawful for the said company to hold such real estate for a longer period than that above mentioned.

3. All persons who shall hereafter insure with the said corporation, and also their heirs, executors, administrators and assigns, continuing to be insured in said corporation as hereinafter provided, shall thereby become members thereof during the period they shall remain insured by said corporation and no longer.

4. All the corporate powers of the said company shall be exercised by a board of trustees and such officers and agents as they may appoint. The board of trustees shall consist of thirty-six persons, all of whom must be citizens of this state. They shall elect a president annually, who shall be a member of this corporation and they shall have power to declare by by-law, what number of trustees less than a majority of the whole but not less than nine shall be a quorum for the transaction of business.

5. The persons named in the first section of this act shall constitute the first board of trustees.

6. The trustees shall, at their first meeting, divide themselves by lot, into four classes of nine each. The term of the first class shall expire at the end of one year, the term of the second class shall expire at the end of two years, the term of the third class shall expire at the end of three years, the term of the fourth class shall expire at the end of four years, and so on successively each and every year. The seats of these classes shall be supplied by the members of this corporation, a plurality of votes constituting a choice, but an insurance of at least one thousand dollars in amount shall be necessary to entitle any member to a vote. This section shall not be construed to prevent a trustee going out from being eligible to a reëlection. The board of trustees may fill any vacancies in their number, occasioned by death, resignation, or removal from the state. The election of trustees shall be held on the first Monday of June in each year at such place in the city of New York as the board of trustees shall designate, of which they shall give at least fourteen days previous notice, in two of the public newspapers printed in the said city, and the board of trustees shall at the same time appoint three of the members of the said corporation, inspectors to preside at such election, and if any of the said inspectors decline or fail to attend, the trustees may appoint others to fill such vacancies.

7. Every person who shall become a member of this corporation, by effecting insurance therein, shall the first time he effects insurance, and before he receives his policy, pay the rates that shall be fixed upon and determined by the trustees, and no premium so paid shall ever be withdrawn from said company, except as hereinafter provided, but shall be liable to all the losses and expenses incurred by this company during the continuance of its charter.

8. The trustees may determine the rates of insurance and the sum to be insured.

9. It shall be lawful for the said corporation to invest the said premiums

in the securities designated in the two following sections, and to sell, transfer and change the same, and reinvest the funds of said corporation when the trustees shall deem expedient.

10. The whole of the premiums received for insurance by said corporation, except as provided for in the following sections, shall be invested in bonds and mortgages on unincumbered real estate within the state of New York; the real property to secure such investments of capital shall, in every case, be worth twice the amount loaned thereon.

11. The trustees shall have power to invest a certain portion of the premiums received, not to exceed one half thereof in public stocks of the United States, or of this state or of any incorporated city in this state.

12. Suits at law may be maintained by said corporation against any of its members, for any cause relating to the business of said corporation, also suits at law may be prosecuted and maintained by any member against said corporation for losses by death, if payment is withheld more than three months after the company is duly notified of such losses; and no member of the corporation shall be debarred his testimony as witness in any such cause, on account of his being a member of said company. And no member of the corporation not being in his individual capacity a party to such suit, shall be incompetent as a witness in any such cause on account of his being a member of said company.

13. The officers of said company, at the expiration of five years from the time that the first policy shall have been issued, and bear date, and within thirty days thereafter, and during the first thirty days of every subsequent period of five years, shall cause a balance to be struck of the affairs of the company in which they shall charge each member with a proportionate share of the losses and expenses of said company according to the original amount of premium paid by him, but in no case to exceed the amount of the premium. Each member shall be credited with the amount of said premium, and also with an equal share of the profits of the said company derived from investments and earnings in proportion to said amount, and in case of the death of any member of the said company the amount standing to his credit at the last preceding striking of balance as aforesaid, together with the proportion which shall be found to belong to him at the next subsequent striking of said balance, shall be paid over to his legal representatives or assigns within three months after the said last-mentioned balance shall be struck. Any member of the company who would be entitled to share in the profits who shall have omitted to pay any premium or any periodical payment due from him to the company may be prohibited by the trustees from sharing in the profits of the company, and all such previous payments made by him shall go to the benefit of the company.

14. On some day in the first thirty days after the expiration of the first five years from the time when the said company shall issue their first policy, and within the first thirty days of every subsequent five years, the officers of the said company shall cause to be made a general balance statement of the affairs of the said company, which shall be entered in a book prepared for that purpose, which shall be subject to the examination of any member of

the company during the usual hours of business for the term of thirty days thereafter. Such statement shall contain: (1st) the amount of premiums received during the said period; (2d) the amount of expenses of the said company during the said period; (3d) the amount of losses incurred during the same period; (4th) the balance remaining with the said company; (5th) the nature of the security on which the same is invested or loaned, and the amount of cash on hand. The said company shall also make and transmit to the Comptroller of the state on the first day of January in each year a full statement of its affairs in the same manner as monied corporations are required to do under the second title of the eighteenth chapter of the first part of the Revised Statutes. The books of the said company shall be open to the examination of any member thereof during the usual hours of business in the same manner as the books of monied corporations are required by the Revised Statutes to be kept open for the inspection of the stockholders thereof.

15. The sections of the Revised Statutes from nineteen to twenty-five, both inclusive, of the first article of the second title of the eighteenth chapter of the first part, shall not be applicable to the corporation hereby created.

16. The operations and business of the corporation shall be carried on at such place in the city of New York as the trustees shall direct.

17. No policy shall be issued by said company until application shall be made for insurance, in the aggregate for five hundred thousand dollars at least, and the trustees shall have the right to purchase for the benefit of the company, all policies of insurance or other obligations issued by the company.

18. The legislature may at any time alter or repeal this act.

19. This act shall take effect immediately.

Form Used by All Monied Corporations for Reporting to the Comptroller of the State of New York, 1832-1848

A full and perfect statement of the affairs of the
on the first of January, 183 .

FIRST. The amount of the capital stock of the said company, paid in or invested according to the provisions of its charter, actually held on the first day of January, was, and still is . . . .$

SECOND. The real estate belonging to said company consists of, ...
Amounting altogether to the sum of . . . .$
Of which real estate, the portion occupied by the company as necessary to the transaction of its business, is valued at . . . . . .$

THIRD. The shares of stock held by said company absolutely, or as collateral security, were, on the said first day of January, and still are as follows, viz.:

I. *Stock held absolutely.*
shares in the capital stock of the bank of
valued at par, $ each share . . . .$

(In this manner all the shares of stock held by the company are to be entered.)

II. *Stock held as collateral security.*
shares in the capital stock of the banks of
valued at par, $ a share . . . .$

FOURTH. Amount of debts owing to said company on the said first day of January, 183 ; distinguishing the amount of such debts due from other monied corporations, with the names, &c., and amount secured by bond and mortgage or judgment; also the amount which ought to be included in the computation of losses and the total amount of all such debts then collectible:

I. *Debts due from other monied corporations.*
Balance due from the   bank, being amount of cash deposited in said bank to the credit of this company. $
(Here insert all debts due from other corporations.)

II. *Debts secured by bonds and mortgages.*
Bonds and mortgages given by stockholders for their original subscription of stock, on which interest has been paid to the day of
183   . . . .$

Bonds and mortgages given by stockholders for their subscription, on which interest has not been paid for the last year (or two or three as the case may be) ....$

Bonds and mortgages for monies loaned, on which the interest has been paid to the   day of   183   ....$

Bonds and mortgages for monies loaned, on which the interest has not been paid for the last year (or two or three) ....$

III. *Debts secured by promissory notes or other personal security.*

Promissory notes given for monies loaned, on which the interest has been paid to the   day of   183   ....$

Promissory notes given for monies loaned, on which the interest has not been paid for 'the last year; (and if there are any on which installments of principal are due and unpaid, let the amount so due be stated) ....$

(Here add other personal securities held by the company, and state whether the payments of interest and principal are regularly made.)

IV. *Debts in judgment.*

Debts in judgment, supposed collectible ....$

Debts in judgment, supposed not collectible ....$

V. *Debts in suit.*

Debts of every kind in suit, but not in judgment, supposed col-lectible   ....$

Debts in suit but not in judgment, supposed not collectible ......$

FIFTH. The amount of debts which ought, according to the provisions of article first of title second of chapter eighteenth of the first part of the Revised Statutes, to be included in the account of losses, is $; of this sum, $ is considered well secured, but no interest having been paid thereon the last year, it is according to the requirements of the statute referred to, included among losses

SIXTH. The amount of debts owing by said company on the first day of January, 183 , is ....$

Of this sum the amount payable on demand is ....$

The amount due to other moneyed corporations is as follows, viz:

To the bank of   ....$

(Here give the name and the amount due each corporation.)

SEVENTH. Claims against said corporation, not acknowledged by it as debts.

(Here give a description of the claim.)

EIGHTH. The amount for which the said company was, on the said first day of January, bound contingently on policies of insurance, was $

(If the company is in any other manner bound as surety, or can be made liable by contingent events, here state the particulars of the liability.)

NINTH. The amount of losses charged on the profits of the company since the first day of January last, is ....$

The amount of losses charged on the capital during the same
time, is, ...$

TENTH. The dividends which have been made during the year preceding the date of this report, amount to $ on each share, being at
the rate of   percent per annum; amounting, on the whole capital stock
of the company, to the sum of . . . .$

ELEVENTH. The average amount for each month during the year preceding this report, of the debts due to the corporation, was . . . .$
The average amount for each month during the year, of the debts due
from the corporation, was . . . .$

TWELFTH. The aggregate liability of the directors to the company,
as principals, is . . . .$
As sureties   . . . .$
                                                                   $
The aggregate amount of stock of the corporation owned by the
directors, is . . . .$

THIRTEENTH. The aggregate amount of premiums received during
the year preceding this report, on policies of insurance, has been $
The aggregate amount received during the same period for interest on
loans, or other debts due the company, has been . . . .$

The Annual Statement

The present Annual Statement conforms in all respects to that required by the Insurance Department of the State of New York. For many years the statements officially printed by the Insurance Department have differed from the Company's own statements to its policyholders in two respects. In the first place, the Company has computed its insurance reserves according to the standard table of mortality, known as the American Table, and its annuity reserves by a special annuity table, while the State has employed another standard, known as the Actuaries' Table, for both insurances and annuities. The American Table is more modern and more scientific than the Actuaries', and its conservatism is shown by the fact that in every year the death losses of the Company have fallen considerably below the amount expected according to the American Table. The annuity table employed by the Company secures larger reserves than those computed by the State standard, experience having shown that, on the average, persons who buy annuities live longer than those of like ages who insure their lives. But the sum of the reserves computed by the Company according to the two tables has always been decidedly smaller than the State reserve, because the Actuaries' table is, on the whole, still more conservative than the American, in the sense that it allows for a heavier mortality. The Company has however, for many years, held extra or special reserves to meet particular risks assumed for extra rates of premiums, for which the State computes no extra reserve, and it has also provided in its reserves for other contingencies, such, for example, as the cost of collecting outstanding premiums which are counted as an asset.

In the second place, the State has for many years ruled out one or two items of assets claimed by the companies, and also the cost of collection above referred to. The net result of all the differences was that the assets and liabilities both appeared larger in the Company's own statement than in the report of the Insurance Department. To secure uniformity, it was this year decided to publish the Company's statement hereafter in accordance with the State form, both as to assets and liabilities, reserving the right to increase the State liabilities whenever the Company's figures should exceed the State's, but retaining for the Company's interval uses its own long-listed standards conforming both to scientific accuracy and sound business judgment.—*Fifty-Fourth Annual Report,* pp. 15–17.

President McCurdy stated to the Board that, the advantage gained being that the statement of the Company will in the future conform to the published statements of the Insurance Departments of New York, Massachusetts, and other states and there will be no further opportunity of explanations of seeming differences. *Minutes of the Board of Trustees,* Nov. 25, 1896.

Tontine Policies [1]

During the past year, a new application of the old idea of Tontine insurance has been made by this company. The plan of Lorenzo Tonti, a Neapolitan, who lived about two centuries ago, was as follows: A certain number of persons contributed a specified sum of money, without reference to age or sex; upon the expiration of a given number of years, this sum, with its accumulations, was divided among the survivors. What are now called Tontine Dividend Policies are merely the ordinary policies of the company, with substantially the foregoing plan applied to the dividends. We found that many persons whose inherited traits and personal vigor gave reasonable assurance of long life, if not cut off by casualty, were attracted by the plan of accumulating the dividends on their policies for a given period—say ten years—and then dividing the result among the survivors. A certain number out of any one class will inevitably die before the expiration of the Tontine period; and these receive only the face of their policies. A certain other number will inevitably allow their policies to lapse, and in this case no surrender value is paid. In the case of the first, the payment of the face of the policy is an ample return for the money invested, and the loss of the dividend is no hardship. In the case of the second, it is a matter of voluntary contract, so that no injustice is done. But the savings from these two sources can hardly fail to be large; and when distributed among those who are fortunate enough to survive, must largely increase their dividends. There can be no doubt that the dividends on these policies, when declared, will exceed those upon the ordinary policies. So far, these policies have been popular, and are being taken in many cases by persons already insured for twenty thousand dollars, and who prefer the remainder of the company's full limit—thirty thousand dollars—on this plan.

1 *Twenty-Eighth Annual Report* (1870), pp. 9–10.

Commission Rates on Different Types of Policies, 1904[1]

CLASSES A, B AND C.

Twenty-year distribution policies, all forms except single premiums, 80 percent first year, 10 percent second year and 7½ percent for six years thereafter.

Fifteen-year ·distribution policies, all forms except single premiums, 70 percent first year, 10 percent second year and 7½ percent for six years thereafter.

Ten-year distribution policies, all forms except single premiums, 65 percent first year, 10 percent second year and 7½ percent for six years thereafter.

Five-year distribution policies, all forms except single premiums, 35 percent first year, 7½ percent for six years thereafter.

CLASS D.

Single premium policies, life policies, 10 percent, endowments 7½ percent. Mortuary allotments, contingent upon conditions, 7½ percent. Annuities of all kinds 5 percent.

If combination policies are issued for single premiums the separate parts of each premium will carry commission same as above.

CLASS E.

Annual distribution and all other forms of policies, not above provided for, 35 percent flat, no renewals.

. . .

Note.—Business will be regarded as "established" in 1893, when the full first year's premium on policies issued in that year shall have been paid in cash.

In the event of your death while general agent, the Company will pay to your heirs, executors, administrators or assigns your renewal interest in said business.

If any of your sub-agents should be dismissed for breach of trust, or dishonesty, or shall go into the service of another life insurance company, all his renewal interests in said business shall revert to The Mutual Life Insurance Company of New York.

Across that paragraph is written in red ink "Canceled, W.R.G."

In the event of the death of any one of your sub-agents while in the service of the company, his renewal interests shall be paid to his heirs, executors or administrators.

Very truly yours,
WALTER R. GILLETTE, *General Manager.*

1 Memorandum to Raymond Agency. Armstrong Investigation, *Exhibits*, No. 260.

Life Insurance Company State Reports [1]

(1) All the real property held by the corporation, the dates of acquisition, the names of the vendors, the actual cost, the value at which it is carried on the company's books, the market value, the amounts expended during the year for repairs and improvements, the gross and net income from each parcel, and if any portion thereof be occupied by the company the rental value thereof, a statement of any certificate issued by the superintendent extending the time for the disposition thereof, and all purchases and sales made since the last annual statement, with particulars as to dates, names of vendors and vendees, and the consideration.

(2) The amount of existing loans upon the security of real property, stating the amount loaned upon property in each state and foreign country.

(3) The moneys loaned by the corporation to any person other than loans upon the security of real property above mentioned and other than loans upon policies by the actual borrowers thereof, the maturity and rate of interest of such loans, the securities held therefor, and all substitutions of securities in connection therewith, and the same particulars with reference to any loans made or discharged since the last annual statement.

(4) All other property owned by the company or in which it has any interest (including all securities, whether or not recognized by the law as proper investments), the dates of acquisition, from whom acquired, the actual cost, the value at which the property is carried upon the books, the market value, the interest or dividends received thereon, during the year; also all purchases and sales of property other than real estate made since the last annual statement, with particulars as to dates, names of purchasers and sellers, and the consideration; and also the income received and outlays made in connection with all such property.

(5) All commissions paid to any persons in connection with loans or purchases or sales of any property, and a statement of all payments for legal expenses, giving particulars as to dates, amounts and names and addresses of payees.

(6) All moneys expended in connection with any matter pending before any legislative body or any officer or department of government, giving particulars as to dates, amounts, names and addresses of payees, the measure or proceeding in connection with which the payment was made, and the interest of the corporation therein.

(7) The names of the officers and directors of the company, the proceedings at the last annual election, giving the names of candidates and

[1] Each company was to report annually on a form provided by the Superintendent of Insurance according to this excerpt from the New York Insurance Law, 1906, section 103.

the number of votes cast for each and whether in person, by proxy or by mail.

(8) The salary, compensation and emoluments received by officers or directors and where the same amounts to more than five thousand dollars that received by any person, firm or corporation, with particulars as to dates, amounts, payees and the authority by which the payment was made; also all salaries paid to any representative either at the home office, or at any branch office, or agency, for agency supervision.

(9) The largest balances carried in each bank or trust company during each month of the year.

(10) All death claims resisted or compromised during the year, with particulars as to sums insured, sums paid and reasons assigned for resisting or compromising the same in each case.

(11) A complete statement of the profits and losses upon the business transacted during the year and the sources of such gains and losses, and a statement showing separately the margins upon premiums for the first year of insurance ascertained according to the select and ultimate method of valuation as provided in section eighty-four of this chapter and the actual expenses chargeable to the procurement of new business incurred since the last annual statement, as enumerated in section ninety-seven of this article. A foreign corporation, issuing both participating and nonparticipating policies, shall make a separate statement of profits and losses, margins and expenses, as aforesaid, with reference to each of said kinds of business, and also showing the manner in which any general outlays of the company have been apportioned to each of such kinds of business.

(12) A statement separately showing the amount of the gains of the company for the year attributable to policies written after December thirty-first, nineteen hundred and six, and the precise method by which the calculation has been made.

(13) The rates of annual dividends declared during the year for all plans of insurance and all durations and for ages at entry, twenty-five, thirty-five, forty-five and fifty-five, and the precise method by which such dividends have been calculated.

(14) A statement showing the rates of dividends declared upon deferred dividend policies completing their dividend periods for all plans of insurance and the precise methods by which said dividends have been calculated.

(15) A statement showing any and all amounts set apart or provisionally ascertained or calculated or held awaiting apportionment upon policies with deferred dividend periods longer than one year for all plans of insurance and all durations and for ages of entry as aforesaid, together with the precise statements of the methods of calculation by which the same have been provisionally or otherwise determined.

(16) A statement of any and all reserve or surplus funds held by the company and for what purpose they are claimed respectively to be held.

Contemporary Description of The Mutual Life Building

The original Mutual Life Building, as occupied in 1884, consisted of 8 stories facing on Nassau Street, with what were then known as "pavilions" extending down Cedar and Liberty Streets. In an early description (1884) the following observations were made with regard to its construction:

The work is of the most solid and enduring character. The foundations have been designed with great care to insure equal pressures under every part of the superstructure. The piers are properly proportioned to sustain the weights, in their sectional areas and heights, according to the several materials of which they are built. The basement and first stories are of granite. The other stories, up to the eighth, are of a beautiful limestone from Indiana.

The interior construction is mainly of iron, consisting of rolled beams supported on plate girders which rest on cast and Phoenix wrought-iron columns. The building is entirely fireproof, the spaces between the beams being spanned with fire brick, and the bottoms of the beams being protected with the same material, which is an unusual precaution. Most particular attention has been given to ventilation, and the heating will be complete, although by direct radiating coils, yet from the manner of introducing fresh air the best effects will be obtained. Steam will be furnished by the Steam Heating Company, although boilers will also be provided. Provision will be made for both gas and electric lighting, as well as for all the latest appliances, such as telephones, electric call-bells, etc. An artesian well will assist in supplying the building with water, and now yields an ample supply of pure water.

The style is an adaptation of the Italian Renaissance. The façade is divided into three features, the central part recessed and flanked by pavilions on Cedar and Liberty Streets. An arcade, the pilasters of which will be ornamented with flutings and richly carved capitals, has arches spanning the spaces between. The main cornice is bold in design.

The portico is the most highly wrought feature of the façade, and is both striking and imposing. It is two stories in height, flanked by massive granite columns. The capitals of both columns and piers are executed in white marble. The ceiling is vaulted and panelled, and the piers are covered with Renaissance carving. The capitals of the piers have heads typical of Europe, Asia, Africa, and America carved upon them, modelled and executed in a masterly style. This work was done by Mr. Samuel Kitson, from Rome. There will be an ornamental bronze gate at the portico entrance.

The main entrance hall leading to the elevators will be finished most substantially in white marble, to make it as light as possible. The elevator doorways will be trimmed with the above-named material and the openings guarded by strong and ornamental brass grill work. The finish of the main office of the company, on second and third floors, will be handsome and dignified, while being free from extravagance. The columns will be of scagliola, with Corinthian capitals. A white marble wainscot of plain design will surround the room. The offices for renting will be most attractive in finish. A noticeable feature is the ample provision for light and air, the windows being unusually large in proportion to the piers, although the grouping and the depth of joints of the piers are so arranged as to give them great solidity in appearance as well as in fact.

The engineering throughout the work has been most thorough, the architect having placed Thomas E. Brown, Jr., C.E., in charge of this work.

The impression produced so far gives promise that the work when finished will be imposing and elegant, with sufficient plainness or severity to give dignity, relieved in certain parts with enrichments, giving value to the rest; a work of which the city may well be proud.

Memorandum by the President of The Mutual Life, 1858

TO THE MEMBERS OF THE FINANCE COMMITTEE

Believing that the time has arrived when you should deliberately mature and settle the question of the propriety of loaning a more considerable amount of the funds of this Company on improved Farming lands in the best sections of this state, I beg to call your attention to some facts and considerations upon this subject; and, upon our loans generally.

The class of securities held by this Company on Real Estate is unquestionably of a high order. But while no loan is made where the security, at the time, is not entirely satisfactory to the Finance Committee, and where they do not deem the property mortgaged abundantly sufficient, at a forced sale for cash to repay the loan and all charges connected with it, yet there is a decided difference in the *intrinsic stability* of the different classes of property mortgaged to this Company.

The highest grade of security for loans, is, a mortgage on cultivated and productive land worth enough in cash at all times to repay the loan upon it,—with a good personal bond attached.

Such property is ordinarily indestructible, and does not require any collateral support like Fire Insurance. This class of security is very limited in our cities, and when offered is usually taken at a low rate of interest.

In this Company we are practically obliged to forego another class of securities, named in our charter, of a very high order—the Stocks of the United States and of the State of New York, and for this reason:—

These Stocks are issued bearing a low rate of interest, and in addition they ordinarily bring a premium upon their *par* value, thus reducing still further the net income received from such investment.

As these Stocks are made by law the basis of Banking operations, it is obvious that such Institutions or individuals who use them for this purpose can afford to pay more for them than this company can, as they not only receive the income they pay, but also the Bankers' profit they bring. Large amounts of these securities also go abroad where parties are content with a small interest and a safe investment—but whether this Company shall invest in securities of this description paying from 4 to 5 percent per annum, or upon others believed to be equally safe at 7 percent is a question of very easy and prompt solution.

Whether the advantage offered by City property, of ready sale for Cash on a given emergency, at a moderate concession from the market estimate of value, more than counterbalances the greater liability to depreciation and loss from any great national calamity, like war, or from municipal disturbance, or from the ravages of epidemic or pestilential disease, is a question which we have not the data to determine.

Of one thing we may be certain; that in a Company like this, where funds must necessarily increase rapidly, and to a large amount for a time, but which funds are sure to be needed in discharge of absolute liabilities, it is not wise to place all, or nearly all, our assets on securities in any one locality or upon any one class of Real Estate.—

The next class of property in point of security is, good, convenient, moderate-priced dwellings or warehouses in this City well situated, and with a satisfactory Bond, and Fire Insurance Policies properly guaranteed and assigned. This is and has been, a favorite class of security with this Company.

The class next to this which we are asked to receive as security, is high-priced property in particular localities, often of a fancied value and liable to fluctuation, or tenement houses where the wear and tear and depreciation is often rapid; or buildings used for hazardous mechanical, or other purposes. The liability to deterioration and loss in one case cannot well be provided against, and in the other the hazard can only be covered through the uncertain resource of Fire Insurance. Such loans we endeavour to avoid, and if taken for security, only for a moderate percentage upon our own valuation.

Another class of Securities is, vacant lots in this city. These we have as a rule avoided, because they yield no income, while the taxation, assessment, interest, etc. subject them to a heavy annual tax, which if the Bondsman fails to pay, might throw an inconvenient amount of unproductive property on the Company.

Another class of Bonds and Mortgages have been of late frequently offered to the Company. These are upon Country Seats in the vicinity of the City, on which in many cases large sums have been expended in ornament and buildings, and where the land is valued at a price far beyond what it could be made to yield an income on, for any farming or horticultural purposes.

The stability of the present values of such property depends very much upon the caprices of fashion, or upon ascertained causes regarding the healthfulness of the Situation.

That, as the City increases in population and business and in wealth, these Country-residences will be multiplied in some form and in some positions cannot be doubted: but the means of locomotion are so various and extended, that a large area of country with a great variety of choice is opened to our citizens, and it is therefore quite probable that the high value now placed upon property in some fashionable positions may not be long sustained.

The Company is also constantly called upon to make loans on property in the cities in the interior of this State. Loans have from time to time been made in the Cities of Buffalo, Rochester, Oswego, Syracuse, Utica and Albany. In some or all of these Cities the loans where the property is well situated, may be as stable as in any other. We ought not however to lose sight of the fact that many of our interior cities were founded to meet the necessities and convenience of our citizens before our Railways were constructed.

That system of travel and conveyance has wrought a prodigious change, and has been as destructive to many of our interior cities and villages, as it has been to stage coaches and canal packet-boats.

New towns have sprung up under the Railway system and a few of the old have increased in population and business under it, but it is believed that its effect upon many of our cities will be gradually to destroy them. Some, indeed, have all the elements of solidity and prosperity within themselves in their central position, agricultural and mineral wealth, like Syracuse: or like Buffalo, in its frontier position and its large commerce: while Rochester, Oswego and Albany have some peculiar advantages from their positions, or water-power for manufacturing purposes, or from agricultural wealth, which will be permanent to a certain extent.

While the history of the effects of our Railway system upon the cities of the interior is undeveloped and unwritten, it would be manifestly unsafe to extend to any very considerable number of them loans on securities which are liable to be quite shifting and uncertain. In the cities above named we have made loans to the extent of about $400,000.

The Company has occasionally had applications for loans on Farms.

Whenever made they have, in compliance with the rule of the Finance Committee, never exceeded 40 percent of the value of the land; excluding the Buildings.

While the Finance Committee have always conceded the great stability and safety of these loans depending upon land which is ordinarily indestructible, and needing no collateral security, except the Bond that accompanies the Mortgage—yet they have almost universally declined these applications, either because they were not personally acquainted with the value of the property proposed, or did not know of safe and competent persons to make the appraisal, and present the facts; the Committee very properly declining to loan the money to the Company unless they were fully satisfied of the security offered.

Two other considerations have also influenced them to a certain extent, viz.—the smallness of the loans sought, and an anticipated want of promptitude in the payment of the semi-annual interest.

While satisfactory securities for the larger proportion of our funds could be obtained as heretofore in this city, there has been no particular pressure upon us to seek to remove these difficulties to loans upon Farms.

But we have now arrived at a period (of uncertain duration) when we must further *lower our rate of interest* or take *securities of an inferior class* or *loan upon Farming lands.*

The present abundance of money and the scarcity of first-class Bond and Mortgage securities in this city, will render this for the present inevitable.

The *first* alternative should be avoided if possible, as the present low price of money, it is believed, is to be of but transient continuance; while it would be very difficult after reducing the rate of interest to get it back to the full legal standard. The *second* alternative being wholly inadmissible, the *third* alternative then demands our deliberate consideration.

Without admitting the claim made by the citizens of the interior of the State that as this Company was chartered by its Legislature, and that a portion of the funds being drawn from all parts of it, all have therefore a right to a distribution of its loans, yet as this institution has much to maintain in its present position in freedom from taxation, and other advantages, it is wise and proper where it can be done without any sacrifice of principle, or of security to its funds, to create friends in every section who may be called to the aid of the Company in case of any threatened invasion of its present chartered and legal rights.

From inquiries recently made, it is believed that Farmers in the central counties of Oneida, Onondaga, Cayuga, Seneca, Yates, Ontario, Monroe, Genesee, Livingston, Niagara and Erie (where the lands are highly productive and their produce is readily marketable), are willing to mortgage their farms to the Company for $\frac{1}{3}$th to $\frac{2}{5}$ths of the value of the land and to make the interest payable semi-annually in New York. In these counties the titles are mostly direct, simple and easy to be verified.

After much inquiry of Trust Companies and individuals who have loaned largely to Farmers, I have been led to the belief that while no class of securities is more safe than farming land the interest on none is more promptly and cheerfully met.

Many substantial Farmers desire money to buy more land adjoining theirs; to start a son in business; or to improve or extend their farming operations; and in giving security on their Homestead, where they expect to live and die, give the best pledge for promptitude in responding to all demands for principal and interest.

It is believed that men of sound judgement and integrity may be found to act as appraisers of property in several sections of this State, and that lawyers of prudence and skill may also be found who, under the direction and superintendence of our Counsel here, may furnish such titles as will prove entirely satisfactory; and without cost to the Company.

Awaiting the action of the Finance Company before proposing for approval the names of persons to act as appraisers, or any general system for the management of these loans, if authorized.

I am very respectfully,
Your obt. Serv't.
[Signed]   F. S. WINSTON,
President

Reflections on Investments in Securities, 1889 [1]

It is reasonable to believe that the evils which have resulted from reckless railroad management are reaching their culmination: certainly they have attained an extent and enormity which now command the serious attention of investors and will compel the adoption of legal remedies. For some time the State of Massachusetts has followed the excellent practice of Great Britain, by placing restrictions upon railroad building. Last year an attempt in the same direction was made in this State: and it is a reasonable hope that not only will other states adopt a like course, but that even the United States Government will, through its control of interstate transportation, enact such restrictive laws as to prevent the reckless and unnecessary construction of roads which can never be profitable in themselves and serve to destroy the value of other properties—which in fact are frequently built not with the object of furnishing transportation facilities, but simply to enrich their projectors.

Not only in this feature of railroad management are we as investors interested, but also in the irresponsible method of keeping accounts by which often those who own the railroad properties are kept in ignorance of their true condition.

When we consider that nearly six hundred varieties of bonds are dealt in upon the New York Exchange, it becomes evident that the adoption of a uniform system of audit or of some certified method of showing the tangible assets and business of a corporation, is a matter of first importance to those who are expected to buy its securities.

[1] *Minutes of the Finance Committee,* Jan. 23, 1889, treasurer's report.

Tables 46-59

TABLE 46

GROWTH OF LIFE INSURANCE IN AMERICA, 1840–1870 [a]

Year	Total Companies Failing	Number Reporting	Number Policies	Amount of Insurance	Number Companies	Number New Policies Issued	Amount New Insurance Issued	Reference Dates of the Business Cycle
1840	1	...	...	...	...	...	...	Peak, 1839
1841	...	...	...	...	...	...	...	
1842	...	...	...	...	...	...	...	
1843	...	...	...	...	...	...	...	Trough
1844	...	...	...	...	...	...	...	
1845	...	...	...	...	...	...	...	Peak
1846	...	...	...	...	...	...	...	Trough
1847	...	...	...	...	...	...	...	Peak
1848	...	...	...	...	...	...	...	Trough
1849	...	...	...	...	...	...	...	
1850	1	...	...	...	...	...	...	
1851	2	...	...	...	...	...	...	
1852	4	...	...	...	...	...	...	
1853	5	...	...	...	...	...	...	Peak
1854	1	...	...	...	...	...	...	
1855	1	...	...	...	...	...	...	Trough; revival
1856	4	...	...	...	...	...	...	
1857	4	...	...	...	...	...	...	Peak, June; recession, July
1858	1	...	...	...	...	...	...	Trough, Dec.
1859	...	...	...	...	...	...	...	Revival, Jan.
1860	...	17	56,046	$ 163,703,455	17	12,639	$ 35,589,934	Peak, Oct.; recession, Nov.
1861	...	17	57,202	165,256,052	17	9,563	24,978,444	Trough, June; revival, July
1862	2	18	65,252	183,962,577	18	17,430	43,471,429	
1863	...	22	98,095	267,658,677	22	35,224	89,812,093	
1864	1	27	146,729	395,703,054	27	59,198	155,803,897	
1865	2	30	209,392	580,882,253	30	86,261	245,427,057	Peak, April; recession, May
1866	2	39	305,390	865,105,877	39	134,300	404,508,474	
1867	3	43	401,140	1,161,729,776	43	158,605	471,611,744	Trough, Dec.
1868	6	55	537,594	1,528,084,685	55	201,922	579,657,871	Revival, Jan.
1869	10	69	656,572	1,836,617,818	70	231,269	614,762,420	Peak, June; recession, July
1870	8	71	747,807	2,023,884,955	71	237,180	587,863,236	Trough, Dec.

[a] Statistics taken from the New York Insurance Department reports. The turning points of the business cycle are those made public by the National Bureau of Economic Research (1941).

TABLE 47

GROWTH OF THE MUTUAL LIFE INSURANCE COMPANY OF NEW YORK
1843–1870 [a]

	NEW BUSINESS		INSURANCE IN FORCE	
YEAR	No. of Policies	Amount	No. of Policies	Amount
1843	470	$1,640,718	400	$1,480,718
1844	616	1,968,922	908	2,960,083
1845	1,047	2,858,817	1,873	4,896,190
1846	1,086	2,594,195	2,710	7,785,236
1847	1,467	3,756,603	3,620	9,997,813
1848	1,505	3,427,428	4,739	12,102,258
1849	1,756	4,074,490	5,799	14,044,213
1850	1,363	3,103,200	6,242	15,886,181
1851	978	2,284,344	6,473	16,326,275
1852	1,061	2,967,133	6,773	17,560,633
1853	1,259	3,679,744	7,390	19,642,833
1854	1,567	4,720,600	8,118	22,082,633
1855	1,698	5,498,545	8,778	24,904,110
1856	2,041	5,878,457	9,794	28,024,012
1857	1,863	5,852,087	10,390	30,481,302
1858	1,728	5,476,230	10,993	32,575,099
1859	1,721	5,343,325	11,832	35,319,279
1860	1,701	5,051,291	12,591	40,159,123
1861	1,221	3,816,325	12,095	38,188,122
1862	1,833	4,812,750	12,972	39,989,692
1863	2,842	8,594,175	15,044	52,615,656
1864	3,998	13,178,195	17,943	61,968,708
1865	7,339	26,415,057	24,143	84,651,136
1866	14,783	51,706,133	36,430	120,281,062
1867	19,056	62,061,915	49,407	164,107,469
1868	18,877	59,022,136	60,872	199,818,578
1869 [b]	15,445	42,232,872	68,119	216,943,902
1870 [c]	12,463	33,458,217	71,271	242,004,489

[a] The figures used in this table are from the New York Insurance Department. This source, rather than the Company's books, is employed because the state has used the same basis of valuation for all companies, whereas the various companies have at times employed different bases of valuation. To use figures that are arrived at by the same method allows intercompany comparison. The state itself has changed its basis of valuation. Until the founding of the state insurance department in 1860, company figures were, of course, the only ones available. In 1866 New York adopted the English Life Table No. 3 for Males (Farr No. 3 Table) with interest at 5 percent as the basis of valuation, that is, of estimating the amount of reserve which with future net premiums and interest is necessary to pay the claims which are going to fall due. In 1868 New York changed to the American Experience Table. For further changes see pp. 156, 357. Other differences between New York State Insurance Department figures and company figures are owing to items disallowed or corrected by the state.

[b] Year ended January 31 up to this year.

[c] December 31.

TABLE 48

GROWTH OF LIFE INSURANCE IN AMERICA, 1870–1906 [a]

Year	Total Companies Failing	ORDINARY AND INDUSTRIAL INSURANCE			NEW ORDINARY INSURANCE (Includes renewals and additions)			Business Cycle Reference Dates
		No. of Companies	Ordinary	Industrial	No. of Companies	Number New Policies Issued	Amount New Insurance Issued	
1870	8	71	$2,023,884,955	...	71	237,180	$587,863,236	Revival, Jan.
1871	9	68	2,101,461,834	...	68	209,753	488,655,022	
1872	16	59	2,114,742,591	...	59	201,366	489,924,857	Peak, Oct.; recession, Nov.
1873	19	56	2,086,027,178	...	56	199,050	405,614,001	
1874	5	50	1,997,236,230	...	50	144,783	351,803,670	
1875	11	45	1,922,043,146	...	45	133,995	299,276,337	
1876	9	39	1,735,995,190	443,072	38	99,036	232,665,489	
1877	8	35	1,556,105,323	1,030,655	34	81,999	178,289,617	
1878	8	35	1,480,921,223	2,027,888	34	67,040	156,501,129	
1879	2	44	1,510,239,906	5,334,531	34	67,399	167,865,390	Trough, Mar.; revival, April
1880	2	44	1,559,314,103	19,590,780	34	72,267	187,504,256	
1881	2	44	1,644,284,403	32,641,798	30	80,929	222,584,483	Peak, Mar.; recession, April
1882	3	44	1,742,633,440	55,514,798	30	91,945	257,517,216	
1883	...	44	1,873,246,208	86,321,162	29	110,302	308,061,893	
1884	1	44	1,985,041,190	108,451,099	29	127,905	321,310,170	
1885	...	44	2,155,968,963	144,101,632	29	156,214	378,214,523	Trough, May; revival, June
1886	1	48	2,230,897,416	196,694,876	29	151,102	448,514,242	
1887	3	49	2,587,956,258	254,104,877	29	174,675	531,170,783	Peak, Mar.; recession, April
1888	4	48	2,828,802,098	305,201,610	29	204,365	631,731,701	Trough, April; revival, May
1889	3	50	3,217,386,436	365,841,267	30	249,297	786,096,741	
1890	3	50	3,620,789,225	428,789,342	40	299,530	902,167,799	Peak, July; recession, Aug.
1891	...	53	3,966,303,495	480,107,214	44	345,009	961,311,684	Trough, May; revival, June
1892	2	56	4,314,197,614	583,533,745	44	374,894	988,066,419	
1893	3	56	4,628,939,120	662,647,864	42	421,748	1,090,002,107	Peak, Jan.; recession, Feb.
1894	3	56	4,769,099,069	803,067,595	43	412,502	1,014,575,827	Trough, June; revival, July
1895	1	56	4,917,688,210	820,746,562	45	385,100	894,575,268	Peak, Dec.
1896	3	57	5,055,949,508	887,117,984	46	369,045	827,951,111	Recession, Jan.
1897	3	60	5,339,478,658	995,642,014	45	448,182	953,306,017	Trough, June; revival, July
1898	...	60	5,714,959,068	1,110,078,702	46	507,083	1,059,645,104	
1899	4	69	6,481,523,963	1,292,756,042	53	649,833	1,324,041,326	Peak, June; recession, July
1900	4	76	7,093,211,398	1,468,028,342	56	729,864	1,407,609,490	Trough, Dec.
1901	5	80	7,953,019,494	1,640,827,454	65	888,848	1,595,600,732	Revival, Jan.
1902	5	80	8,698,587,912	1,806,804,473	64	983,697	1,726,754,525	Peak, Sept.; recession, Oct.
1903	7	92	9,559,296,851	1,977,884,624	77	1,120,628	1,908,085,679	
1904	2	93	10,412,078,838	2,135,859,103	76	1,196,376	1,990,205,121	Trough, Aug.; revival, Sept.
1905	2	112	11,504,231,621	2,309,754,235	93	1,135,042	1,913,628,636	
1906	7	138	11,253,194,077	2,453,603,707	118	839,899	1,450,829,425	Peak, May, 1907

[a] From Frederick L. Hoffman, "Fifty Years of American Life Insurance," *Quarterly Publications of the American Statistical Association*, 1911, pp. 716, 717, 727. Business cycle reference dates are from the National Bureau of Economic Research.

TABLE 49

GROWTH OF THE MUTUAL LIFE, 1870–1906 [a]

YEAR	NEW BUSINESS		INSURANCE IN FORCE	
	No. of Policies	Amount	No. of Policies	Amount
1870	12,463	$33,458,217	71,271	$242,004,489
1871	12,189	35,357,683	73,864	228,770,367
1872	12,184	39,365,277	78,146	264,593,682
1873	16,416	56,560,598	86,416	289,505,739
1874	12,756	38,126,906	90,914	301,878,726
1875	9,843	28,081,122	92,393	305,057,221
1876	9,344	32,127,693	92,125	301,278,037
1877	8,494	20,491,920	91,553	294,488,311
1878	8,870	28,299,818	91,828	290,774,315
1879	12,210	38,394,554	95,423	298,760,867
1880	10,106	33,700,759	97,978	306,002,164
1881	10,607	34,760,755	101,490	315,900,137
1882	11,416	37,234,458	106,214	329,554,174
1883	11,533	37,820,597	110,990	342,946,032
1884	11,197	34,687,989	114,804	351,789,285
1885	14,330	46,548,894	120,882	368,952,337
1886	18,681	56,898,214	129,846	393,776,174
1887	22,323	69,641,110	140,830	427,583,359
1888	32,597	103,346,034	158,190	482,050,579
1889	44,533	151,962,063	182,013	565,839,387
1890	48,973	161,365,921	205,564	638,041,180
1891	53,132	172,708,868	224,815	695,484,158
1892	57,186	162,929,748	246,650	745,780,083
1893	76,369	212,426,850	273,213	802,867,478
1894	82,132	211,551,887	298,515	854,710,761
1895	59,312 [b]	158,361,032 [b]	314,024 [b]	898,458,857 [b]
1896	53,786	135,679,834	326,775	917,930,911
1897	57,641	140,632,461	342,642	935,602,381
1898	54,182	134,118,295	359,758	970,496,975
1899	69,487	169,246,871	397,340	1,051,247,540
1900	75,881	176,006,030	439,440	1,139,940,529
1901	83,148	194,371,100	488,613	1,241,688,430
1902	92,537	206,676,185	543,194	1,340,748,659
1903	98,865	215,102,648	598,972	1,445,228,681
1904	109,967	231,508,259	659,544	1,547,611,660
1905	88,971	183,265,162	689,321	1,589,549,468
1906	41,667	90,550,892	664,925	1,517,257,180

[a] *Spectator Insurance Yearbook,* 1911.
[b] Change made from "issued" to "paid for" basis. This change resulted in a reduction of about 20 percent. *Minutes of the Agency Committee,* January 24, 1898.

TABLE 50

GROWTH OF LIFE INSURANCE

Year	Number of Companies Discontinued	Number of Companies	Ordinary Insurance in Force	New Insurance Ordinary Written	Industrial Insurance in Force	Group Insurance in Force
1907 b	4	160	$11,486,115,758	$1,345,147,040	$2,577,246,881	...
1908	9	171	11,850,032,581	1,468,934,726	2,668,919,696	...
1909	5	189	12,452,089,063	1,655,899,059	2,967,596,031	...
1910	5	214	13,227,213,168	1,822,260,287	3,177,047,874	...
1911	9	240	14,578,410,598	2,097,156,590	3,424,369,841	...
1912	13	250	15,555,901,171	2,240,434,665	3,708,892,514	...
1913	19	260	16,587,378,943	2,549,816,531	3,997,091,002	...
1914	13	250	17,425,501,137	2,456,548,936	4,163,671,236	...
1915	20	238	18,307,041,164	2,599,719,781	4,427,469,245	$42,244,175
1916	15	241	19,806,566,920	3,171,392,083	4,811,041,900	61,703,505
1917	12	241	21,933,103,782	3,727,635,244	5,223,415,465	32,490,450
1918	8	244	23,954,716,389	3,847,234,670	5,703,198,032	212,395,513
1919	8	266	28,169,156,207	6,476,213,982	6,607,011,093	1,103,958,473
1920	1	272	33,454,645,628	7,916,755,633	7,189,852,248	1,636,892,651
1921	7	288	36,378,537,873	6,635,840,279	8,006,119,747	1,598,742,713
1922	7	286	39,557,051,825	7,160,327,248	8,886,519,078	1,847,139,277
1923	15	291	44,227,342,307	8,611,795,436	10,107,256,433	2,468,935,567
1924	17	297	49,241,424,055	9,301,477,191	11,343,740,085	3,194,576,412
1925	13	308	54,519,175,903	10,563,127,810	12,823,680,595	4,299,271,187
1926	14	322	59,031,334,698	11,014,741,923	14,187,164,765	5,425,987,646
1927	14	319	65,043,872,587	11,404,908,728	15,548,488,326	6,429,742,511
1928	21	331	70,486,443,610	12,257,461,655	16,685,581,197	8,034,289,884
1929	24	353	76,122,995,815	12,957,511,853	17,901,996,673	9,121,447,985
1930	25	352	79,774,840,870	12,604,028,847	18,287,408,290	9,886,028,572
1931	37	342	80,657,119,445	11,321,430,409	18,274,432,216	9,954,011,233
1932	35	328	73,780,240,425	8,911,083,197	17,265,389,781	9,108,742,326
1933	27	318	71,918,829,182	8,292,524,912	17,154,472,848	8,911,741,717
1934	16	313	71,298,680,254	8,312,739,221	17,650,708,523	9,593,022,369
1935	14	340	71,963,295,305	8,113,266,242	18,297,543,092	10,469,576,619
1936	19	315	73,737,604,620	8,072,896,785	19,463,951,533	11,465,649,771
1937	14	308	76,071,004,279	8,151,282,602	20,591,183,413	12,910,263,267
1938	21	306	77,265,493,802	7,506,256,192	20,985,704,708	12,803,490,400
1939	19	306	78,813,619,059	7,260,195,023	21,140,150,492	14,022,748,996
1940	30	305	81,069,214,925	7,505,726,736	21,343,634,075	15,381,535,063
1941	...	304	84,363,734,575	8,374,867,503	22,280,022,213	18,029,480,782
1942	...	303	87,125,338,117	7,386,570,013	23,345,412,020	19,862,098,178

a From Stalson, *Marketing Life Insurance*, pp. 752–753, and the *Spectator Insurance Year Book.*

b All companies on a paid for basis after 1906.

c National Bureau of Economic Research.

Total Insurance in Force	DISTRIBUTION AS PERCENTAGE OF TOTAL			Reference Dates of Business Cycle c
	Ordinary	Industrial	Group	
$14,063,362,639	81.67	18.33	...	Peak, May; recession, June
14,518,952,277	81.62	18.38	...	Trough, June; revival, July
15,419,685,094	80.75	19.25	...	
16,404,261,042	80.63	19.37	...	Peak, Jan.; recession, Feb.
18,002,780,439	80.98	19.02	...	
19,264,793,685	80.75	19.25	...	Trough, Jan.; revival, Feb.
20,584,469,945	80.58	19.42	...	Peak, Jan.; recession, Feb.
21,589,172,373	80.71	19.29	...	Trough, Dec.
22,776,754,584	80.38	19.44	0.18	Revival, Jan.
24,679,312,325	80.26	19.49	0.25	
27,189,009,697	80.67	19.21	0.12	
29,870,309,934	80.20	19.09	0.71	Peak, Aug.; recession, Sept.
35,880,116,583	78.51	18.41	3.08	Trough, April; revival, May
42,281,390,527	79.12	17.01	3.87	Peak, Jan.; recession, Feb.
45,983,400,333	79.11	17.41	3.48	Trough, Sept.; revival, Oct.
50,290,710,810	78.66	17.67	3.67	
56,803,534,307	77.86	17.79	4.35	Peak, May; recession, June
63,779,740,552	77.20	17.79	5.01	Trough, July; revival, Aug.
71,642,127,685	76.10	17.90	6.00	
78,492,142,387	75.21	18.08	6.91	Peak, Oct.; recession, Nov.
87,022,103,424	74.74	17.87	7.39	Trough, Dec.
95,206,314,691	74.04	17.52	8.44	Revival, Jan.
103,146,440,473	73.80	17.36	8.84	Peak, June; recession, July
107,948,277,732	73.90	16.94	9.16	
108,885,562,894	74.08	16.78	9.14	
100,154,372,532	73.67	17.24	9.09	
97,985,043,747	73.40	17.51	9.09	Trough, Mar.; revival, April
98,542,411,146	72.35	17.91	9.74	
100,730,415,016	71.44	18.17	10.39	
104,667,205,924	70.45	18.60	10.95	
109,572,450,959	69.43	18.79	11.78	Peak, May; recession, June
111,054,688,910	69.57	18.90	11.53	Trough, May
113,976,518,547	69.15	18.55	12.30	Remaining years are not available.
117,794,384,063	68.82	18.12	13.06	
124,673,237,570	67.67	17.87	14.46	
130,332,848,315	66.84	17.91	15.25	

TABLE 51

GROWTH OF THE MUTUAL LIFE, 1907–1943 [a]

YEAR	NEW BUSINESS No. of Policies	NEW BUSINESS Amount	INSURANCE IN FORCE No. of Policies	INSURANCE IN FORCE Amount
1907	19,524	$48,720,050	641,213	$1,452,752,408
1908	34,229	93,926,992	639,746	1,438,399,803
1909	43,809	102,040,633	645,328	1,441,323,848
1910	47,593	117,990,428	654,683	1,464,024,396
1911	54,817	137,576,110	671,053	1,504,974,662
1912	62,385	153,475,812	691,047	1,550,888,063
1913	65,739	160,035,366	712,527	1,598,466,078
1914	61,231	147,720,038	723,829	1,612,574,168
1915	61,330	148,176,711	734,560	1,636,538,117
1916	70,921	175,377,932	756,623	1,687,797,276
1917	74,303	201,320,720	783,899	1,773,411,526
1918	65,642	201,809,064	802,366	1,861,881,953
1919	108,696	347,639,513	864,539	2,089,171,357
1920	121,950	415,684,409	929,511	2,357,973,121
1921	95,415	332,116,624	947,900	2,472,651,779
1922	104,937	369,645,678	976,358	2,630,603,737
1923	121,482	424,184,966	1,016,053	2,817,761,195
1924	123,249	426,577,372	1,056,973	3,008,991,612
1925	131,496	467,357,946	1,112,680	3,255,615,753
1926	130,835	486,544,777	1,171,263	3,513,573,813
1927	130,615	494,733,652	1,227,698	3,762,898,499
1928	131,056	512,340,104	1,286,016	4,025,874,008
1929	135,896	530,447,168	1,347,097	4,298,774,546
1930	124,392	467,580,119	1,388,448	4,464,278,069
1931	95,188	359,619,757	1,384,815	4,450,294,284
1932	84,008	296,624,031	1,336,382	4,226,616,174
1933	93,965	264,703,489	1,270,351	3,903,658,890
1934	87,351	252,965,171	1,233,706	3,744,186,170
1935	83,611	266,097,986	1,222,570	3,708,081,401
1936	84,744	250,663,340	1,227,629	3,712,259,614
1937	87,308	269,154,537	1,242,531	3,758,762,033
1938	92,818	267,461,084	1,260,818	3,787,704,506
1939	75,017	201,732,621	1,257,221	3,740,731,467
1940	74,766	193,449,925	1,259,354	3,705,911,798
1941	66,712	187,808,605	1,257,901	3,678,249,263
1942	59,454	164,810,502	1,257,496	3,644,202,486
1943	56,160	177,482,626	1,264,209	3,659,982,397

[a] Includes dividend additions; excludes revivals and increases. Source: Mutual Life annual statements.

TABLE 52

SURRENDERS AND LAPSES, 1870–1906 [a]

All Companies Reporting to New York Insurance Department

Year	Surrenders	Lapses [b]	Year	Surrenders	Lapses [b]
1870	$53,805,449	$175,888,860	1889	$56,897,965	$138,996,777
1871	78,457,761	214,919,514	1890	67,323,414	171,674,879
1872	74,078,715	190,283,427	1891	69,760,365	256,821,703
1873	86,541,535	186,716,581	1892	92,663,678	261,764,011
1874	92,796,824	179,023,161	1893	111,351,382	290,939,614
1875	79,774,666	142,903,483	1894	136,091,827	334,048,737
1876	84,548,242	123,652,153	1895	135,022,326	282,768,964
1877	89,017,554	98,800,015	1896	136,630,809	288,107,830
1878	72,489,046	78,936,466	1897	131,457,523	274,288,306
1879	54,257,456	54,066,929	1898	105,048,285	289,118,285
1880	37,453,801	42,787,694	1899	105,462,261	285,204,282
1881	33,046,732	41,809,149	1900	89,436,052	335,423,323
1882	38,120,541	48,678,171	1901	99,305,385	299,712,956
1883	36,708,240	57,236,963	1902	110,417,008	334,420,876
1884	42,103,980	77,850,963	1903	128,379,968	352,843,070
1885	43,882,293	79,268,220	1904	151,214,509	422,366,968
1886	45,035,381	80,895,034	1905	191,416,929	452,759,491
1887	48,356,157	91,400,252	1906	234,115,452	452,215,839
1888	54,153,514	121,013,284			

a Source: New York Insurance Department reports.

b Lapse in this case means voluntary termination, usually during the first three years that a policy is in force, without surrender value.

TABLE 53

SURRENDERS AND LAPSES, 1870–1906 [a]

The Mutual Life

Year	Surrenders	Lapses [b]	Year	Surrenders	Lapses [b]
1870	$10,289,591	$9,394,825	1889	$9,514,813	$20,995,423
1871	8,281,805	13,724,050	1890	12,843,914	28,537,548
1872	12,949,000	5,103,595	1891	. . .	59,309,726
1873	8,299,110	8,407,210	1892	19,221,306	44,138,940
1874	9,476,700	9,531,200	1893	24,464,505	59,170,813
1875	10,300,666	8,183,499	1894	27,721,360	62,873,450
1876	14,413,880	8,252,170	1895	30,353,488	48,063,353
1877	21,157,922	. . .	1896	32,408,046	64,141,163
1878	19,585,632	4,962,732	1897	32,102,401	71,223,270
1879	14,456,338	5,880,344	1898	9,708,959	68,810,705
1880	10,627,073	6,735,110	1899	21,872,288	43,395,006
1881	9,196,259	5,150,394	1900	6,465,105	60,892,223
1882	8,893,235	5,154,454	1901	7,634,134	57,608,548
1883	7,321,129	5,502,813	1902	11,149,372	61,701,961
1884	8,171,214	6,405,779	1903	15,492,944	62,012,378
1885	9,529,905	7,001,784	1904	16,896,941	74,909,054
1886	10,595,373	6,997,160	1905	23,759,386	82,116,481
1887	9,341,038	9,773,791	1906	34,810,023	85,212,351
1888	9,632,833	14,896,223			

[a] Source: Mutual Life annual statements.

[b] Lapse in this case means voluntary termination, usually during the first three years that a policy is in force, without surrender value.

TABLE 54

SURRENDERS AND LAPSES, 1907–1941 [a]

All Companies Reporting to New York Insurance Department

Year	Surrenders	Lapses [b]	Year	Surrenders	Lapses [b]
1907	$211,008,495	$307,639,953	1925	$748,157,393	$1,458,221,877
1908	246,053,655	307,831,148	1926	860,611,009	1,796,390,357
1909	250,031,006	270,909,576	1927	1,065,588,555	2,151,573,164
1910	236,729,678	276,196,939	1928	1,125,595,550	2,044,182,536
1911	252,334,180	325,738,487	1929	1,357,285,345	2,252,412,351
1912	276,616,499	366,276,434	1930	1,691,816,280	2,769,950,898
1913	339,862,748	383,606,555	1931	2,240,324,172	2,918,178,716
1914	362,744,884	427,675,869	1932	3,509,363,836	3,230,040,897
1915	387,696,748	430,697,208	1933	3,581,186,621	2,533,596,360
1916	341,762,213	384,087,776	1934	2,599,712,027	1,892,061,856
1917	284,834,404	397,357,094	1935	1,947,635,105	1,736,624,759
1918	269,162,300	448,047,649	1936	1,436,047,145	1,440,251,725
1919	318,621,289	475,949,527	1937	1,231,999,770	1,421,151,169
1920	330,146,683	749,985,625	1938	1,406,920,691	1,573,753,170
1921	440,616,139	1,403,796,369	1939	1,338,739,820	1,111,673,600
1922	613,563,184	1,226,094,007	1940	1,231,288,915	993,172,759
1923	639,069,095	1,154,569,325	1941	1,066,320,926	903,299,588
1924	697,930,539	1,414,912,635			

[a] Source: New York Insurance Department reports.

[b] Lapse in this case means voluntary termination, usually during the first three years that a policy is in force, without surrender value.

TABLE 55

SURRENDERS AND LAPSES, 1907–1943 [a]

The Mutual Life

Year	Surrenders	Lapses [b]	Year	Surrenders	Lapses [b]
1907	$38,466,712	$36,005,622	1926	$96,283,339	$75,782,468
1908	49,513,535	21,743,383	1927	92,043,486	83,459,713
1909	42,834,678	19,477,463	1928	87,305,916	74,639,129
1910	36,462,861	24,899,559	1929	98,913,272	71,324,677
1911	36,653,721	27,817,299	1930	115,296,810	94,795,864
1912	39,077,507	34,906,007	1931	161,600,349	107,847,769
1913	41,891,128	36,510,971	1932	287,594,951	106,986,671
1914	54,031,855	33,028,898	1933	361,114,092	87,892,943
1915	56,278,957	31,502,069	1934	219,307,910	71,994,218
1916	51,602,771	28,364,211	1935	141,980,021	60,696,743
1917	47,060,502	27,177,426	1936	107,847,217	45,568,351
1918	40,485,067	29,193,212	1937	95,497,127	41,190,559
1919	48,234,562	27,337,085	1938	104,310,031	51,122,614
1920	57,663,230	43,041,372	1939	109,975,056	52,227,632
1921	76,190,514	94,149,626	1940	97,906,562	46,355,722
1922	90,252,933	66,675,016	1941	90,897,977	41,070,267
1923	92,870,797	64,153,304	1942	75,296,916	37,524,958
1924	99,380,733	72,865,733	1943	46,696,835	37,121,491
1925	94,061,479	71,664,328			

[a] Source: The Mutual Life annual statements.

[b] Lapse in this case means voluntary termination, usually during the first three years that a policy is in force, without surrender value.

TABLE 56

GROWTH OF THE ANNUITY BUSINESS, 1907–1943 [a]

The Mutual Life

Year	Premiums Received for Annuities	Total Life Insurance Premiums and Annuity Premiums	Percentage
1907	$540,364	$55,335,353	1.0
1908	606,136	58,446,907	1.0
1909	606,342	52,478,968	1.2
1910	524,367	52,630,796	1.0
1911	447,123	53,630,518	0.8
1912	864,506	55,690,287	1.6
1913	498,308	57,022,800	0.9
1914	485,761	57,010,963	0.9
1915	513,959	58,226,106	0.9
1916	546,422	60,352,991	0.9
1917	559,440	63,564,255	0.9
1918	454,549	66,214,098	0.7
1919	667,934	77,038,618	0.9
1920	539,505	85,652,598	0.6
1921	838,208	90,309,699	0.9
1922	373,083	97,387,905	0.4
1923	583,840	104,268,100	0.6
1924	773,862	112,678,870	0.7
1925	1,294,939	123,019,771	1.1
1926	1,054,008	132,462,732	0.8
1927	1,663,606	143,664,178	1.2
1928	3,750,929	157,682,175	2.4
1929	3,774,391	165,412,110	2.3
1930	4,751,168	170,050,704	2.8
1931	6,402,883	171,679,938	3.7
1932	5,887,512	162,425,330	3.6
1933	12,603,026	153,655,234	8.2
1934	22,343,637	164,132,881	13.6
1935	39,772,968	187,126,716	21.3
1936	21,694,820	159,575,600	13.6
1937	16,230,830	154,524,584	10.5
1938	12,839,809	149,731,771	8.6
1939	13,182,807	144,077,389	9.1
1940	6,279,607	138,944,112	4.5
1941	6,591,383	132,325,326	5.0
1942	5,325,233	127,436,189	4.2
1943	4,585,413	126,616,902	3.6

[a] Excludes supplementary contracts. Source: The Mutual Life annual statements.

TABLE 57

NEW YORK STOCK EXCHANGE, 1870–1905 [a]

Year	Number of Bond Issues Listed	Bond Transactions, Par Values (In thousands of dollars)	Par Value of All Listed Bonds (In thousands of dollars)	Number of Stock Issues Listed	Stock Transactions (In thousands of dollars)	Number of Shares Listed
1870	200	...	...	143	...	...
1871	203	...	...	147	...	...
1872	230	...	...	158	...	...
1873	274	...	...	158	...	...
1874	279	...	...	152	...	...
1875	348	...	...	163	...	...
1876	345	...	...	160	...	...
1877	334	...	...	163	...	...
1878	329	...	...	159	...	...
1879	347	571,307	...	174	...	...
1880	408	643,657	...	219	72,766	...
1881	445	486,300	...	250	95,737	...
1882	533	293,459	...	284	117,079	...
1883	571	313,893	...	304	116,733	...
1884	610	526,926	...	315	97,939	...
1885	628	681,823	...	310	95,947	...
1886	639	649,304	...	293	92,987	...
1887	678	373,604	...	308	103,953	...
1888	704	363,483	...	338	85,819	...
1889	727	414,831	...	346	65,825	...
1890	742	406,101	...	354	73,220	...
1891	760	392,163	...	342	70,579	...
1892	833	500,349	...	375	68,962	...
1893	874	364,957	...	388	86,498	...
1894	900	358,222	...	387	80,645	...
1895	924	520,399	...	370	49,317	...
1896	936	393,695	...	383	66,630	...
1897	905	544,443	...	379	54,448	...
1898	884	913,729	...	390	77,545	...
1899	881	835,056	...	388	113,685	...
1900	839	579,293	5,841,042	377	175,389	...
1901	827	994,554	6,045,526	376	138,981	56,090,180
1902	855	893,049	6,833,890	379	264,935	63,069,208
1903	891	686,435	8,337,335	384	186,715	76,186,285
1904	903	1,032,655	8,703,519	383	158,497	81,241,129
1905	907	1,026,254	9,117,263	374	186,921	82,781,445
					260,569	82,475,783

[a] From information provided by the New York Stock Exchange. No official figures have been compiled for dates prior to those given in the table.

TABLE 58

TOTAL CAPITAL ISSUES, BY KINDS, 1919-1943 [a]

(In millions and tenths of dollars)

Year	Total Issues	New Capital	Refunding	CORPORATE				Farm Loan and Gov't Agencies	State and Municipal	Foreign Government
				Railroads	Public Utilities	Industrials [b]	Miscellaneous			
1919	4,286.2	3,588.4	697.8	208.1	462.3	1,691.6	377.7	110.0	703.2	533.3
1920	4,010.0	3,634.8	375.2	377.9	496.8	1,627.6	464.0	...	699.5	344.3
1921	4,203.8	3,576.7	627.1	655.3	671.1	848.6	215.9	121.9	1,235.7	455.3
1922	5,235.9	4,304.4	931.5	651.5	980.4	915.8	525.5	386.4	1,143.7	632.4
1923	4,989.7	4,304.4	685.3	518.2	1,138.4	1,044.8	531.4	392.5	1,071.3	293.1
1924	6,352.5	5,593.2	759.3	940.3	1,529.6	805.7	563.0	179.1	1,407.8	927.0
1925	7,126.0	6,220.2	905.9	514.7	1,710.0	1,270.2	1,243.2	188.2	1,408.4	791.3
1926	7,430.3	6,344.1	1,086.1	422.6	1,968.0	1,610.2	1,298.8	131.3	1,375.5	623.9
1927	9,933.7	7,791.1	2,142.6	962.8	2,977.4	1,673.8	1,705.2	179.6	1,522.5	912.4
1928	9,991.8	8,114.4	1,877.5	727.7	2,552.3	1,816.9	2,710.9	63.9	1,420.9	689.2
1929	11,592.2	10,182.8	1,409.4	817.2	2,442.8	2,459.8	4,306.6	...	1,435.7	130.1
1930	7,677.0	7,023.4	653.7	1,026.5	2,566.2	1,151.9	728.6	86.5	1,497.6	619.6
1931	4,022.9	3,115.5	907.4	516.5	1,538.9	329.6	204.0	125.6	1,258.0	50.4
1932	1,730.3	1,192.2	538.0	61.0	540.3	20.9	21.8	169.6	850.8 [c]	66.0
1933	1,053.7	709.5	344.2	99.9	92.7	186.6	2.3	90.2	522.0 [c]	60.0
1934	2,212.8	1,386.8	825.9	249.2	158.4	53.2	30.2	721.7	939.5 [c]	60.0
1935	4,752.3	1,412.1	3,340.2	1,067.7	1,289.8	706.5	80.4	1,137.1	1,231.8 [c]	116.0
1936	6,254.3	1,973.3	4,281.0	796.1	2,125.3	1,258.0	452.6	375.2	1,120.7 [c]	126.5
1937	4,001.3	2,100.7	1,900.6	356.7	827.5	1,036.9	212.5	437.7	907.7 [c]	222.3
1938	4,459.2	2,355.0	2,104.1	72.4	1,222.6	798.1	47.3	1,146.0	1,107.6 [c]	65.0
1939	5,853.1	2,298.4	3,554.7	185.6	1,327.0	512.2	171.4	2,461.6	1,125.9	67.5
1940	4,805.9	1,950.5	2,855.4	372.3	1,274.1	764.2	352.0	804.3	1,233.7	...
1941	5,545.9	2,853.9	2,692.0	365.3	1,383.0	675.5	195.0	1,969.0	952.6	4.0
1942	2,114.5	1,075.1	1,039.4	48.6	467.2	490.1	36.6	548.2	523.7	...
1943	2,228.2	643.5	1,584.7	152.4	399.1	503.2	26.1	622.1	435.2	90.0

[a] Data cover domestic and foreign issues in the United States. Preferred stocks of no par value and all common stocks are taken at their offering price, other issues at par, except that in the figures for corporate issues for 1916 to 1918 all stocks are included at their market value. Corporate issues for 1916 to 1918 exclude real estate offerings and privileged stock subscriptions included in figures beginning 1919, and issues of less than $100,000. State and municipal issues include bonds issued by states, territories and possessions, counties and municipalities, and by school and road districts and other independent governmental bodies.

[b] Comprises the following classifications given in the original detailed statements: Iron, steel, coal, copper, etc., equipment manufactures, motors and accessories, oil, rubber, and miscellaneous industrials.

[c] These figures do not include funds obtained by States and municipalities from any agencies of the Federal Government.

TABLE 59

CORPORATE ISSUES BY CLASS OF SECURITY (NEW CAPITAL AND REFUNDING), 1912–1943 [a]

(In millions and tenths of millions of dollars)

Year	Total	Long-term Bonds & Notes	Short-term Bonds & Notes	Stocks
1912	2,253.6		1,349.5	904.1
1913	1,645.7		1,193.9	451.9
1914	1,436.5		1,174.7	261.8
1915	1,435.4		1,110.6	324.7
1916	2,186.5		1,405.0	781.5
1917	1,530.0		1,075.5	454.5
1918	1,344.8		1,047.1	297.7
1919	2,739.7	633.7	540.2	1,565.8
1920	2,966.3	1,234.4	660.8	1,071.1
1921	2,390.9	1,896.2	215.4	279.3
1922	3,073.3	2,304.3	145.0	624.0
1923	3,232.8	2,316.4	180.5	736.0
1924	3,838.6	2,569.3	403.0	866.3
1925	4,738.1	3,040.2	386.9	1,311.0
1926	5,299.6	3,648.0	333.8	1,317.8
1927	7,319.2	5,190.4	355.5	1,773.3
1928	7,817.9	3,916.6	274.1	3,627.2
1929	10,026.4	2,842.3	262.6	6,921.4
1930	5,473.3	3,248.0	657.0	1,568.3
1931	2,589.0	1,840.8	405.1	343.1
1932	643.9	405.8	214.0	24.0
1933	381.6	138.5	90.4	152.7
1934	491.1	287.0	169.5	34.6
1935	2,267.4	2,066.1	50.5	150.8
1936	4,631.9	4,001.3	62.8	567.9
1937	2,433.7	1,578.6	94.7	760.4
1938	2,140.5	2,032.3	10.5	97.7
1939	2,196.2	1,883.4	78.8	233.9
1940	2,762.6	2,396.1	38.6	327.9
1941	2,618.8	2,276.5	43.1	299.1
1942	1,042.5	908.4	4.7	129.4
1943	1,080.9	869.1	38.0	173.8

[a] Figures for 1917–1918 are from the New York *Journal of Commerce*. Source: *Commercial and Financial Chronicle*, except as noted.

Index

Index